COLLIS' ZOUAVES

COLLIS' ZOUAVES

The 114th Pennsylvania Volunteers in the Civil War

EDWARD J. HAGERTY

Louisiana State University Press • Baton Rouge and London

Designer: Michele Myatt Quinn
Typeface: Adobe Goudy Old Style
Typesetter: Impressions Book and Journal Services, Inc.
Printer and binder: Thomson-Shore, Inc.

Portions of unpublished letters by Edward E. Williams and Willie Williams are reproduced with the permission of John B. Sidebotham, Holland, Pennsylvania.

Library of Congress Cataloging-in-Publication Data

Hagerty, Edward J., 1955–
    Collis' Zouaves : the 114th Pennsylvania Volunteers in the Civil
  War / Edward J. Hagerty.
      p. cm.
  Includes bibliographical references and index.
  ISBN 0-8071-2199-1 (alk. paper)
    1. United States. Army. Pennsylvania Infantry Regiment, 114th
  (1862–1865)—History.   2. United States—History—Civil War,
  1861–1865—Regimental histories.   3. Pennsylvania—History—Civil
  War, 1861–1865—Regimental histories.   I. Title.
  E527.5 114th.H34   1997
  973.7'448—dc21   97-16226
                                                           CIP

Contents

Illustrations

TABLES

Preface

With the exception of a three-year tour of duty with the air force, I lived and worked in Philadelphia all my life until moving to Virginia's Shenandoah Valley in the winter of 1994. Despite the beauty, solitude, and pristine rural surroundings of the valley, I still feel a compelling attachment to the place of my birth. I am intimately familiar with the streets and neighborhoods of Philadelphia: Kensington, Southwark, Bustleton, Roxborough, Manyunk, and the many others from which the soldiers of the 114th Pennsylvania Volunteers hailed. With the exception of overhead electric wires, asphalt streets, and concrete pavements, many of those neighborhoods look much the same as they did in 1862. One can still walk their streets, see the houses where the soldiers lived, the factory buildings and offices where they labored, and the churches in which they held their weddings and funerals.

After several years of reading and rereading the letters, diaries, memoirs, and newspaper accounts of the men of the 114th, I feel I have grown to know them. By virtue of my having trod the same streets and seen the same sights; by having visited the scenes of their camps, their marches, and their battles; and by meeting and talking with their descendants, I have formed a sort of kinship with them. I know them largely to be good and honorable men, though I make no extraordinary claims about their qualities as soldiers. They were average men—some of them so young as to be barely qualified to claim the honor of being called a "man," others old enough to be well established in their careers, with wives and children to support. Yet these average men came when their country called, much as their citizen-soldier forebears did, and as their descendants have continued to do. They faced the travails of army life and the storms of shot and shell that flew in their direction. Most gritted their teeth and pressed onward, doing what had to be done. The men of the 114th cannot be credited with stemming any desperate attacks in order to save the day, nor with contributing decisively to the success of a particular battle by an impetuous charge on the enemy. They cannot even lay claim to having held a position against all odds. They performed admirably, to be sure. But in the seesaw confusion of battle, they did what the men of most regiments can be said to have done. They gave some, and they took some. They advanced when they were able, and they withdrew when they had to. In short, they did their duty.

What is it, then, that makes the 114th Pennsylvania Volunteers worthy of an in-depth study? I have said that these were average men, but they served in singular times and experienced spectacular events. Their writings have captured with precision the impact of those events. As a line regiment in the Army of the Potomac, and later as a component of Major General George G. Meade's headquarters guard, the 114th occupied a front-row seat in the grand drama that unfolded on the American stage. Whether it was the ignominy of being heckled by gleeful Confederates as the downcast Zouaves trudged back to camp after Major General Ambrose E. Burnside's infamous "Mud March," or the glory and inspiration of seeing the national colors grasped firmly in the hands of their young mounted colonel while storms of lead and iron flew around them, the men of the 114th experienced war from every perspective.

The Civil War regimental history as a genre has undergone a gradual metamorphosis in the 132 years that have passed since the end of that conflict. Books detailing the exploits of Civil War regiments began to make their appearance soon after war's end, but the vast majority of them were published between the years 1880 and 1910. By then, the passage of time had largely dulled the vivid sense of war's horror. Events could be written about with less passion and more impartiality, less criticism and more charity. The histories were typically written either by a former soldier from the ranks of the regiment or by a professional writer engaged by the regiment's survivors. The results were varied. Some were histories only in the loosest sense of the word, and many were merely panegyric testimonials to the heroic deeds of the regiment. Almost universally, however, they were composed equally of nostalgia and propaganda. The resulting concoction usually tended to overlook any serious shortcomings of the men or of the regiment as a whole. Desertion was rarely mentioned. Poor performance was rationalized. Thus, when evaluated in light of other primary-source information, some late-nineteenth-century regimental histories are more useful to scholars for the information discerned to have been omitted than for what they actually contain.

The quality of modern twentieth-century works examining Civil War regiments is varied; but because their authors have relied on a wider scope of source materials and have made more detached observations, the resulting works tend to be of a quality superior to that of their predecessors. The best of the modern regimental histories typically possess three characteristics: they are well written; they are analytical, not simply narrative, in form; and they incorporate some measure of social history in their portrayal of the common soldier of the Civil War. I have tried to construct this history within that framework, adding one more characteristic that played an undeniable role in the story of the 114th Pennsylvania: a discussion of politics, or political influence. Mid-nineteenth-century politics played an enormous part in the prewar army, with many officers capitalizing on government contacts to secure advantage in assignments and promotions. Politics played a major role in the civilian sector as well, as will be seen from the description of its importance in daily life in Philadelphia. That citizen-soldiers should be no less influenced by it in their lives and careers than were the professional military men of the day is no surprise.

The men of the 114th saw active service from the fall of 1862 until the spring of 1865. They directly participated in four major battles: Fredericksburg, Chancellorsville, Gettysburg, and the final assault on Petersburg. They sustained light combat casualties in two other engagements: Auburn and Guiney Station. In those thirty-one months, they saw six days of direct combat. The remainder of that time was spent trudging along roads that were sometimes dust choked, other times slick with mud, ice, or snow. They marched over mountains and through valleys, and forded streams or tramped over bridges. They camped in woods and fields, pitching tents or shivering under thin blankets. They stood huddled around smoky campfires in winter, stamping their feet for warmth and waiting anxiously for the comforting heat of freshly made coffee in a tin cup. In summer, they sweated beneath the wool fezzes that crowned their heads and the woolen jackets and trousers that clung to their skin. Belts, straps, and slings cut and chafed them on the march. They bathed contentedly and dried on the banks of the same icy streams they had forded with difficulty in winter. These and a hundred other minor irritants and small pleasures constituted the minutiae of their lives. Army life for these Philadelphia Zouaves, as for most men who served, was characterized by months of stifling boredom punctuated by moments of sheer terror.

The pleasure of getting to know the men of the 114th has been rivaled only by my acquaintance with the historians, archivists, and librarians who have assisted me with this project. Those to whom I have become indebted during the course of this work are legion. In naming a few whose assistance has been invaluable, I intend by no means to lessen the credit due others whose guidance was instrumental at some point. It must suffice, however, to say here with heartfelt appreciation that I am deeply grateful to all of them for their help.

First and foremost, I must thank Russell F. Weigley of Temple University for overseeing my work on the 114th from its very beginning, as a twenty-page paper. His inspiration both in the classroom and in private conversations helped sustain me through difficult periods, and I have appreciated his assistance more deeply than I can express. Also at Temple, I would like to thank Dennis Rubini for his insightful guidance and support.

At the United States Army Military History Institute, Richard Sommers' gracious hospitality as well as his and his staff's patient guidance as I worked with the institute's extensive manuscript collection were very much appreciated. I am also grateful to the Harrisburg Civil War Round Table for awarding me the James F. Haas Fellowship in 1990, which provided me with the opportunity to conduct my research at the institute.

To Russ Pritchart, former curator of the Civil War Library Museum in Philadelphia, I owe a debt of gratitude for suggesting Charles H. T. Collis as the subject of a research paper. Russ even permitted me a close examination of a uniform of the 114th in the museum's possession. Russ's help, along with that of Steve Wright and other staff members, was instrumental in steering me to appropriate sources.

I must also thank my good friend and fellow historian Mike Cavanaugh, whose expertise in tracking down sources was willingly shared with a novice. In addition, Mike graciously reviewed portions of the manuscript.

Other readers of the manuscript whom I am delighted to acknowledge are Robert K. Krick, Chief Historian of the Fredericksburg and Spotsylvania National Military Park, and Brian Pohanka of Time-Life Books. Mr. Krick offered perceptive comments that were most valuable in preparing the manuscript for publication, and Mr. Pohanka's extensive knowledge of Zouaves was evident in his keen observations and helpful suggestions.

General Collis' grandson, Charles Collis, has been gracious in sharing his time in corresponding with me and relating his knowledge of family history. Jack Sidebotham, whose relatives Edward, Edmund, and Willie served with the 114th, was also generous with his time and knowledge. My appreciation goes, too, to the many others who supplied photographs and leads to source materials.

At Louisiana State University Press, editor Catherine Landry expertly guided the manuscript through the various production stages and patiently provided thorough answers to my seemingly endless list of questions and concerns. For that I am grateful. Donna Perreault deserves special praise for her proficient copy editing of the text. Her keen eye and perceptive questions led to a number of corrections and the inclusion of explanatory material that greatly improved the work.

These acknowledgments would not be complete without my sincere thanks to a supportive wife and family. To Regina, to my daughters Katie and Meghan, and to my son Brendan, all of whom endured much during the course of this work, I am deeply grateful. Despite my frequent need to travel and other myriad distractions that detracted from our time together, the love, support, and understanding of my family provided an unshakable foundation to this work and to all my efforts.

Abbreviations Used in Notes

CMSR	Compiled Military Service Records
CWLM	Civil War Library Museum, Philadelphia
CWMC	Civil War Miscellaneous Collection
CWTI	*Civil War Times Illustrated*
DEB	Philadelphia *Daily Evening Bulletin*
FSNMP	Fredericksburg and Spotsylvania National Military Park
HCWRT	Harrisburg Civil War Roundtable
HSP	Historical Society of Pennsylvania
LC	Library of Congress
MOLLUS	Papers of the Military Order of the Loyal Legion of the United States
NARA	National Archives and Records Administration
OR	*The War of the Rebellion: A Compilation of the Official Records of the Union and Confederate Armies*
PHMC	Pennsylvania Historical and Museum Commission
USAMHI	U.S. Army Military History Institute

I

Antebellum Philadelphia

Early on the morning of May 7, 1853, the passenger steamship *City of Glasgow* out of Liverpool, England, sailed past the Cape Henlopen lighthouse at the entrance to the Delaware Bay, beginning the last leg of its seventeen-day journey to the bustling port city of Philadelphia. Sailing under the flag of the Inman Line, this ship of experimental design had been constructed in 1850 in the vast Tod and MacGregor shipyards of the Scottish city whose name she bore. Unlike the side-wheel steamers typical of the era, the 237-foot-long iron-hulled *City of Glasgow* harnessed the power of two engines to the shaft of a single screw propeller located beneath the stern. The vessel weighed over 1,600 tons, and her two massive engines produced a total of 350 nautical horsepower. She was able to attain a speed of nearly nine knots, which was not so fast as the wooden paddle steamers of the competing Cunard Line, but comparable to the numerous sailing packets then carrying passengers back and forth across the oceans of the world. Since her maiden voyage from the Clyde River on April 15, 1850, the vessel had successfully plied the cold Atlantic waters between Liverpool and Philadelphia on a regular basis, first in a series of transoceanic trial runs, and then as a passenger liner after her acquisition by the Liverpool, New York, and Philadelphia Steamship Company (Richardson Brothers), known more widely as the Inman Line. On this trip in May, 1853, she was under the watchful eye of Captain William Wylie, and slumbering in the berths below were Wylie's 430 passengers, many of whom would awaken that day to their first view of America.[1]

Many of the passengers aboard the steamer were immigrants from Ireland who had booked passage in the steerage class accommodations located far beneath the upper decks. While the *City of Glasgow* could hardly be compared to the "coffin ships" that nearly a decade earlier had brought by the thousands the sons and daughters of a famine-stricken nation, she was nevertheless a vessel in which confinement to steerage class was likely to be a nightmarish experience. Crowded in dank conditions deep in the bowels of the heaving ship, contending with poor ventilation and inadequate facilities, the plethora of seasick humanity on such journeys quickly grew weary of the adventure and grimly resigned themselves to their fate. The busy decks of a steamship on a trans-Atlantic journey were little different from those of the sailing ships that had for centuries preceded them. The *City of Glasgow*, in fact, was "barque-rigged" and carried "an enormous press of canvass" as well as a crew of seventy. Sailors were therefore scurrying around constantly performing the many tasks necessary for the vessel's operation, leaving little space or time for passengers to come topside. Only the lucky few who filled the higher class cabins, such as the "Saloon Berths," were generally permitted to stroll about the decks, and those only if the weather cooperated. One such fortunate person was William E. Collis, a merchant who was en route to Philadelphia with his fifteen-year-old son Charles to embark upon a new life in America.[2]

Though born in Ireland, William Collis was not the typical Irish immigrant of the mid-nineteenth century. Unlike the majority of his transplanted countrymen, he was neither poor nor Roman Catholic. In fact, William descended from a fairly prominent Irish Protestant family, two

1. Charles Herking, *Dictionary of Disasters at Sea* (2 vols.; London, 1962), I, 233; Ship Passenger Records, Name Index, 1800–1906, Microfilm Publication No. M360, and Ship Passenger Lists, 1800–1882, Microfilm Publication No. M425, NARA, Philadelphia; N. R. P. Bonsor, *North Atlantic Seaway: An Illustrated History of the Passenger Services Linking the Old World with the New* (5 vols.; Prescot, Lancashire, 1955), I, 54.

2. Thomas Gallagher, *Paddy's Lament: Ireland 1846–1847, Prelude to Hatred* (New York, 1982), 171–233; Cecil Woodham-Smith, *The Great Hunger: Ireland, 1845–1849* (New York, 1962), 206–41; G. Gibbard Jackson, *The Story of the Liner* (London, n.d.), 88–89; Passenger Lists, Microfilm Pub. No. M425, NARA, Philadelphia; Circular No. 57, Series of 1902, MOLLUS, Headquarters Commandery of the State of New York (N.Y., October 31, 1902), CWLM.

members of whom were "eminent barristers at the Irish bar," and another of whom was described as "one of the most celebrated surgeons in Great Britain."[3]

William himself had been able to attend Trinity College, Dublin, which then admitted only members of the Church of Ireland. Upon graduation, he worked for several years as a clerk in the Irish adjutant general's department. Eventually, he married Mary A. Lloyd, and the couple's first son, Charles Henry Tuckey Collis, was born on February 4, 1838, in Cork. A year after Charles' birth, William moved the family to England, where five additional children were born. While little is known about the family's circumstances during their time in England, they were situated comfortably enough to support six children and send Charles to school. Nevertheless, in the spring of 1853, William and Charles boarded the *City of Glasgow* and sailed off for Philadelphia. Once established there, William intended to have his wife and the remaining children join them. In thus transplanting itself in stages, the family bore great resemblance not only to other contemporary Irish immigrants, but also to a great diversity of immigrant families in America then and since.[4]

Steaming steadily through the bay and into the mouth of the Delaware River, the *City of Glasgow* glided past one of the first of the river's defensive barriers, Fort Delaware. Built in 1848 on Pea Patch Island, the fort was designed to protect the river's ports. It was never used for that purpose. Instead, it was destined to house a great many southern soldiers during the approaching conflict.

Shipborne travelers fortunate enough to be permitted on deck that early May morning would have encountered their first glimpse of an American city when New Castle, Delaware, appeared off the port side ten miles upriver from the fort. Located on a saltwater portion of the lower Delaware, New Castle was home to many of the fishermen who sailed the bay and river seeking shad and sturgeon; it was also an important port of entry, particularly in winter, when freshwater Philadelphia might be dangerously iced over. A few miles farther and the thriving port of Wilmington, Delaware, at the juncture of the Brandywine and Christina Rivers, would come

3. Circular No. 57, Series of 1902, MOLLUS, New York Commandery (N.Y., October 31, 1902), CWLM.

4. *Ibid.*; William Collis to John M. Read, January 24, 1862, in John M. Read Papers, HSP.

into view; then Marcus Hook, which would develop into a vast oil refining and storage area after Edwin L. Drake's 1859 oil strike in Titusville, Pennsylvania, helped to make oil a profitable commodity.[5]

This final portion of a sea journey to Philadelphia was complicated, requiring the ship's pilot to make a number of skillful course changes in order to remain safely within the river's dredged channel. Such precision sailing was certainly more easily accomplished by a steam-powered vessel like the *City of Glasgow* than by the many wind-powered craft on the river; nevertheless, it was necessary to watch carefully for the channel markers such as buoys or range lights. Once the ship's pilot reached Fort Mifflin, the scene of a British siege during the American Revolution, and spotted the blockhouse light looming oddly from the river's middle on its own palisaded island, he knew that his task was nearly done. He needed only to navigate the river's final segments, or ranges, between Eagle Point, Horseshoe Bend, and Horseshoe before the crowded docks of the city appeared.

Excited passengers crowding the decks of arriving ships would also begin to see prominent landmarks that indicated the imminent end of their journeys. Shortly after passing the sloping stone walls of Fort Mifflin, the traveler would come upon the United States Navy Yard, located at the foot of Federal Street in Southwark. It was marked by enormous and distinctive twin ship houses, with double rows of hatch windows lining the rooftops to provide illumination. Just beyond lay the city itself, its buildings crowding close to the waterfront where row upon row of tall-masted ships of every description lined the wharves and docks that stretched its length.

The river would have become increasingly crowded as the ship neared Philadelphia, and the pilot would have crept cautiously along the channel, wary and vigilant for approaching craft. Fortunately, ships of the Inman Line docked at the foot of Queen Street, at the southern portion of the city's wharves. Otherwise, the pilot would have had to exercise even more care as he approached the waterfront at the center of the town. At this point, it was necessary not only to watch for river traffic, but to navigate by a series of wooded alluvial islands lying in the river's center and separating the city of Camden, New Jersey, from Philadelphia. To compound

5. Philip Chadwick Foster Smith, *Philadelphia on the River* (Philadelphia, 1986), 32–35.

the problem, ferries plying the river between those two cities crossed directly between them by steaming through a narrow channel bisecting the islands. Thus a ferry from Camden making its way to its dock at the foot of High Street in Philadelphia could emerge suddenly from the island's channel and dart dangerously into the path of passing ships.[6]

Travelers from Liverpool landing at the Queen Street wharves would have been greeted by the sight of busy waterfront warehouses and shops, boardinghouses, and immigrant depots. Many of these establishments were constructed so near the piers that passage along the waterfront was often obstructed by ship's jib booms that protruded several yards into the street. Beyond the immediate dockside area, those disembarking from the ship would have seen a vast array of businesses, churches, and dwellings that stretched from the Delaware River westward to the Schuylkill, and from Southwark north to Kensington.

After clearing through customs, health, and immigration stations, the recently arrived travelers might have clustered together discussing what to do next. To the south, they could see large piles of lumber deposited on the docks by coasting vessels, around which was a "colony of spar-makers, boat-builders, [and] architects of stiff-looking figure-heads." To the north could be seen the city's busiest wharves, with row upon row of anchored ships of all descriptions lining the dockside, their canvas furled and their spars and masts now naked against the sky. At the foot of Walnut Street, one might see the steam packets from New York loading or discharging passengers, while several blocks farther, near Vine Street, one might encounter the *State of Georgia* or the *Keystone State* just arrived from Savannah or Charleston. Somewhat farther northward, in Kensington, the traveler would come upon another expanse of lumber yards and shipbuilding facilities, as well as foundries, mills, and machine shops. Finally, at Richmond, one would see the darkened coal wharves where the black diamondlike cargo was received from the mines in and north of Schuylkill County and loaded onto the many vessels lying in wait.[7]

To the east lay Smith's Island, where in the summertime youthful bathers and picnickers who had neither the time nor the resources to take the steamer to the oceanfront resorts of Atlantic City or Cape May flocked to the floating bathhouses for amusement. To the west, sprawling in front of

6. *Ibid.*, 35–41, 134–35.
7. *Ibid.*, 65–87; Philadelphia *Inquirer*, December 13, 1861, p. 2.

the immigrants' eyes, lay Philadelphia itself and the several subdivisions that would be incorporated by the city in 1854. Philadelphia's rapidly growing population, which stood at 408,762 in 1850, made the city one of the largest in North America, second only to New York. In the previous decade, its white population had increased by nearly 35 percent. The number of free blacks in the Quaker City had risen by slightly over 12 percent during that same period. The 1850s would continue to witness phenomenal growth in the city, not only in terms of population—which would reach 565,529 in 1860—but also in terms of industrialization. As the fourth largest city in the Western world—ranked only behind New York, London, and Paris—Philadelphia was "at the forefront of northeastern industrial development" in America.[8]

Though many of the city's subdivisions and much of the surrounding area were still largely rural and devoted to farming, its central portion was increasingly devoted to industrial manufacture. By 1860, Philadelphia's 6,314 manufactories were producing goods worth nearly $120 million. The largest share of that product came from the city's gigantic textile and shoe industries. Men's and boy's clothing alone accounted for over $11 million worth of manufactured goods, while cotton and woolen products accounted for over $6 million and $4 million, respectively. Boot and shoe manufacture contributed over $5 million to the total. Philadelphia's next largest industrial concern, sugar refining, produced sugar worth over $6 million. Wartime increases in sugar consumption and manufacture were to make this food substance the city's single largest item of production by 1866, and undoubtedly did much to establish Philadelphia as one of the country's premier sugar-refining centers—a status that it maintained well into the twentieth century. The phenomenal growth of the sugar industry, however, pales in comparison to the wartime growth in the city's iron production, which experienced an increase in manufacturing dollars between 1860 and 1866 of 353.8 percent. Finally, the city's printing businesses were responsible for over $5 million of the total manufacturing production in 1860. In addition to these larger industries, a host of small but growing concerns added millions more to the city's economy. From

8. *Seventh Census of the United States, 1850*; Russell F. Weigley, "The Border City in Civil War, 1854–1865," in *Philadelphia: A 300-Year History*, ed. Russell F. Weigley (New York, 1982), 363; J. Matthew Gallman, *Mastering Wartime: A Social History of Philadelphia During the Civil War* (Cambridge, Mass., 1990), 1.

cigar makers to gunsmiths, hundreds of Philadelphians toiled in small shops, many of which would also undergo rapid growth during the coming war years. Tobacco and snuff production, for example, saw a percentage increase in manufacturing dollars between 1860 and 1866 of nearly 2,000 percent. Overall, Philadelphia businessmen and financiers reaped a handsome profit supplying the needs of the massive armies and navies fighting to preserve the Union.[9]

Operating the looms, wheels, and other machinery that produced this growth was a workforce as varied as the industries themselves. When the Collis family and their migrating shipmates reached Philadelphia, the city was already making a substantial contribution to the total foreign-born population of Pennsylvania. That population would exceed 430,000 by 1860, second once again only to New York State, which contained nearly a million foreigners. Of Pennsylvania's non-native population, those born in Ireland comprised the largest number by 1860, with 201,939; nearly 17 percent of Philadelphia's population was born in Ireland. Germans, the next largest immigrant group in the Keystone State, numbered 138,244; over 7 percent of Philadelphia's foreign population. No other ethnic group at that time came close to matching those numbers; nevertheless, many other ethnicities were represented in the state. And because Philadelphia was the state's primary port of entry and a source of cheap housing and ready employment, it absorbed a large number of those who disembarked from the steadily arriving ships. In 1860, these new arrivals amounted to somewhere around 30 percent of the city's population.

In addition to the variety of languages and accents heard throughout the city and its workplaces, a racial diversity characterized its inhabitants. By 1860, its free black and mulatto population numbered 22,185: less than 4 percent of the total, but a highly visible and provocative number nevertheless. The combined presence of such disparate groups served to render the city vulnerable to a great deal of ethnic, racial, and class tension.[10]

9. Lorin Blodget, *Manufacturers of Philadelphia, Census of 1860* (Philadelphia, 1861), 1–11; Gallman, *Mastering Wartime*, 253–59. Gallman has extracted this data from Edwin T. Freedley, *Philadelphia and Its Manufactures: A Handbook Exhibiting the Development, Variety, and Statistics of the Manufacturing Industry of Philadelphia in 1857* (Philadelphia, 1867), 581–84.

10. *Statistics of the United States in 1860* (Washington, D.C., 1866), 439; U.S. Civil War Centennial Commission, *The United States on the Eve of the Civil War as Described in the 1860 Census* (Washington, D.C., 1963), 63; Gallman, *Mastering Wartime*, 1; William Dusinberre, *Civil War Issues in Philadelphia, 1856–1865* (Philadelphia, 1965), 20.

More generally, deteriorating housing, a rapidly increasing population, an influx of non-native residents—especially the large numbers of formerly rural and largely unskilled Irish—and often unstable economic conditions all contributed to the fluidity and stress in prewar Philadelphia. Its residents were highly mobile; their frequent moves were often related to changes in wealth and economic status. Generally, Philadelphians lived in three broad zones that radiated out from the center of the city. The zones roughly corresponded to divisions in economic status, as based on an analysis of tax assessments per inhabitant in each ward. Those wards in the central portions of the city showed the highest average assessments; those immediately surrounding the city's center show the next highest assessments; and the wards farthest away show the lowest assessments. The exception to this general pattern was the suburb of Germantown, which by 1860 had become the full-time residence of a number of well-to-do Philadelphians. During the decade preceding the war, far more city dwellers moved outward, away from the city's center—hence economically downward—than moved into its affluent inner-most wards. Downward mobility, in fact, was experienced with nearly triple the frequency of upward mobility in the 1850s. This data seems to "reflect a real shift in the social structure toward a large wage-earning, poor and near-poor, unskilled and semi-skilled, native and immigrant work force."[11]

As immigrants began to arrive in the city in large numbers, nativist sentiment among the existing population led to outbreaks of violence. In the 1840s, anti-Catholic nativists acted on their contempt for and fear of the rapidly increasing numbers of foreigners in their midst. They engaged in large-scale, prolonged rioting in the spring and summer of 1844. After the loss of thirty or more lives and the burning of two Catholic churches and a number of homes, order was restored. This feat was accomplished with little help from the city's police force, whose sentiment was largely nativist. It was necessary to call out the state militia, a move which prevented a third church from going up in flames and eventually quelled the disturbances. The prejudice of the nativists stemmed not only from their antipathy toward non-Protestants, but from their fear that the immigrants would provoke unfair competition among laborers as a result of their will-

11. Stuart M. Blumin, "Residential Mobility Within the Nineteenth-Century City," in *The Peoples of Philadelphia: A History of Ethnic Groups and Lower-Class Life, 1790–1940*, ed. Allen F. Davis and Mark H. Haller (Philadelphia, 1973), 41–45.

ingness to work for low wages. The unskilled workers who were flocking to the city thus seemed to pose an economic threat to the Protestant artisan class.[12]

Despite the fears of the city's longtime residents, Philadelphia was largely able to absorb the unskilled laborers into its workforce with little consequence to the Protestant artisans. The city's expanding industries provided an outlet for the flood of job-seeking immigrants. In addition, the mobility of much of the city's established population provided housing opportunities for the poorer immigrants. Philadelphia, in comparison to other large eastern port cities, accommodated expansion relatively easily. It is not geographically isolated in any way: it lies neither on an island, as does Manhattan, nor on a peninsula, as does Boston. Its only substantial barrier—the Schuylkill River, extending along its antebellum western edge—was easily bridged. Finally, the rise of an effective urban transportation system enabled residents to relocate from one neighborhood to another while remaining within an easy commute of the city's heart. However, the result of these geographic and technological advantages for the middle and upper classes was that the immigrants were relegated to the least desirable areas of the city. Urban slums grew up in districts including Moyamensing, Southwark, Gray's Ferry, and Port Richmond, and were occupied—if not exclusively, then largely—by the immigrant newcomers.[13]

The political allegiance of the majority of these newcomers lay with the Democratic Party. Jacksonian appeals to workingmen and objections to perceived Whig privilege formed the basis of this allegiance. It would be further promoted by party efforts to dispense patronage among the faithful. For the large Irish population in the city, the Democratic Party represented hope. It proved to be a tremendous source of power for many of them.

12. Michael Geldberg, "Urbanization as a Cause of Violence: Philadelphia as a Test Case," in *The Peoples of Philadelphia*, ed. Davis and Haller, 56–57; Russell F. Weigley, "'A Peaceful City': Public Order in Philadelphia from Consolidation Through the Civil War," ibid., 156; Weigley, "The Border City," in *Philadelphia: A 300-Year History*, 368–69; Dusinberre, *Civil War Issues in Philadelphia*, 21–22.

13. Dennis J. Clark, "The Philadelphia Irish," in *The Peoples of Philadelphia*, ed. Davis and Haller, 136–39; Dennis J. Clark, *The Irish in Philadelphia: Ten Generations of Urban Experience* (Philadelphia, 1973), 41–44.

The Irish were able to harness two standard neighborhood institutions to the yoke of political power in their attempt to pull themselves out of the miasma of their poverty. The first was the saloon, and the second was the volunteer fire company. Saloons provided a political forum for their working-class patrons; and the saloonkeeper, by virtue of his relative wealth, independence, and familiarity with his neighbors, became a figure of some stature within the community. For their part, the fire companies, which were very large owing to the numbers of men required to pull the apparatus rapidly and pump water effectively, gave new meaning to "beating" the rival political faction; violence and politics seemed synonymous then. Nevertheless, they also provided fertile ground for a burgeoning political infrastructure. As such, the fire companies served to propel a number of Irishmen to prominence in ethnic politics. The career of William McMullen exemplifies the point. From his early affiliation with the Moyamensing Hose Company, "Bull" McMullen rode the wave of street-gang violence into the political arena. His reward for supporting Democrat Richard Vaux for mayor in 1856 was a position on the board of prison inspectors for Moyamensing Prison. The following year he was elected to the position of alderman. Because of the enormous judicial power held by aldermen, he became the most influential man in Moyamensing. He was reelected steadily and held the position into the 1870s. Throughout his career, McMullen was able to capitalize on his background as the son of an impoverished immigrant. His appeal among the common people of Moyamensing was strong because he was one of them.[14]

The strong-arm tactics and lawless shenanigans of the volunteer fire companies and street gangs were primary considerations in the implementation of the Consolidation Act of 1854. Under the terms of the act, twenty-nine subdivisions were brought into the jurisdictional boundaries of the city. Their inclusion eliminated "an impediment to law enforcement which had aggravated all the major riots"—namely, their insulation from the powers of a police force—yet at the same time increased "the area of the city at one stroke from two to 130 square miles." The consolidated city was to be governed by a mayor, elected at two-year intervals, and a bicameral council. Much to the chagrin of the Democrats who supported

14. Clark, *The Irish in Philadelphia*, 115–17. See also Harry C. Silcox, *Philadelphia Politics from the Bottom Up: The Life of Irishman William McMullen, 1824–1901* (Philadelphia, 1989), 37, 49–76.

consolidation and hoped to derive some benefit from its success, the first mayor of the enlarged city proved to be the candidate of the American Party, who promptly gave notice of his intent to enlist a nine-hundred-man police force of fellow nativists. Two years later, however, Democrats, including men like Bull McMullen, triumphed in the election of Richard Vaux.[15]

The year of Vaux's election, 1856, was also a presidential election year. According to one historian, "anti-negro impulses, fear of secession, determination to assert the rights of Northern white men, and anti-Catholic nativism were respectively the dominant motives of Philadelphia's four major political groups." City Democrats were the most vitriolic critics of abolitionism. In this sentiment they were joined by a number of former Whigs, who, in a less radical manner, adhered to the ingrained belief in black racial inferiority. The American Party, while primarily concerned with the containment of the rights and influence of foreigners, also appealed to those who feared offending the South on the issue of slavery. For its part, the Republican Party was only nascent in 1856, and its candidate for mayor attracted less than 1 percent of the vote. When prominent local politicians, largely former Whigs, became attracted to the party, however, its radical stance against slavery was somewhat softened. In effect, then, while a minority of Philadelphians harbored some genuine concern for the condition of African Americans, the generally supposed antislavery sentiment among antebellum northerners seems not to have prevailed in the city. Such a social climate might have had ominous portent for the coming crusade to extend freedom to the oppressed.[16]

For William Collis and his teen-age son, no such thoughts must have disrupted their wonderment on arriving early that May morning in 1853; rather, hope for a bright new beginning must have suffused their perceptions of the strange American city. While many of their shipmates very likely joined the multitudes in the squalid streets of Southwark and Moyamensing, Collis and his son found more favorable accommodations near the center of town. Father and son soon settled into more permanent

15. Weigley, "'A Peaceful City,'" in *The Peoples of Philadelphia*, ed. Davis and Haller, 157; Dusinberre, *Civil War Issues in Philadelphia*, 22.

16. Dusinberre, *Civil War Issues in Philadelphia*, 27–47. In Philadelphia's polls of the 1856 presidential election, Democrat James Buchanan garnered 53 percent of the vote; Millard Fillmore, the American Party candidate, 36 percent; and Republican John C. Fremont only 11 percent.

lodging; introductions were made and employment found. Within a year, William thought his position secure enough to send for his wife and children still in England. The Collises were destined, however, never again to be united as a family. On March 1, 1854, Mrs. Collis and her children, along with 474 others, boarded the *City of Glasgow* and set out from the docks of Liverpool bound for Philadelphia. The vessel was never heard from again; young Charles' mother, two brothers, and three sisters were all lost at sea. Ships arriving in Liverpool later that month reported sighting a number of large icebergs, and it seems likely that the iron-hulled ship encountered one that sent it sinking to the depths of the cold Atlantic waters.[17]

The effects of this disaster on young Charles and his father are not recorded; but, emotions aside, one might conjecture that had they been faced with the prospect of supporting the other six members of the family, their lives might have been decidedly different. Had the family survived intact, it is possible that the eldest son might have been required to seek some employment not of his choosing in order to help support them. Whether or not he could have overcome those circumstances and risen to the status he later attained both in civil and military life is questionable. Perhaps the young man's loss was later to be the country's gain. When Charles did eventually find employment, it proved to be a momentous and fateful occasion, for the relationship that developed between the young immigrant and his employer was one that so influenced his future that it might credibly be said that the luck of the Irish was with him. For his employer and benefactor, Charles could hardly have done better than gain the interest of the influential attorney and politician John Meredith Read. A newspaper account written in 1864 describes this event in Charles's early life in glowing if half-truthful prose:

> Gen. Collis, then an obscure, penniless Irish boy, landed upon our republican soil, to work out for himself, in this free land, the bright destiny which dawns upon him to day. At first but a mere squalid errand-boy, in the employ of our distinguished fellow-townsman, the Hon. Judge John M. Read, he was soon discovered by this employer to possess talents of no ordinary de-

17. MOLLUS (N.Y., October 31, 1902), Circular No. 57, Series of 1902, CWLM; Herking, *Dictionary of Disasters at Sea*, I, 233.

scription. Judge Read became his instructor and protector, and ere many years the emigrant boy stood prominently before the public as a distinguished member of the Philadelphia bar.[18]

John Meredith Read was a third-generation American whose great-grandfather had come from Dublin, Ireland, in the early part of the eighteenth century. That earlier Read had settled in Cecil County, Maryland, and later founded the city of Charlestown on the Chesapeake Bay. John M. Read's grandfather, George, was a respected attorney in New Castle, Delaware, and was elected to the provincial assembly in 1765. He was a delegate to both Continental Congresses and a signer of the Declaration of Independence. Read's father, John, moved to Philadelphia in 1789, where John was born eight years later. John was admitted to the bar in 1818, six years after graduating from the University of Pennsylvania. He made his debut in politics in 1822 when he was elected to the General Assembly of Pennsylvania. A dissident Democrat, Read later became one of the founders of the free-soil wing of the party. His political views regarding slavery—views which would soon lead him to oppose the extension of that evil into the territories acquired after the Mexican War—probably triggered some disfavor in the Senate to his nomination to the United States Supreme Court in 1845. Read stood by his antislavery convictions on that occasion and withdrew his name from consideration as a result of the opposition offered.[19]

Read joined many former "conscience" Whigs, disaffected Democrats, and free-soilers when he embraced the Republican Party in the mid-1850s. Read belonged to the more moderate class of Republicans who opposed the expansion of slavery into the new territories but declined to interfere with the institution as it already existed. In 1856, he delivered a speech on the "Power of Congress over Slavery in the Territories." Two years later, he was elected to the Pennsylvania Supreme Court in the Republican Party's first major victory. By 1860, Abraham Lincoln's political allies were considering Read's nomination for president, with Lincoln to be his run-

18. *DEB*, November 1, 1864, p. 3.

19. *Appleton's Cyclopaedia of American Biography* (3 vols.; New York, 1888), s.v. "John M. Read"; *Webster's American Biographies*, ed. Charles Van Doren (Springfield, Mass., 1975), 859–60.

ning mate. Read, however, was defeated by the ambitions of fellow Penn-
sylvanian and powerful Republican senator Simon Cameron at the party's
national convention in Chicago that year. Thereafter, Read used his considerable personal influence in favor of Lincoln.[20]

The opinions rendered by Judge Read during his time with the Supreme
Court of Pennsylvania run through forty-one volumes of reports. His opinion "Views on the Suspension of Habeas Corpus" was adopted by Lincoln
as the basis for his proclamation of March 3, 1863, which suspended habeas corpus throughout the Union in cases of suspected treason. Both the
Pennsylvania and New Jersey constitutions of the time came to contain
many elements of his thought in their amendments, and his ideas had
significant impact on the formulation of numerous federal statutes.[21]

Young Collis was indeed fortunate to acquire a friend and mentor of
such influence and renown. Charles read law in the judge's Philadelphia
office and was admitted to the bar in 1859 under Read's tutelage. The
young attorney's star was beginning its ascent.

During this period, moreover, Charles met and fell in love with a pretty,
former Charlestonian belle, Septima M. Levy. It was a grand time for
courtship, for much of the country was gripped by romance. Already
steeped in the knightly tales of Sir Walter Scott, Americans derived their
notions of honor and chivalrous conduct from the pages of his influential
novels. Although the couple would eventually wed, it was unfortunate for
Miss Levy and her suitor that more of the ambient romance was not of
the type engendered by moonlit nights along the scenic Schuylkill. Instead, it was born of notions of banners waving gaily on the battlefield
while fancily bedecked heroes fought their way to a bloodless victory. Such
was the innocence of the country's youth on the eve of the Civil War. An
unsuspecting generation was on the verge of an inferno that would consume many of them while violently altering the course of the nation's
history.

Charles Henry Tuckey Collis was only one of many Philadelphians who

---

20. *Appleton's,* s.v. "John M. Read." At the Republican convention, Cameron threw
his support to Lincoln in return for a promised cabinet post. Lincoln's reluctance in naming
him secretary of war proved well grounded, and Cameron was offered the post of minister
to Russia after ten months so as to make way for an abler secretary of war candidate, Edwin
McMasters Stanton.

21. *Ibid.*

were thus swept up in the deceptive fantasy of war. Thousands of other young men would join him in voicing initial enthusiasm to preserve the Union. And when the time came to defend the country, Collis would enlist with those from the immigrant neighborhoods of the city as well as those from the older, more established sections and the newer, largely affluent suburbs.

2

With Lincoln and Hamlin We'll Conquer or Die

> The war drums are beating;
> Prepare for the fight!
> The people are gathering
> In strength and in might;
> Fling out your broad banner
> Against the blue sky,
> With Lincoln and Hamlin
> We'll conquer or die!
> —*Song of the People's Campaign Club, printed*
> *during the People's Procession, November 2, 1860*

Early on the morning of April 12, 1861, anxious southerners peered out into the darkness of Charleston Harbor in South Carolina, waiting to catch a glimpse of Fort Sumter as it appeared in the coming dawn. At 4:30 A.M., just as the outline of the fort could be distinguished, a signal gun was fired and the war was begun. From Cummings Point, on the south side of the harbor, Virginia's elderly, ardent secessionist Edmund Ruffin was said to have been given the honor of pulling the lanyard on one of the eight-inch Columbiads aimed at the fort. The cannon belched forth its deadly projectile, which lodged in Sumter's masonry wall. The bombardment continued unabated until dark and resumed at daylight on the thirteenth. A relief expedition sent by President Abraham Lincoln was forced to remain outside the harbor and watch in helpless despair, much like the rest of the North, as the fort succumbed. After thirty-four hours, during which neither side suffered a casualty, Major Robert Anderson, the former slaveholding Kentuckian who commanded Sumter, agreed to surrender.[1]

On Sunday, April 14, Anderson's command was drawn up for a final salute as the United States flag was lowered. Captain Abner Doubleday, second in command, directed the preparations for a one-hundred-gun salute, but on the fiftieth round the ceremony was abruptly halted. One of the guns had discharged prematurely, killing a cannoneer, Private Daniel Hough. Several others were wounded when sparks from the charge ignited some nearby cartridges. In an incongruous incident at the start of a war to be filled with such scenes of pathos, the first death occurred after the battle itself was done. Anderson struck his tattered flag and marched the defenders out of the fort to the tune of "Yankee Doodle." Behind them, the fort's new garrison of Palmetto Guards raised their own silken banner. "Tremendous shouts of applause were heard from the vast multitudes of spectators," wrote Captain Doubleday, "and all the vessels and steamers, with one accord, made for the fort."[2]

The soldiers tramping aboard the waiting transport ship that morning were a reflection of the United States Army in general. That army contained fewer than sixteen thousand men and was woefully unprepared to oppose a rebellion by hundreds of thousands of southern militiamen eager to support with arms their states' bid for freedom. To compound problems for the regular army, its officer corps would be torn by resignations. A third of the officers, some of the most promising and talented men in uniform, would follow their home states and serve the Confederacy. In addition, the army's general-in-chief, Winfield Scott, was then seventy-four years of age; and several of his subordinate commanders had served, like him, as long ago as the War of 1812.[3]

1. "The Bombardment and Surrender of Fort Sumter, April 12–14, 1861," *Blue and Gray*, I (May, 1984), 25–33; Abner Doubleday, "Abner Doubleday Defends Fort Sumter," in *The Blue and the Gray*, ed. Henry Steele Commager (Indianapolis, 1950), 35–38.

2. "The Bombardment and Surrender of Fort Sumter," 25–33; Doubleday, "Fort Sumter," in *The Blue and the Gray*, ed. Commager, 38.

3. Gallman, *Mastering Wartime*, 11.

Despite the regular army's lack of readiness to meet the crisis of secession, the North was making feverish military preparations. Like their
southern countrymen, northerners everywhere who were not already committed were quick to join one of the hundreds of local state militia or
volunteer units that were prevalent in nineteenth-century America. In
fact, the North had much greater potential manpower than the South.
There were over three-and-a-half times as many eligible white men in the
North than in the South, though when adjustments were made to discount
those who would not actually be available to fight, the North's ratio of
superiority was reduced to two-and-one-half to one.[4] Although the Union
was fortunate to have retained the loyalty of the vast majority of the
regular army's enlisted force, it ultimately pinned its hopes on the ranks
of its militiamen and volunteers.

One day after Sumter's fall, Lincoln sent out a call to the states for
75,000 militia to serve the federal government for three months. This call
was based on the provisions of the Militia Act of 1792, under which each
state was assigned a quota of men that must be furnished for the nation's
defense. Lincoln eventually accepted nearly 92,000 men from the states
as a result of this initial plea for assistance. Pennsylvania purportedly contained an "actual and uniformed State force" of 56,500 men who were
organized into 476 companies; in Philadelphia, the militia organization
consisted of eight complete regiments of all branches of the service: infantry, cavalry, and artillery, and one infantry battalion. In addition, the
city boasted several renowned independent militia units, including the
First Troop Philadelphia City Cavalry, the Scott Legion, and the Washington Grays.[5]

However, much of Philadelphia's militia strength in early 1861 still
existed largely on paper. In response to Lincoln's first call for troops, men
all over the city flocked to recruiting stations, eager to fill the ranks of the
regiments. As a result, Philadelphia sent eight regiments of infantry, one
of cavalry, and one of artillery. In addition, one independent company of
Moyamensing Hose Company rowdies-turned-infantrymen enlisted under

4. James M. McPherson, *Battle Cry of Freedom: The Civil War Era* (New York, 1988),
322.

5. Russell F. Weigley, *History of the United States Army* (New York, 1967), 198; Frank
H. Taylor, *Philadelphia in the Civil War, 1861–1865* (Philadelphia, 1913), 16–18.

the command of that belligerent Irish alderman Captain William "Bull" McMullen.[6]

One of the Pennsylvania regiments mustered into Federal service upon Lincoln's request for assistance was the 18th. It included troops from many of Philadelphia's volunteer militia units, such as the State Fencibles, the Washington Blues, and the National Grays—the last, an organization that dated from the American Revolution. Among the ranks of the regiment was the young barrister Private Charles Collis, who, like so many others, had forsaken his profession for that of the soldier. Such a thing was easy to do during the initial patriotic rush to defend the colors. In fact, many men would have considered it disgraceful not to volunteer their services at such a moment. Within weeks of the president's call, Philadelphia still had a large surplus of eager volunteers who chafed under Pennsylvania's restriction by law to field a fixed number of men. In their eagerness to enlist, men traveled to New York or signed on with enlisting agents representing other states with larger unfilled quotas.[7]

Just as the election of the "Black Republican" Abraham Lincoln had provided the impetus for southern secession, the fall of Fort Sumter inflamed patriotism in the North. Peace rallies and public denunciations of the use of force and coercion on the part of the Union gave way to cries for war. All over Philadelphia there "was the most tremendous excitement. Thousands assembled furious at the news of the surrender, swearing revenge on all disunionists or disaffected." Only a short period of time elapsed before "recruiting tents dotted the landscape, volunteers drilled wherever they could find open space, and hundreds of women flocked to the recently vacated Girard Hotel to sew uniforms."[8]

Private Collis' regiment went into camp at Washington Square, near Independence Hall, where the men spent the first month of enlistment learning the rudiments of soldiering. By the time the regiment was mustered in on April 24, 1861, Collis had been appointed to the position of

6. Gallman, *Mastering Wartime*, 12–14; Weigley, "The Border City," in *Philadelphia: A 300-Year History*, 395.

7. F. H. Taylor, *Philadelphia in the Civil War*, 35–36, 41; Samuel P. Bates, *History of Pennsylvania Volunteers*, (5 vols.; Harrisburg, 1869), I, 168.

8. Fanny Kemble Wister, "Sara Butler Wister's Civil War Diary," *Pennsylvania Magazine of History and Biography* (July, 1978), 273; Diary of Henry C. Benners, April 28, 1861, in HSP.

sergeant major. Camp life in the midst of a metropolitan area was probably not extremely taxing for the new soldiers. They were well supplied with all the necessities of comfort, and undoubtedly spent a good deal of their time visiting with friends and well-wishers or parading about town in their handsome new uniforms. In mid-May, the regiment received orders to move to Perryville, Maryland. When the men arrived at Perryville, however, they were immediately boarded onto a steamer and taken to Locust Point, near Baltimore. The regiment then marched to the vicinity of Fort McHenry, where it remained performing guard duty and drill until May 22. On that day, the 18th marched into Baltimore and encamped on Federal Hill, overlooking the city and the harbor.[9]

For the next several weeks, "the monotony of camp life was little varied" for the regiment, with guard and military police duties occupying nearly the whole of its time. But on June 12, two companies were detached from the regiment and sent to perform garrison duties at the Pikesville arsenal, about sixteen miles northwest of the city. The novice soldiers probably undertook this task with far more seriousness than any yet assigned to them, as the threat of seizure of United States property in the unstable and highly charged political atmosphere of the Old Line State, lying, as it did, so near the area of active rebellion, was no inconsiderable one. Military officials must have perceived the threat as imminent. The men of the 18th Pennsylvania spent their time at the arsenal packing government property and transporting it to Fort McHenry.[10]

Although the Philadelphians left little record of their stay at the National Arsenal at Pikesville, others testified to their impressions of the place. The 18th left Pikesville on July 23, and was later replaced by Company A of the 20th Indiana. Private William C. H. Reeder of that regiment wrote that the arsenal was "one of the nicest places you ever saw."

We have the arsnel houses to sleep in and eat in so that we do not have to tent. I tell you it is like a pallace here we have everything we want the slavewomen and boys bring berries here for 3 cents a quart and peaches pears and of the finest kind for cent a piece. I tell you the Niggars are thick here . . . there is a good manny free blacks here there is some of the prettiest

9. Bates, *Pennsylvania Volunteers*, I, 168; MOLLUS, Membership Application No. 8636, Philadelphia, CWLM.

10. Bates, *Pennsylvania Volunteers*, I, 168.

Creole girls here you most ever saw you can hardly tell that some of them has . . . Negro blood about them only by the chalk in the eye.[11]

Whether the Philadelphians ever found the environs and its inhabitants so agreeably beneficent is not known. The 18th returned home and was mustered out of service on August 7, ten days after the expiration of its three-month enlistment period. The men had learned something of military life, with its endless drills and customs; and more importantly, they had been introduced to some of the many regulations to which a regiment must adhere. In retrospect, the three-month regiments were mere stopgaps given the later manpower needs generated by the war; but they had the important function of protecting the capital and other vital cities as well as forts, arsenals, and—most critical of all—railroad lines. Many of the men who served in those early regiments would go on to serve with distinction in the three-year regiments that began to be recruited later in the spring of 1861.

Immediately upon his discharge, Collis set about raising a company of Zouaves, which would be modeled on the French military units that had so recently captured the fancy of many Americans. Upon the request of Major General Nathaniel Prentiss Banks, then commanding the Union forces on the upper Potomac, this nascent company was to serve as his bodyguard. On August 13, Collis received notification from Assistant Secretary of War Thomas Alexander Scott that the company of Zouaves d'Afrique that he offered was "accepted for three years or during the war, provided you have it ready for marching orders in twenty days."[12]

One need not stretch the imagination to see Judge Read's powerful influence in this decision, innocuously appealing to General Banks's political acumen on behalf of Collis. It must have seemed personally expedient and of no great possible military consequence to the general to appoint an obscure Pennsylvania sergeant major with only three months' experience as a soldier to recruit and train a company of Zouaves that would serve as his personal bodyguard. As an attorney, former congressman, and governor of Massachusetts, Banks himself had little experience with soldiering, a fact that would eventually prove disastrous to his command. Collis, for his part, quickly proved that he was equal to the ap-

11. William C. H. Reeder to Dear Father and Mother, August 6, 1861, in Personal Correspondence, William C. H. Reeder Papers, 1861, USAMHI.

12. *DEB*, August 14, 1861, p. 1.

pointment. Only three days after he received authorization to raise his company, the Zouaves d'Afrique were mustered into service. Although they did not yet possess uniforms or arms, the company paraded briefly after being mustered in, and were complimented as being "a fine looking body of men."[13]

Zouaves were then the latest rage in military circles, and Collis' company was no less popular than the many others forming both in the city and throughout the North. Just a few weeks before in Philadelphia, Colonel David Bell Birney was putting the Zouave "scouters" of the 23rd Pennsylvania through their paces, much to the delight of the public. "The members are going through with their drill rapidly," wrote one correspondent. Their drill consisted of physical exercises "such as running and gymnastic feats, in order to give them 'wind,' and test the capacity of their lungs for long marches and active movements incident to their duties." This unit was rather conservatively dressed in plain dark blue Zouave-style uniforms with red trim on the jacket, vest, and pants. Nevertheless, they attracted the awe of onlookers and even performed a "farewell benefit" at the Walnut Street Theater. It was billed as "Musical Zouave and Gymnastic Entertainment," for it included drill and gymnastic performances by the soldiers.[14]

The Zouaves that Collis envisioned were to wear uniforms more in keeping with the traditional garb favored by the fierce Frenchmen. His men would each be outfitted with baggy red pantaloons, a short blue Zouave jacket with a distinctive lighter blue cuff, white leggings, and a light blue merino sash around the waist, topped by a red fez and white turban. In addition, Collis even attempted to make his unit's composition authentic by attracting men of French descent. His second-in-command, First Lieutenant Severin A. Barthoulot, who would later become captain of Company A, 114th Pennsylvania Volunteers, was a native of France. This forty-year-old teacher was undoubtedly instrumental in drawing a number of his countrymen into the ranks of the company. For men like Christian Rochrig, a thirty-one-year-old shoemaker; Philip Rhem, a twenty-seven-year-old machinist; William Lambrecht, twenty-three, a baker; John Alff, thirty-eight, a gold melter; or Jacques Metzger, a twenty-

13. *Ibid.*, August 19, 1861, p. 1.

14. *Ibid.*, July 9, 16, 1861, p. 1; Michael J. McAfee, *Zouaves: The First and the Bravest* (Gettysburg, Pa., 1991), 71.

one-year-old machinist—all of whom were born in France—the uniform of the Zouaves must have evoked fond memories and proud recollections of the Empire. The company also contained a small number of musicians, and Frenchmen Emile Jonan and Eugene Brousard were among them. Some of the Frenchmen of the company were reputed to have seen "actual service in the French army," and thus may have had some firsthand knowledge of French Zouave dress and drill.[15]

The Zouave craze began in the United States after the Crimean War, although French Zouave troops came into existence long before that time. Zouaves of the French army were first recruited from native Algerian troops in North Africa after the French occupation of Algiers in 1830. They were officially accepted for service by King Louis Philippe in March of 1831, and over the next ten years the Zouaves expanded into three battalions totaling nine companies. By that time, however, only one of those companies contained native troops; the rest were Europeans. Eventually, all of the Algerians were placed into independent battalions of sharpshooters, and by 1852, the Zouaves were authorized to expand into three entire regiments. All of the men, nearly 10,000 by the time of the Crimean War, were to be Europeans.[16]

Two battalions of each of the Zouave regiments were mobilized and sent to Constantinople in June, 1854. As a result of the widespread photographic and newspaper coverage of the war in the Crimea, the Zouaves' "gaudy, oriental uniforms coupled with their roguish behavior and unquestioned bravery" were brought prominently before the public eye. No doubt the impression of young Captain George Brinton McClellan furthered the reputation of the Zouaves. His report concerning his official visit to the Allied forces in the Crimea was published in 1857 as a congressional document. McClellan's overall praise for the Zouaves included the remark that "with his graceful dress, soldierly bearing, and vigilant attitude, the Zouave at an outpost is the beau-ideal of a soldier."[17]

15. Regimental Records, 114th Pennsylvania Volunteers, in Record Group 94, NARA; Frank Rauscher, *Music on the March, 1862–65, with the Army of the Potomac: 114th Regiment Pennsylvania Volunteers, Collis' Zouaves* (Philadelphia, 1892), 11.

16. McAfee, *Zouaves*, 9–10.

17. *Ibid.*, 14; Stephen W. Sears, *George B. McClellan: The Young Napoleon* (New York, 1988), 44–49. McClellan was picked by Secretary of War Jefferson Davis to accompany Majors Richard Delafield and Alfred Mordecai. Both men were considerably older than McClellan, and he railed at "these d——d old fogies!! I hope that I may never be tied to

Following close on the heels of the Crimean War came the 1859 battles of Magenta and Solferino, in which Franco/Sardinian forces, including the Zouaves, contended with Austrian troops attempting to suppress rebellious Italian patriots. During the course of this war, *Harper's Weekly* devoted eight issues largely to the fighting. Illustrations of Zouaves or Turcos (native descendants of the original Algerian troops) could be found in seven of those issues.[18]

Such illustrations fired the imagination of Americans like Elmer E. Ellsworth, who in 1859 created the United States Zouave Cadets from a company of the 60th Regiment, Illinois State Militia. Their uniforms were a fanciful combination of conservative military clothing and traditional Zouave regalia, and their drill and gymnastics were derived from French examples. In July, 1860, Ellsworth and his men embarked on a grand tour of the East, which included a stop in Philadelphia. By the time they returned home several weeks later, newspaper coverage had made Ellsworth and his Chicago Zouaves popular national heroes. Though Ellsworth's company was not the country's first Zouave organization, its fame undoubtedly did more than that of any other group to spawn imitators. By May, 1861, New York City alone fielded four complete Zouave regiments in response to the president's call: In Philadelphia, newspaper correspondents extolled the virtues of the French methods of preparing soldiers: "The French Zouaves have been trained to gymnastic exercises and to the most thorough development of muscular strength and activity. In every French barrack . . . there are gymnasia, where the soldiers are afforded the finest facilities for practicing. This system of exercise has given the French soldiers an advantage over many others. Gymnastic training should be established among all our troops. Not only will the soldiers be made more efficient for service in the field, but their general health and their capacity for endurance will be greatly promoted."[19]

Gymnastic training might very well have promoted general fitness and health among the army's new recruits, but getting them to perform the complicated evolutions of regulation drill efficiently was in itself an immense and worthwhile task. Many of the soldiers apparently found no

---

two corpses again—it is a hell upon earth"; George B. McClellan, *The Armies of Europe* (Philadelphia, 1861), 61.

18. McAfee, *Zouaves*, 15.

19. *Ibid.*, 25–26, 40; *DEB*, August 19, 1861, p. 1.

complaint in the fact that much of their time was taken up in drill practice. One novice of the 57th Pennsylvania, for example, writing from Camp Curtin near Harrisburg in 1861, informed a friend at home that he liked soldiering "first rate so far and I never felt better in my life. We drill about 10 hours a day which is first rate exercise."[20] Not all regiments followed such a rigorous daily regimen, to be sure, but all would have benefited greatly had they done so. Many a commander who struggled vainly in the heat of battle to align his men properly in a desired formation must have mourned time wasted at their camp of instruction.

Rather than joining General Banks's division immediately, as expected, Collis' independent company of Zouaves d'Afrique departed for Fort Delaware within several days of being mustered in. The men bid farewell to Philadelphia at noon on August 25 and steamed downriver for their first real taste of military duty. Fort Delaware was a masonry fortification located on mosquito-infested Pea Patch Island, Delaware. The irregularly shaped pentagonal fort on its 125-acre island was situated midstream in the river between New Jersey and Delaware. The Zouaves were probably sent there as reinforcement for the fort's permanent garrison; however Collis' men apparently made good use of their time in preparing for the rigors of the field and quickly became proficient in drill. By Tuesday, September 24, 1861, the Zouaves had been relieved from their tedious duty and were scheduled to arrive back in Philadelphia prior to joining Banks's command.[21]

The return of the colorful Zouaves was quite an event, typical of such occasions during the early war period when enthusiasm, confidence, and patriotism ran high. The boat carrying the Zouaves from Fort Delaware was expected at the Arch Street wharf at 11:30 A.M., and a large crowd assembled to greet them. A detachment of soldiers under the command of a captain, and consisting of a sergeant, corporal, and ten men from each company of Philadelphia's First Regiment, Reserve Brigade, was also drawn up on the wharf to salute the Zouaves' arrival. It was a festive occasion, one that might lead an unknowing onlooker to believe that Collis' small band of men had already captured Richmond single-handedly. Of course, they had done no such thing, but in September, 1861, it was important

20. Ellis C. Strauss to "Dear Friend," October 21, 1861, in Ellis C. Strauss Papers, 57th Pennsylvania Volunteer Infantry, Letters, 1861–1865, *CWTI* Collection USAMHI.

21. F. H. Taylor, *Philadelphia in the Civil War*, 196, *DEB*, September 24, 1861, p. 6.

to buck up the spirits of the northern people. After all, it was they who had been called upon to supply their sons—or selves—for the country's cause, and many more would soon be asked to follow their example. Union arms had already met with disaster on the banks of Bull Run Creek in Virginia only two months before, and the confidence of the North was justifiably shaken. Just a few weeks prior to that first major clash of arms, a Philadelphia newspaper article confidently expounded on the fine qualities of the Union soldier: "a majority of our Northern soldiers have been laboring men. The Southern army is not largely composed of laboring men and the chivalry howl dolefully about the labor of making fortifications. They might do tolerably well in a fight, but would faint on a march and fizzle at an entrenchment. The Soldiers of the Union would thus have important advantages over the rebels on their own ground and in their own climate." Many other articles in a similar vein had appeared in newspapers throughout the North prior to the defeat of Union General Irvin McDowell's army at Bull Run on July 21; afterward, it was only with grim resolution that many northerners determined, "we must pick up our flint and try again."[22]

And so, on that clear late-September day, with the temperature hovering in the midseventies, citizens flocked to the docks to see the flag-bedecked steamboat *Major Reybold* sidle up and disembark its cargo of Zouaves. The boat arrived about an hour later than expected, and the crowd endured another long delay while the company was formed into line and marched off. Complete with glistening Enfield rifles topped with enormous sword bayonets, the spectacle of gaudily dressed Zouaves proved to be a real crowd-pleaser. As the soldiers headed toward the Volunteer Refreshment Saloon at the foot of Washington Street, with the noted Pennsylvania Cornet Band in accompaniment, their appearance "elicited remarks of commendation at every point."[23] Many of the spectators had come to see the Zouaves in anticipation of their scheduled exhibition of

22. *DEB*, July 9, 1861, p. 7. Interestingly, this article shows the direct contrast of opinions between the country's two contending sections. Southern editorialists universally proclaimed the superiority of their manhood based on their upbringing and rigorous outdoor lifestyle. Conversely, northern workers were demeaned as being physically weakened and corrupted by the conditions of industrial labor. Diary of Katherine Brinley Wharton, July, 22, 1861, HSP, quoted in Gallman, *Mastering Wartime*, 5.

23. *DEB*, September 24, 1861, p. 1. The band was hardly a complimentary welcoming surprise. It was arranged and paid for in advance by the company.

drill at the Academy of Music that evening. While a large number of those at the wharf would be among the crowd at the evening performance, others likely attended the colorful Zouaves' arrival so as to save the twenty-five-cent expense of admission to the show.

After a dinner at the Volunteer Refreshment Saloon in Southwark that afternoon, the Zouaves visited with friends and family, and prepared themselves for their performance. Dinner at the refreshment saloon, through which thousands of volunteers from the northeastern states passed during the course of the war, typically consisted of beef, ham, bread and butter, potatoes, pickles, coffee and tea, and occasionally a dessert such as cake or pie. Early in the war, local businessmen and patriotic citizens—who sought no funding from either city or state—had set up the Union Volunteer Refreshment Saloon and provided meals, washing facilities, writing paper, and envelopes to the men. Letters written by the soldiers were mailed without charge to them, and many of those letters tell of the kindness of Philadelphians in providing volunteers with a much needed respite from an arduous journey. A stop at the Volunteer Refreshment Saloon or its neighbor, the Cooper Shop Refreshment Saloon, was an event stamped indelibly into the memories of thousands of young soldiers.[24]

The doors to the Academy of Music opened at 7:15 that evening, and by the time the performance got underway at eight o'clock, the "house was crowded to the utmost capacity." The entertainments provided by both the Zouaves and the accompanying band were termed "delightful" and "marvelous specimens." Billed as a "Grand Exhibition Drill and Musical Entertainment," much like the earlier performance by Birney's Zouaves, the program included musical pieces interspersed with performances by the soldiers. It began with an overture from the famous 1830 comic opera *Fra Diavolo*, by French composer Daniel Auber, and was followed by a "Dress Parade as a Battalion of Four Companies." The program called for a continuation of that pattern, with musical pieces and military drills alternating. At the program's end, Captain Collis was called before the curtain by the cacophony of whistles, cheers, and calls. "In a modest and thoroughly soldierly speech," according to one account, Collis voiced his thanks to the audience for their attendance and appreciation of his men's performance. The show lasted fully three and one-half hours, after which

24. F. H. Taylor, *Philadelphia in the Civil War*, 206–207; Gallman, *Mastering Wartime*, 127–29.

many of the Zouaves very likely took advantage of their remaining time at home to say goodbye to friends and loved ones. The following day, the company boarded a train that took them to the town of Frederick, Maryland. From there, the men marched thirty-four miles to Darnestown, where they reported to General Banks's division.[25]

There was little activity in Banks's army that fall. Collis was on detached service in Philadelphia from the fourth through the tenth of October. His courtship of Miss Levy was in all likelihood being carried out with great urgency, and he undoubtedly found sufficient time to combine pleasure with military business while in the city. Later that month, the Zouaves missed their first opportunity to engage the enemy when the company came rushing to the support of Major General Charles P. Stone's forces during the fight at Ball's Bluff. The Zouaves marched to Seneca at the head of the division, but the men were not called into action. They took up a position at Edwards' Ferry, lying about four miles south of the point of the Union attack. From that spot, the Zouaves could see across the Potomac where Goose Creek entered the river, and just to the north, they could discern the road to Leesburg, Virginia. Leesburg, a town of three or four thousand, was the Loudoun county seat and the objective of a "slight demonstration" by Stone's troops. Stone commanded a division that was termed—like Banks's—a Corps of Observation, and his mission was to guard the Potomac from Point of Rocks to Edwards' Ferry. To his north was a regiment under Colonel John W. Geary, and to his south was Banks's division. Although Collis' men may have been anxious to pitch in and enter the fray—and perhaps a strong demonstration at Edwards' Ferry might have prevented the calamity that was about to befall the Union forces upstream—they were relegated to the sidelines.

At Ball's Bluff, a reconnaissance force under the command of Lincoln's close personal friend Colonel Edward D. Baker, a United States senator from Oregon, was decimated by Colonel Nathan G. "Shanks" Evans' Confederates. Baker was killed, Stone was arrested, and Union morale plummeted. Throughout the North, the "melancholy disaster" on the Potomac caused consternation almost equal to that following the defeat at Bull Run three months earlier. One soldier probably summed up the general feelings among the ranks when he opined, "There does not seem to be one re-

25. *DEB,* September 24, 1861; Gerhart von Westerman, *Opera Guide* (1964; rpr. London, 1973), 181; *DEB,* September 25, 1861; Bates, *Pennsylvania Volunteers,* I, 1183.

deeming feature in the whole business. They went on a fools [*sic*] errand—went without means, and then persisted in their folly after it became clear."[26] The Union army was off to setting a poor record in its contests with the southerners—one that would plague it continually for the next few years—but, for a time, the fighting was suspended.

By early December, Banks had gone into winter quarters at Frederick, Maryland. Captain Collis promptly took advantage of the lull in campaigning and returned to Philadelphia, where he married Septima M. Levy on December 9, 1861. Although his bride had resided in Philadelphia for several years prior to the outbreak of war, she had been born and raised in that hotbed of secession, Charleston, South Carolina. Her sympathies were naturally with the South, and she later wrote that she had become a "Union" woman only by marrying a northern soldier. While staying with her husband near Petersburg, Virginia, in April of 1865, Mrs. Collis had occasion to defend her change in loyalties. Upon meeting her, the dour, recently surrendered Confederate lieutenant general Richard S. Ewell expressed dismay at the willingness of a southern woman to adopt the Union cause. Mrs. Collis attempted to coax him into a more cheerful mood by retorting that she had merely followed the example of many other southrons and gone with her state, hers being the state of matrimony.[27]

Showing her rather adventurous spirit, Mrs. Collis insisted on accompanying her husband back to Frederick when he returned there on December 10. Yet it was not uncommon for officers to bring their wives to join them while in winter quarters, and this practice persisted throughout the war. Mrs. Collis joined her husband in the field on several occasions, and she spent the final months of the war at City Point with him, even after the birth of a daughter. During the winter of 1861–1862, the newlyweds set up house in a small apartment in Frederick, which Mrs. Collis later described as consisting of "two very modest third-story rooms, sparsely furnished, with the use of a kitchen, at a cheap rent, for we neither of us had any money."[28]

Money was scarce for the young couple, but entertainment among the townspeople and the officers' wives was not. That first winter of the war

26. Quoted in Byron Farwell, *Balls Bluff: A Small Battle and Its Long Shadow* (McLean, Va., 1990), 129.

27. Septima M. Collis, *A Woman's War Record, 1861–1865* (New York, 1889), 1–2.

28. *Ibid.*, 2.

proved to be great fun. Mrs. Collis had enlisted the services of Nunzio Finelli, a private in her husband's company, who only months before had been employed in the kitchen of one of Philadelphia's most fashionable hotels. He was then considered "the best cook in the army," and his skills were greatly appreciated. Writing to Judge Read in January, 1862, Captain Collis described the festive New Year celebration that had taken place: "My wife received yesterday, with Mrs. Maj. Genl Banks, and was the admiration of all, as she might well be. Every officer in the Division waited upon them, and partook of an entertainment at the General's expense, but cooked and set out by one of my men, Nunzio Finelli, late chief cook at the Girard House, and probably the best Cuisinier in the United States. It was a grand affair, imagine a consumption of 2,000 oysters in four hours."[29]

In addition to the parties and receptions among the military men at Frederick, there were also numerous dress parades and imposing reviews of the troops when weather permitted. Mrs. Collis and the other wives found such martial displays to be fine entertainment as well. The former recalled that "we women cantered in the saddle, and stood beside the generals while the troops marched by in their picturesque uniforms to splendid music." The citizens of Frederick probably observed many of these parades and reviews also. They proved to be excellent hosts—especially to the officers—and there were many balls and parties given by the people of the town. Several regiments returned the courtesy in turn, "by such improvised hospitality as the scanty accommodations of the camp would afford." When ragged and odorous Rebel troops marched through the town several months later in September, 1862, their reception was somewhat cold. General Robert E. Lee's hopes that Marylanders would flock to the southern cause at the sight of his hitherto victorious army were most conspicuously dashed by the stony silence of the majority of Frederick's residents. The hard-marching, battle-worn soldiers who passed through the town on the way to Antietam Creek must have looked shockingly like rabble, and nothing at all like the smartly clad, blue-suited men the residents remembered from the previous winter. Lee found few recruits for his army in the city of Frederick.[30]

29. Charles H. T. Collis to John M. Read, January 2, 1862, in Letter Books, Charles H. T. Collis Papers, HSP.

30. S. Collis, *War Record*, 1–4; Stephen W. Sears, *Landscape Turned Red: The Battle of*

Despite the opportunities for diversion in Frederick, Captain Collis had been neglecting neither his military duties nor his career. To the captain's normal duties, General Banks added another time-consuming task when he appointed Collis Judge Advocate for his division in late December, 1861. In this position, the young attorney could draw on his previous legal background. He was responsible for trying, at courts-martial, all those accused of violating either the law or the rules of military behavior. As in all situations where large numbers of men are thrown hastily together, a few assaults and thefts would occur among the men. Some would chafe under military discipline and disobey their superiors; others would strike out at them physically; but more commonly, men would simply leave camp without permission. During winter quarters, when the dull routine of camp life became too much for the men to bear, the temptation to slip away—either temporarily or permanently—also often overwhelmed them. Much of Collis' time was undoubtedly spent in the prosecution of those men who were apprehended either as deserters or as absent without leave.

Throughout the fall and winter of 1861, Collis also made time to attend to his own business. He was then campaigning heavily to have the size of his force increased from a company to a battalion, which he proposed to outfit as sappers and miners. As early as November 1, he had been to Washington to discuss with Major General George Brinton McClellan and his chief of staff, Brigadier General Randolph Barnes Marcy, the prospect of organizing such a command. The idea to recruit a "Corps of 'Sappers Miners and Pontoniers'" was attributable to General Banks himself, who believed that such a force was "much needed in the service."[31]

Before Collis could carry out this plan to enlarge his command, he had to obtain the governor's approval. Collis' first step after gaining the support of Generals McClellan and Marcy was to write immediately from Wash-

---

Antietam (New Haven, 1983), 85–86; James V. Murfin, *The Gleam of Bayonets: The Battle of Antietam and Robert E. Lee's Maryland Campaign, September, 1862* (1965; rpr. Baton Rouge, 1982), 105; John W. Schildt, *September Echoes: A Study of the Maryland Campaign of 1862* (Shippensburg, Pa., 1980), 9–11.

31. John M. Read to "My Dear Meredith," December 29, 1861, in William M. Meredith Papers, HSP; C. Collis to "My Dear Governor," November 4, 1861, in Records of the 114th Pennsylvania Volunteer Infantry, Record Group 19, PHMC, Harrisburg. By raising a battalion, which consisted of three companies, Collis would have ensured himself a ready promotion to the rank of major.

ington to his mentor, Judge Read, with the request that Read appeal to Pennsylvania Governor Andrew Gregg Curtin on his behalf. This Read gladly did. Collis then returned to General Banks's headquarters at Muddy Branch, Maryland, on November 4. As he sat conversing with the general, Collis composed his own letter to Governor Curtin. In it, he explained that he had been given "full authority to raise the necessary men" provided that he first obtain the governor's sanction. "You have already been so instrumental in my success," he continued, "that I am sangine [sic] of your approval now." In commending his plan to the governor, Collis made a comment also designed to appeal to Curtin's state pride. General Banks, he wrote, had "complimented Pennsylvania not a little by making her the offer in preference to Massachusetts."[32]

Whether he was sanguine of Curtin's approval or not, Collis was not one to leave his career to fate alone. Only five days after posting his letter to the governor, he again appealed to Judge Read in a telegram urging him, "Please see or write Gov. C. concerning the acceptance of engineer corps." The following day, November 10, Read—then in Pittsburgh— again wrote to Curtin, enclosing the telegram from Collis in his letter. Collis also wrote the governor that day, stating that he was "particularly anxious to organize . . . and instruct" his command before the onset of winter weather, "as their services will be indispensable should we be compelled to erect winter quarters." This time, General Banks added his endorsement to the letter, in which he explained that the proposed corps would "consist chiefly of theoretical and practical Engineers, making an effective Battallion . . . which cannot fail to confer honor upon the Keystone State."[33]

Despite the flurry of requests, over two weeks passed before Collis finally received a response from Harrisburg. The letter from Curtin's staff stated that Collis had permission to change the name of his company from "Zouaves d'Afrique" to "Sappers and Miners." The frustrated captain quickly wrote back to the governor. "This is not exactly my object," he explained; "I propose to increase my Company to a Battalion and can raise the men

32. Read to "My Dear Meredith," December 29, 1861, in Meredith Collection, Read Papers, HSP; C. Collis to "My Dear Governor," November 4, 1861, in Records of the 114th P.V., PHMC.

33. C. Collis to Read, November 9, 1861, in Read Papers, HSP; C. Collis to "His Excellency," November 10, 1861, in Records of the 114th P.V., PHMC.

in ten days." He went on to declare that several men in Philadelphia were waiting to hear from him in reference to joining his new organization.[34]

Those anxious to join Collis were not only Philadelphians. Frederick J. Amsdeu read a newspaper article concerning the formation of an engineer corps, in which a letter from Banks was cited that expressed his approval and requested the same from Governor Curtin. Amsdeu addressed a letter to Curtin from Scranton on November 16, asking to be commissioned a second lieutenant in Collis' battalion. Judging from the number of other letters in the records of the 114th Pennsylvania from men seeking commissions, it is likely that the governor was besieged with similar requests.[35]

Nevertheless, several more weeks passed without appearance of the desired response, and again Collis requested Judge Read to use his influence to attain the goal. Read wrote to the State Attorney General, William M. Meredith, on December 29, explaining that Collis had received the sanction of all involved save Governor Curtin. He went on to praise Collis as "a most meritorious officer highly esteemed by his commanding general," who was "beloved and respected by his men who form the best disciplined company in the service." Finally, he requested that Meredith "call the attention of the Governor to this matter."[36]

Meredith was finally able to clear up the matter when he ascertained that a letter from Governor Curtin authorizing the increase of Collis' force had been sent but had "miscarried." Read notified Collis of the results of his inquiry, and finally in mid-January, 1862, the official authorization was received in a letter from Pennsylvania Adjutant General A. L. Russell. Collis responded that he would commence recruiting as soon as possible and that he hoped to have his full command in the field within a month.[37]

Still, things did not proceed smoothly for the young captain. Although General Banks had professed anxiety to field a corps of engineers, his

34. C. Collis to "Hon A. G. Curtin," November 27, 1861, in Records of the 114th P.V., PHMC.

35. Frederick J. Amsdeu to "Gov. Curtin," November 16, 1861, in Records of the 114th P.V., PHMC. Collis would need two hundred men in addition to those in his original company to compose a full battalion.

36. Read to "My Dear Meredith," December 29, 1861, in Meredith Collection, Read Papers, HSP.

37. William M. Meredith to "My Dear Read," January 7, 1862, C. Collis to Read, January 2, 1862, in Correspondence, 1861–62, Read Papers, HSP; C. Collis to A. L. Russell, January 18, 1862, in Records of the 114th P.V., PHMC.

immediate need for a competent judge advocate was apparently more pressing. Upon receiving the authorization from Harrisburg, Collis attempted to resign his position as judge advocate for the division. Banks disapproved his request, advising Collis that "he did not know at present how he could supply [Collis'] place." Even so, Collis hoped to be able to obtain at least a week's leave of absence so that he could return to Philadelphia to recruit the necessary men. His hopes were dashed when he encountered yet another obstacle to his battalion's creation: Governor Curtin's authorization needed an endorsement by the Secretary of War. Collis forwarded the appropriate papers to Edwin M. Stanton, and with due pragmatism settled down to await a response before running any risk or incurring an expense in recruiting.[38]

In the midst of this frustrating series of events, Collis was exposed to severe criticism in the press when a letter that was supposedly written by one of his men appeared in a Philadelphia weekly. The January 5 edition of the *Sunday Dispatch* carried the article, which alleged that there was some impropriety in the handling of company funds. The anonymous writer complained that while in Philadelphia, most of the men did not utilize their full allotment of rations. Eight days' worth were sold, it was alleged, and the profit was used to set up a "sinking fund for the benefit of the company," which was to be controlled by the captain. In addition, while at Fort Delaware, the men were reportedly able to save four or five barrels of "mess pork," which was also sold in Philadelphia. Prior to leaving the fort, each enlisted man was assessed a "tax" of twenty-five cents, and noncommissioned officers were assessed fifty cents. This money was to be used to defray the expense of the band that accompanied the men through the city on their return parade. Finally, the exhibition at the Academy of Music reportedly netted a profit of $305. All of this money was supposedly placed in the company fund; however, the disgruntled letter-writer went on, it had been circulated that the fund was in debt. In response, some of the men held a meeting at Darnestown, during which a committee was appointed "to wait on the Captain to see what condition we were in." Collis apparently never met with the committee, and a few days afterward the Zouaves moved to Edwards' Ferry. Later, while at Muddy Branch, Collis "was again waited on by a committee but vouchsafed no answer." The writer concluded this portion of his criticisms by claiming that since the

38. C. Collis to Read, January 11, 20, 1862, in Read Papers, HSP.

company encamped at Frederick, a new committee had been appointed but had yet to receive a response.[39]

There were other allegations leveled against the captain in the letter:

> Since we left Philadelphia, Captain Collis has not drilled us ten times. While on a march from one place to another he will mount a horse and ride ahead of his company and not show himself for days. Since we have been here [Frederick] he has never drilled the men, nor looked after their comfort or improvement in any manner whatever. We are pronounced by all military men to be one of the most thoroughly drilled companies in the service (thanks to our Lieutenants and our own pride as soldiers and Philadelphians). If we do not soon get justice and treatment as men, the company will be entirely demoralized.[40]

Collis took immediate action designed to protect his reputation, and solicited support from those who could vouch for his character and actions. He wrote to Judge Read on January 11, hoping that "the slander . . . has made no greater impact upon you, and my friends in Philadelphia than an anonymous letter ought to do." He further expressed his wish that "the refutation of it by men, not ashamed to show their names, has properly vindicated my character." But he also noted that he had contacted two fellow attorneys in the city "to take the matter in hand for me against the Journal in question." The "Journal in question" had a distinctly Democratic Party bias, and Collis—a loyal Republican supported by his party fellows—had likely run afoul of its editors. Like so many newspaper editors of the period, those of the *Sunday Dispatch* were often eager to print derogatory news concerning the opposition. Nevertheless, after several days, Collis reconsidered his course of action—perhaps at the suggestion of Judge Read and other supporters—and decided that he had been "a little hasty in writing [his attorneys], but would write them . . . to do nothing in the matter." It proved to be the proper course of action. The issue was dropped, with no apparent ill effects, and was not publicly heard of again.[41]

As can be seen, Collis relied greatly on the advice and beneficence of Judge Read. Without his political influence, the young captain's career would likely have been less auspicious. But Captain Collis was not the

39. Philadelphia *Sunday Dispatch*, January 5, 1862, p. 2.
40. *Ibid.*
41. C. Collis to Read, January 11, 20, 1862, in Read Papers, HSP.

only member of his family to rely upon and benefit from Read's sponsorship. Charles' father, William, had gone to Washington the previous November in search of employment with the rapidly expanding bureaucracy of the federal government. He was too late to find a vacancy, however, and by January was becoming almost desperate. Upon learning that a bill had recently passed enabling the Secretaries of War and of the Navy to appoint additional clerks in their departments, Mr. Collis wrote Read to inform him of the results of an interview he had obtained with Senator Charles Sumner. "On [my] mentioning your name he desired me [to] write you at once, as your recommendation would be all powerful." The senior Mr. Collis also received a recommendation from General Banks, and with the backing of two such powerful politicians, he very likely managed to secure a position.[42]

Read's influence apparently was not enough to persuade General Banks to allow Charles Collis to return to Philadelphia to recruit the balance of men authorized to fill his battalion. It is also possible that the captain may have encountered another series of complications in procuring the final necessary approval from Secretary of War Stanton. In any event, Banks's force was soon on the move. On February 23, 1862, the Zouaves received orders to be ready to move. On February 27, Collis and his Zouaves departed Camp Read and marched through Frederick to Sandy Hook. There they crossed the Potomac to Harpers Ferry and the following day moved to Charlestown. Within three months, Banks's shortcomings as a military commander and strategist would be prominently illustrated by his defeat at the hands of Confederate major general Thomas J. "Stonewall" Jackson.[43]

The move to the south also brought an end to the bucolic domestic life that the captain and his wife had experienced in Frederick. Mrs. Collis was reluctant to return to Philadelphia; upon doing so, however, she was surprised at the changes that had taken place in the Quaker City. The town was fully mobilized for the war effort by then. Its people were no longer caught up in the first euphoric burst of war fever, but had rather settled into the grim realization that a long ordeal lay ahead. Oddly enough, Mrs. Collis had little appreciated the meaning of war while

42. William Collis to Read, January 24, 1862, *ibid.*

43. Morning Reports of Captain Collis' Company of Zouaves d'Afrique, in Ac. 6267, LC.

"among the light-hearted soldiers in the field." It was upon viewing the warlike visage of the normally peaceful city that the reality of current events finally struck her fully. She found that many of the stores in the prominent shopping district along Chestnut Street had been transformed into recruiting stations, and public meetings were held daily to encourage enlistments. The music of fife and drum and the cry "On to Richmond!" were heard constantly. The Girard House on Chestnut Street had been converted from a hotel into a vast workshop, "where the jingle of the sewing-machine and the chatter of the sewing girl . . . gave evidence that the government was in earnest."[44]

One of the items produced in prodigious quantities during that early period of the war, Mrs. Collis later recalled, was the havelock: a cotton cap-cover with a long tail designed to shade the neck from the sun. The item was soon found by the soldiers in the field to be more irritating than useful, and "the poor fellows in the army were so inundated with them that those who had the fewest relatives and sweethearts were much the best off." The Zouaves, with their turbans and fezzes, probably never received havelocks, which were made for wear with the regulation army forage cap. Those who did receive them, however, quickly discovered that although useless for the purpose for which they were originally designed, they otherwise came in handy. When cut to the proper size, for instance, they made superb gun-cleaning patches.[45]

Philadelphia, as Mrs. Collis noted, was indeed a changed city by early 1862. Although it would be universally praised and noted for its benevolent activities during the war, it also profited greatly from the many government contracts allotted to its firms. Mrs. Collis had perhaps failed to notice earlier that the quartermaster general of the state militia had established an emergency clothing depot at the Girard House during the opening months of the war. Philadelphia women from the upper class worked side by side with those from the working class to meet the initial demand for uniforms. In addition, sewing circles and independent workers stitched away in their homes—many of them on a contract basis. Such improvised manufacture carried the army through its initial shortage of materiel, but not always satisfactorily. Fraud and abuse among unscrupulous contractors abounded. Uniforms made with shoddy were unable to

44. S. Collis, *War Record*, 12–13.
45. *Ibid.*

withstand the rigors of field usage, and the governor appointed a committee to investigate the inadequacy of uniforms manufactured at the Girard House. In the summer of 1861, the committee reported that while it had discovered no clear evidence of intentional fraud, it had found "ample evidence of poor judgement and unpatriotic profiteering."[46]

After March 31, 1862, when the inventory of state military goods was turned over to Quartermaster General Montgomery C. Meigs of the Federal army, all wartime contracts fell under the purview of a centralized Federal bureaucracy. Thenceforth, all materiel was issued to state troops by the U.S. army quartermaster's department.[47] The Zouaves were not affected by the earlier complaints about uniforms and equipment, however; their materiel was procured before shortages of quality cloth became common. And since it was rarely the workmanship that was faulted, the Zouaves found themselves comfortably clothed.

46. Gallman, *Mastering Wartime*, 286–88. See also *Report of the Commission Appointed to the Governor of Pennsylvania to Investigate Alleged Army Frauds, August, 1861* (Harrisburg, 1861), 42–43.

47. Gallman, *Mastering Wartime*, 288.

3

The Din of War's Alarms

In the early months of 1862, General McClellan was developing a plan to transport his massive army by sea to the Virginia Peninsula lying between the York and James Rivers. From there, supported by a sea-borne line of communications, he hoped to advance rapidly to Richmond—only sixty miles to the west. President Lincoln, however, favored an overland assault against the Rebel capital and feared that an amphibious operation down the Chesapeake might leave Washington dangerously exposed to attack. The general was eventually able to win over his doubting commander-in-chief, but not without making some concessions to the defense of the capital. Part of these concessions concerned the safety of the Baltimore & Ohio Railroad line, and Secretary of War Stanton, who seconded the president's concerns, insisted on the security of the lower Shenandoah valley, through which the line passed.[1]

1. The Shenandoah Valley, or the Valley of Virginia as it is sometimes called, lies between the Blue Ridge and Allegheny Mountains and extends in a southwesterly direction for over 150 miles from the Potomac River to the James River. Because the Shenandoah River and its tributaries run generally northward toward the Potomac, the northern portion of the valley is called the "lower" valley. Therefore, when traveling northward through the valley, one is said to be going "down" the valley. For an overview of the history and importance of the valley, see Robert G. Tanner, *Stonewall in the Valley: Thomas J. "Stonewall" Jackson's Shenandoah Valley Campaign, Spring 1862* (Garden City, N.Y., 1976), 7–28.

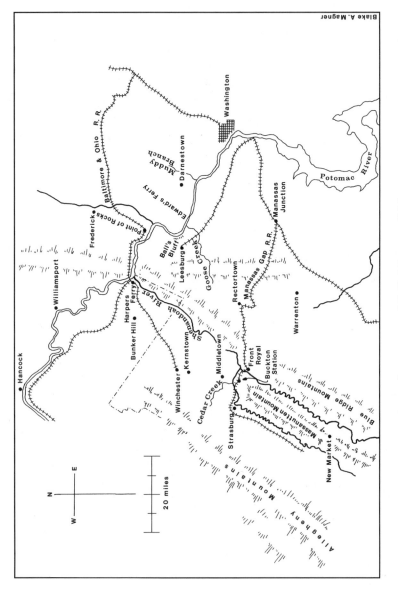

Blake A. Magner

Area of operations of Collis' Zouaves d'Afrique

In order to satisfy Stanton's concern for the Baltimore & Ohio, as well as to allay Lincoln's fears for the safety of Washington, McClellan proposed to dispatch General Banks into the valley, where he would drive the Confederate forces under Stonewall Jackson from the town of Winchester and garrison that place with a portion of his own army. From that strategic location, Banks's forces would be able to defend the line of the Baltimore & Ohio and the Chesapeake & Ohio Canal, which paralleled the Potomac River. Once his garrison was secure in Winchester, the majority of Banks's command would be expected to move to Manassas Junction, where it would be largely responsible for defense of the capital.[2]

Lincoln's concern regarding Washington's possible capture played unwittingly into the hands of the Confederates. The primary mission of Stonewall Jackson's tiny Valley Army was to protect the left flank of the main Confederate force to the east under General Joseph Eggleston Johnston. In addition, his force was to protect the fertile breadbasket of the Shenandoah Valley from destruction. Jackson hoped to accomplish both tasks by reinforcing his own army and attacking Banks. By occupying as many Federal troops as possible in the valley, he expected to prevent Union forces from leaving there to join McClellan, as well as to maintain the vital supply of foodstuffs to the Confederacy. Little did either commander know it, but the simple presence of their armies in the valley was sufficient to accomplish their respective basic missions. Banks was to clear the lower valley, then hold his position and protect Washington. Jackson's mission was to keep Banks occupied in the lower valley and prevent him from joining McClellan. Unlike more cautious commanders, however, Jackson would not be content merely to hold Banks in check.

Thus it was that Banks crossed the Potomac and occupied the town of Harpers Ferry. By March 6, he had moved portions of his force south to the town of Bunker Hill, twelve miles north of Winchester. On the eleventh, he dispatched Collis with a force of twenty Zouaves to conduct a reconnaissance of the roads leading to Winchester from the east. From their camp near Berryville, the men moved to within a few miles of the city. Banks was joined that day by an eleven-thousand-man division under Brigadier General James Shields. The combined force was soon afterwards designated the Fifth Corps.[3]

2. *OR*, Ser. I, Vol. V, 56–57. Unless otherwise indicated, all further citations are to Series I.

3. Morning Reports of Captain Collis' Company, March 11, 1862, LC; *OR*, V, 18.

Jackson's meager force was far outnumbered by Banks's army, and with Shields now in the field, the odds against him were nearly ten to one. Despite Banks's initial success, however, he was still a somewhat timid commander. Jackson had every intention of contesting his advance to Winchester in spite of the odds, and it was only because of a misunderstanding that Stonewall's army withdrew without a fight. Jackson had ordered his men to join their wagons and rest while he formulated his plan of attack, ignorant of the wagons' retreat to a distance of about eight miles south of Winchester. Despite his railing, Jackson could do little to correct the mistake. He had hoped to pull back only far enough to make his opponent believe that he was in full retreat. He then planned to fall on the Union forces in a surprise night attack. Instead, Banks entered Winchester nearly unopposed, doubtless unaware of his good fortune; and the angry, outnumbered Jackson fell back toward Strasburg and his supplies at Mount Jackson.[4]

Jackson continued to retreat in the face of Shields's pursuing division of 11,000 men, and Banks now dismissed the threat from his adversary's small army as negligible. Confident that he could hold the lower valley, Banks compliantly dispatched two of his three divisions to Fredericksburg to aid McClellan's campaign against Richmond, and he ordered Shields to withdraw to the security of Winchester. Jackson now became the hunter, and Shields the quarry. The indomitable rebel turned and marched his men at a grueling pace in pursuit of Shields's division, and late in the afternoon of March 23 rushed into an impetuous attack against the Federals at Kernstown. After three hours of fighting, Jackson was forced to retire his badly outnumbered force; but he had accomplished his purpose. Federal troops intended to support McClellan were ordered to remain in the valley.[5]

In the meantime, Collis and his men had encamped near Winchester on March 14. New tents were delivered there on the following day, and on March 21 the men received a shipment of new rifles. They departed camp that day and started out for Berryville, wading the icy Opequon Creek where it intersected the Berryville Pike. The company had been

4. Tanner, *Stonewall in the Valley*, 106–109; James I. Robertson, Jr., "Stonewall in the Shenandoah: The Valley Campaign of 1862," special issue of *CWTI* (Harrisburg, 1979), 8–10; Frank E. Vandiver, *Mighty Stonewall* (College Station, Tex., 1957), 200.

5. Robertson, "Stonewall in the Shenandoah," 10–17.

detached temporarily from Banks's service and assigned to Brigadier General John Joseph Abercrombie's brigade of Banks's division. The Zouaves trudged their way up the Blue Ridge through Snicker's Gap on the twenty-second and that evening enjoyed the scenic view from their camp on the summit. While the battle raged at Kernstown the following day, Collis wound his column of men down the eastern slopes of the Blue Ridge and into the town of Aldie, nestled in the bosom of the Bull Run Mountains about fourteen miles from Snicker's Gap. The men then backtracked and spent a few days at Goose Creek, scouting the area toward Middleburg. Finally, on the twenty-eighth, the Zouaves continued eastward via Aldie on the Little River Turnpike to the Fairfax courthouse, nearly twenty miles distant. The footsore soldiers remained there only a day, however, and March 29 saw them encamped at Centerville, in the vacated huts of the 8th South Carolina. Over the next several days the Zouaves continued their seemingly aimless marching over the Virginia countryside. They finally were given a respite on April 1 when they boarded the cars of the Orange and Alexandria Railroad at Bristoe Station. The train took them west to Warrenton Junction, where they remained for a few days and received a new supply of sorely needed uniforms.[6]

On April 7, the Zouaves d'Afrique set out to join Colonel Geary of the 28th Pennsylvania Volunteers, who was then near the town of Warrenton commanding a detached brigade from Banks's division. A violent spring snowstorm overtook the plodding column during the march, and Collis was forced to halt the men for a few days until it passed. The company reached Geary's command on the eleventh, immediately set out for White Plains, and eventually settled into a camp near Rectortown that the men called Camp Pardee. Geary's forces were kept busy guarding and rebuilding roads and bridges in the area while constant attempts were made by Confederate cavalry forces to destroy them. Nature also continued to work against the Union engineers and laborers. Continual storms between April 18 and 22 swelled streams beyond passage. Several recently repaired or newly constructed bridges were washed out or damaged. During the lull in activity caused by the incessant rains, the Zouaves received their pay. More importantly, they were issued much needed new footwear to replace that which constant marching was rapidly wearing thin.[7]

6. Morning Reports, March 14–April 1, 1862, LC.
7. Morning Reports, April 7–23, 1862, LC; OR, V, 515–16.

By mid-April, Jackson had reorganized his army and received nine thousand reinforcements under Major General Richard S. Ewell. Jackson first moved to secure his left flank by defeating the Union forces of Major General John C. Frémont's newly formed Mountain Department at the Battle of McDowell on May 8. He then concentrated his army for an assault on Banks, now commanding the Department of the Shenandoah. Still believing that he outnumbered the Rebel forces arrayed against him, Banks had again agreed to transfer Shields's division to McClellan's army. By mid-May, the hapless politician turned general had only eight thousand men left in the vicinity of Strasburg. He was about to receive a lesson in the art of war at the hands of his scorned enemy, whose reinforcements meant that the balance had tipped in favor of the Confederates. It was Jackson who now possessed the numerical advantage, two to one.

Captain Collis' Zouaves finally moved to rejoin Banks's command in early May. Collis had been attached to Colonel Geary's forces for over a month, and the colonel's correspondence of May 6 and 8 reflected that the Zouaves were still temporarily at his headquarters, "but are expected soon to report to Gen'l Banks." By then, Geary had the bridges repaired and the railroad "in good running order." Still, there were incessant attacks and probes by Confederate guerrillas, "rendering it necessary to maintain a very vigilant surveillance of the entire line." Though the Zouaves were assigned to Geary's headquarters near the bridge spanning Goose Creek and saw no action, such service was not entirely without hazard. Illness and disease constantly threatened the well-being of the soldiers, and the Zouaves proved unexceptional in this regard. On May 9, the company buried Private Christian Wall near the railroad line. The thirty-three-year-old soldier had died the previous day of "congestion of the bowels." Three days later the Zouaves boarded the cars of the Manassas Gap Railroad once again and chugged off slowly for Strasburg, where they arrived on May 13. They were back in the valley with Banks, in time to share in the inglorious fate of that general's army.[8]

Banks had been as far south as New Market with his corps; but after losing Shields's division to the effort against Richmond, he fell back to Strasburg. It was there that Collis found him, and the position was hardly a strong one. Banks's army was dispirited by the retreat, during which they had been subjected to the taunts of valley residents who watched gleefully

8. *OR*, V, 515; Vol. XII, Pt. 3, p. 136; Morning Reports, May 9, 1862, LC.

as the northerners returned whence they came. To make matters worse, the small, "shiftless town" of Strasburg offered little in the way of diversion to the thousands of Union troops spreading out across the valley floor in vast assemblages marked by row upon row of white canvas tents. Finally, Banks's lack of acumen in military matters was beginning to set the stage for disaster. Although he himself considered his position "dangerously exposed," he took little corrective action, and his men waited passively in their hazardous state of ignorance. Perhaps a nagging sensation of vulnerability added to their unease at Strasburg.[9]

Meanwhile, Jackson marched his men into the Luray Valley, the portion of the Shenandoah Valley east of Massanutten Mountain, thereby screening his northward progression from the Federals on the western side of the mountain. His objective was the Union outpost at Front Royal, which stood guard over the left flank of Banks's position. At Front Royal, Jackson would be just east of Banks at Strasburg, and directly astride the Manassas Gap Railroad and Banks's line of communication in that direction. With Confederates at that location, Banks's position would be untenable, for Jackson could easily race farther northward to Winchester, capturing the Union supply depot there and severing completely Banks's lines of communication. This outflanking would then have left the unwary general no choice but to retreat either into western Virginia or through Manassas Gap to the east. Either option would represent a serious setback for Union plans.[10]

On Friday morning, May 23, 1862, Jackson's men began their final advance on Front Royal. It was a clear day and scorchingly hot. Exhausted Rebel soldiers dropped by the score along the line of march. Jackson's cavalry pushed ahead toward the Union outpost at Buckton Station, lying midway between Strasburg and Front Royal. There they burned the depot and severed telegraph communications between the towns. Confederate infantry east of Front Royal fell on the railroad line there and completed the isolation of the town. At 2 o'clock that afternoon, Jackson began his attack on Front Royal. He quickly pushed Union troops back through the town and across the vital bridges spanning the Shenandoah. Retreating Federals stalled the attack long enough to set fire to the bridge over the North Fork of the river; but concerted pressure soon drove the northerners

9. Robertson, "Stonewall in the Shenandoah," 24–28.

10. *Ibid.*, 28; Tanner, *Stonewall in the Valley*, 210–16.

back, and the charred span was saved. Without the bridges, Jackson's progression toward Winchester would have been greatly slowed.[11]

In Strasburg, meanwhile, Banks refused to believe that the Rebels at Front Royal were a real threat to his army. Perhaps he wished not to believe it because he realized that in his present perilous position, a determined effort on Jackson's part would surely spell disaster. He procrastinated—in a very worried state no doubt—while his situation grew even more precarious. In addition, political considerations may have clouded his judgment at this time. Having determined unadvisedly that any attack by Jackson would be made on Strasburg, he had taken steps to make that place as defensible as possible. His belief, however, had no reasonable basis in fact, and now he shuddered at the thought of being outflanked from his position and driven northward without a fight. "By God," exclaimed the Waltham general, "I will not retreat!" Banks's fear that censure by the press would follow a Union retreat led him to state to a fellow officer, "We have more to fear from the opinion of our friends than from the bayonets of our enemies." While his political judgment was later vindicated, his military foibles were to cost his army dearly.[12]

On the night of May 23, Banks was still uncertain as to the enemy's intentions—this despite early word from a courier, and later telegraphs from the Front Royal detachment that had escaped to Winchester, indicating Jackson was present in full force. At about 10 P.M., Captain Collis volunteered to take a small escort and determine the situation at Front Royal. Returning at daylight the following morning, Collis informed his commander that the attack on the outpost at Front Royal was indeed "no raid, but an army . . . determined to seize Winchester before the arrival of Banks." Collis' report served only to reinforce what the general had come to realize. While Collis was conducting his reconnaissance, Banks had already begun to remove his sick and wounded to the safety of Winchester in anticipation of having to make a run for it himself.[13]

By midmorning of Saturday, May 24, over twenty hours after Jackson's attack on Front Royal, Banks finally started his entire division on the road to Winchester. By that time, he probably understood that his initial delay

11. Tanner, *Stonewall in the Valley*, 211–14.

12. Fred Harvey Harrington, *Fighting Politician: Major General N. P. Banks* (Philadelphia, 1948), 69–70; Robertson, "Stonewall in the Shenandoah," 30.

13. Charles H. T. Collis, *1st Brigade, 1st Division, 3rd Corps* (New York, 1891), 13; Harrington, *Fighting Politician*, 72; Robertson, "Stonewall in the Shenandoah," 30.

might have been a fatal mistake. If the Confederates had pushed forward with purpose, they could have already occupied Winchester or at least be positioned to contest Banks's retreat in that direction. Once aware of this possibility, Banks also knew that he could not afford to abandon completely his route back to Strasburg should it become necessary to return there and strike east or west in order to escape Jackson's clutches. To preserve that option, he deemed it necessary to ensure that the bridge carrying the Valley Turnpike over Cedar Creek remain intact.

Only after his division was well on the road to Winchester did Banks find that he was not the only general guilty of indecision that day. After taking Front Royal, Jackson paused to consider which course of action would next be best. It was a difficult choice, and Jackson sought guidance through prayer. If he pushed north toward Winchester, he would leave open a route of escape to the east that would allow Banks to flee through Manassas Gap and join Major General Irvin McDowell's division. This would defeat his strategic purpose of drawing Union troops away from the effort to take Richmond. If he moved directly against Strasburg to the west, Banks would then be able to retreat northward to Winchester in time to occupy the high ground west of the city. Jackson groped tentatively northward on the Front Royal–Winchester road on the morning of the twenty-fourth, hoping that his cavalry would discover the enemy's intentions yet fearful that Banks would press eastward and escape.[14]

Jackson's delay allowed a good portion of Banks's force to pass the critical points along the Valley Turnpike where it might have been halted and decimated. As it was, it was a near miss when Jackson did strike at Banks. He sent the Federals scurrying northward in a panic with Rebels nipping at their heels and isolated a sizable rear guard south of Middletown. Among this rear guard were Captain Collis and his Zouaves.

Banks had assigned one of his staff, Captain James W. Abert of the Topographical Engineers, to remain behind at the Cedar Creek bridge in order to destroy it once word arrived that the army would not need it for a return to Strasburg. Captain Abert attempted to retain a detachment of men from one of the rear-guard regiments to assist him in his task but had limited luck. He found that only Captain Collis "was willing and con-

---

14. Tanner, *Stonewall in the Valley,* 217–19. See also Tanner's Appendix A, "Jackson's Plans and Marches, May 24, 1862," 333–43, for a more detailed discussion of the reasons for Jackson's delay in reaching the Valley Turnpike and intercepting Banks.

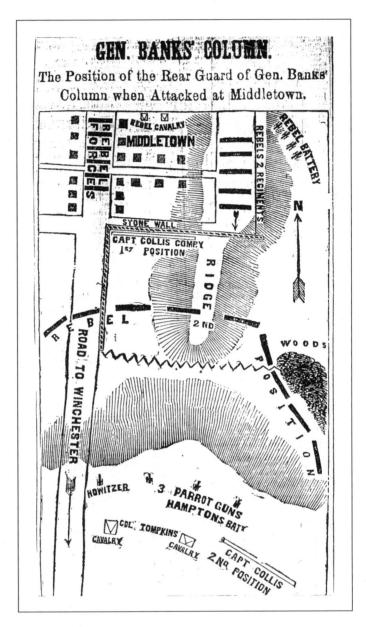

The fight of the Zouaves at Middletown on May 24, 1862
Reproduced from Philadelphia Inquirer *May 31, 1862*

sented to remain." Thus while the army pushed toward Winchester, Captains Abert and Collis, with the Zouaves d'Afrique, halted at the bridge, which lay about midway between Strasburg and Middletown.[15]

Abert sent the Zouaves into a neighboring barn, where they found a tar barrel, straw, and some "commissary pork." The men lit a fire nearby for use when the order was given, prepared the bridge for burning, and settled down to await word from General Banks. None was forthcoming. The captains waited there from about 10:00 A.M. until 3:30 or 4:00 P.M. without further communications from a higher authority. By that time, Captain Abert had determined that a nearby ford was in better condition for crossing than the bridge itself. After consultation with Captain Collis, he decided to leave the bridge intact and push on after the main body of the army.[16]

The small band of soldiers arrived in the vicinity of Middletown in time to see what Collis believed was Jackson's reserve, consisting of four infantry regiments, some cavalry, and four artillery pieces around the town. From the top of the ridge, Collis could see that the Rebels were advancing from the east, while in the town, it could also be seen that a regiment was marching along the main street "in column by company." Confederate guns posted on a ridge to the east were shelling Brigadier General John Porter Hatch's cavalry, which charged up the main street but was unable to proceed. Gun- and rifle fire from Confederates concealed behind one of the stone walls that abounded in the area left a "shrieking, struggling mass of men and horses, crushed, wounded and dying." Hatch then turned westward to escape the barrage. While the Zouaves moved cautiously forward, unable to determine the exact situation in their front, the "excited and terror stricken cavalrymen, who were galloping away, [were] unwilling to halt a single instant."[17]

Collis quickly deployed his company behind the cover of a stone wall that ran eastward across the ridge from the Valley Turnpike and awaited the arrival of the Confederate regiment then in the town. The Rebel force

15. C. Collis, *1st Brigade*, 14; George B. Davis, Leslie J. Perry, and Joseph W. Kirkley, *Atlas to Accompany the Official Records of the Union and Confederate Armies* (Washington, D.C., 1891–95), plate 99, number 2.

16. OR, Vol. XII, Pt. 1, pp. 568–69, 572; C. Collis, *1st Brigade*, 14.

17. C. Collis, *1st Brigade*, 12–14; Henry Kyd Douglas, *I Rode with Stonewall* (Chapel Hill, 1940), 60; Philadelphia *Inquirer*, May 30, 1862, p. 4; OR, Vol. XII, Pt. 1, pp. 568–69, 572.

proved to be the hard-bitten Louisiana battalion known as "Wheat's Tigers," commanded by the battle-seasoned veteran of several armies, Major Chatham Roberdeau Wheat. The "Tigers" advanced to within a hundred yards of Collis' position, close enough for the Union men to see that one of Wheat's companies, the "Tiger Rifles," was also clad in Zouave garb. The southerners unleashed an ineffective volley that slightly injured only one man. From the cover of the stone wall, the Philadelphians fired three volleys that staggered the advance of the exposed infantrymen. Collis later opined that the combination of "cool aim, short range, and grand position must have had terrible effect." Nevertheless, numbers quickly began to tell, and he was forced to withdraw his men from their position in the face of a flanking attempt on his right. Collis deployed the company as skirmishers and fell back in good order, firing steadily. "This movement was as orderly as though executed upon the drill ground," he reported, echoing Captain Abert's judgment that it was "the most orderly movement of the kind on record." The Louisianans, meanwhile, as befit their reputation, "were looting right merrily," and did not follow the retreating Federals aggressively.[18] Collis and his men moved steadily southward, losing three men thought killed by the Rebels who had taken up for the plundering Louisianans.

On a hill nearly a mile south of Middletown, the Zouaves were relieved to find four pieces of Captain Robert B. Hampton's 1st Pennsylvania Artillery Battery firing at the advancing graycoats. Collis formed his men once again in line of battle on the right of the battery. Hampton continued shelling the oncoming lines of the enemy, temporarily checking their advance with canister as they approached the skeleton force obstructing their way.[19]

General Jackson, after observing the situation at Middletown and the apparently large Federal formation south of town, was once again unable to ascertain the whereabouts of Banks's force. Thinking that the force fleeing northward in disarray from that point was only the lead portion of Banks's division rather than the tail of his column, Jackson concluded that his adversary was still concentrated in force somewhere between Middle-

18. C. Collis, *1st Brigade*, 12–15; OR, Vol. XII, Pt. 1, pp. 568–69, 572–73; Philadelphia *Inquirer*, May 30, 1862, p. 4; Terry L. Jones, *Lee's Tigers: The Louisiana Infantry in the Army of Northern Virginia* (Baton Rouge, 1987), 75–78; Richard Taylor, *Destruction and Reconstruction: Personal Experiences of the Late War* (New York, 1879), 55.

19. OR, Vol. XII, Pt. 1, pp. 568–69, 572–73.

town and Strasburg. The appearance of Collis' company, Hampton's battery, and a small force of cavalry and miscellaneous infantry to the south seemed to confirm this conclusion. Jackson turned the bulk of his army toward Strasburg. He then dispatched a message to Major General Ewell, instructing him to halt his division and advance no farther in the direction of Winchester. "There still seems to be a considerable body of the enemy advancing on us from Strasburg," he wrote. Over an hour would pass before Jackson discovered that the force he was pursuing was merely a fragment of Banks's army, and that the bulk of the Federal corps had already passed through Middletown in its rush for the safety of Winchester.[20]

Meanwhile, Collis continued to fall back toward Strasburg along with the artillery and other miscellaneous remnants of the rear guard. In the face of the overwhelming concentration of Confederate troops arrayed against them, the small Federal force finally took up position on a hill north of the Hupp house, about one-quarter mile north of Strasburg. With a steep hill anchoring their left flank, and the north branch of the Shenandoah River on their right, it would have proven to be a defensible position. In addition, the men were joined by about five hundred troopers from Colonel Charles H. Tompkins' 1st Vermont Cavalry along with the 5th New York Cavalry under Colonel Othneil De Forest. By this time, however, Jackson had realized his error and had begun to turn northward to resume his march to Winchester. The little band was spared, and a "final struggle" was averted.[21]

Once the immediate danger had passed, Collis intended to reach Banks at Winchester by an alternate route. He and Captain Abert determined to march northward on roads lying to the west and paralleling the Valley Turnpike. Captain Abert offered to guide the artillery to safety, but Hampton declined upon learning that the proposed route would be within three or four miles of the turnpike and would dangerously expose his flank. Both Hampton and Colonel Tompkins decided to seek a less hazardous path, leaving the foot soldiers on their own. With Abert, his own company, and about fifty men of various other regiments who had been left guarding the commissary stores at Strasburg, Collis struck off westward, probably to the Cedar Creek Grade and Middle Road to Winchester. By midnight,

20. Tanner, *Stonewall in the Valley*, 221–22; *OR*, Vol. XII, Pt. 3, p. 899.
21. *OR*, Vol. XII, Pt. 1, pp. 569, 572, 581; Davis, Perry, and Kirkley, *Atlas to Accompany the Official Records*, plate 99, number 2.

the Zouaves had slogged along uneventfully to within three miles of their objective, meeting along the way with a detachment of Colonel De Forest's cavalry and a train of thirty-eight commissary wagons commanded by a lieutenant.[22] Their luck, however, turned when they found their path blocked by the enemy's pickets. Collis and his companions retraced their steps and headed farther north to the Romney Pike. As they approached Winchester from the west that Sunday at midmorning, they came to realize that their efforts to rejoin Banks would be frustrated once again.

The sounds of battle carrying over the mist-shrouded mountains to the east had been furious since the fighting began at 5 A.M. The tiny remnant of the rear guard arrived within sight of the town in time to see Banks's outnumbered division fleeing toward the Potomac. His lines had been flanked by nearly one-half mile on either side, and his men streamed fear-stricken to the north, many of them discarding their weapons and equipment in an effort to speed their escape. Banks's best attempts to rally his division accomplished nothing. "Stop, men!" he shouted to one Wisconsin regiment; "don't you love your country?" "Yes, by God," came the reply from one of them, "and I'm trying to get back to it just as fast as I can!"[23]

Collis abandoned all hope of rejoining Banks at that time. He then had over twenty men who were too fatigued to walk placed into the commissary wagons. Perhaps he, too, was stunned and unnerved by the sight of Banks's division fleeing pell-mell for safety. "I was at last compelled to provide for our own personal safety," he reported, and, leaving the wagons to fend for themselves, "took to the woods." With a pocket compass and map, he and Captain Abert succeeded in reaching the Potomac at Hancock, Maryland, at 2 P.M. on the following day, where they were joined by the wagons. After a march of 141 miles in forty-seven hours, as measured by Captain Abert, Collis reported with his Zouaves to General Banks near Williamsport, Maryland, at noon on May 27.[24]

Banks was no doubt surprised to see Collis, as he had been given up for lost. Colonel John S. Clark, an additional aide-de-camp to Banks, had reported to Secretary of War Stanton on May 26: "Captain Collis and his company of Zouaves d'Afrique taken prisoners." A similar report was published in the newspapers in Philadelphia, where friends of Mrs. Collis—

22. OR, Vol. XII, Pt. 1, pp. 569, 572–73; C. Collis, *1st Brigade*, 15.
23. OR, Vol. XII, Pt. 1, p. 573; Robertson, "Stonewall in the Shenandoah," 32.
24. OR, Vol. XII, Pt. 1, p. 573; Philadelphia *Inquirer*, May 30, 1862, p. 4.

who was anxiously awaiting news of her husband's fate—purposely kept the information from her. Although Collis later reported a final loss of three men killed, one wounded, and two taken prisoner, one correspondent gloomily wrote that the Zouaves had been "cut to pieces." Mrs. Collis was greatly relieved when Judge Read called late one evening to relate the news of her husband's successful evasion of the enemy. In reality, the loss among the Zouaves was not even so great as Collis originally surmised. Private Charles Fedalen had been wounded and taken prisoner during the withdrawal from the stone wall at Middletown. Collis also reported the deaths of William McClane, James Britton, and Jacques Laurier. Of the three, only McClane had been killed; the other two men had been captured. Both later served with the 114th Pennsylvania and were discharged on surgeon's certificates in the spring of 1863.[25]

Collis was not alone in praising Banks when he finished his official report of May 28 by congratulating the general "upon the success of your unparalleled retreat." Banks even deluded himself into thinking that the debacle was not very serious. He wrote his wife that he was "delighted with our success." Friends, however, called for the general to protest the mismanagement of the War Department, whose blundering policies they alleged had left his weakened forces at the mercy of Jackson's minions. Banks would have none of it, and Stanton thought the general's behavior admirable. The secretary rewarded the soldier's silence by declining to censure him for his mishandling of the affair.[26]

In the eyes of Banks, Collis and his men had performed their duties well during the retreat of his corps; for his valuable service in the valley, the captain was given permission to increase the size of his command to a full regiment. He quickly took advantage of the opportunity to return to Philadelphia to begin recruiting the necessary men.

Banks reentered Virginia on June 10, and on June 26 his force was absorbed into Major General John Pope's Army of Virginia as the Second Corps. Collis' company, rather than returning to Philadelphia with their leader to assist in recruiting, accompanied Banks, under the command of forty-year-old First Lieutenant Severin A. Barthoulot. He and Second

25. *OR*, Vol. XII, Pt. 3, p. 136; S. Collis, *War Record*, 14; Philadelphia *Inquirer*, May 30, 1862, p. 4; Bates, *Pennsylvania Volunteers*, I, 1188.

26. *OR*, Vol. XII, Pt. 1, p. 573; Harrington, *Fighting Politician*, 78–79. Nathaniel P. Banks to his wife, May 28–29, June 6, 1862, quoted in Harrington, *Fighting Politician*, 78.

Lieutenant George Heimach would share the leadership responsibilities in the company while Collis was in Philadelphia. During the summer campaigning of 1862, the Zouaves remained with the Third Brigade, First Division, Second Corps, suffering thirteen casualties at Cedar Mountain on August 9 while attached to the 2nd Massachusetts. The reorganization of the army just prior to the battle at Antietam on September 17 caused the Zouaves to be placed in the Third Brigade, First Division, Twelfth Corps, where they remained attached to the 2nd Massachusetts. With neither of their officers present, the Zouaves suffered three additional casualties at Antietam. The situation in which they were left would become the source of much dissatisfaction among some members of the original company. They would later voice their displeasure at being abandoned in the field without what they felt was competent leadership, and some of them would request a transfer to another regiment, where they hoped to be treated more equitably. Collis would eventually soothe their ruffled feathers, but it was obviously a disgruntled group of Zouaves who were tramping around the Virginia and Maryland countryside that summer.[27]

27. OR, Vol. XII, Pt. 2, pp. 137, 155; Vol. XIX, Pt. 1, pp. 179, 501.

4

Star of the Keystone State

After the rout of Banks's division at Winchester, Union commanders in the Shenandoah Valley continued to suffer defeat at the hands of Stonewall Jackson. Both Shields and Frémont were chastened in early June by the Confederate warrior and his hard-marching "foot cavalry."

Meanwhile, on the Virginia Peninsula, General McClellan was inching toward the Rebel capital with his ponderous army. He was destined to be the first of many Union generals who faced the combined strategic and tactical talents of Stonewall Jackson and General Robert E. Lee. The strange lethargy that Jackson exhibited during the coming contests was of tragic proportions but a poor indicator of the magic that he and Lee would later generate on the battlefields of Maryland and Virginia. This lethargy notwithstanding, by the end of the Seven Days' Battles from June 25 to July 1, McClellan was compelled to execute his infamous change of base and retreated to Harrison's Landing on the James River to seek solace in the safety of the Navy's gunboats there.

McClellan's army was soon withdrawn to cooperate with Major General John Pope's Army of Virginia, into which Banks's corps had been absorbed. The bombastic style of the Kentuckian Pope, who boasted of maintaining a headquarters in the saddle and chided his troops for their defeatist attitude, did little to foster a cooperative spirit among the easterners. Stung by his pompous rebukes, Pope's army experienced an alienation that would have telling effects on the battlefield.

In response to the fruitless campaigning in Virginia that spring and summer of 1862, a despairing President Lincoln was forced to call on northern states for an additional 300,000 volunteers. Each state was again given a quota by the Federal government that was based on the state's total eligible population, and again the responsibility of recruiting the regiments fell to the individual governors. For ambitious soldiers like Captain Collis, the call for more men signaled a golden opportunity.[1]

In Philadelphia, whose portion of the state's quota amounted to 33,414 men, city officials watched apprehensively for the response of its eligible citizens. The early war fever of the previous year had begun to die down as the harsh reality of armed conflict became apparent. Besides witnessing the obvious effects of death, destruction, and grief, many Philadelphians already in the army made it clear in letters home that army life was difficult and unrewarding, and thereby fostered little enthusiasm for enlistment. In addition, the wartime economy was swelling enormously. The increasing number of jobs available corresponding to the rise in production that was necessary to sustain the massive armies removed another incentive to enlist. As might be expected under such conditions, the response to President Lincoln's third call to arms was far less ardent and impetuous than to his previous requests for troops.

Government efforts to spur enlistments came in both positive and negative forms. On the positive side, the War Department authorized an advance bounty payment of twenty-five dollars, with the remainder of the normal inducement of one hundred dollars to be paid upon honorable discharge. On the negative side, Congress enacted the Militia Act on July 17, 1862, which strengthened the president's hand by permitting him to call state militia units into Federal service for up to nine months at a time. The War Department quickly sought to take advantage of the leverage this act provided, and on August 4, called for 300,000 nine-month militia from the states in addition to the three-year volunteers. Though every three-year volunteer enlisted above a state's quota would count as four militiamen, any number of volunteers short of the quota would require an equal number of nine-month men in their place. In addition, states who failed to mobilize the required number of militiamen would be faced with the prospect of the War Department stepping in to take over the recruiting

---

1. Gallman, *Mastering Wartime*, 16–17; James M. McPherson, *Ordeal by Fire: The Civil War and Reconstruction* (New York, 1982), 251.

process. This threat amounted to a quasi-draft, and the possible enactment of a full-fledged draft loomed ominously.[2]

Seeking to avert both a draft of men from Philadelphia and the resultant "stigma" that such a draft might incur, the city councils appropriated funds necessary to provide a municipal bounty of $20, $30, or $40 for nine-month, one-year, or three-year recruits, respectively. It was hoped that this City Bounty Fund, totaling $500,000, would provide sufficient incentive to enlist.[3]

While city officials were fretting over the possibility that a draft might occur and beget violence, Captain Collis was offering to do his part to ensure that Philadelphia met its quota. He again appealed to Harrisburg for permission to increase the size of his command, this time to a full regiment. No delays or miscarried communications thwarted his ambitions on this occasion, and he soon received the authorization to carry out his plans.

Leaving Lieutenant Barthoulet in command of the company of Zouaves d'Afrique, Collis returned to Philadelphia to begin recruiting. His task would be slightly less difficult than that of other prospective colonels seeking to enlist men. First, it would be necessary only to enlist a number of men equivalent to nine companies—about nine hundred soldiers—rather than the normal ten. The original Zouaves d'Afrique were to comprise nearly all of Company A of the new regiment, and several experienced men would be advanced in rank and dispersed among the regiment. In addition, since the new regiment was to be modeled after the original company of Zouaves, its current reputation, which had been enhanced by local newspaper accounts of its actions, would go a long way toward attracting recruits. They would be joining men with experience, would be officered by veterans, and would assume heroic stature by virtue of their association with the well-known Zouaves d'Afrique. Finally, the Zouave craze was still a powerful force in influencing young men to enlist in a particular regiment. The thought of wearing the regulation dark blue wool, four-button sack coat and sky blue kersey trousers must have paled in comparison to that of the colorful and flamboyant uniform of the Zouaves.

Raising a regiment of troops, however, was not possible to do on a shoestring and could prove to be very costly. There were musical bands to

2. McPherson, *Battle Cry of Freedom*, 491–93; McPherson, *Ordeal by Fire*, 251–52.

3. Gallman, *Mastering Wartime*, 17, 271–98; F. H. Taylor, *Philadelphia in the Civil War*, 267–68.

be hired, advertisements to be printed, and numerous other expenses that could soon drive all but the wealthiest seekers of rank into financial distress. On July 25, Collis accordingly appealed to his fellow members of the Philadelphia Bar for assistance in raising funds not only for general recruiting expenses, but also to offer a "premium" to recruits that was designed to attract a "superior class of men" to his regiment. "I trust I am well enough known to you to merit your confidence in my present undertaking," he wrote to the city's attorneys. Hoping that their patriotism would manifest itself in pecuniary assistance, he appointed one of their number to serve as treasurer of a fund to which he wished them to subscribe. As no documentation can be found that shows any member of his regiment's having received an additional monetary inducement to enlist, it is unlikely that Collis was able to generate much by this means. What money, if any, that was raised through this appeal was likely used for general recruiting purposes, or possibly to obtain the specially imported cloth used for the Zouave's trousers.[4]

Collis' first step was to begin to recruit officers willing to serve under him as company commanders in the new regiment. Each of those officers would have the responsibility to recruit the number of men required to muster an entire company into service. Often this challenge entailed convincing a number of men who knew and respected the potential officer that they should follow him and join his regiment. An officer could also make every effort to secure a position in the noncommissioned officer (NCO) ranks of his company for his friends who followed him. Once this nucleus was formed, the initial stages of enlisting recruits might proceed fairly rapidly, as each of the men was expected to appeal to others whom he knew to join him. Because much of the early recruiting took place through this initial word-of-mouth system, many companies contained men who were members of the same families, the same occupational groups or workplaces, or the same neighborhoods. If this method failed to provide sufficient numbers, officers, often accompanied by the colonel, could sponsor and participate in rallies, speeches, concerts, and war meetings designed to generate enough interest to fill out their companies.

A recruiting rendezvous for the Zouaves was established at the Old Military Hall at Fifth and Locust Streets in Philadelphia, and substations

---

4. C. Collis to "the members of the Bar," July 25, 1862, in Simon Gratz Collection, HSP.

were quick to appear throughout the city. The populous areas near the center of town were likely to contain the most recruiting stations, and those of the Zouaves could be found at 109 South Third Street, Third and Gaskill Streets, and Sixth and Chestnut Streets. They were also found as far south as 723 South Third Street and as far west as Nineteenth and South Streets. By July 30, there were three recruiting stations opened near the Union Volunteer Refreshment Saloon in the Southwark section of the city, one of which belonged to the Zouaves; and on August 5, it became necessary to open another station on Chestnut Street, this one in a tent in the yard of the Customs House between Fourth and Fifth Streets. Others were established in more distant parts of the city, such as at Lyceum Hall in Roxborough, and in rooms over a coal office on Main Street in Germantown.[5]

On July 14, Colonel Collis reported that he had recruits joining him so rapidly that he thought he might have to ask the governor for authority to raise up to five additional companies. He further reported that he could muster as many as forty men per day; however, competition from other regiments and exhaustion of the initial word-of-mouth resources would soon slow his regiment's growth.[6]

Assisting in the recruiting of the regiment was Captain Federico F. Cavada of Company K, 23rd Pennsylvania Volunteers. Collis initially offered Cavada the position of major but subsequently raised him to lieutenant colonel of the Zouaves. Collis was aware that Governor Curtin wished to promote officers who had already served in the field and gained some experience. Cavada not only fit that description, having served in the Peninsular campaign under a prominent Philadelphia attorney and former colonel of the 23rd Pennsylvania, Brigadier General David Bell Birney, but he also possessed the advantage of claiming friendship with the governor. Events would prove that neither his experience nor his connections would make Cavada an adequate leader, however much they made him seem a good choice at the outset.[7]

Other officers detached from their regiments to recruit for the Zouaves were Second Lieutenants Charles B. Sloan and Edward R. Bowen of Com-

5. Philadelphia *Weekly Times*, April 24, 1886, p. 1; Philadelphia *Inquirer*, July 30, 1862, p. 8.
6. C. Collis To "General," July 14, 1862, in Records of the 114th P.V., PHMC.
7. *Ibid.*

panies G and D, 75th Pennsylvania. Sloan was mustered into the new regiment of Zouaves as captain of Company H, Bowen as first lieutenant of Company B. Other members of the 75th to join the Zouaves were Captain Joseph S. Chandler of Company H, who was appointed to the rank of major, and First Sergeant Francis Fix of Company I, appointed as captain of Company E. The latter's brother, Augustus W. Fix, then in the field with the Zouaves d'Afrique, would serve under him as first sergeant of Company E.[8]

The 75th Pennsylvania, which had been recruited largely from the German population of Philadelphia and its environs in 1861, seems to have been followed by a black cloud during its early period of service. Many of those transferring to the Zouaves were undoubtedly hoping to put this bad luck behind them. In April, 1862, for instance, two officers, a first sergeant, and fifty enlisted men of Companies I and K were drowned in the Shenandoah River while attempting a crossing of the turbulent stream at Berry's Ferry, Virginia. The regiment lost heavily at the battles of Cross Keys and Port Republic in the Valley Campaign of 1862 while part of Major General Frémont's command, and at the second battle of Bull Run in August its casualties amounted to 133. Among those killed was Lieutenant William Bowen, whose brother Edward was then in Philadelphia recruiting for the Zouaves.[9]

Sergeant George J. Schwartz of the original company of Zouaves d'Afrique was also detached for recruiting in the city that summer. Schwartz was mustered in as first lieutenant of Company B and then promoted to captain of Company G in December, 1862, after the dismissal of a fellow member of the original company, Alexander T. Mitchell. Several other men in the original company were also promoted to officer and NCO positions in the new regiment. Still others joined the Zouaves who had served together with Colonel Collis and Lieutenant Barthoulot in the 18th Pennsylvania. E. Forrest Koehler, who, like Barthoulot, had served as a first sergeant in the 18th, became Captain of Company C, the Zouaves' color company.[10]

8. Philadelphia *Inquirer*, July 19, 1862, p. 8; Bates, *Pennsylvania Volunteers*, II, 1188–1207.

9. F. H. Taylor, *Philadelphia in the Civil War*, 99–100.

10. Philadelphia *Inquirer*, July 19, 1862, p. 8; Bates, *Pennsylvania Volunteers*, I, 168–75, II, 1188–1207.

The life and career of Alexander Wallace Given is perhaps illustrative of those of the new regiment's recruits who had no prior military experience. Given was mustered in as sergeant major on July 22, 1862, and later promoted to first lieutenant of Company F. He was born in Philadelphia on June 29, 1838, slightly over four months after the birth of Collis, and was educated in the city's public school system until 1850. At that time, he was forced by his family's financial needs to take employment with Howell and Brothers wallpaper manufactory. Given then tried the printing business, but finding indoor work too "confining," he sought employment at a brickyard where he sometimes loaded carts from 4 A.M. until 6 P.M. Eventually, he returned to the wallpaper trade, binding himself as apprentice for three years and six months to Joseph E. VanMeter, whose shop was located on the southeast corner of Sixth and Arch Streets. His apprenticeship completed on February 21, 1859, Given took a position as head paperhanger for John Brockbank of Manayunk and boarded at the home of Richard Patton, "whose daughter, Annie, [he] was paying attention to." At that time, Given was able to average one hundred dollars per month, being "strong and temperate" as well as paid by the piece. With these wages, he was able to pay off his family's debts and have two houses constructed in Manayunk—one for himself and one for his parents and brothers.[11]

Given never moved into his house, however. On the moonlit evening of December 15, 1859, he and Annie Patton became husband and wife. In February, 1860, they rented a store at the corner of Ridge Avenue and Lyceum Street in Roxborough; they occupied the store's two additional rooms, which they used as living room and bedroom, respectively. It was in the bedroom, Given later wrote, that he determined to answer President Lincoln's call for troops and enlist in the 114th Pennsylvania Volunteers:

A singular dream or vision came to me the night before [the decision] while asleep in my little home. I thought while in conversation with my wife that Genl. Washington appeared to me [and] looking me in the eye said as he raised his hand in a solemn manner, "This country must and shall be free," then vanished. When I awoke and told the dream to my wife, I said that means for me to go and fight for my country and my flag. My wife said, "Go and God be with you." I enlisted the next day.[12]

11. Diary of Alexander W. Given, n.d., in Alexander W. Given Collection, CWLM.
12. *Ibid.*

While many of the men who enlisted that summer of 1862 probably recollected the call to arms far less melodramatically than Given did, it seems that some force more powerful than economic necessity or self-preservation commonly possessed a good number of them. Given's paper-hanging business had expanded rapidly in the months immediately preceding his enlistment. He would be turning his back on prosperity for the prospect of thirteen dollars per month, poor food, and hard marching. These were to be his rewards, provided he did not succumb to disease or enemy lead. In general, the men preparing to don the Zouave uniform at the many recruiting stations throughout Philadelphia seem to have been gainfully employed at the time of their enlistment. A local newspaper correspondent even noted on July 24: "We are informed that the class of men enlisting [in the 114th Pennsylvania] are of a superior order, whether this is because the organization is to be officered by gentlemen of experience, or that the uniform is to be that of the original Zouaves D'Afrique of France, we do not know, but true it is that this appears to be a favorite regiment." [13]

Whatever his reasons for doing so, Given apparently worked in the regiment with an energy similar to that which had made him a successful businessman. Captain Frank A. Elliot of Company F, a Germantown wool merchant whose offices were on North Front Street near the Delaware River wharves, appointed Given as second sergeant and authorized him to open a recruiting office in the twenty-first ward. This was the office in Roxborough's Lyceum Hall, where Given quickly enlisted thirty men. [14]

Captain Elliot also proved to be a popular recruiter. On Tuesday, July 29, he and Lieutenants Charles A. Robinson—who later became the adjutant of the regiment—and George P. Anderson of Company F took advantage of the impetus provided by a war meeting held the previous Saturday to enlist twenty-two men. Company F then numbered over sixty men. Other Zouave companies were recruiting quickly as well. On August 5 it was noted that the color guard, Company C, which was under the command of another former attorney, Captain Koehler, and was also "reported to be the best in the regiment," contained ninety-six men. That company took the name "Coopers Guard," supposedly because it was composed mostly of men belonging to that occupation. It was further alleged:

13. Philadelphia *Inquirer*, July 24, 1862, p. 8.
14. Given Diary, n.d., in Given Collection, CWLM.

"With the exception of four of the members they have all left good situations to serve their country. Of those four, two are Rebel deserters, who have taken the oath, joined our army and now intend fighting for the Union."[15]

As August progressed, Philadelphians were still responding eagerly to calls to join the ranks of the Zouaves d'Afrique. At a war meeting in Bustleton on Wednesday, August 6, at which Collis delivered an address, another large number of recruits was enlisted—16 on the spot. The following morning, another successful recruiter, Captain Albert G. Rowland of Company I, a thirty-eight-year-old former clerk, reported to the regiment with a full complement of 114 men, most of them residents of the Frankford section of the city.[16]

By mid-August, however, enthusiasm had waned, and recruiting had slowed almost to a standstill. Recruits at that time were eligible to receive "a premium of $3.00 for enlisting, one month's pay in advance ($13.00), bounty from the general government of $25.00, and bounty of $50.00 from the city." As mentioned earlier, soldiers would also receive the balance of their $100.00 bounty from the Federal government at the expiration of their enlistment. Philadelphians had the choice of joining any one of five regiments recruiting in the city that summer. While Collis' Zouaves proved to be one of the most popular of them, competition from the 118th and the 68th Pennsylvania especially drew a good many potential recruits away from the 114th.[17]

The 118th, known as the "Corn Exchange Regiment," did not begin recruiting actively until over a week after the 114th did so, yet by August 16, the 118th contained 864 men while the 114th had only 649. The primary reason for the disparity was undoubtedly that the Corn Exchange of Philadelphia, which sponsored the 118th, had offered the "inducement of a liberal bounty," in addition to the regular government-funded sum.

15. Philadelphia *Inquirer*, July 29, p. 8, August 5, p. 8. A review of the muster rolls for Company C reveals that only 11 men of a total of 87 whose occupations could be determined described themselves as coopers. While this is not an insignificant number, comprising over 12.6 percent of the company, it is indicative of the often-misleading nature of such company names. Though coopers may have predominated among the early enlistees and formed the nucleus of the company, the sheer numbers alone do not seem to warrant the title adopted by the group.

16. Philadelphia *Inquirer*, August 8, 1862, p. 8; *DEB*, August 7, 1862, p. 5.

17. Philadelphia *Inquirer*, August 5, 1862, p. 8.

The men were derisively referred to as "the $200.00 boys from Philadelphia" by some of the veteran regiments they initially encountered in their brigade. But after the 118th suffered casualties of 262 men at the hard-fought but disastrous battle of Shepherdstown less than three weeks after taking the field, no one dared chide them again.[18]

Other regiments recruiting in the city during the same period were the 68th, which later would be brigaded with the 114th; the 116th, destined to join the ranks of the famed Irish Brigade; the 119th, known as the "Gray Reserve" regiment because it contained a number of men from Philadelphia's prominent First Regiment Militia of the same name; and the 121st, raised and commanded by two members of the influential Biddle family of Philadelphia, Chapman and Alexander. This last regiment was never filled to capacity, and it was necessary to complete its rolls by including three companies of men enlisted from the mountains of distant Venango County, Pennsylvania.[19]

With five regiments vying for the city's eligible male population, by mid-August commanders increased the types of recruiting activities designed to spur enlistments. On August 11, Collis paraded those of his men for whom he was then able to furnish uniforms. He had hoped that nearly the entire regiment would be able to turn out for this event, but many were still without complete uniforms. A parade was also held the following day "through the upper part of the city," but again the full regiment was unable to participate. "In consequence of the delay in the manufacture of the uniforms," it was reported, "the grand parade of the regiment will not take place until later in the week."[20]

Local newspapers did their part to stimulate interest in the regiments then recruiting. They faithfully announced the upcoming parades and reported those performed by the regiments. Journalists complimented the men and officers on the "fine display" they made during such events. Collis himself was touted as having displayed "a wonderful amount of energy in rallying his command in so short a time," while the men of his regiment were praised individually for their fine qualities. The command received

18. *DEB*, August 16, 1862, p. 1; F. H. Taylor, *Philadelphia in the Civil War*, 130–31; Survivors' Association, *History of the 118th Pennsylvania Volunteers, Corn Exchange Regiment* (Philadelphia, 1905), 71.

19. *DEB*, August 16, 1862, p. 1; F. H. Taylor, *Philadelphia in the Civil War*, 83–136.

20. Philadelphia *Inquirer*, August 12, 1862, p. 1; *DEB*, August 8, 1862, p. 3.

much acclaim in the press, and one reporter evinced little doubt that it would "bid fair to be one of the star regiments of the Keystone State."[21]

Collis continued to stage parades throughout the city, sometimes accompanied by the regimental band. Individual companies also paraded in an effort to fill their ranks, occasionally escorted by the band as well. Still, enlistments continued to be slow in the latter days of August. As reports began to reach the city of the battle at Cedar Mountain, the press took the opportunity to extol further the virtues of the original company of Zouaves d'Afrique, which was still in the field. In an effort to spur enlistments in the regiment so that their comrades in arms could soon join them, one reporter remarked:

> Thrown into the front ranks, they bore the brunt of a close and fierce assault with genuine Zouaveism. Their numbers previously depleted by promotions and recruiting squads, it is feared, will be thinned by the wounded and disabled in this encounter. Only one killed is reported, Arthur H. Coxe, of this city, who fell pierced through the body, after fighting nobly from the opening of the fire. Collis' surviving heroes of Culpeper, promoted to position in the new regiment, will add a glorious prestige to the already popular command.[22]

In addition to appearing in parades, rallies, and speeches, the nattily dressed Zouaves freely strolled the streets of Philadelphia. It was hoped that, in addition to attracting the admiring glances of young ladies and the compliments of patriotic citizens, they would elicit the envy of impressionable young men and send them scurrying to the recruiting stations. To that end, passes were liberally granted to the enlisted men of the 114th, and they were provided with transportation on the Germantown–Philadelphia streetcar system.

One young Philadelphian, twenty-one-year-old artist Joseph Boggs Beale, was able to withstand the pressure of seeing his cousin William Palmer in the uniform of the Zouaves without himself succumbing to a desire to enlist. But Beale's cousin did made a considerable impression on him. While in Philadelphia, "Cousin W. Palmer" came often to visit the Beale home on Walnut Street, and the two young men were often out together. Beale and his friends also traveled to the camp of the Zouaves

21. *DEB*, August 7, 1862, p. 1, August 8, 1862, p. 1.
22. *DEB*, August 14, 1862, p. 1, August 15, 1862, p. 5, August 18, p. 1.

to visit Palmer. On Saturday, August 9, Beale noted that his cousin had returned "from camp near Germantown" to see them. "He is in his uniform which he got today," he penned in his diary, and then went on to describe the uniform in detail. The following day, Beale accompanied Palmer to see his father, after which they attended church services in the evening. On Wednesday of that week, Beale and four friends went up to Germantown to see Palmer in camp. "Their supper was over when we got there," he noted, "and we saw them receive their band of music and start in a regimental parade for a 'War Meeting' at Germantown."[23]

On Thursday, August 14, while the regiment was parading past the Beale residence, Palmer got permission to leave the ranks and visit. "William was in uniform and had his turban on," his cousin wrote, and while the regiment dined at the Volunteer Refreshment Saloon, Palmer enjoyed dinner in the company of his family. He returned on Saturday, and a group of friends and family went out to Darby to see the young men's grandfather. It must have excited Beale just to be in the company of the dashing Zouave, for he again noted the fact that "Cousin William had on his turban and uniform." On Sunday, Palmer and Beale attended three church services over the course of the day, and Beale recorded that "William was spoken to from the pulpit, because he was in the U.S. uniform, by a chaplain from Harrison's landing." Palmer stayed at the Beale home that night and did not return to camp until the following morning.[24]

Whether Palmer's visits to the city were ever responsible for enticing anyone into the ranks is not known; however, it is significant both that he was permitted the freedom to roam so widely and often from camp and that Beale considered his cousin's visits noteworthy enough to preserve them carefully in his diary. Beale's entries paid particular attention to the fact that his cousin was wearing his uniform and perhaps had attracted some public attention as a result of his appearance. Nevertheless, Beale continued to document such events until his cousin departed with the regiment. On two occasions, he noted that Palmer brought photographs of himself in uniform and requested that the artist Beale color them. Beale saw his cousin off to the war at the train station, but he remained in the

23. Diary of Joseph Boggs Beale, August 9, 10, 13, 1862, in Joseph Boggs Beale Collection, HSP.

24. Beale Diary, August 14, 16, 17, 1862, *ibid.*

city and soon secured a position as an art teacher at Central High School. He was chosen over another young local artist, Thomas Eakins.[25]

Some men could not escape the lure of the Zouave mystique, while still others were attracted by the bounty. One soldier even deserted his regiment to join the 114th under an assumed name. That man, William K. Magradey, had joined the "California Regiment" under the command of Oregon senator Edward D. Baker in May, 1861. Baker was later authorized to recruit an entire brigade. Nine of his original regiment's ten companies had been raised in Philadelphia—as had most of the other regiments—and when Baker was killed the men were claimed by Pennsylvania. The "Californians" then became the 71st Pennsylvania, which along with Baker's three other regiments became part of the "Philadelphia Brigade."

Magradey undoubtedly encountered the Zouaves d'Afrique during their service under Banks. Perhaps he even had friends or relatives in the company. When the 71st was transferred to McClellan's army to take part in the Peninsular Campaign, Magradey and his fellow Philadelphians saw some hard fighting. Somehow, he must have heard about the formation of the new regiment of Zouaves and determined to join them. He left the 71st on June 25, 1862, the day of the battle at Oak Grove that marked the start of the Seven Days' Battles. Magradey might have become separated from his regiment during the confused action around Allen's Farm, where the 71st was engaged that day. He managed to make his way to Philadelphia, where he enlisted in the 114th on August 27 under the name William K. Martin. Historians can only speculate on the reasons for Magradey's decision, but it seems possible that having friends or relatives in the 114th might have enticed him away from the immediate danger and drudgery of combat. The bounty, not available at the time of his original enlistment in 1861, might also have been a factor in his regimental shift. Magradey was discharged in May, 1865, having served nearly the entire war period in active campaigning.[26]

A detailed look at the prewar life and career of a recruit such as Alexander Given may be useful in creating a profile of a young man in mid-nineteenth-century Philadelphia. However, Given's story is not apparently representative and should not alone lead us to any conclusion about what

25. Beale Diary, August 27, 28, 31, September 1, October 11, 1862, *ibid.*
26. Pension file of William K. Magradey, NARA.

life was like for men of backgrounds and economic circumstances very different from his. It is only through an examination of the available information concerning these men that one arrives at an authentic picture of their overall lives in the antebellum city. The information that is usually available most readily from the military records is their age, occupation, birthplace, and date and place of enlistment. Even these scanty facts are often not available for some men of the regiment. In any event, precisely what use can be made of these data when they are available?

Most simply, the age data will illustrate that the men who enlisted in the 114th in the summer of 1862 belonged primarily to a single age cohort. This information may then be compared with data from other sources to determine if there was a significant difference between the original men of the 114th and those who enlisted later in the war or in a different geographic location. Age data can also be compared with occupational information to determine whether age can be said to be related to occupational skill level and financial or class status. Finally, both age and occupational data can be compared with place of birth. A comparison between immigrant soldiers and native-born soldiers can then be made in an effort to determine whether that information has any relationship to age and occupation.

From the comparisons made of the information in these categories, many issues can be addressed. If the 114th was an elite organization that recruited its members from the higher strata of society, for example, it would seem likely that the regiment contained a high number of persons who were somewhat older than the average recruit, of better economic circumstances, and more highly skilled. Furthermore, such persons were unlikely to be immigrants; thus it might be expected that the regiment would contain fewer foreign-born members than on average.

In any Civil War regiment, one might expect to find a diverse group of men: a few old men, a few young boys, but mainly a group between the ages of twenty to twenty-four years. This composition would probably differ little from that of previous wars. A survey of colonial troops from Massachusetts Bay who fought in the Seven Years' War during the year 1756 revealed that 31.7 percent of the men fell between the ages of twenty- and twenty-four. The age group of fourteen- to nineteen-year-olds contained the next highest percentage, 24.7 percent; and only 16.5 percent composed the group of twenty-five- to twenty-nine-year-olds. Thus nearly 73 percent of those eighteenth-century soldiers were under thirty years of age. This is hardly a surprising statistic, and it appears to closely approximate age groups of soldiers who enlisted during the Civil War.[27]

Other recent studies have shown that analysis of age data has been a successful source for determining which groups were most likely to have enlisted during the Civil War. In one recent essay, the author analyzes six variables that might have affected the enlistment of soldiers and sailors in Newburyport, Massachusetts: age, ethnicity, occupation, wealth, school attendance, and education level. It was found that, "as expected, age was the best predictor of whether or not someone enlisted in the armed forces."[28]

An analysis of age data might serve more uses than simply as a predictor of which age groups were more likely to be represented in the military. Joseph F. Kett expands the relevance of age data in explaining nineteenth-century ideas about the nature of youth. It was generally viewed then that the postponement of the choice of a profession or occupation and the postponement of "fixed purpose [was] inconsistent with the protection of young people from worldliness." Conversely, twentieth-century thinking now adheres to the view that protectiveness can be better achieved by a "prolongation of adolescence." Perhaps those of the Civil War era felt that the idleness resulting from a youth's failure to engage in some useful occupation would increase his vulnerability to be led astray. Kett's thesis therefore suggests that nineteenth-century youths—those of an age to enlist in the military during the Civil War—might have viewed their enlistment as an opportunity to enter upon a new stage of life. There are several reasons why they might have broken their ties with adolescence in this way.[29]

It must first be more precisely understood how greatly the nineteenth-century concept of adolescence differed from our current notions. While we now commonly use the term *adolescent* to describe persons in their early teen years, previous meanings encompassed a much broader span of

27. Fred Anderson, *A People's Army: Massachusetts Soldiers and Sailors in the Seven Years' War* (Chapel Hill, 1984), 231.

28. Maris A. Vinovskis, "Have Social Historians Lost the Civil War? Some Preliminary Demographic Speculations," in *Toward a Social History of the American Civil War: Exploratory Essays*, ed. Maris A. Vinovskis (Cambridge, Mass., 1990), 40.

29. Joseph F. Kett, "Adolescence and Youth in Nineteenth-Century America," in *The Family in History: Interdisciplinary Essays*, ed. Theodore K. Rabb and Robert I. Rotberg (New York, 1971), 110.

years, usually from the late teens to the mid-twenties, with primary emphasis on the late teens and early twenties. As an illustration of this trend in thinking, Kett cites an 1860s Currier and Ives series entitled *The Four Seasons of Life*. In the series of prints, childhood is depicted by a group of small children at play, while youth is symbolized by a sober figure of about twenty years of age walking arm in arm with a female companion. This, Kett maintains, is an indicator that the focus of youth was primarily on those in their late teens and early twenties, and that a youth was seen more as a "burgeoning independent than a frustrated dependent."[30]

It may seem strange to us, considering our modern-day use of the terms, to refer to Civil War soldiers as "youths" and "adolescents." Nevertheless, many of those soldiers did fall within the range of adolescence by contemporary standards. They were probably assisted in their transition from civilian to soldier life—perhaps even propelled into that transition—by the idea of embracing a "fixed purpose." If Kett's assessment of nineteenth-century views is accurate, then perhaps those who sent their sons off to war felt somewhat relieved by the concomitant effect of seeing them engaged in a transition from adolescence to adulthood.

If nineteenth-century concepts of the progression of the stages of life were based on clearly defined transitions between them, it is likely that military service would be seen as an ideal opportunity for those on the verge of making the jump to adulthood to accomplish their goal. Further, if these young men were expected to be sheltered by their adult experiences, rather than seeking shelter from them, it is less difficult to understand how the seemingly incongruous pairing of army service and protection came to be accepted. This pairing also hinges on the fact that knowledge of what army service entailed was not particularly clear, despite increasing apprehension over the possibility of death or maiming in battle by the summer of 1862. While ignorance of the hardships of military life might account in some part for adolescents' eagerness to enlist, and patriotism or peer pressure for the tendency to overlook the known possible consequences of military service, it is also possible that perceptions of the military as an institution would contribute to its acceptability as well. The military was considered capable of protecting youths, because, by its nature, it was characterized by order and discipline. Furthermore, this order

30. *Ibid.*, 105

and discipline was enforced through a rigid hierarchy, which ensured compliance with established standards of behavior and conduct and would view the effects of "worldliness" as being detrimental to proper military decorum.

Considering what we now know of army life in the 1860s, and of the horrors awaiting the young men on the battlefields of the war, it hardly seems plausible that anyone could send his son off to war with the idea that the young man would be significantly protected there from "worldliness." Yet, as another example of this belief reveals, most people had little knowledge of life in the army prior to the Civil War. J. Matthew Gallman reports how one Philadelphia mother, concerned about the well-being of her son, wrote to ask the youth if the military "houses" had windows.[31] Soldiers themselves proved ignorant as well, knowing little of what to expect of military life. The heavily laden troops issuing forth from every northern town, burdened with all the comforts of home in their knapsacks, soon became savvy veterans who had learned to discard nearly everything that could be neither eaten by a soldier nor fired from the muzzle of his rifle. They learned and adapted rapidly, and of necessity; but they learned by experience.

Another factor that may have lessened fear for the welfare of loved ones in the army was the fact that enlistment was something of a community affair. As noted previously, the word-of-mouth methods of recruiting generally led to group enlistments: men who knew each other, worked together, or lived in the same neighborhoods. Though less frequently a factor in the formation of regiments recruited from small towns or rural neighborhoods, this phenomenon prevailed in the neighborhoods of Philadelphia and its surrounding areas, and was most evident at the company level. Many of the company commanders and those who assisted them in recruiting were typically men of some prominence in their communities. While this standing may not have been directly related to social class or status, it probably did derive from the degree of power that the person wielded in his neighborhood. First Lieutenant Edward E. Williams of Company K, for instance, was a sergeant of police in Philadelphia's Fifteenth District, located in the Frankford section of the city. This civic position probably conferred on Williams some measure of status that helped him

31. Gallman *Mastering Wartime*, 72.

to convince a number of Frankford men to join him—including his two brothers, Sergeant Edmund Williams and Private William F. Williams.[32]

Many recruits thus found themselves serving in close proximity to friends, neighbors, schoolmates, and co-workers. In this way, the organization of companies often resulted in the reproduction of the local community within the army structure. Certainly, not all eligible members of a community responded to the call to arms; but for the families of those who did, some support and comfort must have come from the knowledge that they were sharing similar experiences with neighbors. In many respects, they were all in this together. Such a feeling of mutual commiseration among the parents of those in the army may also have served to mask temporarily any uncertainty about their sons' transition to adulthood. Eventually, however, the broadened personal experiences of the young men, and their exposure to an expanded circle of comrades upon whom they need rely, would have tempered their provincialism and hastened their transition to the next stage of the lifecourse. War has an uncanny power to change exuberant boys into sober men.[33]

Determining the ages of recruits by reviewing the information contained on muster rolls would seem to be a fairly straightforward task; in fact, calculations can entail much imprecision. Though easily obtained from muster rolls or from the descriptive data contained in the compiled military service records of the regiment, age information is, alas, only as accurate as the statements given by the recruits and recorded by the mustering officer. Without making painstaking comparisons to census records, it is nearly impossible to determine from these sources how many eighteen-year-olds misrepresented their age in order to enlist. While many were able to pull off the deception, at least one private of the 114th was discharged after his mother appeared with conclusive proof that her son was underage. Furthermore, statistics compiled by the United States Sanitary Commission for 1,012,273 Union soldiers indicate that 10,233 were under the age of eighteen at the time of their enlistment, and Bell I. Wiley's examination of 123 company lists describing 14,330 men reveals 246 underage soldiers. These figures indicate that somewhere between 1.0 and

32. CMSR, 114th Pennsylvania Volunteer Infantry, in Record Group 94, NARA; DEB, August 15, 1862, p. 5.

33. See Thomas R. Kemp, "Community and War: The Civil War Experience of Two New Hampshire Towns," and Reid Mitchell, "The Northern Soldier and His Community," both in Toward a Social History of the Civil War, ed. Vinovskis, 31–77, 78–92.

1.6 percent of all recruits may have been underage, and it would not be unreasonable to assume that this estimate would also apply to the 114th Pennsylvania. In addition, both Wiley's and the Sanitary Commission's figures indicate that of those recruits who were underage, a majority were just barely so. Of the 10,233 soldiers mentioned in the Sanitary Commission survey, 6,425, or 62.7 percent, were seventeen years old. Of Wiley's 246 underage soldiers, 160, or 65 percent, were seventeen.[34]

At the other end of the spectrum, a small percentage of soldiers were over the age of forty-five. After September, 1862, these men also had to misrepresent their age to circumvent War Department orders that prohibited mustering men above age forty-five. The Sanitary Commission survey found .005 percent over forty-five, while Wiley discovered only .006 percent. In the 114th Pennsylvania, one officer—Colonel Collis' father, who served as quartermaster—was forty-eight when he was commissioned. Several enlisted men were also in their forties. At least three of the men in this age group were members of the original company of Zouaves d'Afrique, and several were professional men: two, for example, were engineers and another a doctor. It is likely that many of the men in the army over the age of forty-five served in capacities that did not require direct exposure to battle in the front ranks of the regiment, such as surgeons, musicians, teamsters, or chaplains. Only four enlisted men of the 114th who were age forty-five or over served in the ranks as privates. One was fifty-two years old, the oldest man in the regiment. A handful of other men between the ages of forty and forty-five served as privates. As might be expected then, the great majority of men serving in the Union Army were between the ages of eighteen and forty-five.[35]

On the basis of information compiled from the Sanitary Commission's survey of over one million men, it has been estimated that the average age of the Union Army in July, 1862, was 25.10 years. According to age data from the records of the 114th Pennsylvania, this would appear to be a fairly accurate figure. Of the fifteen field and staff officers on the rolls of the 114th in 1862, the average age was 24.84 years. This figure excludes Collis' 48-year-old father and the 38-year-old chaplain; but when those two men are included, the average age is raised to 27.26 years. Unfortu-

---

34. CMSR, 114th PV, Record Group 94, NARA; Bell Irvin Wiley, *The Life of Billy Yank: The Common Soldier of the Union* (Baton Rouge, 1952), 298–99.

35. CMSR, 114th PV, Record Group 94, NARA; Wiley, *Billy Yank*, 302–303.

nately, previous work in this area has relied on the somewhat misleading figures produced by averaging the ages of the men. Similar information has been included here in order to facilitate comparison with earlier estimates; however, a more authentic measure of age in the regiment would be the median age of the soldiers. Use of this figure would reduce the tendency for the data to be skewed by soldiers like Collis' father, who is far outside the expected range and raises the average age of the staff officers by more than two years. The median age of staff officers, at 25 years, turns out to be much closer to the average age calculated prior to the inclusion of Lieutenant Collis and the chaplain.[36] (See Table 1.)

The twenty-six company officers on the rolls of the 114th in 1862 whose ages can be determined were an average of 26.23 years old. The median age, however, reaches only 24 years. Most company officers fell within the 21–24 age range, with the two youngest being only 18, while the oldest was 40. Ages for NCOs were found to be slightly higher than those considered thus far. The average age for NCOs of the 114th Pennsylvania in 1862 was 24.70, with the majority falling within the more restricted age range of 21–22 years old. The median age was 23 years, with the youngest NCO being 18 and the oldest 42.[37]

Finally, the average age of an enlisted man of the 114th in 1862 was 24.37, while the median age was 22. The 21-year-olds formed the largest age group with 120 men. The next largest group was that of 18-year-olds, of whom there were 86. Well over one-half of the men (64.9 percent) were under 25 years old, while only 6.5 percent were over age 36. (See Table 2.) Taken together then, the average age of all members of the 114th—officers, NCOs, and privates—was 25.03 years; their median age, however, was only 22 years. The largest group remains the 21-year-olds, with 19-year-olds following closely behind. (See Table 3 for age distribution of personnel by age groups.) This distribution comports closely with the Sanitary Commission figures, which Wiley used to estimate that the largest single age group during the war's first year was that of 18-year-olds, with 21-year-olds the next largest. He further concluded that the average age of the soldiers "increased slightly with the progress of the war," owing to the maturation of veterans, and in spite of the fact that "the age pattern of men coming into the service remained fairly constant."[38]

36. CMSR, 114th PV, Record Group 94, NARA; Wiley, *Billy Yank,* 302–303.
37. CMSR, 114th PV, Record Group 94, NARA.
38. *Ibid.;* Wiley, *Billy Yank,* 303.

Table 1

Ages by Rank Groupings in the 114th Pennsylvania, 1862

Rank	Number	Average Age	Median Age
Field and staff officers	15	27.26	25
Company officers	26	26.23	24
Noncommissioned officers	135	24.70	23
Privates	690	24.37	22
Totals	866	25.03	22

Table 2

Age Distribution of Privates in the 114th Pennsylvania, 1862

Age Group	Number (%)	Cumulative %
17–20	197 (28.5)	28.5
21–24	244 (35.4)	63.9
25–28	104 (15.0)	78.9
29–32	65 (9.4)	88.3
33–36	34 (4.9)	93.2
37–40	21 (3.0)	96.2
41–44	22 (3.1)	99.3
45–48	3 (.4)	99.7[a]

[a]Deviations from 100.0 in percentage totals here and elsewhere are a function of rounding.

While the median age of soldiers in the 114th was twenty-two years, what is more significant is the fact that fully one-half of them were between the ages of eighteen and twenty-two. In light of the foregoing observations concerning nineteenth-century perceptions of youth and adolescence, what this fact meant in 1862 was probably very different from what it might mean by modern standards. A large number of the regiment's men were thus potentially in a position to be affected by the factors explained in Kett's hypothesis.

Table 3

Age Distribution of All Members in the 114th Pennsylvania, 1862

Age Group	Number (%)	Cumulative %
17–20	218 (25.2)	25.2
21–24	324 (37.4)	62.6
25–28	142 (16.4)	79.0
29–32	84 (9.7)	88.7
33–36	41 (4.7)	93.4
37–40	27 (3.1)	96.5
41–44	26 (3.0)	99.5
45–48	4 (.5)	100.0

First, those in the eighteen- to twenty-two-year-old age group would fall into the category of youth or adolescent in accordance with Kett's thesis of the nineteenth-century lifecourse. In this respect, all could theoretically have felt the impact of desire to move into the next stage, adulthood. Second, it seems likely that few of the men in this group would have been deterred in their desire to enlist by financial commitments at home. Though strict confirmation would require an extensive examination of census data, it is unlikely that many of the men in this age group would have been married. Rather, it seems more plausible that many were still living at home with their parents. In such a situation, they probably contributed to domestic income but were not supporting their families alone. Thus they would have been in a position to enter the army without undue concern for the financial well-being of those at home. In order to explore further whether contemporary attitudes toward the concept of adolescence bore any relationship to the life experiences and motivations of Civil War soldiers, it will be necessary to examine the type of life those men were leaving. Were they taking a step toward adulthood by enlisting in the army, or had they already crossed the threshold of that life-stage? An examination of the occupational data contained in the muster rolls of the regiment may reveal some conclusions as to how many men had engaged in a "fixed purpose" by 1862.

An examination of the compiled military service records of the 114th disclosed 402 soldiers whose occupations at the time of enlistment can be determined. One factor that must be considered prior to proceeding, however, is that some of the men listed may not actually have been gainfully employed in their occupation at the time of enlistment. There is, of course, no way to determine how many men may have fit this description, but the number was probably not significant. The economic crisis in northern industries precipitated by the secession of the South signaled a bleak future for workers in the spring and summer of 1861, but the rebound fostered by wartime production and by a reduced labor pool—owing to the siphoning off of increasingly large numbers of men by the army—soon reversed fortunes for laborers. Workers now in demand found that they could expect higher wages. Unfortunately, they also discovered that because of inflation, their money enabled them to buy little more than they had previously. In short, there is no evidence to suggest that unemployment was pervasive in the summer of 1862; thus it was probably not a condition relevant to those enlisting at that time.[39]

The 402 men of the 114th whose occupations are known were engaged in 115 distinct types of work. The single most common occupation was that of clerk, in which capacity twenty-seven men were employed. Clerical jobs often served as entrance points and training grounds for the sons of those higher up in the business class, and those fortunate enough to find themselves in these positions could realistically count on their upward mobility. While working conditions and prospects for advancement for many clerks may hardly have exceeded "those of dockworkers," they nevertheless "stood much closer to the employer than to factory labor," and they certainly could read and write. This distinction is significant in that mid-nineteenth-century clerks can therefore be considered as skilled workers and members of the business class. While their current clerical jobs would surely place them in the lower ranks of the skilled class, the fact that they stood to advance to the class of proprietors is also important.[40]

The twenty-seven clerks found on the rolls of the 114th ranged in age from 17 to 31. As should be expected, 67 percent of them fell between the ages of 17 and 21 with the 19- and 21-year-old age groups containing the largest number. The average age was 20.8 years, while the median age

39. Gallman, *Mastering Wartime*, 223–24.

40. Michael B. Katz, "Social Class in North American Urban History," *Journal of Interdisciplinary History* XI (Spring, 1981), 594–98; Harry Braverman, *Labor and Monopoly Capital: The Degradation of Work in the Twentieth Century* (New York, 1974), 293–94.

was 21. Clerks constituted not only the largest group of skilled workers, but the youngest as well. Again, these men would constitute the lowest category of skilled laborers and would be judged as less skilled than teachers or lawyers. Twenty of the distinct occupations found within the ranks of the men of the 114th can be considered those of skilled workers. Sixty-seven men, or 16.7 percent of the 402 men with known occupations, were placed in this category. (See Table 4.) Ages for men in nonclerical skilled occupations were significantly higher than those of the clerks, and, at 25.6 years of age, conformed more closely to the average age of the regiment as a whole. Their median age of 24, however, is fully two years older than the median age for the regiment as a whole, and identical to the median age found for company officers. When clerks are included in that calculation, the median age for skilled workers is only 23 years. Only 33.3 percent of nonclerical skilled laborers fell within the 18- to 21-year-old age group, as compared with 67 percent for clerks.[41]

At the other side of the regiment's socioeconomic scale are grouped those members classified as unskilled. One might have expected to find that soldiers classified as skilled were generally older than the majority of men in the regiment given that the skills necessary to their professions took time to acquire; similarly, it would seem probable that many of those considered unskilled would be younger than most in the regiment in reflection of the fact that they had not worked long enough to learn a skill. Of course, not every person would have had an equal opportunity, regardless of time, to learn a skill. However, because the men examined in this study provide a more or less random sample of workers who fall into the eligible age category for enlisting in the military, the idea that unskilled workers are apt to be found among the regiment's younger members is not likely to be attributable mainly to their lack of opportunity. All workers between the ages of eighteen and forty-five, while they might not have enjoyed an equal opportunity to learn a skill, had an equal opportunity to enlist in the 114th.

In fact, the subcategory of unskilled workers containing the largest number of men (twenty-two) was that of common laborer. These men largely listed no definable trade as their primary occupation and referred to themselves only as laborers. Others listed occupations that obviously required no skills. Several were categorized as "day laborers" who would have

41. CMSR, 114th PV, Record Group 94, NARA.

Table 4
Occupational Skill Levels of Members of the 114th Pennsylvania

Skill Level	Number (%)		Median Age
Skilled	67	(16.7)	23
Semiskilled	298	(74.1)	22
More	(154/51.7%)	(38.3)	
Less	(144/48.3%)	(35.8)	
Unskilled	37	(9.2)	21
Totals	402 (100.0)		22

worked at a variety of ever-changing menial jobs wherever they could be found. Even those with a continuing association with a trade, however, routinely would have performed the most onerous of required tasks. In the regiment, the average laborer was only 22.8 years of age. Eighteen-year-olds comprised the majority of laborers, and exactly 50 percent of the laborers were in the 18- to 21-year-old age group. The median age for laborers, 21 years, was significantly lower than the group's average age and was two years younger than the median age of skilled workers. Also important is the fact that 64 percent of the laborers were foreign-born, a finding to which we shall later return for further analysis.[42]

Thirteen additional men were found to have been engaged in occupations that may be categorized as unskilled labor. The total number of men generally classified as unskilled was thirty-five, and as expected, they were younger than their skilled counterparts. The average age of all unskilled laborers was 22.6 years, and, once again, the majority belonged to the 18-year-old age group in 1862. The median age for all unskilled workers was 21 years, two years lower than that for skilled workers. (See Table 4.) The presence of numerous native-born workers in unskilled subcategories other than laborer causes the percentage of foreign-born workers to fall to 40 percent of the total number of unskilled workers found in the sample. Even so, this percentage may still be considered high as foreign-born soldiers represented only about 28 percent of the regiment.[43] (See Table 6.)

42. *Ibid.*
43. *Ibid.*

The vast majority of men in the regiment who were sampled fill the vaguely delimited category of semiskilled labor (74.1 percent). The difficult distinction between skilled and semiskilled work is made even more ambiguous in the context of the mid-nineteenth century because many occupations then were undergoing the transformation from artisanal or crafts trades to larger manufacturing industries. Whereas an eighteenth-century shoemaker made an entire shoe from beginning to end, one cannot claim with certainty that a man designated a shoemaker in 1862 possessed the skills to do the same. He may have worked in a shoe factory, where he performed only part of the task of making a shoe. The same ambiguity obscures the nature of other occupations during this period; although many workers may have retained their status as individual craftsmen or artisans, it is difficult to tell precisely how many did so. Given the fact that the majority of men in the 114th were from Philadelphia—a highly industrialized city containing numerous factories and mills—I have chosen to include such occupations as shoemaker, glassblower, and blacksmith in the category of semiskilled labor. In contrast, had these soldiers come from a rural or non-industrialized area, one might reasonably have classified them as skilled.[44]

Eighty-seven of the occupations listed on the rolls for men of the 114th (75.6 percent of the total known occupations) have been classified as semiskilled. It is possible to divide further those semiskilled workers into subcategories of more skilled or less skilled. Those professions typically requiring a training period or apprenticeship—a shoemaker or carpenter, for example—will, for the purposes of this analysis, be considered more skilled than those which were less likely to require an entry-level training period or apprenticeship, like a boxmaker or a corkcutter. By classifying the eighty-seven semiskilled occupations as either more skilled or less skilled, I have determined that of the 298 men in the more general grouping, 51.7 percent were more skilled, and the remaining 48.3 percent were less skilled.[45] (See Table 4.)

Nearly 30 percent of the 402 men sampled were employed in six different occupations and could be linked to occupational groups that comprised only 5.2 percent of the total number of groups. (See Table 5.) More

44. Daniel E. Sutherland, *The Expansion of Everyday Life, 1860–1876* (New York, 1989), 158–62.

45. CMSR, 114th PV, Record Group 94, NARA.

Table 5
Most Common Occupations Represented in the 114th Pennsylvania

Occupation	Number (%)	Cumulative %
Clerk	27 (6.7)	6.7
Laborer	22 (5.4)	12.1
Farmer	21 (5.2)	17.3
Shoemaker	19 (4.7)	22.0
Carpenter	16 (3.9)	25.9
Blacksmith	15 (3.7)	29.6

significantly, of the 30 percent in those six most common occupations, fully 64 percent were in occupations that could be classified as skilled or more semiskilled. Only 18 percent were in unskilled occupations, and 17.5 percent in less semiskilled. It would appear that the overall skill level for the men of the regiment as sampled was high. This ratio was probably not unusual for a regiment recruited from a highly urbanized area.

But comparison with results of similar studies for regiments recruited in other areas reveals that the 114th Pennsylvania, along with other urban regiments, was composed of men significantly different from the majority of the army. An analysis of the data compiled for Company A of the 57th Massachusetts Veteran Volunteers, which was recruited in the towns and surrounding rural areas of Fitchburg and Worcester, illustrates the point. Using the same criteria and classification system as those used for the present study, that analysis revealed that 4.8 percent of the company's men were in skilled occupations, 81.8 percent in semiskilled (47.6 percent more skilled, 34.3 percent less skilled), and 13.4 percent in unskilled. The 114th had not only a much higher percentage of personnel in the skilled category, but also a slightly higher percentage in the more semiskilled subcategory. (See Table 5.) Using data based on the number of men in the entire 57th Massachusetts regiment, all of whom enlisted in the same area in the winter of 1863–1864, it was found that there were 158 laborers (15.2 percent), 238 farmers (22.1 percent), and 156 boot/shoemakers (15 percent); but only 43 clerks (4.1 percent), and a smaller percentage of blacksmiths. The tendency for significant proportions of Civil War regiments to be comprised of farmers and laborers is borne out in other studies.

The principally urban 114th Pennsylvania, however, contained a comparatively small proportion of farmers—only 5.2 percent.[46] (See Table 5.)

Wiley's sample of 14,000 Union soldiers from a variety of areas reveals that farmers (less semiskilled) composed over 50 percent of the total, while laborers (unskilled) constituted the next most numerous occupational group with over 10 percent. Thus, over 60 percent of his sample could be classified as unskilled or less semiskilled, while only 35.5 percent of the 114th could be so classified. One significant commonality between the sample of men from the 114th and Wiley's sample of 14,000 soldiers is that they share the same six most frequently named occupations. In Wiley's sample, however, approximately 72 percent of the men could be placed in these six occupations, as opposed to only 30 percent of the 114th. This difference is due to the large number of farmers found in Wiley's sample. In addition, only 2.5 percent of that sample's six most common jobs were held by skilled and more semiskilled men. This finding probably reflects the fact that the majority of Union soldiers did not come from cities or highly industrialized areas where skilled workers were common. This statistic is further indication that the army as a whole tended to be more rural than urban or industrial, while also illustrating that the occupational and skill-level structure of the 114th Pennsylvania was markedly different from that of most of the Federal army.[47]

Studies of Confederate regiments have revealed that their occupational distribution was fairly similar to that which Wiley arrived at for Union soldiers. James I. Robertson, Jr., has analyzed a sample of the 19th Virginia, of which 40.3 percent were farmers and 10.7 percent laborers. Thus, 60 percent of the regiment was in either the unskilled or less semiskilled categories. In addition, his separate survey of 2,639 members of the Stonewall Brigade revealed that farmers composed 30.73 percent of the brigade, and laborers 18.1 percent, for a total of 48.83 percent in the unskilled or less semiskilled categories. The six occupations most commonly repre-

---

46. *Ibid.*; Warren Wilkinson, *Mother, May You Never See the Sights I Have Seen: The Fifty-Seventh Massachusetts Veteran Volunteers in the Last Year of the Civil War* (New York, 1990), 412–32. While it is not surprising that the urban 114th Pennsylvania contained so few farmers, it should be noted that as late as 1860, census records indicated the presence of over 1,600 farms within Philadelphia's limits. The more rural surrounding counties of Bucks, Montgomery, and Delaware, from which some recruits were drawn, contained over 12,000 farms; *Eighth Census of the United States, 1860.*

47. Wiley, *Billy Yank*, 303–304.

sented among the members of the Stonewall Brigade can also suggest a further comparison between data on my sample and Robertson's figures for the Virginians. Only 23 percent of the southerners held those occupations that would place them in the category of skilled or more semiskilled, as opposed to 64 percent of the Pennsylvanians working at those skill levels.[48]

As mentioned previously, many of those giving their occupations as unskilled laborers were foreign-born. Let us now examine the composition of the regiment in terms of place of birth. A common complaint voiced by southerners during and after the war was their assertion that the Union Army was composed largely of foreign-born mercenaries. In fact, the army was overwhelmingly native-born, although the comparatively large immigrant population in the East was naturally reflected in the makeup of regiments from that area, and the percentage of immigrants probably increased as the war went on. In the 114th Pennsylvania, 71.3 percent of those whose place of birth could be determined were native-born, with 47.3 percent born in Philadelphia itself. The largest of its foreign-born groups had come from Ireland (10 percent), England (6.5 percent), and Germany (5.6 percent). In all, 19.8 percent of the men of the 114th hailed from the countries of Great Britain and its Celtic fringe. Only 8.7 percent of the regiment's men claimed origins in other European countries. (See Table 6.)[49]

Comparisons with other northern regiments from the East show that the 114th Pennsylvania was typical with respect to the distribution of natives versus non-natives. Wiley's survey of Company F, 46th Pennsylvania, shows that 81 percent were natives, with Irish-born (8 percent) constituting the most numerous non-natives. Company B, 5th New York, included 48.6 percent native-born, with Irish-born again representing the

48. James I. Robertson, Jr., *Soldiers Blue and Gray* (Columbia, S.C., 1988), 25; James I. Robertson, Jr., *The Stonewall Brigade* (Baton Rouge, 1963), 15–16.

49. CMSR, 114th PV, Record Group 94, NARA; Wiley, *Billy Yank*, 306–11. Although eastern regiments generally contained more immigrants than those from other sections of the country, many northern volunteer regiments from the Midwest also contained a large number or were composed wholly of immigrants. Just prior to the Pea Ridge Campaign in Arkansas in early 1862, for example, Brigadier General Samuel Ryan Curtis upon taking command was faced with the task of placating German immigrant volunteers and their popular leader, Brigadier General Franz Sigel, to whom many—including Sigel—felt the command rightfully should have gone. See William L. Shea and Earl J. Hess, *Pea Ridge: Civil War Campaign in the West* (Chapel Hill, 1992); and William L. Burton, *Melting Pot Soldiers: The Union's Ethnic Regiments* (Ames, Iowa, 1988).

Table 6
Place of Birth of Members of the 114th Pennsylvania

Place of birth	Number (%)
Philadelphia	160 (47.3)
Pennsylvania (other counties)	50 (14.8)
Other states	31 (9.2)
Total (Native-born)	241 (71.3)
Ireland	34 (10.0)
England	22 (6.5)
Scotland	8 (2.4)
Wales	3 (.9)
Total (Great Britain)	67 (19.8)
Germany	19 (5.6)
France	10 (2.9)
Switzerland	1 (.2)
Total (Continental Europe)	30 (8.7)
Total (Foreign-born)	97 (28.5)
Totals	338 (99.8)

most numerous non-native group at 23 percent. While certain regiments and companies were filled predominantly with foreign-born soldiers, it is equally true that many were filled mostly with men born in this country. For example, Company H of the 8th Michigan was composed of 85 percent natives, with Canadians (5.4 percent) constituting the most numerous group of foreigners. In addition, data for the 57th Massachusetts show that 65.6 percent of the men were natives, while 34.4 percent were foreign-born. Eighteen percent of this regiment's men came from Ireland and 9.4 percent from Canada. In all, men from Britain and its Celtic fringe composed 21.2 percent of the 57th. Many more were first-generation natives, their parents having arrived in the United States in the early 1840s.[50]

50. Wiley, *Billy Yank*, 311; Wilkinson, *Mother*, 630. Extant muster rolls and descriptive lists, from which the bulk of the information in these tables was extracted, do not contain complete data for each soldier. As a result, the ages of 866 men could be determined, while the place of birth was listed for only 338 men. Occupations, facilitating a determination of skill level, were given for 402 men.

What kind of portrait evolves from an examination of the muster rolls and military service records of Collis' regiment of Zouaves? The "average" soldier of the 114th Pennsylvania, appears to have been a native Philadelphian, about twenty-five years old, employed in a semiskilled occupation. It is interesting to note that the average age of the regiment was fairly high; although there were large numbers of young men, there were also significant groups of men who were well past the age where soldiering would be considered an attractive diversion. Given Philadelphia's healthy economy in 1862, it is further likely that this older man not only possessed a skill, but also actively employed it for pay at the time of his enlistment. In addition, it is reasonable to suspect that as this soldier was born in this country, he might have possessed patriotism enough to have felt some personal interest in the preservation of the Union.

When one combines these statistically derived attributes, it is then possible to theorize about this "average" man's motivation for enlisting. Although he received a bounty, he was far from a mercenary. He could undoubtedly have benefited financially by staying at home. Although the threat of a draft was looming in the late summer of 1862, this man probably could have avoided military service. One Philadelphia newspaper speculated that a worker making $10 a week could afford to purchase a substitute for $300 to release him from his three-year obligation under a draft, and still come out ahead of the enlisted man in spite of the government pay and bounties. It is not certain that the average man in Collis' regiment was motivated by patriotism, war fever, or peer pressure, but a combination of these factors was more likely to have influenced his decision to join than financial interest or fear of the draft.[51]

Yet this portrait only begins to demonstrate the usefulness of the data that have been presented. By exploring the interrelationships among the data, we will arrive at more incisive conclusions about their meaning. I should first like to return to Kett's assumptions concerning the nature of adolescence during this period. The analysis of age groups within the 114th revealed that over 50 percent were under the age of twenty-three, with twenty-one-year-olds and eighteen-year-olds composing the largest groups. Again, these age groups fall into the category of adolescent or youth according to nineteenth-century standards. To test whether Kett's hypothesis applies to this particular situation, it will be necessary to de-

51. Gallman, *Mastering Wartime*, 36.

termine how age groups corresponded to occupation. It would seem reasonable to conclude that younger recruits would have been slightly more motivated than their older peers to enlist for reasons outlined in Kett's thesis. They were less likely than the others to be employed in a skilled occupation, to be property owners, or to be sole supporters of a family. In contrast, they were more likely than the others to be starting out in a career or moving from job to job and living with their parents or other family members. Therefore, they more likely than not viewed military service as a severance of home ties and an embarkation on a "fixed purpose." In addition, the previously estimated 1–1.6 percent of the recruits who were underage were probably the group most likely to have been influenced by the factors that Kett elaborates.[52]

Analysis of the relationships between age and occupation reveal that skill level increased in accordance with age. This fact further confirms Kett's thesis by establishing the conditions that would be necessary for it to work. Military rank—a fair predictor of social class and occupational status—also serves to strengthen the connection between age and occupation. Not only were officers and NCOs older than privates, they were also more highly skilled. (See Table 7.) From this correlation, one might conclude that a more skilled occupation corresponded equally to a higher age and a higher social status, which then resulted in the likelihood of obtaining rank in the regiment. A brief look at the field and staff personnel and members of Company A, the 57th Massachusetts, reveals that all of the skilled workers in those positions were officers or NCOs. There were no skilled workers at all among the enlisted men of Company A. Of thirty-six officers and NCOs listed, 61 percent were skilled and the remainder were semiskilled.[53]

Unskilled laborers of the 114th Pennsylvania were also unlikely to rise above the rank of private. (See Table 7.) Those who did so attained only corporal rank. As we saw earlier, over 40 percent of all the unskilled laborers were foreign-born; although foreign-born soldiers made up over 28 percent of the regiment, few were in positions of rank.

In conclusion, most of the men of the 114th Pennsylvania were young—between the ages of seventeen and twenty-five; they had most

---

52. Kett, "Adolescence and Youth," in *The Family in History,* ed. Rabb and Rotberg, 109–10.

53. CMSR, 114th PV, Record Group 94, NARA; Wilkinson, *Mother,* 412–32.

Table 7
Ages and Skill Levels in the 114th Pennsylvania, by Rank

Rank	Number	(% by Skill Level)			(% by Age Group)		
		Skilled	Semiskilled	Unskilled	18–22	23–27	28+
Colonel	1	100	0	0	0	100	0
Lt. Colonel	1	100	0	0	0	0	100
Major	2	100	0	0	0	50	50
Captain	10	60	40	0	10	60	30
Lieutenant	12	42	58	0	8	58	33
1st Sergeant	9	33	66	0	56	33	8
Sergeant	27	26	74	0	55	22	22
Corporal	35	8.5	83	8.5	60	20	20
Private	305	16	73	11	52	23	25

likely worked in a semiskilled occupation that required more skill than not; and they were largely native-born with roots in or near Philadelphia. Those few privates who were able to advance in rank had to have possessed education to some degree as well as social status. In general, the men who enlisted in the 114th were probably not motivated by economic self-interest or fear of the draft, but rather by a combination of patriotism, war fever, peer pressure, and—in the case of the younger recruits—a desire to break free from home ties and embark on the path to adulthood and independence.

In the summer of 1862, the psychological impact of war meetings, rallies, parades, flag waving, and speechmaking must have overwhelmed many of the military-aged residents of the city. Such activities had continued almost unabated since the fall of Fort Sumter in April, 1861, when "riotous crowds filled the streets," and "thousands assembled furious at the news of the surrender, & swearing revenge on all disunionists or disaffected." It was not long before "recruiting tents dotted the landscape, volunteers drilled wherever they could find open space, and hundreds of women flocked to the recently vacated Girard Hotel to sew uniforms."[54] With the

54. Wister, "Sara Butler Wister's Civil War Diary," entry of April 15, 1861; Benners Diary, April 28, 1861, in HSP.

114th Pennsylvania participating in a large number of patriotic meetings and parades, and individual soldiers like the cousin of young Joseph Boggs Beale exerting some influence—either directly or indirectly—on his friends and relatives, it seems assured that such displays affected impressionable young Philadelphians.

How Beale was able to resist the desire to enlist in 1862 is a mystery; however, his attraction to the soldierly displays is evident in his diary. "Bands of music have paraded about with whole companies of soldiers with them & the drums & fifes can be heard all day in any part of the city. Men are enlisting fast," he wrote that summer. Later that same week he noted the enthusiasm that accompanied a parade of the 114th and two other regiments when they marched to Independence Hall to welcome returning prisoner of war Brigadier General Michael Corcoran. Along with the soldiers, he noted, was nearly "a regiment of citizens with 2 flags and music." Much of the excitement of this occasion was undoubtedly generated by the notorious ordeal endured by General Corcoran. The fiery Irishman, former colonel of the 69th New York Militia, had been captured at the first battle of Manassas and then held hostage as a pawn to guarantee the safe treatment of captured Rebel privateers.[55]

Such fanfare, coupled with the influence of peer pressure—ranging from outward haranguing and needling to subtle persuasion, like that which Beale's diary evidences—seem likely to have spurred enlistments. Judging from the youth of the men of the 114th, it may even be said that peer pressure was one of the major factors in the Zouaves' decision to enlist. Both co-workers and employers possibly fostered this pressure. The word-of-mouth style of generating recruits, and the fact that men of certain occupations appear in significant numbers in some companies but not at all in others, seem to indicate that a number of men enlisted together through this informal recruiting system. In addition, several patriotic employers in the city promised financial assistance to the families of employees who decided to join the military, thus removing one barrier to enlistment: financial opportunity cost. One might sympathize with the plight of a healthy military-aged male in the summer of 1862 as he stood watching a regiment of soldiers march proudly past on the way to defend the country. Perhaps, to the young civilian, the soldiers appeared as they did to one Quaker observer, "to be going 'like lambs to the slaughter.'" More

55. Beale Diary, August 18, 21, 1862, in Beale Collection, HSP.

likely, though, it was the idly watching civilian who felt more like the lamb; he may have wondered self-consciously whether those standing around him were asking themselves why he was not among the soldiers. In such situations, guilt and peer pressure probably worked closely together.[56]

In addition, during that summer of 1862, officials in Philadelphia may also have had some effect on the complex motivational factors that led men to enlist. They may well have communicated their fear to the citizens that their city would fall short of its quota of volunteers, thus compelling the government to exercise its authority to draft men from the militia— which theoretically was composed of all able-bodied men between the ages of eighteen and forty-five. It would seem, however, from an analysis of the occupational structure of the 114th Pennsylvania that such fears would have played a small role—if any—for those men. Had an actual draft been implemented, many of them probably could have earned enough money to pursue the earlier discussed course of hiring a substitute or paying a commutation fee. Such practices had been a sine qua non in all previous instances of drafts in America, and like many other policies of the Federal government, were grounded in European tradition. In addition, because the volunteers were relatively young and largely gainfully employed but not yet fully established on their own, it is likely that, had they wanted to avoid a military draft, they could have secured assistance from parents or relatives as well in order to pay for a substitute or a commutation fee. Finally, the fact that many men of the regiment possessed a fairly high degree of skill in their occupations makes it more likely that their earnings were high enough to reduce the attractiveness of enlistment bounties and military pay. The majority of them, like Alexander Given, would have been financially better off at home.

One final factor concerning the enlistment of soldiers should receive our attention. Although many of the regiment's men were young, spirited, and sometimes irreverent, there is ample evidence in letters and diaries to suggest that they also possessed a considerable degree of religious senti-ment. The religious revivals that swept the armies on occasion throughout the war constitute a further indication that the soldiers provided a fertile ground for cultivating such sentiment. Many men carried bibles and read them faithfully. Like Stonewall Jackson, often labeled as something of a

56. Jacob Elfreth, Sr., Diary, May 18, 1861, HSP, quoted in Gallman, *Mastering Wartime*, 109.

religious fanatic, many men believed that God had ordained their life's plan. When it was their time to die, there was nothing that could be done about it. Their fates were in the hands of the Creator. An extension of this belief caused many to expect that when God's will was done, the deceased would be carried into a hereafter that would be a considerable improvement over earthly existence with its difficulties and sorrows. As Jackson is reported to have said on his deathbed, "I will be an infinite gainer to be translated."[57]

The religious atmosphere of mid-nineteenth-century America thus might have played a significant role both in the process of enlistment and in the behavior of men on the battlefield. Young men of 1862 very likely felt themselves no less impervious to danger than do young men of today. Yet when the shot and shell began to fly thickly around them and comrades were torn by ghastly wounds, those with religious convictions could draw upon the common faith that their struggles and suffering were preordained. Along with peer pressure, the belief that they were always safe in God's hands must surely have served to strengthen many soldiers during battle.

57. Douglas Southall Freeman, *Lee's Lieutenants: A Study in Command* (New York, 1942–44), II, 679. Also, for a general discussion of the importance of religion among Civil War soldiers, see Wiley, *Billy Yank* and *The Life of Johnny Reb: The Common Soldier of the Confederacy* (Baton Rouge, 1943), as well as Robertson, *Soldiers Blue and Gray*.

5

To the Seat of War

They are coming from their firesides,
From the hallowed light of home,
Looking back with tearful vision
On the blessings they have known.
—*"Our Volunteers," n.d., newspaper clipping*

Throughout the heat of July and August, 1862, recruits for the 114th Pennsylvania continued their training at a camp located in lower Germantown, or Nicetown, at the intersection of Nicetown Lane and Germantown Road. It was named Camp N. P. Banks in honor of Collis' former commander. Situated on a flat plain surrounded by tall trees, the camp was laid out in strict military fashion. Long rows of white canvas A-frame tents for the enlisted men neatly lined the aisles formed by the company streets. The larger wall-tents of the officers were placed perpendicularly at the ends of the streets, with several yards separating them from the tents of the enlisted men. The entrances of the officers' tents faced the open company streets so that their residents could easily observe the activities of the men. Several yards beyond the tents of the company officers lay those of the field and staff officers of the regiment. At the opposite end of the company streets were the parade ground and flagpole.[1]

1. F. H. Taylor, *Philadelphia in the Civil War*, 113.

One of Colonel Collis' first steps after seeing to the arrangement of the camp was to issue a general order to the regiment on August 8, 1862. It contained the daily schedule that the men were to follow:

Reveille and Roll Call ....at daybreak
Breakfast 6AM
Guard Mounting and Drill...................................... 7AM
Dinner.. 12M
Drill 5 1/2PM
Supper 6 1/2PM
Tattoo... 9PM
Taps 10PM

Immediately after roll call, tents and bedding will be well dried, and accoutrements neatly arranged.

After every meal camp kitchens will be swept clean and utensils thoroughly scoured and properly put away . . . no fragments of food to be left lying about the kitchens or tents.[2]

Colonel Collis was no doubt intent on preserving the good appearance of the camp; and the proper preparation, eating, and disposal of food was of primary importance not only for appearances' sake but for sanitary purposes as well. In the case of regiments like the 114th, which was encamped close to an urban area and within easy visiting distance of civilians, cleanliness was likely given particular emphasis. Some men in other regiments were not so fortunate, and one complained that his first impression of camp life was anything but agreeable. "The great greasy black kettles strung on a pole over an open fire, and tended by a cook who much resembled the kettles, put a damper on my appetite. When meal time came each one marched to the fire with his tin cup and plate, and received his share, and then went away to sit on the ground to eat, while the wind seasoned his 'mess' with dirt and camp rubbish."[3]

By August 26, Collis had added a surgeon's call at 9:00 A.M., an "Inspection of Arms by Company Commanders" at 5:30 P.M., and a dress parade at 6:00 P.M., and had also sent the men to their tents earlier by moving taps up to 9:30 P.M.[4]

2. General Order Number 1, August 8, 1862, Order Books, 114th PV, in Record Group 94, NARA.
3. Diary of Nicholas Rice, in Nicholas Rice Papers, USAMHI.
4. General Order, August 26, 1862, Order Books, 114th PV, in Record Group 94, NARA.

Having adopted nearly the same uniform as that of the original Zouaves d'Afrique for the new regiment, Collis ensured that his men would be suitably clothed throughout their term of enlistment. He had imported from France a sufficient quantity of material for this purpose, securing it by unknown means—possibly by the citizens of Philadelphia, Collis' fellow members of the bar, or other benefactors of the regiment. But though cloth was on hand, uniforms were slow in coming. Government operations such as the Schuylkill Arsenal, on Grays Ferry Road between Carpenter Street and Washington Avenue, were important Federal depots for uniforms, blankets, and equipment. Though many of the Zouave uniforms were manufactured by that arsenal, such facilities were simply overwhelmed by the early demands for military items. Hence the need for regiments to resort to individual contractors, as previously mentioned. Nevertheless, as a result of Collis' foresight in stockpiling quantities of materiel—and thanks to the generosity of the unknown benefactors who made that purchase possible—the 114th Pennsylvania was one of the few Zouave regiments able to maintain its distinctive apparel throughout the war.[5]

In addition to the single uniform issued to each man of the 114th, Collis required his soldiers to purchase an extra set of clothes so that they would have on hand the proper outfit to replace those parts that became unwearable. At $5.25, the jacket was the most expensive part of their attire. The trousers and the fez, both made from specially imported brick red wool, were the next most costly items at $2.84 and $1.99, respectively. Each shirt cost $1.67; turban, $1.00; and sash $.88. The total cost for these uncommon parts of the Zouave uniform equaled nearly a month's pay.[6]

In keeping with their Zouave identity, the regiment also adopted another "accessory" peculiar to the French forces: a vivandiere, or canteen manager. Vivandieres originated, like the Zouaves, with the military forces in France. In their original capacity, they functioned much like sutlers, following the armies in the field while selling food and supplies to the soldiers. They were distinguished from cantinieres, or canteen keepers, who remained in camp or barracks. After 1800, French vivandieres came to be recognized as legitimate military figures and were permitted to wear uniforms that resembled in cut and color those of their units. During the

5. Rauscher, *Music on the March*, 13; F. H. Taylor, *Philadelphia in the Civil War*, 322.
6. Order Books, 114th PV, in Record Group 94, NARA.

French conquest of Algeria, the unavailability of women's clothing forced the vivandieres to substitute military-issued items. This well-established French tradition was carried over to the Zouave organizations in the United States and made a significant impact on women's clothing styles during the 1860s, popularizing pantaloon skirts and short collarless jackets for women. Contemporary fashion magazines such as *Godey's Ladies' Book* carried numerous illustrations of the latest styles based on the Zouave military uniform.[7]

Mary Tepe, or "French Mary," as the vivandiere of the 114th was more commonly known, was a veteran of several campaigns by the time she joined the regiment. Mary was born on August 24, 1834, in Brest, France, to a French mother and Turkish father. She arrived in America about 1849, and in 1854 married a Philadelphia tailor, Bernardo Tepe. When Bernardo enlisted in the 27th Pennsylvania Volunteers in 1861, he wanted Mary to stay in Philadelphia to manage his tailor shop. Instead, she joined her husband's regiment as a vivandiere. If Mary was in the field with the 27th during their early service, she could possibly have seen active campaigning from the first battle of Bull Run in July, 1861, until near the time of the second battle on that same scarred landscape the following August. In any event, she eventually left the regiment—and her husband as well, apparently—and returned to Philadelphia, where she joined Collis' Zouaves. She would prove to be a colorful addition to the already flamboyant regiment.[8]

Captain Frank A. Elliot of Company F was responsible for another colorful and popular addition to the regiment. Elliot, a resident of Germantown, was able to recruit a full fifteen-piece brass cornet band despite the issuance of General Order Number 151, from the headquarters of the Army of the Potomac, dated August 4, 1862, which prohibited bands below the brigade level. Elliot's efforts eventually produced larger rewards than musical enjoyment, for the future of the regiment became closely intertwined with that of the band, whose good fortune would benefit all those associated with it. In addition to the band, the regiment also boasted a drum and bugle corps.[9]

7. Rauscher, *Music on the March*, 13; H. Sinclair Mills, Jr., *Vivandieres*, (Collingswood, N.J., 1988), 1–3.

8. William Gladstone, "Gettysburg Mystery Photo . . . More Answers and More Questions," *Military Images*, III (March–April, 1982), 18.

9. Rauscher, *Music on the March*, 13–16; Wiley, *Billy Yank*, 157.

While Collis and his officers continued to seek recruits to fill out the ranks of the 114th, events on the battlefields of Virginia were adding to the sense of urgency behind such efforts. More men would be needed to stem the tide of southern victories, and quickly. On August 29 and 30, after a hard-fought battle at Bull Run, General Lee drove Union forces under Major General Pope back to Chantilly, and thence to the defenses of Washington. Lee had not only driven the Union army from the field, but had also driven the man he called a "miscreant," John Pope, from command of that army.[10] Lee then turned northward towards Maryland.

On August 27, a day marked by the return to Washington of Major General McClellan from the Virginia Peninsula and by the feasting by Stonewall Jackson's troops on the vast stores of Union supplies at Manassas Junction, Colonel Collis had hosted an equally well received dinner for his officers at the United States Hotel on Chestnut Street in Philadelphia. Knowing that they would soon be taking the field, the officers lent an air of bravado to the farewell party. With the band present to serenade them, the men toasted and made speeches well into the night. Then, on Friday, August 29, in anticipation of a directive to move at any time, Collis ordered: "All commissioned and noncommissioned officers and soldiers of this command, whether on detached service or otherwise, [to] report to Camp N. P. Banks immediately." Several days prior, he had taken steps to ensure his men could be easily assembled: "As this command may be ordered to the seat of war at any moment," he had proclaimed, "hereafter, no passes will be granted for a longer time than five hours."[11]

Collis' regiment still needed eighty-five men to fill it to its maximum capacity; except for the Corn Exchange Regiment, the other Philadelphia organizations then recruiting were in even worse shape. Finally, on Saturday, August 30, Adjutant General Lorenzo Thomas arrived in Philadelphia to try to salvage something usable from the incomplete units lying about the city. Weary of the delays in forwarding troops to meet the current emergency, Thomas ordered Philadelphia's mustering officer, Lieutenant Colonel Charles Frederick Ruff, to begin consolidating the regiments and sending them to the field. Ruff promptly disbanded some still-skeletal regi-

---

10. John Hennessy, "The Second Battle of Manassas: Lee Suppresses the 'Miscreant' Pope," *Blue and Gray*, IX (August, 1992), 12.

11. DEB, August 28, 1862, p. 5, August 29, 1862, p. 5; General Order Number 8, August 24, 1862, Order Books, 114th PV, in Record Group 94, NARA.

ments and transferred recruits into those, like the 114th, nearly ready to muster in. In one case, Ruff consolidated three companies of a proposed regiment, the 145th—to be commanded by Colonel Elisha W. Davis— with the 121st under Colonel Chapman Biddle. Biddle retained command of the regiment, and Davis became its Lieutenant Colonel. Ruff's labors resulted in the formation of five full regiments: the 68th, 114th, 118th, 119th, and 121st.[12]

On the night of Sunday, August 31, 1862, the long-anticipated order to move was given. The camp was a beehive of activity that night as the men prepared for the coming march. Members of the band, who had been permitted to make the adjustment to military life much more gradually than the average infantryman—and spent most nights in their own nearby homes—were roused from their beds by couriers. The regiment began to break camp around midnight, and by 7 A.M. had marched through the city and reached the Cooper Shop Volunteer Refreshment Saloon at 1009 Otsego Street. They were breakfasting excitedly as scores of friends and relatives arrived to say good-bye. A tremendous crowd was on hand by the time Collis' regiment resumed its march to the Baltimore depot at Broad and Prime Streets and boarded freight cars along with the 68th, 69th, 115th, and 118th Pennsylvania Volunteers. "It is impossible to tell in words that would convey anywhere near an accurate description of the scenes, incidents and excitement attending this embarkation," wrote one chronicler. They were commencing a journey from which far too many would never return, and tragedy struck before the train was even as far as Perryville, Maryland. Private Mordecai Ryan—at 6 feet 2 1/2 inches, known as "The Bucks County Giant"—was killed after falling from the moving train. Ryan was one of a group of friends from Bucks County, Pennsylvania, who had enlisted in Captain Elliot's Company F. Robert Kenderdine had been the first of the tentmates to enlist, followed by Joseph P. Kitchen, Ryan, then Thaddeus Paxon. Ryan had been sitting in the doorway of the boxcar swinging his long legs back and forth in time to the songs he and his friends had been noisily singing, when his legs crashed into a trackside coal bin, sweeping him from the car and under the wheels. One of the soldiers was immediately lifted to the top of the jolting boxcar, "and by running along the tops of the cars he reached the

12. *DEB*, September 1, 1862, p. 1; F. H. Taylor, *Philadelphia in the Civil War*, 135.

engine and the train was stopped some three or four miles from the scene of the accident." The engineer quickly reversed the train and sped to where the dying soldier lay on the tracks. Kenderdine was tasked with bearing Ryan's body home to his widowed mother while the rest continued sadly on their journey. Several men mentioned the ghastly event in their letters home. "[He was] one of the best and largest men in our company," wrote Sergeant Isaac Fox to his parents a few days afterwards. Some thought his death an ill omen. For the men from Bucks County, it might have been. Paxon and Kenderdine were destined never to return, while Kitchen was discharged on a surgeon's certificate for disability within only a few weeks.[13]

Without further incident, the train pulled into Baltimore that evening in a drenching rain. After marching through the downpour from the Philadelphia depot to the Washington depot, the men found that there were several regiments ahead of them awaiting transportation and that they would be unable to continue their journey that night. Though they were "fed by the citizens" upon their arrival, most of the men spent an uncomfortable night lying on the flagstone floor of the station—if they were fortunate. Others less lucky were forced outside to lie or sit as best they could manage on the damp, cobblestone ground. The men of Company F fared slightly better. Shortly after they spread their blankets on the ground, Captain Elliot roused them and took them to a storehouse where they could be out of the weather. The following morning, the men of the 114th fended for themselves for breakfast; as there was yet no transportation for them, they remained in the city until later that day. Sergeant Given, perhaps not having thought to have it done at home, used the occasion to have his photograph taken "in full uniform standing with my gun at a parade rest."[14]

Finally, the anxious Philadelphians continued on their way by rail to

13. Philadelphia *Weekly Times,* April 24, 1886, p. 1; Robert Kenderdine Papers, HCWRT Collection, USAMHI; Isaac Fox to "My Dear Parents," September 5, 1862, in Isaac Fox Collection, HSP; George Murray to "Dear Father & Mother," September 3, 1862, in George Murray Collection, FSNMP; David M. Mace to "Dear Cousin John," September 12, 1862, in John Bricker Papers, CWMC, USAMHI.

14. Given Diary, n.d., in Given Collection, CWLM; Murray to "Dear Mother & Father," September 3, 1862, in Murray Collection, FSNMP; Rauscher, *Music on the March,* 16–17.

the nation's capital. The short distance from Baltimore to Washington, D.C., took an exhausting ten hours to travel. Upon their arrival, the hungry Zouaves were taken to the Soldiers' Retreat for dinner. It was a government facility, where the fare could not favorably compare to that served at the privately run refreshment saloons. The meal was conducted, wrote one disgruntled Zouave to his parents, "like all the government concerns, nothing to eat but bread and coffee without sugar, and in horse buckets at that." "The impression left upon us, both bodily and mentally," recalled a member of the band, "was not of a very complimentary character."[15]

That night the men encamped within a few hundred yards of the Capitol. For most of them, it was probably an emotional and thought-provoking experience. Now that they had arrived in Washington and were about to begin soldiering in earnest, many wondered fearfully at what the coming days might bring. There would be no turning back now. Alexander Given was one such soldier who was powerfully affected that night, as his future recollections poetically attest: "The stars silently watched over us while we slept and a good God in whose care we were placed held us in the hollow of his hand. Then began an experience of an army life, an experience to be remembered as long as I live and the record of which will be handed down to my children and to the generations to come. The Nation's Capital was in danger and we were there to save it and drive back the enemy to our Country and our dear old Flag."[16]

Daylight shook the men from their reverie, however, and after another poor breakfast at the same Soldiers' Retreat where they had dined the previous evening, the Zouaves started out of the city and headed north about five miles. Across the road from Fort Slocum, on the sandy surrounding ground the men set up camp, which they called Camp Crosman. Although the water was poor, there were plenty of peaches and apples to be had, and the view from the heights was awe inspiring. The city was surrounded by forts and soldiers, and the Zouaves quickly caught on to the generally accepted practices of an army in the field. A number of men went out from the camp each day "to go 'foraging' as they call it. That is 'appropriate' all eatibles they can lay hands on," recalled one of them. "Some poor farmers nearest camp have been stripped of nearly everything," he continued. "The farms on which we encamped, I am thinking,

---

15. Murray to "Dear Father and Mother," September 3, 1862, in Murray Collection, FSNMP; Rauscher, *Music on the March*, 17.

16. Given Diary, n.d., in Given Collection, CWLM.

will need a new set of rails by the time we are through. We burn nothing else." [17]

From their camp, the Zouaves could even see Fort Lincoln near the Baltimore and Ohio Railroad line over four miles away. Some men manning the defenses around the capital were so anxious to see the Rebels that they sometimes climbed high into the trees to catch a glimpse of an enemy camp. Though the Zouaves were probably too far away to see any Confederate soldiers, it was just as well, for such tree-climbing adventures did not always end safely. One man from the 50th Pennsylvania, which had been encamped in the Washington vicinity the previous year, recalled an incident where youthful exuberance to see the enemy ruined the health of one of his friends: "Reed and I climbed some trees near camp, and saw camps among the hills south of the river, three or four miles away, which I know now were those of our own troops, but passed for rebels then. While coming down, Reed fell and broke his arm, which a drunken surgeon pretended to set, but left him a cripple for life." [18]

As the Zouaves began to settle into their new camp, Confederate forces were crossing the Potomac River and heading to the north in hopes of luring the Union army out of its fortifications around Washington. General McClellan, now restored to command of the Army of the Potomac, was putting that force into motion to meet the Rebels. When the two armies did meet near the sleepy town of Sharpsburg, Maryland, and the meandering stream called Antietam Creek, the single bloodiest day of the war would ensue.

On Sunday, September 7, the 114th Pennsylvania was ordered to move to join the main army in the field. The previous day, orders had been issued assigning them to Major General Fitz John Porter's 5th Corps; but those orders had been quickly countermanded, and the Zouaves found themselves under the command of Major General Banks. The 114th thus marched out of Camp Crosman en route to Rockville, Maryland, and covered twenty-two miles; but they were then recalled. "I expect it [was] thought we were most too green to enter the field," wrote Private George Murray from Company B, while a disappointed Sergeant Given recalled,

17. Mace to "Dear Cousin John," September 12, 1862, in Bricker Papers, CWMC, USAMHI.

18. Rice Diary, n.d., in Rice Papers, USAMHI. Camp Crossman, as it was commonly spelled by the men, was named in honor of George Hampton Crosman, a Regular Army officer who was in charge of the quartermaster's department in Philadelphia.

"As the troops passed us going into the Battle we cheered them all we could."[19] As for Banks, he was temporarily relieved from command of his corps on September 8 and placed in charge of the defenses of Washington.

The Zouaves returned to the safety of their camp near Fort Slocum, passing along roads choked with troops, wagon trains, horses, and artillery "all hastening to the scene of action." Over the course of the next several days, however, despite their deliverance from the inferno of battle, a large number of men deserted the regiment. "There are but about four hundred and twenty men in camp, all the rest have left for home because they didn't get their bounty," wrote Private Murray. Apparently, men began to desert as early as September 6. Eleven enlisted men of Company B, all from the town of Hanover in York County, Pennsylvania, gave the excuse that, after reading in the papers that the Confederates had invaded the North and that Rebel pickets were within a few miles of their home town, "they were much excited, and in conversation with others of the company stated that they thought their proper place was at home, defending it."[20]

A short time before deserting, one of the men from Company B, who supposedly spoke for all, had discussed the bounty situation with their captain, Edward R. Bowen. The captain was assured that the nonpayment of the bounties was of no importance to the men and that they would stand by him with unabated confidence. "To all this, they have given the lie," wrote Bowen after receiving a letter from one of the deserters, Private Theodore N. Bain, who was then at Hanover. The letter-writer contended, however, "It was spoken of in the company that as the men did not get their bounty and were not regularly mustered in the service that the men could not be held." Furthermore, he maintained that the captain was fully aware "that we intended to leave as we were deceived in every respect."[21]

Bain further alleged that so many men from the 114th had left the regiment with no effort on Collis' part to prevent them from doing so that Federal pickets had received orders to allow the Zouaves to pass freely through the lines. Bowen's eleven men absent without leave, however,

19. OR, Vol. XIX, Pt. 2, pp. 197, 202; Murray to "Dear Father & Mother," September 12, 1862, in Murray Collection, FSNMP; Given Diary, n.d., in Given Collection, CWLM.

20. Murray to "Dear Father & Mother," September 12, 1862, in Murray Collection, FSNMP; Edward R. Bowen to "Col. C. H. T. Collis," September 16, 1862, in records of the 114th PV, PHMC.

21. Bowen to "Col. C. H. T. Collis," September 16, 1862; Theodore N. Bain to "Capt. E. R. Bowen," September 14, 1862, both in Records of the 114th PV, PHMC.

passed not only through the Union lines, but into the hands of Major General James Ewell Brown Stuart's "sable Cavalry" at Westminster, Maryland. The fast-moving cavalrymen quickly paroled the men, who then made their way unmolested to Hanover. Captain Bowen was wholly unsympathetic. He requested that every effort be made to effect the exchange of the deserters and that "they be apprehended and made to suffer such punishment as their crime deserves."[22]

An additional eighty-five men had been apprehended in Baltimore and returned to Fort Slocum, where they were held under guard. By September 15, those of the regiment who had remained in camp and were now standing guard over their errant comrades had at least received their bounty from the Federal government. Private Murray also expressed little sympathy for the prisoners. "One or two of them will be shot," he wrote matter-of-factly to his parents; "a couple of them are chained together." The fate of those who had encountered Stuart's horsemen was unknown, but the rumor had spread that the men of Company B had not only been captured but had been sent to languish in a Richmond prison. Such a fate probably would not have seemed too severe to men like Sergeant David M. Mace of Company H, who likewise expressed his contempt for those who had deserted the regiment. "I have been cursing and swearing for three days hardrunning at these *creatures* styling themselves men," he wrote on September 12. "There we were," he continued, "one of the finest set of men in the service, the rebels crossing the Potomac, and threatening even their native state, and they refusing to move, because a few paltry dollars have not been paid as soon as promised, or as soon as they expected them! Ye Gods! save me from such patriotism. It is time indeed for republican institutions to fail when they depend on such men to preserve them from ruin."[23]

Even before it had lost a large number of men through desertion in early September, the 114th Pennsylvania had suffered the desertion of many other soldiers during the preceeding weeks. Some men deserted from Camp Banks within days of their enlistment. These men probably decided that they had made a terrible mistake in joining the regiment, but the

22. Bowen to "Col. C. H. T. Collis," September 16, 1862, Bain to "Capt. E. R. Bowen," September 14, 1862, both *ibid*.

23. Murray to "Dear Mother & Father," September 15, 1862, in Murray Collection, FSNMP; Mace to "Dear Cousin John," September 12, 1862, in Bricker Papers, CWMC, USAMHI.

possibility also exists that they were prospective bounty jumpers. After realizing that the bounties were not to be paid immediately, however, they may have simply tired of waiting and tried their luck elsewhere. At least 105 men of the regiment are known to have deserted between July and September of 1862. The 114th was thus short the equivalent of one full company before it even took the field. The subsequent desertions from Camp Crosman were thus a severe drain on the regiment's manpower. Had it been sent into battle, its numbers would have been comparable to those of the veteran regiments that had suffered legitimate losses in action. It would have been a disgraceful debut.[24]

The fact that so many men deserted—ostensibly because of the non-payment of bounties—would seem to imply that those men enlisted in the 114th were motivated by financial self-interest. This hypothesis contradicts the earlier assertion that pecuniary issues probably had little influence on the majority's decision to join the regiment. Rather than view the problem strictly in terms of its financial implications, however, we do well to regard it in terms of a violation of contract made between the men and their government—in this case, the city of Philadelphia most conspicuously. Previous studies of regiments composed of citizen-soldiers have shown that throughout the history of armed conflict in North America, from colonial times through the Civil War, volunteer soldiers viewed themselves simply as civilians who were engaged in performing work for their government. The terms and conditions of that work were made clear in the provisions of their "contract," or enlistment. In the case of colonial troops, for example, the unstated expectation that they could be utilized on expeditions into Canada seemed to violate the provisions of their enlistment. Many of those soldiers believed that they had enlisted to provide for the defense of their colony, hence their homes, and could not be forced to engage in invasions of foreign territory. Even during the Civil War, this contractual attitude must have been present to some extent in the Confederate army. A considerable number of soldiers fell out of the ranks on the way north, citing their belief that they had enlisted to defend their homes against northern aggression, not to return that aggression in kind.

Other factors that gave pause to the commitment of some early citizen-soldiers included the quality of care taken by the government to provide for the needs of the volunteers, and the strict conformity to terms of en-

24. Descriptive list of deserters, Records of the 114th PV, in Record Group 94, NARA.

listment. Many men of the colonial forces were prepared to go home at the moment their term expired, no matter where they were or what actions they were then engaged in, or whether the long-anticipated battle was to take place imminently. They had been bound by a contract. For many, when the contract expired, their commitment to fight patriotically did likewise. Conflict between the volunteers and the government was never uncommon; and while the views of the citizen-soldiers were sometimes seen as petty, they nevertheless indicate the strength of their belief that they had entered into a set and inviolable pact. Many a provincial soldier in colonial times was held to his duty at the point of a bayonet despite his businesslike protestations that his "contract" had in some way been violated and was thus void.[25]

While a number of those who deserted the 114th Pennsylvania may have been influenced to some degree by the failure of the government to pay the bounties, it is more likely that the failure struck the soldiers' sense of fairness more than their economic condition. In this light, the decision to desert the regiment probably derived from the feeling that the contract into which they had entered with the government had been violated rather than from their immediate need for the money promised. Hence, the men believed they were free to absolve themselves of their obligation on that basis.

As it was, many of the deserters were subsequently captured and returned to the regiment. Not only did their professed reasons for leaving carry little weight with military authorities, but the unfortunate timing of their actions made it appear that they had deserted at a moment of crisis. This circumstance undoubtedly disqualified their explanations in the eyes of their comrades and superiors. On September 16, the brigade commander and fellow Philadelphian, Colonel Augustus A. Gibson, issued orders that the 114th would be paraded at retreat that day, with the prisoners in front. It was a "painful task," he wrote, "to render a public exposure of the disgraceful conduct of a portion of the 114th Pennsylvania Volunteers."

25. For a full discussion of the background of early American militia and the implications of contractual obligations on their performance, see Anderson, *A People's Army;* John Shy, *A People Numerous and Armed: Reflections on the Military Struggle for American Independence* (London, 1976); John Shy, "A New Look at Colonial Militia," *William and Mary Quarterly,* 3rd ser., XX (April, 1963), 175–85; Howard H. Peckham, *The Colonial Wars, 1689–1762* (Chicago, 1964); and Lawrence Delbert Cress, *Citizens in Arms: The Army and the Militia in American Society to the War of 1812* (Chapel Hill, 1984).

Gibson intended to release the prisoners to the custody of their company officers, but he felt compelled first to issue a stinging rebuke.[26]

With the regiment assembled, Gibson began his reprimand by reminding them that they had been received into the brigade "with drums beating and colors flying—challenging the admiration of every spectator to the scene." But three days later, he recollected, upon the reception of "orders to take the field against an invading army of traitors, whose insolence and audacity for the moment appalled the country,"

> nearly two hundred enlisted men, like cowards or poltroons—more likely both—threw down their arms, deserted their colors, and retired in infamy. Was ever an act on record so disgraceful? And to make the deed doubly damning the paltry plea was put forth that the State bounties had not been paid in full at the moment stipulated. The man that must be bribed to his country's rescue is more than mean, vile despicable.
>
> Such is the terrible stigma which justice pronounces upon the conduct of these men. It can be washed out only by the blood of the 114th. Let every man consecrate his life to regain the lost place and redeem the lost name which the regiment assumed when honored with its colors by the proud patriotic State of Pennsylvania.[27]

Gibson then released the prisoners from confinement and decreed that the reprimand given by him be copied into the order books of every company of the 114th. It must have been a humiliating experience for Colonel Collis and the loyal men of the regiment. They would anxiously await the opportunity to prove themselves worthy in battle and remove this blemish from their record. "Washed out only by the blood of the 114th!" Those powerful words would no doubt resound within the minds of many Zouaves as they formed in line of battle for the first time.

Two days later the regiment packed up and marched back through Washington, down Pennsylvania Avenue past the White House, then by the Smithsonian Institution and the Washington Monument to the Long Bridge and "the sacred soil of Virginia at last." By 5 o'clock that evening, the Zouaves had arrived at Camp Prescott Smith near Arlington Heights.

26. Special Orders Number 8, Headquarters 1st Brigade, Defenses of Washington North of the Potomac, Fort Lincoln, D.C., September 16, 1862, Records of the 114th PV, in Record Group 94, NARA.

27. *Ibid.*

Rumor had it that the men were to push on to Fort Lyon, south of Alexandria, but instead they were ordered to remain where they were. The 114th took up temporary residence in the camp of their Philadelphia neighbors, Scott's Legion, the 68th Pennsylvania. That regiment was then on picket duty. The camp lay on high ground, and the men enjoyed the view of the capital lights at night and the serenades played by the many bands encamped nearby. "There is nothing but music . . . till nine or ten o'clock at night, drum, fifes, and bands," wrote Private Murray. The men enjoyed this idyllic respite for a few days before receiving orders to ready themselves to march at a moment's notice with three days' rations in their haversacks and one hundred rounds of ammunition in their cartridge boxes.[28]

On September 25, the regiment moved out of camp to perform picket duty southwest of the city, three or four miles past Bailey's Crossroads. It was then that the men of the 114th first saw the scenes of devastation that would soon become commonplace to them. Along the Bull Run Road, Private Murray reported "such a sight . . . I never saw in all my life, horses had been gutted, and horses laid dead along the road." Thus far, the regiment's experience with the effects of warfare had been confined to the accidental deaths of Private Ryan, who had fallen from the train on the way south, and Corporal John Bell of Company B, who died on September 8 after a careless comrade shot him in the head at Camp Crosman. "The ball penetrated [Bell's] left eye and took away the left side of his head. It was a ghastly sight," wrote Sergeant Mace.[29]

By the time the regiment was sent on picket duty, they had received their winter overcoats and turned in their large A-frame tents for smaller three-piece shelter tents. There were to be three men to a tent, with each man carrying a piece of the tent while on the march. The Zouaves had also been formally mustered into United States service during this period, and were placed in the 1st Brigade, 1st Division, 3rd Corps. Strangely, their comrades from the original company of Zouaves d'Afrique had yet to join them.

After the battle of Antietam, in which they had fought side by side with the 2nd Massachusetts, those early Zouaves unwisely decided to re-

28. Murray to "Dear Father & Mother," n.d., in Murray Collection, FSNMP.

29. Murray to "Dear Mother & Father," September 12, 30, 1862, *ibid.*; Mace to "Dear Cousin John," September 12, 1862, in Bricker Papers, CWMC, USAMHI.

turn to Philadelphia to find out why their assignment to the 114th Pennsylvania had not yet taken effect. From there, a letter was sent to Governor
Curtin detailing the plight of the unassigned men. The letter was hardly
complimentary to their former commander, Colonel Collis, or to the first
lieutenant, Severin A. Barthoulot. It was alleged that the company had
fought only one engagement under the command of then-captain Collis,
and that since that time it had been under the command of Second Lieutenant George Heimack, "Barthoulot being generally in a state of intoxication and consequently unfit for duty." The disgruntled men resented
being left under charge of an officer whom they little trusted, "Barthoulot
. . . at times when most needed refusing to take command" of the company.
In particular, they disliked the fact that Collis had been "generally engaged
elsewhere," and that they had been "kept in a perfect state of ignorance
as to [his] whereabouts." They claimed never to have heard a word of his
doings until the end of July, when the newspapers reported that he was in
Philadelphia recruiting a new regiment! At that point, they must have
made an effort to contact him, for the letter next claimed that Collis
informed them in writing that they would be made officers and NCOs in
the new regiment. "But in this [he] has not fulfilled his promise," they
averred, and the company was "left to take care of themselves the best
way possible."[30]

The writer continued to chronicle the complaints of the company and
the ordeal they had suffered at the hands of the incompetent Barthoulot.
At the battle of Cedar Mountain, they were under the command of Lieutenant Heimack. Barthoulot was then under arrest for drunkenness and
disorderly conduct. Heimack was wounded and taken prisoner during that
engagement, however, and the command then devolved upon Fifth Sergeant George Doriot. Doriot continued in command of the company at
the battle of Antietam, "Barthoulot absolutely refusing to take
command."[31]

Finally, the letter considered the fate of the neglected company. Its
remnants, then numbering about sixty-five men, were in Philadelphia. The
twenty-six members of the company who signed the letter to Governor
Curtin requested that, in light of the treatment received thus far, they be

30. "To the Honorable Andrew G. Curtin," Records of the 114th PV, in Record Group
19, PHMC.
31. *Ibid.*

permitted to transfer intact under command of Lieutenant Heimack to an existing regiment—preferably the 110th Pennsylvania. Many of them had served under that regiment's colonel, William D. Lewis, Jr., when he commanded the 18th Pennsylvania in the three months' service. But if a position within a regiment other than the 114th could not be found, they would seek authority to expand the company into a battalion, also to be commanded by Heimack.[32]

It was not until early October that the whereabouts of Collis' independent company were made known to him. He received an inquiry concerning them from the assistant adjutant general, Major Thomas McCurdy Vincent, a regular army officer in charge of the organization of volunteer troops. Collis quickly responded that the original company "should now constitute Co. A of my regiment. I have recruited only nine additional companies." In addition, Collis contended that he had made repeated though unsuccessful efforts to have the company ordered to him, and that it had "dwindled down by casualty, promotion and desertion to a mere Corporal's Guard." He trusted that "what is left of it may be ordered to me at once."[33]

Collis then dispatched Barthoulet, then acting as Captain of Company A, to Philadelphia to retrieve his men. The incompetent captain apparently made no new impression on the Zouaves and was probably starting to trouble Collis as well. The Colonel expressed exasperation in a letter he fired off to Barthoulot on October 16: "I am surprised that you should write me asking 'What are you to do' with the members of Co. A of this Regiment. You will immediately send them to these Head Quarters, and unless they report soon they will be arrested and sent to Harpers Ferry to work on the fortifications. These men are in Philadelphia *without authority*, and unless you do something promptly to make their services available to the government, you may get yourself into serious trouble."[34]

Collis followed up this letter soon afterward with one to Lieutenant Heimack. In it he requested Heimack to furnish a written statement detailing his efforts to arrest and return to duty those men then absent without leave from Company A. It still took several more weeks before Collis

32. *Ibid.*

33. C. Collis to "Major Thomas M. Vincent," October 8, 1862, Records of the 114th PV, in Record Group 94, NARA.

34. C. Collis to "Capt. Barthoulot," October 16, 1862, *ibid.*

was able to obtain his men from Philadelphia. He complained of the situation to Adjutant General Thomas, and as late as November 25, was forced to request that Major Joseph S. Chandler of his regiment travel to Philadelphia to ensure the company's return.

The allegation by men of the original company that Collis intended for all of them be promoted to some position of rank in the 114th hardly seems credible. In fact, a number of those early Zouaves d'Afrique did become officers and NCOs in the new regiment, but it would have been impossible for all of them to have been placed in such positions. Whether Collis naïvely presumed otherwise and actually promised them advancement cannot be determined. The allegation may have stemmed from a misunderstanding of his intentions. What is certain, however, is that when the dispute was finally settled, there were six men from the original company on the rolls of the 114th as company officers, twenty-three as NCOs, and one as quartermaster sergeant. In the coming months, eight of the men who assumed NCO positions would advance to become officers.[35]

During all this confusion over the whereabouts of Company A, Collis received further discouraging news from Major General Seth Williams, adjutant general of the Army of the Potomac. Williams questioned Collis about a statement made by one of the deserters from Company B, Private Theodore N. Bain. The private alleged that as a result of the dispute over the payment of bounties, the colonel ordered 250 men to take their arms to Fort Slocum and "to remove all on their persons belonging to the US and do as they please hereafter." Bain's attempt to rationalize his actions and put a portion of the blame on his colonel left Collis nonplussed. He simply replied that a few days before Bain "*deserted,* a mutiny occurred in my Regiment" over the nonpayment of bounties: "having no force on hand on which I could rely to enforce obedience the best I could do was to secure the Government property which they had in their possession." He went on to say of the fewer than 200 men who deserted, that 150 of them had been returned and punished, with the ringleaders tried by general court-martial. After securing the government property, Collis wrote, he then "cautioned the mutineers that they deserted at their peril and ordered them to the ranks but they refused upon the plea that the City of Philadelphia had violated its contract. I should most certainly have used

35. Muster Rolls of the 114th Pennsylvania Volunteers, Records of the 114th PV, in Record Group 19, PHMC.

force, but there were not other troops in the vicinity." As for Bain, Collis maintained that he was not part of the group that had deserted on account of the bounties, but had stated to his captain that he was going home to Hanover to protect his family. As a consequence, Collis contended, when exchanged he should be treated as a deserter. Bain was eventually apprehended in Hanover on January 27, 1863. He was tried by general court-martial and sentenced to forfeit all pay and allowances then due him until April, 1863. He returned to his company, was captured at Gettysburg in July, and paroled in September. He mustered out with the regiment in 1865.[36]

During the time that Collis was busy with these administrative matters, the regiment continued a routine of serving picket duty and digging entrenchments. They quickly grew tired of the view of Washington and found cause to complain about their new camp. Prohibited from leaving it to get water, to bathe, or to pick grapes—as they had done at Camp Crosman—the men groused that they were not so clean as they were in the other camps and hoped to move soon. They were then encamped inside of entrenchments at the foot a hill, atop of which was a fort. Surrounding them were the other regiments of their brigade: the 63rd, 68th, 105th, and 141st Pennsylvania, and the 20th Indiana. The Zouaves were particularly impressed by the colors of the veteran 20th Indiana. "You ought just to see their flags," wrote Private Murray; "they are cut to pieces so that you can hardly see what they are."[37]

Other regiments, in turn, were struck by the appearance and military bearing of the Zouaves. Private James P. Coburn of the 141st Pennsylvania took particular notice of the cornet band of the 114th, and wished that all his friends at home could see the wonderful spectacle of dress parade. "Each regiment is drawn up in a line by itself," he wrote to his friends, "& I tell you a thousand men make quite a line, but there were 10 such regiments in view from our camp." He continued:

> That which would please you most is the 114th from Philadelphia . . .
> & when drawn up in line . . . their guns glittering in the rays of the setting
> sun—O! Isn't it nice! And then their band marches the whole length of

36. C. Collis to "Maj. Gen. S. Williams," October 23, 1862, and other records of the 114th PV, in Record Group 94, NARA.

37. Murray to "Dear Father & Mother," September, 1862, in Murray Collection, FSNMP.

the line playing such pieces as any patriot loves to hear. "Fix bayonets" & a thousand bristling bayonets are drawn from their scabbard & "fixed" in less time than it takes me to write it. "Shoulder arms!" & a thousand white-gloved hands grasp a thousand muskets at the same instant looking as though they were moved by a machine so perfect are their movements.

"Order arms" and a thousand muskets strike the ground so nearly at the same time that you could hear but one sound. They are beauties I tell you— but when they "Charge bayonets" with such a yell as Zouaves only can give, the rebels'll skedaddle even if the greybacks have five times as many men as the red breeches have.[38]

The anticipated power of the Zouave charge would not be confirmed for some time yet. In the meantime, the brigade packed up their belongings once more on October 11, and started out for Poolesville, Maryland. Re-crossing the Potomac on the aqueduct, the men continued through Georgetown and up the Rockville Road, reaching Rockville itself after a march of about fourteen miles. The following day, the Zouaves were aroused at 2 A.M. and were on the march again by 4 A.M. It was the first forced march that the regiment would undertake, and they were ill pre-pared for the exertion. By the time they halted in midafternoon two miles beyond Poolesville, straggling had reached crisis proportions. One com-pany of eighty-nine men was found to contain only sixteen who were able to keep up the pace. A good number of the latecomers caught up with the regiment during this one-hour respite, but they were still footsore and weary. Twenty-pound knapsacks were lightened by disposing of nonessen-tial items, and most men took advantage of the halt to tend to blistered feet. Afterward, the regiment was marched another four or five miles to the Potomac River, where it was rumored that they were to prevent the recrossing of Rebel cavalry then engaged in raiding in Maryland and Penn-sylvania. The Zouaves remained picketing the river and the Chesapeake and Ohio Canal until about 10 P.M. that night. They then returned to the vicinity of Poolesville without seeing a single Rebel.[39]

38. James Parly Coburn letter, n.d, in Correspondence, 1862, James Parly Coburn Pa-pers, USAMHI.

39. Murray to "Dear Father & Mother," October 25, 1862, in Murray Collection, FSNMP; Fox Diary, November 6, 1862, in Fox Collection, HSP; Bucks County *Intelligencer*, October 28, 1862, p. 3.

In fact, two thousand hard-riding raiders under Major General J. E. B. Stuart had crossed into northern territory on October 10. Despite the best efforts of the Union cavalry to catch them, the Rebels were able to slip back across the Potomac virtually unmolested at White's Ford. One veteran of the 57th Pennsylvania lamented the wasted effort and the escape of the horsemen, and placed the blame on a regiment of fellow Keystone State Volunteers: "We were unable to come into contact with [them] although we tried their wind . . . we had them bagged and could have taken them all prisoners just as well as not had one Regt of our men held the position that was assigned to them, but no the cowards run letting them pass unmolested on the Va side. How mad we were when we learnt the fact for we anticipated quite a time but had none but a great march amounting to nothing only making us very tired." The soldier was so incensed that he thought the men responsible should be sent home disgraced. "Had I the power," he wrote to his wife, "I would put the 99th Reg't P. Vols to hard labor for the rest of their three years for deserting their post and letting the enemy through."[40]

Unfortunately for the 114th and the rest of the brigade, the several days following their picketing on the Potomac consisted of hurried marches to various points along the same river—all to no avail—then a return to camp. One Zouave estimated that during a three-day period the regiment had marched eighty miles. He claimed to have felt pretty well despite the effort, "My feet did not blister much, for these big army shoes are very easy," he wrote. "I have no trouble with wakefulness or indigestion now-a-days." The only digestive problems that the regiment experienced during this period stemmed from the fact that the men had very little to eat. On the second day of their forced marches, they even lacked hard crackers to eat. Fortunately, they eventually came upon some deserted provisions and were able to fill their haversacks with crackers and their tin cups with rice and beans. Some of the men also found salted pork, which they carried stuck onto the ends of their bayonets. The march continued with the column of soldiers trudging along with several pounds of the greasy meat swinging over their heads.[41]

40. Luther A. Granger to "Dear Wife," October 14, 1862, Luther A. Granger Papers, CWMC, USAMHI.

41. Fox Diary, November 6, 1862, in Fox Collection, HSP; Bucks County *Intelligencer,* October 28, 1862, p. 3.

The Zouaves remained encamped near Poolesville for some time, re-covering from the hard marching of the previous week. Despite the op-portunity for rest, at least one Zouave found cause for complaint. On October 19, Private Jacob B. Donnaker of Company E began a letter by telling his mother that he and many other men of the regiment had just returned from church services in Poolesville, "so you may know how re-ligious I am. But it was a very poor specimen of a church," he griped. "There was only about a dozen people there besides the soldiers. There seems to be nobody about here. I never saw such a half dead and alive kind of place in my life. But its like all the south I expect." Notwithstand-ing his disenchantment with the surroundings, Donnaker admitted that the respite from tramping up and down the river was a welcome one. "That march pretty near killed us all," he exclaimed. "I have not hardly got over it yet, but I think in a few days I will be ready to go again." The ability of some of the men to keep up with the grueling pace was not strengthened merely by patriotism or sense of duty, he wrote. "We had to keep up with the regiment under the penelty of being sent to Harpers ferry to work on the entrenchments. . . . two fellows out of our company have been sent there already so you see that they are very strict."[42]

One unfortunate soldier who could not withstand the rigors of the brief campaign was Robert Kenderdine, who fell ill while at Poolesville. Word was sent to his home in Bucks County, where his father and brother-in-law, Eastburn Reeder, made hasty preparations to go to him immediately. By the time they arrived in Poolesville, however, the army was gone. Following to Leesburg, Virginia, the two men found Robert "under an orchard tree . . . wrapped in a blanket, on the bare ground and unable to rise." Hospital tents soon reached the army, and conditions improved slightly. Kenderdine's condition apparently worsened, however. Efforts were made to secure his temporary release from the army so that he could be taken home and cared for properly. Failing that, Eastburn Reeder jour-neyed several miles to a Friends settlement on Goose Creek to make ar-rangements for Robert's care there. The hospital's medical director agreed, and the ailing soldier was moved to the home of Rachel Hoag. Reeder, meanwhile, fearful of capture by Rebel cavalry, returned to Philadelphia with the elder Kenderdine, leaving Robert in the attentive care of the

42. Jacob B. Donnaker to "My Dear Mother," October 19, 1862, in Jacob B. Donnaker Papers, CWMC, USAMHI.

Quaker community. Reeder had been right to fear his capture, for soon after his departure a group of southern horsemen made their appearance inquiring about a federal soldier at Hoag's house. Taken to where the stricken Zouave lay, the cavalrymen remarked that he was indeed a very sick man. Still, they made him prisoner and immediately paroled him. "A parole for a sick man meant a chance to get home and exemption from service until exchanged; but Robert protested and demanded the officer's authority. He, however, signed the necessary papers and the rebels left." In less than two weeks, Kenderdine was again well enough to travel. This time a respite in Philadelphia was approved. He arrived there on November 19 and remained confined to the hospital for most of his stay. He would not return to the regiment until mid-February, 1863.[43]

Kenderdine's fellow Zouaves had in the meantime enjoyed a visit at Poolesville from Governor Curtin, who on October 23 had presented the regiment "with a handsome state flag." The following day, the men were treated to the "splendid sight" of a review of the entire brigade by the division commander, Brigadier General George Stoneman. Finally, on October 27, the Zouaves started on the move again, crossing the Potomac near Leesburg, Virginia. From then on, their marching would take them steadily southward, to the banks of the Rappahannock River.[44]

43. Kenderdine Papers, HCWRTC, USAMHI.

44. Murray to "Dear Father & Mother," October 25, 1862, in Murray Collection, FSNMP; Fox Diary, October 27, 1862, in Fox Collection, HSP.

6

Hell on the Rappahannock

The 114th Pennsylvania spent the last few days of October, 1862, en-camped in the vicinity of Leesburg, Virginia; but on Sunday, November 2, they marched out to a small settlement called Mount Gilead, which lay in the shadow of Hog Back Mountain just to the east. The following day saw the Zouaves continuing southward until they arrived at Pleasonton Mills, near Middleburg, where they took prisoner four or five Confederate soldiers who were hidden in one of the local residences. The next morning the men struck west on the Ashby's Gap Turnpike for a short distance, passed through Middleburg, then turned south for Salem, where they halted for the night. On the morning of the fifth, the 114th passed through the mountains to the southeast of Salem until they reached the town of Waterloo, near Warrenton.

The weather was steadily turning worse, and the men approached War-renton the next day huddled against the force of a driving snow squall. "It snowed most all day and it was as cold as Greenland," wrote one man in the brigade, who hoped "we shall all go into winter quarters for it is too cold to be on the road." Some men complained not only of the cold, but of the incessant marching as well. It had been "hard and rough march-ing," they said, "between the rocks and creeks." But there were to be no winter quarters, not yet at least. The Army of the Potomac had a new commander, and he meant to test them.[1]

---

1. Fox Diary, October 27–November 7, 1862 in Fox Collection, HSP; Murray to "Dear

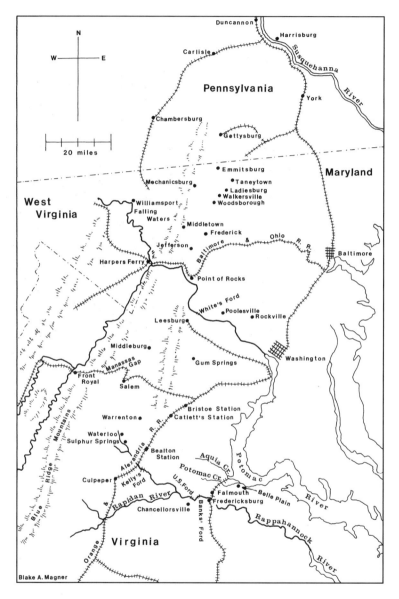

Area traversed by Collis' Zouaves between August, 1862, and August, 1863

Bewhiskered Major General Ambrose Everett Burnside had already twice declined command of the army, but early in November, 1862, he relented. On November 5, General in Chief Henry Wager Halleck sent two orders to Burnside: one that directed him to take command of the army, and one that instructed him to report both the position of his troops and what he proposed doing with them. General McClellan had already started the army moving toward Warrenton for the purpose of concentrating there and gathering needed supplies for a campaign against the Confederates at Culpeper. Burnside allowed the movement to continue as planned. Upon formally taking command of the army on November 9, he arranged a meeting with Halleck during which he proposed moving the army to Falmouth and there crossing the Rappahannock River to Fredericksburg. Halleck, in his usual way, demurred, refusing to commit himself until the president had reviewed the plan. Soon after Halleck returned to Washington, however, Burnside received a telegram informing him that Lincoln had agreed to his proposal. "He thinks it will succeed if you move rapidly; otherwise not," warned the general in chief. Three days later, the 114th began moving southward again, toward Fredericksburg. The night prior to the advance of Zouaves, Private Donnaker wrote facetiously to his mother from Warrenton: "We have it quite nice, about half enough to eat and when we get up in the morning froze stiff so we have to make a fire and thaw ourselves." He then turned to serious news, telling her that "we are ordered to have five days rations and to march at daylight tomorrow morning so I expect there is something up."[2]

General Burnside had started others of his army on the road to Fredericksburg before the 114th began to move. Within just a few days after receiving approval for his plan, the general was on the banks of the Rappahannock ready to cross a portion of his troops to the south side. Unfortunately for him, his rapid marching had come to naught. The pontoon bridges, boats, timbers, and engineers that had allegedly been promised to be waiting on his arrival there were nowhere to be found. It would be days before they would even begin to arrive, and the army could do nothing but wait and watch in paralyzing disbelief as Lee's Confederates on the

Mother & Father," November 9, 1862, in Murray Collection, FSNMP; Granger to "Dear Wife," November 8, 1862, in CWMC, USAMHI.

    2. OR, XXI, 82–84; Donnaker to "My Dear Mother," November 16, 1862, in Donnaker Papers, CWMC, USAMHI.

south side of the river caught up with them and filed into lines of en-trenchments on the hills overlooking the town.

Collis' Zouaves arrived near Fredericksburg on November 22 and settled down to wait. Many of the men again hoped to go into winter quarters. They complained about the insufficiency of their shelter tents, lamenting that it was "getting pretty cold in these dog houses." Soldiers contended with the weather and boredom as best they could, and most had little else to do but maintain that ever-important connection with loved ones at home. The letter-writers struggled on in the cold, but complained that it was "sharp on the fingers." One man resignedly begged pardon for his poor handwriting, but his "fingers were too stiff to write well." Rumor had it, though, that they would soon be supplied with new tents—with stoves in them. In the meantime, the men built fires in front of their cramped canvas quarters to keep warm. One soldier remarked that the fires contributed to the difficulty of writing letters, for though "we can keep warm, it smokes so that I can't see by it."[3]

Food shortages continued for the men encamped in the Fredericksburg and Falmouth area. With the tenuous and overloaded supply line from Aquia Creek to Falmouth struggling to meet the requirements of the mas-sive assemblage of men, supplies were spartan. Moreover, much time had passed since the army had been paid. Many men relied on the few dollars sent from home to see them through with the regimental sutler. Sometimes the sutlers could not keep pace with the soldiers, however, and it was not unusual for them to be separated from the men for weeks. Living off the land was impossible. Virginians in the area had already "'played out' so far as eatables are concerned," wrote one hungry private; "there is 'too much army' here for them to keep much even for themselves." He went on to describe how the army could quickly strip an area of the countryside of its comestibles: "Their pigs, chickens, turkeys, etc. receive 'marching orders' soon after the first Brigade stacks arms on their plantations—unless the Gen. posts his 'provost guards' in advance. He always posts them as soon as possible but sometimes the soldiers get in advance of them & roosters forget to crow, pullets to cackle & turkeys say 'quit' for the last time."[4]

3. Murray to "Dear Father & Mother," December 5, 1862, in Murray Collection, FSNMP; Strauss to "Dear Mother," November 26, 1862, in Strauss Papers, *CWTI* Collec-tion, USAMHI.
4. Coburn to "Dear Parents," November 24, 1862, in Coburn Papers, USAMHI.

As the days passed, the men became increasingly cold and uncomfortable. Brigadier General John Cleveland Robinson attempted to keep the men occupied as best he could, and on November 28 even tried conducting a mock battle as a diversion from the cold and boredom. It gave little consolation to the men. An early December storm that left two or three inches of snow coating the already austere landscape, and the uncertainty of when they would move, combined to exacerbate the miserable conditions. The Zouaves had yet to receive their pay, although they expected to do so soon, and some men sent home for boxes in the hopes that they finally would be settling in. The boxes would contain many items that would help to sustain them through the winter months: woolen underwear, mittens, and scarves, but especially homemade foods such as cakes, pies, meats, and preserves. Reading material was also highly prized. "I think that you can send the press here now," wrote one, "as a fellow has nothing to read." Private Murray, however, was not so certain that the time was right to send for the valuable goods from home. "Several of the boys are sending for boxes but I cannot tell whether they will get them or not," he wrote; "you can suit your own pleasure about sending a box now, some say we are going to move."[5]

For some men, the strenuous lifestyle and exposure to inclement weather constituted more than mere inconveniences. Soon after arriving at Falmouth, Colonel Collis was pained to report the death of twenty-three-year-old Second Lieutenant Charles E. Henkell of Company G. The lieutenant had been suffering from a severe cold when he crossed the Potomac River at White's Ford, "preferring to march with his men, than to ride on horseback or be carried in an ambulance." His condition worsened as a result, and a high fever kept him hospitalized until his death—probably from pneumonia. Collis recounted the circumstances of Henkell's death, pointing out the lieutenant's selfless devotion to his duties by stating that he had been so ill that he had been confined to bed, "with the exception of the day upon which we arrived at Salem, when the Regiment being drawn up to resist an anticipated attack of the enemy, he left his sick bed, took his position in line and marched over a severe road during the remainder of the day. This was contrary to my advice and the

5. Diary of James Parly Coburn, November 28, 1862 in Coburn Papers, USAMHI; Murray to "Dear Father & Mother," December 5, 1862, in Murray Collection, FSNMP.

advice of his surgeon."[6] Henkell's body was transported to a Washington embalmer, where it remained until his family retrieved it.

Other officers were not so conscientious in the performance of their duties, however. For example, on December 1, Collis found it necessary to request that the military examination board question Lieutenant David P. Dillington of Company D concerning his fitness to remain in the service. In his request to Brigadier General Robinson, president of the examining board, Collis accused his subordinate of "incompetency, slovenly habits, and negligence."[7]

The examination boards had been authorized by Congress in its act of July 22, 1861, which called forth the first 500,000 three-year volunteers. Containing from three to five officers, the boards were charged with questioning those officers brought before them on subjects such as military tactics, army rules and regulations, personal character, and physical fitness. Individual boards could develop their own criteria for an officer's acceptability; however, it is likely that lieutenants would have had to evince some knowledge in the following areas: infantry tactics through the company level, company organization and related duties, and the discharge of administrative duties related to a company. The boards had the power to recommend dismissal upon approval of the commander in chief, and there were often complaints that they unfairly exercised it to carry out personal or political vendettas. Whether this abuse of authority occurred with Lieutenant Dillington is not known; but he probably presented poorly in front of the board, for the twenty-two-year-old officer was discharged on January 1, 1863.[8]

Many of the other officers of the 114th were then suffering just as severely as their men. Most of their baggage and camp equipage had been left at Poolesville prior to the move south. Collis himself was called to task in early December for leaving not only those items but "about 20 muskets and a box and a half of cartridges," oversights which, according to Brigadier General George Stoneman, had occurred "contrary to orders." Collis had left Privates Zebadee Richards, David Drummon, John Lewis,

6. Order Books, 114th Pennsylvania, November 23, 1862, in Record Group 94, NARA.

7. C. Collis to "Brigadier General Robinson," December 1, 1862, in Records of the 114th PV, Record Group 94, NARA.

8. Stanley L. Swart, "The Military Examination Board in the Civil War: A Case Study," *Civil War History: A Journal of the Middle Period*, XVI (September, 1970), 227–45.

and Jeremiah Flemming at Poolesville on October 24. They were detailed to guard the commissary stores and camp equipage of the regiment. After nearly a month of idleness at that location, Private Richards had penned a letter of complaint to the office of the adjutant general in which he stated that they had been left with no provision made by the quartermaster for rations, and that they had been "paying out of their own pockets in order to sustain themselves." To this complaint Collis replied that he had ordered the detail "some time ago" to store the property and return to the regiment, and furthermore, that he had left them adequately supplied with three barrels each of pork and salt beef, seven boxes of crackers, thirty pounds each of coffee and sugar, twelve pounds of rice, and thirty pounds of dried apples. In a biting style that reveals Collis' contempt for the inefficiency and ineptitude of military regulations and the martinets who enforced them, he appended the following observation to his reply: "I beg to add, that had I been furnished with proper transportation to replace that which had been twice condemned, there would have been no necessity for this detail."[9]

Statements such as this almost proved the young officer's undoing in the near future. He was only slightly less contentious in his reply to General Stoneman's inquiry. There he simply stated that he had left the equipment under a guard of four men. As for adequate transportation, he grumbled, "At the present moment we have not one horse fit for work." Unfortunately for the officers, transportation would have been of no benefit by this time; all of the items left at Poolesville had been captured by the Confederates.[10]

Finally, at 5 A.M. on December 9, Burnside summoned the commanders of his three grand divisions to a noon meeting at his headquarters and instructed them to begin issuing orders to their commands immediately preparatory to a movement to cross the river. They were to be in position by the morning of the eleventh. Each man would carry three days' cooked rations, forty rounds of ammunition in his cartridge box, and twenty additional rounds in his pockets. The uncertainty was now over; men hastily cooked their rations and prepared for a fight.[11]

9. OR, XXI, 803–805; Zebadee Richards to "Dear Sir," November 22, 1862, C. Collis to "General," November 29, 1862, both in Records of the 114th PV, Record Group 94, NARA.

10. OR, XXI, 805.

11. Ibid., 63.

Some of the men mused over the abilities of their new commander. Many had already expressed their dismay at the removal of McClellan. "The men had great confidence in him," wrote Private Ellis Strauss, veteran of the 57th Pennsylvania. "I think that he was to [*sic*] slow at times and that if he would have had a little more dash in him he might have accomplished more." Nevertheless, the soldiers seemed generally pleased with Burnside so far—"though whether he is capable of managing the whole army remains to be seen" qualified Strauss. They were about to find out whether their general was indeed capable, and they expectantly hoped for the best: "I hope that he will prove himself competent to lead the Army, and to lead it to victory." [12]

Even Colonel Collis was engaged in evaluating his superiors. His opinion of his divisional commander and fellow Philadelphian Brigadier General David Bell Birney was uncomplimentary—perhaps for some personal or political reason. "My present *immediate* Commander [General John C. Robinson] I am exceedingly well pleased with," wrote the Colonel, "but I fail to appreciate the true merits of his superior, Genl. Birney. This is no doubt my misfortune," he continued, "he is no doubt an excellent General Officer—but we should not break our hearts on leaving him." From the tone of his criticisms, it would seem that Collis harbored some personal dislike for Birney, whose Zouave regiment had been the first regiment to organize and depart from Philadelphia in the war's first weeks. Whatever animosity may have existed between the men possibly contributed to some of Collis' later difficulties with the general. [13]

After much hectic preparation, the 114th finally moved out of camp at about 5 o'clock on Thursday morning, December 11. They marched about a quarter of a mile to a spot where the men stopped and "laid all of that day till about five o'clock." When the Zouaves resumed their march, they moved to within a quarter mile of the river, near the Richmond, Fredericksburg, and Potomac railroad line that ran from Aquia Creek. There they halted for the night in the road "while the cannons were raining an iron hail storm over the seemingly doomed city" of Fredericksburg. The following day the men resumed their march along the river road

12. Strauss to "Dear Mother," November 26, 1862, in Strauss Papers, *CWTI* Collection, USAMHI.

13. C. Collis to G. K. Warren, October 7, 1862, in Records of the 114th PV, Record Group 94, NARA.

for what seemed to them to be another three or four miles. It was probably only half that distance, but it was "over an awful road," upon which they saw for the first time the lifeless bodies of their blue-clad comrades.[14]

The regiment moved down closer to the river early on the morning of December 13. From their position on the high ground overlooking the Rappahannock and the pontoon bridges that provided the lower crossing, or "Franklin's Crossing," they could clearly see the battle unfolding before them. The morning had dawned brisk and chilly, and the thick fog that had hung over the landscape restricting visibility to less than fifty yards began to burn off as the sun rose higher in the sky. By 10 A.M. the Zouaves could see the two armies drawn up in battle array. The Army of Northern Virginia, some 75,000 strong, stretched along a front nearly five miles in length from Taylor's Hill on the north to Prospect Hill on the south.[15]

From the Rebel position, the view of Burnside's blue-coated soldiers was a sight of terrible beauty. The sun danced and played on thousands of gleaming Union bayonets, while state and national colors fluttered and snapped in the cool morning air. A member of Lee's staff, watching the drama unfold, later wrote that it was a scene "which in point of grandeur has seldom been witnessed." Other Confederates watching the deployment of Union troops on the easternmost portion of the field were equally impressed. A soldier of the 38th Georgia, which moved into position just prior to the Union attack on the Confederate right, recalled the sight. "Away over the undulating meadow they were seen debouching from the woods in solid columns," he wrote. "They came up in fine order . . . and with a courage worthy of a better cause."[16]

The Zouaves watched the battle unfold from their position overlooking the river. The left of the Federal line began moving forward in the face of a withering artillery fire that swept the field. Intense cannonade from the supporting Union artillery caused heavy losses among the Confederate gunners, yet they kept at their grim task and mowed down their attackers

14. Fox Diary, December 12, 1863 in Fox Collection, HSP; Edward E. Williams to "My Dear Wife and Mother," December 15, 1862, in Edward E. Williams and Edmund Williams Papers, Private Collection of Jack Sidebotham, Philadelphia.

15. "From Collis' Zouaves," Philadelphia *Inquirer*, December 19, 1862, p. 2; Vorin E. Whan, Jr., *Fiasco at Fredericksburg* (University Park, Pa., 1961), 1–12.

16. "The Battle of Fredericksburg, December 13, 1862," *Blue and Gray*, I (January, 1984), 28; "Army Correspondence, Near the Battlefield, December 15th, 1862," Sandersville *Central Georgian*, January 14, 1863, p. 1.

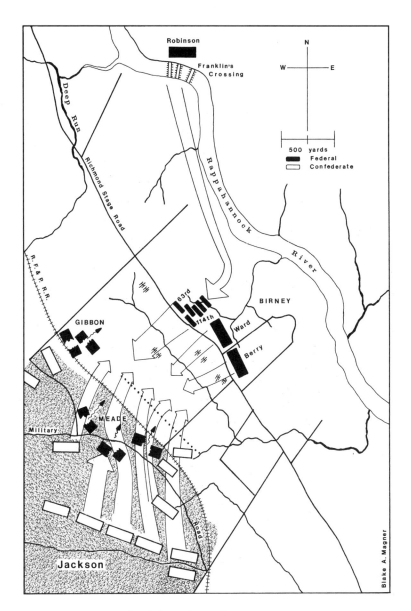

Fredericksburg, December 13–15, 1862

by the score. As the advancing soldiers neared the Rebel lines, they were met by a thunderous volley from those waiting southerners that staggered their lines anew. After a slight pause, the three brigades of Major General George G. Meade's Third Division, First Army Corps, pushed ahead into the maelstrom. The general rode along his lines giving encouragement to each of his regiments. As he passed Colonel William McCandless, commanding the first brigade, Meade alluded to the possibility of promotion: "A star this morning, William," he called. "More likely a wooden overcoat," came the melancholy reply.[17] The first brigade eventually reached the shelter of a wooded area that protruded from the Rebel lines. Here they found that the woods and an oversight on the part of the Confederate commanders had combined to produce a gap in the gray lines that was nearly six hundred yards wide. Meade's men poured into the gap and advanced to a cleared area at the top of the hill and across the military road that ran there.

To Meade's right, another Union brigade, commanded by Brigadier General John Gibbon, also broke through the Confederate defenses and carried the enemy trenches at bayonet point. The attackers fought on, doggedly determined to hold their costly gains until they could be supported. Meade sent urgent requests for reinforcements that would never arrive. The defenders, however, poured support into the threatened area. Gibbon's men were soon flanked on both ends of their line, and they began to withdraw. Meade's men were likewise struggling hand-to-hand with overwhelming numbers of fresh Confederates, who now assailed them from three sides. Finally, at about 2:15 P.M., over an hour after the start of the final push that had carried them into the Rebel lines, Meade's bloodied Pennsylvanians began streaming back out of the woods from the enemy position. They walked slowly and dejectedly across the corpse-strewn fields in a disorganized mass until two Confederate brigades charged and sent them flying to the rear.

The sight of the Confederate counterattack must have alarmed even the most stalwart Union commander. The repulse of Meade and Gibbon had left a gigantic hole in the Federal line that had not been adequately covered by reserve units. Now it was the Rebels' turn to attack an opening in the Union line. As Meade's retreating troops passed through the trickle of men coming belatedly to their support, the angry general requested that

17. St. Clair A. Mulholland, "Fredericksburg," *Grand Army Review* (August, 1886), 1.

the fresh regiments attempt to stop and rally his men. "It was useless," said one Union brigadier, as the dispirited men "sullenly and resolutely marched to the rear."[18]

Most of Brigadier General Birney's division had been ordered to cross the river before noon to support the attack made by Meade and Gibbon. As Birney began to deploy his men, however, it was already too late to make a success of the earlier attack. He deployed the regiments on hand and sent his chief of artillery, Captain George E. Randolph, with Batteries E of the 1st Rhode Island (Randolph's Battery) and F and K of the 3rd U.S. Artillery (Livingston's Battery) into the breach. They were intended to relieve the exhausted gunners of Battery C, 5th U.S. Artillery, whose ammunition was nearly depleted.

Meanwhile, Birney had earlier sent for Brigadier General Robinson's brigade, which had been held in reserve on the north side of the Rappahannock. Robinson ordered his brigade forward at about 1 P.M., and the cheering Zouaves took the lead. With their band playing "Hail Columbia," they filed down to the river in column of fours and crossed the pontoon bridges under heavy artillery fire. Once across, Collis led his men to the left as shot and shell plowed the ground around them or exploded seemingly over their very heads. "It was dreadful to hear and see the wounded lying around us," recalled the former police sergeant from Frankford, Lieutenant Edward E. Williams of Company K.[19]

As the lead regiment, Collis' men would be on the right of the brigade when it formed in line of battle. He pushed his men forward at a double-quick in column of companies until they reached the open field in which Randolph's guns were then deployed. Company F, at the head of the regiment, wheeled into the field, and the right general-guide flag snapped smartly in the breeze as the remaining companies filed into position on their left. Alexander Given recalled proudly that, as second sergeant, he occupied the left guide position of Company F upon which all other companies and regiments of the brigade would form.[20]

By that time, however, a frenzied and impetuous drive by four regiments of Georgians had nearly succeeded in reaching the batteries. Robinson

---

18. OR, XXI, 362.

19. "From Collis' Zouaves," Philadelphia *Inquirer*, December 19, 1862, p. 2; Edward Williams to "My Dear Wife and Mother," December 15, 1862, in Sidebotham Collection.

20. Given Diary, n.d., in Given Collection, CWLM.

waited only long enough to get the 114th and the 63rd Pennsylvania into line before sending them forward to protect the guns. General Meade was then standing, in Collis' words, "brave as a lion . . . under the most terrific artillery fire, in the midst of the Pennsylvania Reserves begging them, 'For God's sake to stand by him.'" Meade himself later remembered "very distinctly" the arrival of the 114th: they "came up in good style—cheering as they passed me and calling out to my men . . . to come back with them, that they were going in."[21]

General Robinson had no sooner given the order for the 114th to wheel into the field than a solid shot ripped through the body of his horse, sending the officer sprawling to the ground. At nearly the same instant, the explosion of another artillery shell killed bugler John McKay and wounded a captain and an aide. Private Samuel Hamilton of Company F "had his head shot off" just then, and the gruesome sight of the blood-spattered men and horses was nearly too much for the inexperienced Zouaves. The advance began to stagger, "and for a few seconds there was an alarming pause in the forward movement."[22]

Sensing the urgency of the situation, Collis galloped to the regiment's standard-bearer, seized the flag, and shouted out to his men, "Remember the stone wall at Middletown." His inspiration made reference to the determined behavior of the men of the independent company of Zouaves d'Afrique during Banks's retreat in the Shenandoah Valley. With their confidence restored by the stirring sight of their young colonel gallantly sitting his horse with the colors in his grasp, the Zouaves now rapidly deployed into line to face the enemy.[23]

While the 114th was waiting for the 63rd to come up into line, some of Randolph's hard-pressed artillerymen appealed to the Zouaves for help. Several of the men rushed forward without orders to fill out the ranks of the depleted gunners. By the time the two Pennsylvania regiments came up to support the batteries, Given recalled, "the Rebels had got to within 20 paces of it and were just on the point of taking it." Halting within a few feet of the belching cannon, the men dropped to the ground while the artillerymen sent five or six last rounds of grapeshot and canister spew-

21. C. Collis to Read, June 29, 1863, General Meade to C. Collis, May 24, 1863, both in Read Collection, HSP.

22. William Grew, "Fredericksburg," Printed leaflet, n.d., n.p.; "Regiment Histories," Philadelphia *Weekly Times*, April 24, 1886, p. 1.

23. Grew, "Fredericksburg," n.p.

ing into the advancing Rebel ranks. "Then the order was given to up and at them; the battery ceased firing, and we charged past it and down to the brow of the hill," recalled Given. "We poured in a volley and gave one yell and rushed at them," wrote Lieutenant Williams. "They turned tail and run and we poured it into them until they reached the woods." Lieutenant George W. Bratton of Company C, then serving temporarily on General Robinson's staff, rode excitedly along the line encouraging the men. "Go in Zoo-Zoos; now is your chance," he called out.[24]

After driving the enemy back to the cover of the woods, Collis' men, now joined by the remainder of the brigade, lay down in the muddy field while both friendly and enemy shells whistled over their heads. Finally, at about 4 P.M., Generals Birney and Robinson rode out to the exposed position of the 114th and ordered Collis to deploy a company of his men as skirmishers, and to occupy a ditch that was located directly in their front, about one hundred yards from a wooded area that protruded from the Rebel line. From these woods, hordes of southern sharpshooters kept up a continuous fire on the exposed men, making any movement hazardous.

Collis turned to Sergeant Given and placed one hand on the sergeant's shoulder. "Given, do you see that tree?" he asked while pointing while to a clump of trees and bushes. "When you reach that point, halt and drop. Hold that position." Given relayed the order to Captain Elliot, who started his men forward. As the Zouaves moved off apprehensively, all was ominously quiet. No fire was received from the Rebels, who probably hoped to entice the group as close to them as possible before shooting. When the company reached the spot indicated by Colonel Collis and dropped to the ground, however, the enemy sharpshooters banged away. "For half an hour it sounded like a nest of bumble bees," recalled one participant.[25]

In the ditch just in front of them, Elliot could see a large number of Confederates, whom they made prisoners. Included in this haul was the wounded colonel E. N. Atkinson, who had been commanding Brigadier General Alexander Robert Lawton's Brigade; Captain Edward Porter Lawton, who was acting as assistant adjutant general to Major General Richard Stoddert Ewell; and about sixty Georgia enlisted men. Also in the ditch

24. Given Diary, n.d., in Given Collection, CWLM; Edward Williams to "My Dear Wife and Mother," December 15, 1862, in Sidebotham Collection; "Regiment Histories," Philadelphia *Weekly Times*, April 24, 1886, p. 1.

25. Given Diary, n.d., in Given Collection, CWLM; "From Collis' Zouaves," Philadelphia *Inquirer*, December 19, 1862, p. 2.

were a number of Federal soldiers who had taken shelter there when over-
run by the mad dash of the Georgians.[26]

The 114th remained on the field with the rest of the brigade for the
remainder of that Saturday and until about 7 A.M. on the following Monday. Even the darkness provided little refuge from the singing projectiles
that whizzed incessantly over their heads. "It is a dreadful duty, but we did
it," wrote Lieutenant Williams. As the stars came out in the clear winter
sky, the sounds of battle slowly abated. With the exception of stray shots,
the only sound then heard was the groaning of the thousands of wounded
men scattered about the field. "Poor fellows," recalled Williams, "we could
not help them." With the other survivors, he could only listen and suffer
with them, thanking God for his own escape from a similar fate. Two days
after the battle, the still-shaken lieutenant wrote in a letter: "Oh Mother
if ever a Mortal offered up a sincere prayer of thanks I did it that night. I
can only atribute my escape to Providence and a Mothers prayers. Men
who have been all through this war say we came in under the hottest fire
they had ever seen. . . . God grant that we may never go into another
Battle. I dont mind it while I am in but going in and coming out is hard
to bear."[27]

The first night was especially uncomfortable. Men froze in the slushy
mud. No one had blankets or overcoats, for all provisions been dropped
when they first swung into line in the field behind Randolph's guns. "It
was awful to have to lay there and freeze or to be shot to death if trying
to gain a more comfortable position," recalled Sergeant Given. Several
sharpshooters' bullets found their mark. One of the men who was struck,
John F. Page, belonged to Given's company: "Early on Sunday morning in
shifting his position [he] raised his head and received a ball in the forehead
which placed him hors de combat. We thought him dead and [were] con-
sulting best where to bury the body when a flag of truce gave us an opportunity to carry him to the rear, where he revived, was sent off to an
hospital, thence home where he died."[28]

Lieutenant Williams recalled a similar incident: "One of our Lieut was
laying alongside of a man who lay with his head on his arm. The enemies

26. *OR*, XXI, 366; Strauss to "Dear Mother," December 19, 1862, in *CWTI* Collection,
USAMHI.

27. Edward Williams to "My Dear Wife and Mother," December 15, 1862, in Sidebotham Collection.

28. Given Diary, n.d., in Given Collection, CWLM.

sharpshooters began firing on them pretty sharp. The Lieut kept ordering him to lie closer down but he would not mind so he took hold of him and found he was dead." Yet Williams, like many others, was so exhausted that he was able to lie down beside his brother Willie and ignore the cries of the wounded that night. "I lay down within a few feet of 3 dead men with the wounded screeching in our front . . . and as soon as the firing ceased I slept as sound as if I had been in bed beside you," he wrote to his wife.[29]

Elliot's company remained on picket duty until about 9 P.M. on Sunday, when it was relieved by Captain Edward R. Bowen's Company B. The only other respite had been the brief truce late that afternoon, during which the ambulance corps removed the wounded. Once relieved, Given and his companions crept cautiously among the sparse bushes back to the regiment. There they flopped down once again in the freezing muck and tried to quiet their growling stomachs with a meal of hardtack and onions. Though the wounded had been removed, the bodies of the dead remained strewn across the disputed field, and even in the cold the sickly sweet stench of death pervaded all.

Finally, early on Monday morning, the men observed the third corps commander, Brigadier General Stoneman, and his staff riding onto the field. Soon after, the 114th was ordered into line. Robinson's First Brigade was relieved by Brigadier General John Henry Hobart Ward's Second Brigade, which had been among the troops initially sent to stem the tide of the Rebel counterattack after the retreat of Meade's Pennsylvanians. The 114th fell back toward the river, and took up position behind the Richmond Stage Road. In this location, recalled Lieutenant Williams, "All kinds of manouvers were practiced all the afternoon and up to nine o'clock at night when we moved off as silently as death."[30]

As the men trudged quietly back across the pontoon bridges, it was only then that they became aware of the fact that they had been "whipped." The weather turned colder as the weary Zouaves marched toward the camps they had so confidently left just a few days before. It soon began to rain as well, and the roads turned quickly into quagmires. "I struggled on until I was completely exhausted and had to give up," recalled Lieutenant Williams. Like many others that night who possessed nothing but their

29. Edward Williams to "My Dear Wife," December 18, 1862, in Sidebotham Collection.

30. *Ibid.*

blankets to protect them from the rain, Williams and his brother Willie
sank to the ground and slept: one blanket in the mire, one on top, and
only the heat of their shivering bodies to keep them warm. Sergeant Given
could do even less. He and Private William J. Craven, who would soon
be discharged on a disability certificate, attempted to sleep on the sodden
ground with only one blanket to cover them. "I could not sleep, so I gave
the blanket to William while I walked to keep warm all night," wrote
Given. The next day he was sick, and remained so for five or six weeks.[31]

When the Zouaves finally staggered into their former campsite the following afternoon, they found it occupied by some troops from the Eleventh Corps, whom Williams described simply as "Sigel's dutchmen." The
unhappy Philadelphians were forced to move "further down on a steep
hill." Their previous campground would have offered little more than familiarity, however, for the men had not had time to build winter quarters
and had taken their tents and belongings with them when they moved.
Now they had nothing at all to shelter them and no implements with
which to start building. All had been lost on the field. The men got by as
best they could until they could obtain the things they needed. That night,
rather than lie in an open field, Lieutenant Williams and his two brothers
went off into the woods, built a fire, and slept there, returning to camp in
the morning.[32]

Although Burnside's attack on the Confederates at Fredericksburg had
been a disaster for the army, the 114th had reason to be proud of its
performance during its baptism of fire. Collis promptly forwarded to Robinson a copy of Special Orders Number Eight—by which the regiment's
deserters had been admonished three months earlier—with a request that
his superiors would testify to the stain on their record "having been oblit-
erated in the engagement of the 13th inst." Robinson gladly endorsed the
order. The stain had been washed out with blood, he wrote, and the "Regiment's gallant conduct and valuable services . . . entitle it to be ranked
equal to any of our veteran Regiments." Birney agreed that the 114th was
"entitled to rank with the veteran Regiments of the Division," while
Stoneman took "great pleasure" in noting that the Zouaves were "conspicuous both in dress and gallantry." Stoneman also took the occasion to

31. *Ibid.*; Given Diary, n.d., in Given Collection, CWLM.
32. Edward Williams to "My Dear Wife," December 18, 1862, in Sidebotham Collection.

note that both the 114th and 63rd Pennsylvania had performed admirably. They "held the crest in advance and on the right most nobly and under a very galling fire," he wrote, "for which both regiments have my warmest thanks."[33]

Though their reputation had been redeemed, it was likely very little consolation to the disheartened and freezing men. Sergeant Given found himself in the hospital, where he was tended by the regiment's hospital steward, John Field, and administered doses of cod-liver oil prescribed by the regimental surgeon, Jacob M. Cummins. It was only after rubbing his chest with an oil treatment that he began to recover. "This was painful but effected a cure," he recalled.[34]

Most of the men in the regiment knew little about the battle except for the small part they had themselves played. It was even difficult to tell how many casualties had been suffered. One Zouave closely estimated that "the loss in our regiment is . . . about thirty five." Many men actually wrote home asking for information about the battle. "I wish you would send me some papers with an account of [it]," requested one. "What do the papers say of us?" inquired Lieutenant Williams. "Send me any extracts you may find." Others in the brigade knew little more. Private James P. Coburn of the 141st Pennsylvania wrote home on the December 17: "You have ere this got the general details of the battle. We have not."[35]

By December 18, the weather had again warmed slightly, and the men were busy erecting their huts and making themselves as comfortable as possible. Still, the mood was somewhat morbid. In a letter whose writing spanned the course of two days, Lieutenant Williams seemed unable to shake the melancholy that followed defeat. "I think this war is played out," he wrote, and in his despondency he encouraged his brothers to "take French leave of the army. You may look for them home soon," he told his wife, "as I think we will be paid next week." He felt certain that the army would go into winter quarters, "for we are decently whipped here." The thirty-year-old lieutenant was himself anxious to return to Philadelphia. "How I am to get out of it I dont know. . . . I still hope that peace will be

33. Endorsements to Special Orders Number 8, Headquarters, First Brigade, December 17–19, 1862, in Records of the 114th PV, Record Group 94, NARA.

34. Given Diary, n.d., in Given Collection, CWLM.

35. Murray to "Dear Father and Mother," December 15, 1862, in Murray Collection, FSNMP; Edward Williams to "My Dear Wife," December 18, 1862, in Sidebotham Collection; Coburn to "Dear folks at home," n.d., in Coburn Papers, USAMHI.

made this winter on some terms or others. At all events I am coming home by spring." His complaints—no doubt exacerbated by thoughts of the approaching holiday, homesickness, and the army's defeat—were bitter:

> This thing is played out. The whole army is disheartened and want peace on some terms. We are not treated right. Thousands of men have not been paid for six months. Their families need the money and ought to have it. I have only got 50 cents left no sutler nor no anything. We are treated like dogs by the Quartermasters and contractors and if things dont mend one day half the army will desert and come home. Home, how well we know how to estimate the value of that little word. It means all that a man need care for. Glory and honor sink into insignificance alongside of it with all its endearments. This is a gloomy letter, but if you could see us crouched around a smoky fire trying to keep warm and our eyes nearly smoked out of our head you would not wonder at it.[36]

During the battle, the Zouaves lost eight enlisted men. In addition, twenty-four enlisted men and three officers were wounded, and seventeen men were listed as missing or captured. Most of the missing men belonged to the regimental band. On the afternoon of the fifteenth, the band performed at General Birney's headquarters and was afterward instructed to remain close to the line of battle. The musicians feared a renewal of the Rebel cannonade, however, and so they found a large ditch where they spent the night without interruption. The following morning they were awakened by a mounted officer in gray who informed them that they were prisoners. The entire army had slipped back across the Rappahannock during the night while the band slept soundly. They were immediately relieved of the fine German-made silver instruments that had been a gift of the citizens of Philadelphia, and were shipped off to Libby Prison in Richmond. It would be several weeks before they were exchanged, and months more before they were properly paroled and reunited with the regiment.[37]

The new camp in which the 114th found itself was named Camp Pitcher, possibly after recently promoted Brigadier General Thomas Gamble Pitcher, who had been wounded at the battle of Cedar Mountain

---

36. Edward Williams to "My Dear Wife," December 18, 1862, in Sidebotham Collection.

37. Rauscher, *Music on the March,* 34.

in August. Located near Falmouth, this camp represented a haven to the men, who began to settle in and to prepare for the possibility of a long respite from the rigors of a winter campaign. Of course, they were still uncertain whether the army would yet move again that winter. One pessimistic soldier of the 141st Pennsylvania summed up the brigade's recent doings very succinctly: "We have crossed the Rappahannock—we have seen a battle—have seen a 'masterly retreat'—have *recrossed* the Rap. & find ourselves on safe ground near our old camp—once more putting up our log huts & making preparations to *live* again—not knowing but we *may* stay here for a time or so." With the Christmas holiday approaching, even those who most anticipated further movement that winter sent for boxes from home. Though many packages would not arrive in time, the expectation of receiving something from home must have gladdened numerous hearts. But, a saddened Private Murray surmised on the twenty-fourth, "I think we will have a poor Christmas this year."[38]

Colonel Collis was occupied with reports and official correspondence for some time after the battle. His first report of the action was returned to him by General Robinson as "unfit in its present shape to forward to higher authority." This would not be the last time the colonel had trouble of this sort. In the present instance, he responded with the nearly impertinent explanation that the report had been "called for on the battlefield and made out and sent to you *at once,* in as 'proper form' and as neatly as circumstances would permit."[39]

In the immediate aftermath of battle, it was also the painful duty of the commander of the regiment to write to the relatives of those of his men who had been killed. Two days before Christmas, Collis penned a letter to the mother of Private Francis Sheridan of Company I. The twenty-three-year-old plasterer had been a member of the original company of Zouaves d'Afrique and had served nearly sixteen months before his death at Fredericksburg. "By his own request," wrote Collis to the grieving mother, "I gave him the post of honor between the two colors of my brave regiment." Knowledge that their son and brother had done his duty and died bravely for his country might in some small way have consoled the

38. Coburn to "Dear folks at home," December 17, 1862, in Coburn Papers, USAMHI; Murray to "Dear Father & Mother," December 24, 1862, in Murray Collection, FSNMP.

39. C. Collis to Robinson, December 19, 1862, in Records of the 114th PV, Record Group 94, NARA.

distraught family. It seems unlikely, however, that such honors did much to allay the sorrow of a family whose loved one lay dead on a field of battle that remained in the hands of the enemy, his body perhaps lying for days unburied or hastily thrown into a mass, unmarked grave. Christmas of 1862 was a bitter one for many.[40]

Sickness, casualties, details, and desertions had all combined to reduce seriously the numbers of men available for service in almost all the regiments. Private Strauss of the 57th Pennsylvania complained that his brigade was "not so large as a full regiment." The size of the 114th was so much diminished that on December 29, Collis wrote to Governor Curtin about the "sad condition of my regiment as regards *numbers.*" As a consequence, he requested that some smaller regiments be merged with the Zouaves. Some companies, he claimed, were reporting only twenty or thirty men for duty. The 114th was by no means alone in this situation, however, and his request was never acted upon. The situation must have been a source of worry for the ambitious colonel.[41]

The Zouaves had not only lost many of the rank and file, but they also stood a good chance of losing their lieutenant colonel, Federico F. Cavada, under less than honorable circumstances. Cavada had been assigned the duty of Brigade Officer of the Day on December 13, and was in charge of the brigade guard when it crossed the Rappahannock that afternoon. The apparently eager Cavada had made it known to all that he "felt very unpleasantly about being kept in the rear [and] that he was very anxious to go into battle with his regiment." After hearing this complaint two or three times from members of his staff, General Robinson sent word to Cavada to stay with the guard while on the march; then, if the brigade was engaged, he had permission to turn over command of the guard to a subordinate officer and to join his regiment. Cavada received this message from Captain Winslow L. Kidder, who was soon to be felled by a Rebel shot.[42]

As Collis led his regiment over the pontoon bridges, he learned that Cavada had permission to join them should they see fighting. "I shall expect to see you there," said Collis. "I shall be there," replied the fiery

40. C. Collis to Mrs. E. Sheridan, December 23, 1862, *ibid.*

41. C. Collis to Governor Curtin, December 29, 1862, in Records of the 114th PV, Record Group 19, PHMC.

42. Testimony of Brigadier General Robinson, January 12, 1863, Cavada Court-Martial Proceedings, in Court-Martial Records, Record Group 153, NARA.

Cuban. When the Zouaves were precipitately thrown into battle, Collis expected Cavada to join him at any moment. It was not until the following morning, he later recalled, that he learned of the whereabouts of the missing lieutenant colonel. It was first reported that Cavada had been wounded in the leg by a shell near the rear of the battlefield. Once the regiment was withdrawn to the north side of the Rappahannock, however, Collis learned from Lieutenant William Morehead of the 63rd Pennsylvania, and from the NCOs of the brigade guard, that Cavada "was seen on and off his horse walking and riding as usual" after his supposed wound was received. Collis immediately reported this information to his superiors and was ordered to prepare charges.[43]

The court-martial convened on January 12, 1863, at the headquarters of the Second Brigade. Brigadier General Ward of that brigade was appointed president of the board, which was composed of six additional officers selected from various regiments of all three brigades within the division. Major P. Allen Lindsay of the 40th New York was appointed judge advocate. Cavada was charged with "misbehavior before the enemy," which included allegations that he absented himself from the battlefield, neglected to join his regiment but remained in the rear in shelter while they were engaged, and deserted the brigade guard while under fire. He was also charged with being absent without leave from his command.[44]

Testimony was first heard from Colonel Collis and General Robinson. Next, Lieutenant Edward R. Robinson, of the general's staff, told of encountering Cavada with the brigade guard during the course of a severe shelling. "I was on horseback and he was on foot," he related, "and I recollect of his stating that he was lame." He testified that Cavada then went off in search of Lieutenant Charles A. Robinson of the 114th, who had been wounded during the battle and taken to a field hospital. Returning later to the guard, Cavada and E. R. Robinson both lay down to sleep. The latter recalled, "About midnight he awoke me and said it was daybreak . . . [H]e said that his leg pained him a good deal and I soon afterwards fell asleep."[45]

43. Testimony of Colonel Collis, January 12, 1863, Cavada Court-Martial Proceedings, *ibid.*

44. Charges and Specifications, January 12, 1863, Cavada Court-Martial Proceedings, *ibid.*

45. Testimony of Lieutenant Robinson, January 12, 1863, Cavada Court-Martial Proceedings, *ibid.*

Prior to encountering E. R. Robinson, Cavada reportedly had made an attempt to find the regiment. Lieutenant Morehead testified that when the brigade guard came under fire, Cavada got off his horse, turned the command over to him, and went forward in search of the 114th. "Take care of my horse," he told Private William Grew of the 114th, "while I go to meet my regiment or see where it is." Morehead stated that Cavada returned about one-half hour later, and when the severe shelling began, he "went over the bank and into the brush."[46]

Not all of the testimony was detrimental to Cavada's case. "French Mary," the vivandiere, testified that she saw the lieutenant colonel as he passed by in search of his regiment. She told him "not to go there, the fire was too heavy," but he went on without heeding her warning. Collis' father, the quartermaster, also testified that he had observed Captain Kidder ride up to Cavada on the morning of the thirteenth to tell him something. Cavada "seemed very much pleased" with the message, said Lieutenant Collis. "What is the good news?" he inquired. Upon learning that Cavada had received permission to join the regiment when they became engaged, the quartermaster added, "I made some remark like this: 'you are easily pleased.'" Later, Cavada claimed to Lieutenant Collis that his injury had resulted from a fall from his horse when the animal had been startled by a bursting shell. Collis went on to describe Cavada's horse as "nice . . . but very nervous—high spirited. . . . I had previously cautioned [him] not to ride the horse into action and offered to leave him mine."[47]

Finally, Private Joseph E. Kelly of the 114th testified that on the night after the battle, while he was sleeping near Cavada, the lieutenant colonel roused him and asked him to accompany him to the divisional hospital. They searched for the hospital until Cavada "laid down declaring he could go no farther on account of the pain in his leg." Kelly found the hospital at daylight and convinced a chief surgeon to send an ambulance for the officer.[48]

The trial ended with a statement by Lieutenant Colonel Cavada, in which he seemingly rebutted all the testimony against him. Testimony

46. Testimony of Lieutenant Morehead and Private Grew, January 12, 1863, Cavada Court-Martial Proceedings, *ibid*.

47. Testimony of Mary Tepe and Lieutenant Collis, January 12, 1863, Cavada Court-Martial Proceedings, *ibid*.

48. Testimony of Private Kelly, January 12, 1863, Cavada Court-Martial Proceedings, *ibid*.

showed, he said, that he had been present on the field when his regiment was engaged, and that he did not leave until after dark. When thrown from his horse, he claimed not to have believed himself seriously injured. It was only later that he began to suffer and sought medical treatment. He also brought attention to the testimony showing why he was unable to find the 114th. As it was his duty to "drive up the stragglers," he said, the guard was delayed in reaching the field: "I hurried the guard after the Brigade, and fearing that I would altogether lose sight of the latter, I gave my horse, which was unmanageable under that heavy fire, to the officer of the guard, and hastened on foot in the direction taken by the Brigade, which by this time was some distance in advance." Unknown to him, however, the 114th had wheeled into the field at some point to face the enemy, while Meade's retreating troops had fallen back in their rear and concealed them from his view. He pushed on in search of them, he stated, until reaching the extreme left of the battlefield. "I found myself without a command," he lamented. "Being neither with my regiment nor with my guard, I subjected myself to the accusation of being absent from both." His defense concluded with the observation that the duties in which he was engaged that day were "by no means enviable." He bemoaned the fact that those duties limited an officer to the rear, "which often a place of safety from the enemy's fire, is also often one of danger to his reputation."[49]

Cavada had good reason to fear for his reputation. Despite his seemingly flawless rebuttal of all charges, he was found guilty of all the specifications related to the charge of "misbehavior before the enemy." His absence from the army was found excusable because of his documented injury, however, so he was exonerated of the charge of being absent without leave. The court sentenced him to forfeiture of all pay and allowances due him "and to be cashiered"—in other words, dismissed.[50]

It took over a month for the proceedings of the court-martial to be transcribed and to travel through the army's chain of command. When they finally reached the headquarters of the Army of the Potomac, Burnside had been replaced by Major General Joseph Hooker. That officer

49. Testimony of Lieutenant Colonel Cavada, January 12, 1863, Cavada Court-Martial Proceedings, *ibid*.

50. Verdict, January 12, 1863, Cavada Court-Martial Proceedings, in Court-Martial Records, Record Group 153, NARA.

forwarded the documents to President Lincoln for review. He recommended that, "owing to the circumstances of the case . . . and the good character proven by Lt Col. Cavada," the sentence be remitted. Cavada's reputation was then in the hands of the harried chief executive. It would be several agonizing months before he was notified of the final decision.[51]

51. Endorsement by Major General Hooker, February 18, 1863, Cavada Court-Martial Proceedings, *ibid.*

Major Joseph S. Chandler, a twenty-eight-year-old Philadelphia salesman when he transferred from a captaincy in Company H, 75th Pennsylvania Volunteers, to the position of major of the 114th in September, 1862, was killed at Chancellorsville on May 3, 1863. *Courtesy Ronn Palm Collection, U.S. Army Military History Institute*

Captain Henry M. Eddy was promoted in August, 1862, from the original company of Zouaves d'Afrique to lieutenant of Company E at the age of twenty-three. In March, 1863, Eddy was again promoted, this time to captain of Company D. He was commissioned a major in October, 1864, but was not officially mustered in at that rank. He died on April 11, 1865, of wounds received in the regiment's final charge of the war at Petersburg on April 2. *Courtesy Ronn Palm Collection, U.S. Army Military History Institute*

Major Jacob M. Cummins, a twenty-six-year-old physician, joined the 114th in July, 1862, and served faithfully as its primary surgeon until mustering out with the regiment in May, 1865. *Courtesy Ronn Palm Collection, U.S. Army Military History Institute*

Augustus W. Fix, a twenty-four-year-old Philadelphia carver shown here as lieutenant of Company E, was promoted from the ranks of the Zouaves d'Afrique to first sergeant. He served in that position and as a lieutenant under the command of his brother, Captain Francis Fix, until the latter's wounding at Gettysburg. Gus Fix was eventually raised to the rank of captain on May 19, 1864, commanding Company D after Henry Eddy's death at Petersburg. *Courtesy Ronn Palm Collection, U.S. Army Military History Institute*

Wounded severely in the buttocks at Gettysburg, twenty-four-year-old Edward T. Marion, a Philadelphia confectioner, had been promoted from the Zouaves d'Afrique to first sergeant of Company I upon formation of the 114th. Marion served in that position throughout the war, recovering from his wound and returning to his company, where he was promoted to first lieutenant in March, 1864. A week later, Marion was killed in the regiment's final assault at Petersburg. Notice Sergeant Marion's non-regulation plaid vest and tie. Such variations in the uniform of the 114th were common throughout the war. *Courtesy Ronn Palm Collection, U.S. Army Military History Institute*

Striking a jaunty, Napoleonic pose, Colonel Charles H. T. Collis, the twenty-four-year-old Philadelphia attorney who organized both the independent company of Zouaves d'Afrique and the 114th Pennsylvania Volunteers, finished the war as a brevet major general. *Courtesy Ronn Palm Collection, U.S. Army Military History Institute*

First Sergeant John R. Waterhouse of Company F enlisted in the 114th in July, 1862, at age thirty-seven. Wounded severely in the thigh at Gettysburg, Water-house returned to the regiment and was promoted to captain of his company. Note his collarless shirt and the absence of buttons. *Courtesy Ronn Palm Collection, U.S. Army Military History Institute*

Private Henry Lyons of Company E, a boyish-looking twenty-four-year-old printer, received a slight leg wound at Gettysburg but later returned to the regiment. Lyons is wearing a non-regulation striped shirt and watchchain. He is not wearing the usual white gaiters over his shoe tops and trousers, again illustrating the variations in uniform styles found in the regiment. *Courtesy Ronn Palm Collection, U.S. Army Military History Institute*

The physical appearance of men like Company K's Captain Almayne H. G. Richardson added in spirit if not in fact to the regiment's claim to be composed in part of Frenchmen infused with Zouave élan. Richardson was a twenty-two-year-old clerk when he joined the 114th. He received a promotion to first lieutenant in February, 1864, after the resignation of Lieutenant Edward E. Williams. Several months later, he was promoted to captain. *Courtesy Ronn Palm Collection, U.S. Army Military History Institute*

Twenty-six-year-old Harry E. Rulon began his service with the 114th as first sergeant of Company B. As first lieutenant, Rulon commanded the company after Captain Edward R. Bowen's promotion to major in September, 1863. Rulon was himself made captain of Company B a year later. *Courtesy Ronn Palm Collection, U.S. Army Military History Institute*

First Lieutenant John A. Tricker of Company A was a twenty-five-year-old confectioner who came to the regiment from the original company of Zouaves
d'Afrique as first sergeant of Company B. He was promoted to first lieutenant of
Company A in November, 1864, then to captain of the company in mid-May,
1865, just prior to mustering out. Tricker followed the company's original captain,
Severin A. Barthoulot, who resigned in mid-1863, and Andrew J. Cunningham,
killed at Petersburg on April 2, 1865. All of them came from Collis' original
company. *Courtesy Ronn Palm Collection, U.S. Army Military History Institute*

Sergeant Henry Smallbrook of Company H was a twenty-eight-year-old cooper from York County when he enlisted in the 114th in August, 1862. Unfortunately, Smallbrook had already enlisted in Company H of the 87th Pennsylvania Volunteers in September, 1861. He deserted the 87th in Baltimore in June, 1862, and apparently went to Philadelphia, where he joined the 114th, listing his place of birth as Baltimore. Smallbrook served honorably with the regiment, mustering out with them in 1865 as Company H's first sergeant. He was wounded in the right thumb at Gettysburg and was compelled to abandon his trade as a cooper after the war, instead working as a blacksmith. Smallbrook is wearing an unusual combination of corps badges, with a white Fifth Corps Maltese Cross superimposed atop a red Third Corps diamond, reflecting the 114th's assignments. *Courtesy Marcus McLemore*

Private Mathias Chadwick of Company F was wounded slightly and captured at Chancellorsville, where twenty-four of the company's fifty-nine men were either killed or wounded. Two more were listed as missing. Born in England, the twenty-nine-year-old Zouave returned to the regiment and mustered out with his company in 1865. Chadwick had this picture taken at the Arch Street studio of noted Philadelphia photographer Frederick Gutekunst. *Courtesy Daniel J. Miller*

Captain Francis Fix of Company E received a severe leg wound at Gettysburg and was discharged for physical disability in December, 1863. The twenty-eight-year-old bar keeper died in September, 1864, but his brother Gus finished the war as captain of Company E. *Courtesy Michael J. McAfee Collection, West Point Museum*

Company B's Private George Murray, an eighteen-year-old Philadelphia carpenter who was severely wounded at Chancellorsville, was a prolific letter writer whose correspondence was preserved by his family. It was donated to the National Park at Chancellorsville, along with the holed uniform Murray was wearing when he was wounded there in May, 1863. *Courtesy Fredericksburg/Spotsylvania National Military Park*

Twenty-year-old Private William "Willie" E. Williams served with Company K, eventually receiving a promotion to corporal before his discharge on a surgeon's certificate in April, 1865. William served in the company with his two brothers, Ned, a thirty-eight-year-old sergeant who transferred to the 40th New York Volunteers in March, 1863; and Edward, who was a Philadelphia police sergeant in 1862 when he was commissioned first lieutenant in Company K. *Courtesy Jack Sidebotham Collection, Philadelphia*

This dramatic painting of the 114th at the battle of Fredericksburg by noted artist Carl Röchling captures the moment when the regiment comes into line just in time to save the battery in its front. Brigadier General John C. Robinson is shown extricating himself from beneath his dying horse, while his adjutant reels backward from his saddle. Collis is depicted with the flag. It is said that he encouraged his men to move forward by shouting, "Remember the stone wall at Middletown!" Regrettably, Röchling's giant canvas cannot now be located; only black-and-white images of it remain. *Courtesy Fredericksburg/Spotsylvania National Military Park*

Colonel Collis and Captain Alexander J. Dallas, seated on folding camp chairs, confer in front of quarters at Petersburg in August, 1864. The high posts surrounding the raised platform in front of the tent undoubtedly supported a canopy of pine boughs that shaded the area from the scorching Tidewater sun. *Courtesy U.S. Army Military History Institute*

The noted band of the 114th poses for a picture at Brandy Station in March, 1864. The musical abilities and repertoire of the Zouave bandsmen were highly regarded in the army, making them a popular choice at headquarters. *Courtesy U.S. Army Military History Institute*

Guard mount of the 114th at Brandy Station in March, 1864, with their winter quarters in the background. Note the log structures atop which canvas tents were affixed and the makeshift chimneys that were sometimes a fire hazard for occupants of the huts. Guard mount was a daily ritual during which the officer of the day and officer of the guard inspected the men selected for guard duty that day. Lieutenant Almayne Richardson, then the ranking officer of Company K, stands near the regimental band at the left in the photograph. Regimental adjutant Charles Watson, recently promoted from the ranks of Company C, stands facing the men toward the right of the picture. In the foreground behind Watson stand captains John Crawford of Company I, recently promoted from first lieutenant, and Henry Eddy of Company D. In the background between those two officers is Sergeant Major Alexander W. Given, soon to be advanced to the rank of lieutenant in Company F. *Courtesy U.S. Army Military History Institute*

Officers of the 114th pose for a picture near Petersburg in August, 1864. *Courtesy U.S. Army Military History Institute*

Officers of the 114th pose under a makeshift sun shelter. *Courtesy U.S. Army Military History Institute*

Captains Almayne Richardson, John Crawford, George Bratton, and Henry Rulon styled themselves the "Four Guardsmen" mess. The officers strike a cavalier pose in camp near Petersburg while being waited on by two Negro servants. *Courtesy U.S. Army Military History Institute*

Captain Crawford, one of the "Four Guardsmen," is shown here in a more soldierly view of camp life. *Courtesy U.S. Army Military History Institute*

Company F of the 114th Pennsylvania poses near Petersburg in August, 1864. The officer with the sword on the far left of the photo is Captain John R. Waterhouse. On the extreme right is Lieutenant Alexander W. Given. *Courtesy U.S. Army Military History Institute*

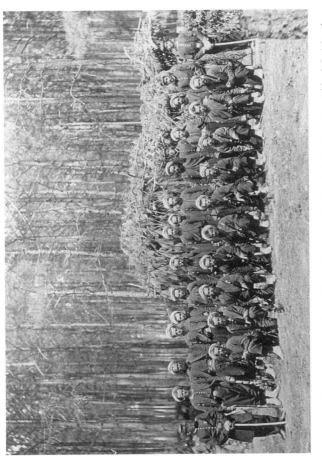

Company G in August, 1864. The officer on the far left is Captain Alfred S. Newlin. Lieutenant Henry C. Munns stands behind the rear rank, while the regimental quartermaster Lieutenant James Hartley and Sergeant Major Joshua G. Bates stand at far right of photo. *Courtesy U.S. Army Military History Institute*

The rather informal-looking group of unarmed Zouaves depicted here is part of Captain Aaron K. Dunkle's Company H. Dunkle is seated on a stump at the left, while Lieutenant Benjamin C. Shermer is seated to the right. Dunkle would be discharged on a surgeon's certificate within the month, and Shermer would advance to his place. Shermer had advanced rapidly from second lieutenant on April 12, 1863, to first lieutenant on April 13, when he replaced Camiel Nifenecker after the latter failed to demonstrate adequate military knowledge to a military examination board. *Courtesy U.S. Army Military History Institute*

This unidentified Zouave is most likely a member of the original Zouaves d'Afrique, as evidenced by his strictly regulation uniform, striped turban, and two-banded rifle, a Belgian-made copy of a British Enfield. *Courtesy Michael J. McAfee Collection, West Point Museum*

Captain Frank A. Eliot of Company F, a thirty-seven-year-old Philadelphia silver-smith, was killed at Chancellorsville in May, 1863. *Courtesy Carl Adams*

Major Edward R. Bowen, shown here wearing a regulation overcoat, was a twenty-four-year-old Philadelphia wool merchant who commanded the regiment for a time as lieutenant colonel, but was never mustered at that rank. As a result of the greatly depleted numbers of men in veteran regiments, it was sometimes difficult to obtain promotion. *Courtesy U.S. Army Military History Institute*

7

Rally Here, Men!

Shortly after arriving at their new campsite after the battle of Fredericksburg, the men of the 114th formed themselves into line for an evening dress parade. It was a ragtag collection of soldiers who stood in the ranks, with their natty Zouave clothing "hanging in ribbons and full of dirt." Nevertheless, the men held their heads high, for they were proud of their appearance "on account of the way they got so." While the men were gathered, the regimental chaplain, John K. Karcher, "made an earnest prayer for the absent ones and thanked God for his mercy towards those of us who were spared." When the parade was over, the Zouaves broke ranks and returned to the tedium of their daily routine. "The whole regiment was in rags," wrote Private Murray to his uncle. They were to remain so until receiving new clothing on January 11.[1]

The army began to recuperate from the shocking repulse on the banks of the Rappahannock. But it would be a long and difficult recovery, slowed by the interminable boredom and routine of camp life in winter quarters. The men struggled against the monotonous repetition of inactive days that dulled the senses and exhausted the body. The sole relief from the tedium was the prospect of picket duty. Typically a three-day detail, this duty required the men to leave behind what little comfort they had in camp

---

1. Edward Williams to "My Dear Wife," December 18, 1862, in Sidebotham Collection; Murray to "Dear Uncle," January 11, 1863, in Murray Collection, FSNMP.

and brave the elements once more. It provided only further annoyance and a change of scenery.

But the Union army had more to contend with than boredom. A logistical logjam prevented the mountain of supplies arriving at Aquia Creek from being rapidly transported to the men scattered in barren camps along the river. "Our government rations are rather course food not as good as last winter," wrote a private in the 57th Pennsylvania. "Any luxury from home would be received with a thankful heart and a willing stomach for we are getting tired of one thing all the time," he continued.[2] Thus the men in blue struggled to subsist on their meager rations. Similarly, they struggled to keep warm, quickly denuding the surrounding landscape of trees, so that details sent out for firewood roamed miles in search of the vital commodity.

Many men, like Lieutenant Williams' two brothers, sought an opportunity to slip away for a visit home. The growing number of soldiers seeking to take a "French leave" presented an increasingly difficult problem for the army that winter. Although the lieutenant's brothers were able to pull off their recess with no ill effects, others were not so lucky. Sergeant Thomas W. Stephens of Company K, 20th Indiana, recalled that at about 2 P.M. on Sunday, January 18, the entire brigade was drawn up to witness the branding of a deserter from the 63rd Pennsylvania. "A letter D was put on his right thigh, and he was drummed out of the U.S. service, to the tune of 'Rogue's March.'" Another man of the brigade, James P. Coburn, of the 141st Pennsylvania, also found the incident noteworthy— and an effective deterrent to those considering desertion. He remarked: "Today I witnessed what I never did before. . . . The prisoner was called out—his head shaven, the iron heated—pants turned down & brand applied, the army buttons cut off his clothes—a squad of soldiers with fixed bayonets placed behind him when the band struck up the 'Rogues March' & the rogue did march all along the line, with hat in hand, a living specimen of the disgraced soldier. I have concluded not to desert this week at least."[3]

Though Lieutenant Williams was convinced that "there will be no more fighting for some time," others were less certain. The activities of

2. Granger to "Dear Wife," January 6, 1863 in Granger Papers, CWMC, USAMHI.

3. Diary of Thomas W. Stephens, January 18, 1863, in Thomas W. Stephens Collection, USAMHI; Coburn to "Dear folks at home," January 18, 1863, in Coburn Papers, USAMHI.

Professor Thaddeus S. C. Lowe's hydrogen-filled observation balloon, *Eagle*, were easily visible to all as the silken behemoth floated high above the river. Some thought the balloon's flights to be the harbinger of an advance. "For several days past the balloon has been going up, and for several nights we have seen signal lights, so that something is going to happen soon," expounded Private Murray. He was not far from the truth.[4]

Burnside had decided that the time for active campaigning had not yet ended. His plan was to create diversions near Fredericksburg with portions of his army and to cross the Rappahannock with the bulk of his force at Banks' Ford, some six miles above the town. By this time, however, he enjoyed the confidence of neither his superiors nor his subordinates. He was doomed to defeat once more, this time at the hands of an unpredictable rainstorm that turned the Virginia roads into impassable quagmires.

The Zouaves began the march upriver late on the morning of Tuesday, January 20. Along with other regiments of General Birney's First Division, they were to assist the engineer officers in getting pontoon bridges down to the river, and were then to cross on the boats in order to establish a beachhead on the opposite bank. Private Murray estimated that the men made fifteen miles that first day, though the actual distance covered was probably only half that. During the night, the Zouaves camped without fires in a dark pine forest, but before midnight the skies opened and there was little rest or comfort thereafter in the sodden woods. As the first light of dawn began to show, the men kindled fires "and got about half dry" before being ordered to pack up and fall in.[5]

Once back on the road, the Zouaves—most of whom were dressed in their newly issued clothing—were ordered to reverse their arms, drive them bayonet first into the ground, and get to work pulling the pontoons out of the mud. "They had all the Zoo Zoos pulling at the Boats like the other jack asses," wrote Sergeant Fox of Company F. "The Zoos were pulling at the Boats from daylight . . . until about 12 O'Clock when we were relieved by another Regiment of Blue Legs, but they could not pull like the Red Boys."[6]

4. Edward Williams to "My Dear Wife," December 18, 1862, in Sidebotham Collection; Murray to "Dear Uncle," January 11, 1863, in Murray Collection, FSNMP.

5. Edward Williams to "My Dear Wife," December 18, 1862, in Sidebotham Collection; Murray to "Dear Uncle," January 11, 1863, in Murray Collection, FSNMP.

6. Murray to "Dear Mother," January 27, 1863, in Murray Collection, FSNMP; Fox to "My Dear Brother Charles," January 27, 1863, in Fox Collection, HSP.

The so-called Red Legs labored in mud up to their knees until a frustrated and angry Colonel Collis called a halt to it: "Seeing that we were
getting our splendid clothes muddy [he] ordered us to drop all and leave
the old things in the mud." The exhausted men gladly did as commanded
and marched back to the pine woods where they waited to see if the
weather would clear up. When it did not, Burnside turned his army around
and retraced his steps to Falmouth. The Zouaves finally reached their old
camp on Friday after an arduous march over mud-choked roads. Their
trek's difficulties were exacerbated by the catcalls and yells that they had
to endure from laughing Confederates on the opposite bank. "The rebels
stuck up a board on the other side of the river with 'Burnside stuck in the
mud,'" mused an irritated Private Murray. Yet the soldiers were not so
humorless that they could not poke fun at themselves in their misery. One
man observed, "It is a common saying among the boys, 'who got stuck in
the mud?' 'Burnside.'" Morale, along with the commanding general's
standing among his troops, plummeted. "I think Burnside will never be
able to command this army," wrote a dejected Zouave. In Washington,
President Lincoln was coming to the same conclusion.[7]

Lincoln removed the hapless Burnside from command on January 25,
elevating Burnside's most vociferous critic, Major General Joseph Hooker,
to the post instead. It was not a moment too soon, for the once "Grand
Divisions" of Burnside's army were dissolving into a formless rabble. Men
were streaming homeward in alarming numbers. Others were succumbing
to exposure and to inadequate nutrition. On January 24, Lieutenant Williams was among those who were struck down by illness, and he found
himself in the division hospital. It was a large tent that had a hay-covered
floor and held a stove and twelve sick officers. Williams described it as
"very nice." In a shaky hand, the fever-racked lieutenant wrote of his
condition: "My nurse is a very good one. Last evening I thought I could
stand alone but his strong hand was on me or I should have fallen. As I
get stronger I'll write more but now I can't. I am near Falmouth." Williams
himself did not then realize just how sick he was. When he finally returned
home and saw the letter he had written that winter, he claimed not to
have had any recollection of it at all. "I don't know what good angel

7. Murray to "Dear Mother," January 27, 1863, in Murray Collection, FSNMP; Fox to
"My Dear Brother Charles," January 27, 1863, in Fox Collection, HSP.

directed for me or how they got the address," he said. "I never knew anything about it until I came home."[8]

On January 27, the weather turned cold again, and the men awoke to find six to eight inches of snow on the ground. By that time, however, they were as comfortably situated as was possible in log houses. Typically, such accommodations were constructed by placing four or five large logs atop one another to form walls, upon which canvas tents were then set to make a roof. Often a chimney was constructed either of small sticks or discarded barrels, or a combination of both. The danger of fire was thus considerable. Most important, though, the soldiers were able to construct bunks in their houses and raise themselves off the cold ground while they slept. Still, the quarters were likely to be disagreeable. In the successive periods of rain and snow, it was nearly impossible to keep the cramped space within their huts dry. "Even if we do succeed in freeing the floor from water," wrote one Zouave, "the damp from the roof is rapidly distilled and pervades all the atmosphere of the little domicile." A further disadvantage stemming from the construction of such accommodations resulted when the men were assigned to picket duty. Private Donnaker of Company E later recollected that duty as "the only hard times we have . . . we have to leave our tents behind for they are nailed fast to our houses."[9]

General Hooker wasted no time in implementing changes designed to stay the decline of his army. He not only reorganized his command into a more efficiently managed force, but also took steps that had a direct influence on his men as individuals. To combat desertion, he instituted a system of rotating furloughs. He ended the corrupt supply system that made some unscrupulous commissary officers rich but left his army hungry. He ordered the construction of brick ovens so that fresh bread could be provided to the men. They even began to receive fresh vegetables twice each week. Finally, he decreed that each of his soldiers would wear a cloth badge designating his unit's corps and division. The Third Corps was to wear a diamond insignia. The First Division of that corps was to wear a diamond cut from red cloth and to carry a flag of the same design. The red patch under which the gallant Third Corps fought proudly in the coming battles became a badge of honor as it waved over the division. Its color was deepened symbolically by the oft-spilled blood of the patriot.

8. Edward Williams to "My Dear Wife," January 24, 1862, in Sidebotham Collection.
9. "From the 'Zouaves D'Afrique,'" Bucks County *Intelligencer*, April 14, 1863, p. 1; Donnaker to "Dear Mother," March 3, 1863, in Donnaker Papers, CWMC, USAMHI.

The condition of the army slowly began to improve. Assisting in this improvement was the arrival both of visitors and long-awaited boxes from home. Private Murray, the eighteen-year-old carpenter from Company B, was visited in January by his father, who stayed for two weeks. "All of the boys have received their boxes," wrote Murray the following month. "I also received some things out of my box, but . . . most of things were spoiled, as the jelly spilt all over them. I received some jellys, doughnuts, ginger cakes, raspberry vinegar, all of which went very good to me. We receive fresh bread three times a week now. I would like to have another box, if you can get it to me, but be sure and fasten the things up tight, and direct to Birney's headq."[10]

Despite the general betterment of conditions, some men were so debilitated by this time that they would be of little further use to the army. Murray's friend and bunkmate, Henry P. Gentry, a nineteen-year-old Holmesburg farmer, was one of them. "Gentry is very poorly," wrote Murray to his mother, "I make him as comfortable as possible, which is not much in these little doghouses of ours." Gentry's father and other family members came to see him in February, and Murray thought that Mr. Gentry would soon procure his son's discharge. In fact, it took several additional weeks, but Henry was finally released from duty on a surgeon's certificate on March 29.[11]

While some of their number were bedridden and ill, most of the Zouaves were fairly healthy. Those men still found themselves periodically on picket duty, but in mid-February, they were also detailed to help construct a corduroy road that ran about four miles on the Belle Plain Road to Potomac Creek Bridge. This project required the felling of even more trees. The trunks were then butted together and laid across the dirt road to provide a hard surface over which the army's wagons could continually ply without fear of sinking hub-deep in mire.

By early March, the shortage of firewood in the area became so critical that relocation was the only solution. The 114th spent the first three days of March on picket duty about eight or nine miles from their camp. After returning from this duty, the Zouaves were abruptly ordered to pack up and move to a new campground, which they named in honor of Major

10. Murray to "Dear Mother," January 27, 1863, Murray to "Dear Father and Mother," February 19, 1863, both in Murray Collection, FSNMP.

11. Murray to "Dear Father and Mother," February 19, 1863, *ibid.*

General Daniel Edgar Sickles, the new Third Corps commander. They moved about four miles, near the Potomac Creek Bridge, where they set up camp in a large wooded area—"it having run out at our other camp," said Sergeant Fox. There the men once again began to construct their log houses, chinking the spaces between the logs with the plentiful mud. "The hills, covered with monster pines and noble oaks when we came here, now let in from all sides the rays of the sun, and every day larger patches of blue sky become visible," wrote Corporal Robert Kenderdine, the twenty-one-year-old teacher from Bucks County. The new camp was laid out on two sides of a valley, with company streets rising by successive terraces up the hills. Kenderdine thought it "one of the most tasteful camps that has come under my notice." Recalling its early appearance, he wrote, "When the companies first wheeled to form lines for streets, they were tripped by underbrush, and twitched in the faces by the limbs of saplings, sprung by some careless file-leader; and when aligned, company F could not see Company B for the dense undergrowth. But two weeks have made a wondrous change."[12]

Most of the building had been substantially completed within four or five days, however, and daily drill was resumed. Picket duty had also been reinstituted quickly. Corporal Kenderdine vividly described the ordeal of such duty:

You have heard many times of Virginia mud. It is the sovereign of all mud— the plastic king of all plastic matter. It is not Springfield mud, nor Solebury mud, nor Buckingham mud, nor Manor mud—it is Virginia's own mud— her sacred mud. It is mud that is muddier than even this very muddy paragraph. We were drawn up in line on the morning of the 10th inst., and started for the picket-posts on the right. At the beginning of our march lay a steep hill, which, though corduroyed, was covered with a coating of moistened clay, several inches in thickness. It was not difficult to get one's foot into this argillaceous trap, but to draw it forth was a question of time and of the relative tenacity of the soil and the shoe-pegs. I have seen men less exhausted from a long march than they were at the top of this slight hill. From this point to the outposts our movements could not be called march-

12. Murray to "Dear Father & Mother," March 2, 1863, *ibid.*; Fox Diary, March 4, 1863, in Fox Collection, HSP; "From the 'Zouaves D'Afrique,'" Bucks County *Intelligencer*, April 7, 1863, p. 1.

ing; it was a process of thrusting one foot into the argillferous compound, and extricating it with the other.[13]

The pervasive mud proved to be a fertile topic in the letters that many of the men wrote. "I am not troubled with my feet, but one thing I am troubled with is mud," wrote Private Murray in March. "Everywhere you go you get over shoetop in it." Sergeant Fox also told his parents that month that "we have very wet weather, and plenty of mud making it impossible for us to move."[14]

In addition to undergoing the sudden relocation of camp on March 4, the Zouaves had been startled by the unanticipated reorganization of their brigade on March 3. "Our brigade is a Pennsylvania Brigade now," wrote Private Murray. "The 20th Indiana has left us and gone into Ward's Brigade, and we took the 57th Pennsylvania out of Ward's." Other moves had also affected the 114th more directly. Brigadier General Robinson had taken command of the Second Division, First Corps, at the end of December. By the end of February, Colonel Collis was made acting brigadier and commander of his brigade in place of the absent Robinson. With Cavada still in Philadelphia awaiting word of the disposition of his court-martial, the Zouaves were commanded by Major Joseph S. Chandler. Chandler had suffered a slight wound during the fight at Fredericksburg, but the veteran officer had quickly recovered. He apparently was a serious and conscientious soldier, but his tenure as commander was not well received. "The major is getting awful strict, so that he is getting the men down on him," contended Murray. One circumstance that might have contributed to the men's ill feelings for Major Chandler was his having to inform the Zouaves in early March that no more furloughs would be permitted. Private Donnaker wrote his disappointed mother: "I can't get [a furlough] for it has been stopped in this regiment for one of the Sergeants got a furlough and has never come back so the major told us the other night that that was the reason we could not get any more as that was Gen. Hooker's orders."[15]

13. "From the 'Zouaves D'Afrique,'" Bucks County *Intelligencer*, April 7, 1863, p. 1.

14. Murray to "Dear Father & Mother," March 22, 1863, in Murray Collection, FSNMP; Fox to "My Dear Father & Mother," March 28, 1863, in Fox Collection, HSP.

15. Murray to "Dear Father and Mother," March 20, 22, 1863, in Murray Collection, FSNMP; Donnaker to "Dear Mother," March 3, 1863, in Donnaker Papers, CWMC, USAMHI.

As the winter progressed, the army recovered its morale and fighting spirit. Although the Zouaves were at least temporarily prohibited from going on furlough, they continued to receive visitors and parcels from home. Private Murray, however, continued to have difficulty getting his longed-for delicacies undamaged. "I lost my jelly as usual," he wrote to his parents. "The lid came off and the jelly spilt over everything; the glass bottle that had the pickles in got broke, but it did not hurt anything." On that occasion, at least, he was more fortunate than eighteen-year-old Joseph Miles, who complained of his box "that half of his things were taken out." Murray experienced similar problems in April when he discovered that not only was his bottle of Jamaica Ginger broken, but his "eggs were pretty well squashed [and] as for cakes I could not find any." A few weeks later he received another box, but "as for the cakes and candies I could not find them." His parents had also taken pity on his friend Miles, and had included some additional items for him. "Joe would not take any of the pickles and eggs. I wanted him to but he would not," wrote Murray. Moreover, despite efforts to revive the spirits of the defeated soldiers, many remained downcast. Private Donnaker's disgust with the privations of army life is evident in a letter he wrote to his parents on March 23. He first inquired about conditions in Philadelphia and about the impact of the draft. Addressing his father, Donnaker then wrote: "I hope they will never draft you because if you ever get down in this damned hole you will never get back alive for I don't think you would be able to stand it. I thought I would of been dead before this, its 7 months since I first went under Uncle Sam, I would advise you to keep from the draft if you possibly can."[16]

Still, the men were somewhat buoyed by a visit on March 26 by Governor Curtin. It was yet another overcast and dreary day, but the soldiers cheerfully marched about four miles to a level plain within sight of the spires of Fredericksburg, where they passed the time "not uncomfortably." Finally, Curtin appeared, and he and Birney rode across the front of each brigade. All of the Pennsylvania regiments in the division (then totaling six) were afterward called up and formed around a central point, where the governor addressed them. "Giving us his blessing in the name of the high position given him by the people, he bade us farewell," recalled Cor-

16. Murray to "Dear Father & Mother," March 20, April 21, 26, 1863, in Murray Collection, FSNMP; Donnaker to "Dear Mother and Father," March 23, 1863, in Donnaker Papers, CWMC, USAMHI.

poral Kenderdine. "I must not forget to say," he continued, "that the Governor was enthusiastically cheered by the soldiers of the 'Old Keystone,' and he seemed well pleased with his reception."[17]

The following day proved to be even more enjoyable for most of the Zouaves. Private Murray and several others were left behind as a guard, but the rest of the regiment marched over to General Birney's headquarters for special duty. "It was to be a gala for our Division," wrote Kenderdine. "There was to be some artistic horse racing among the officers, and other sights, rough and racy withal were to be exhibited to suit the tastes I suppose of us more common soldiery." Governor Curtin and General Hooker were both present to view the festivities.[18]

For the first contest, the Zouaves, along with other regiments chosen for the duty, were formed around the circumference of a large ring nearly a mile in length. The ring was cleared for the exclusive use of numerous mounted officers who were to participate in the races. Outside the ring, other officers and "ladies of high degree" sat upon the boards that had been taken up from the pontoon bridges and set up across the backs of wagons to make benches. Many of the mounted officers declined to race, however, and Kenderdine facetiously opined that it was either because of the formidable nature of the course, the "sight of a suggestive ambulance, or . . . motives, perhaps higher, perhaps lower, that we did not understand."[19]

Only seven anxious officers participated in the first race. Kenderdine graphically described the outcome of the contest, and that of several others to follow:

> Only six reached the goal, one far ahead of all his competitors; one is left maimed and crushed beside his fallen horse, far behind and unnoticed. . . . He disentangles himself from the horse, rises for a moment and falls nerveless to the ground. The ghastly ambulance drives in; he is lifted into it, and when the solemn vehicle scarcely hides itself from sight the game begins anew. Along flies a dashing Colonel; his horse stumbles and the rider lies half buried in a soft cushion of mud; a tall Major's mare sinks in a ditch,

17. Murray to "Dear Father & Mother," March 27, 1863, in Murray Collection, FSNMP; "From the 'Zouaves D'Afrique,'" Bucks County *Intelligencer*, April 14, 1863, p. 1.
18. Murray to "Dear Father & Mother," March 27, 1863, in Murray Collection, FSNMP; "From the 'Zouaves D'Afrique,'" Bucks County *Intelligencer*, April 14, 1863, p. 1.
19. "From the 'Zouaves D'Afrique,'" Bucks County *Intelligencer*, April 14, 1863, p. 1.

rolls over like a playful dog, and sends her rider headlong. The Colonel of the Zouaves takes his round in the exciting arena; he saves his horse till near the goal, when he urges him to the utmost; he doubles some of the racers, when his horse slips and pitches him, crimson cap, red shirt and breeches, boots and all into the open embraces of a huge Virginia mud-puddle. One run after this finishes the horse-racing of the day, which, in some thirty rides, threw four officers—the one thrown first dying the following night from his injuries.[20]

Fortunately for Collis, the only injury sustained in his fall was that to his ego.

Subsequent events proved to be far less hazardous to all than the races and produced a great deal of amusement. The next contest was the climbing of a greased pole. Several men had slid hilariously down the pole when one fellow ingeniously stopped, pulled out his large handkerchief, and proceeded to wipe away the grease as he climbed upward toward the ten-dollar bill at the top.

Next came the sack race, and more bloodletting. The participants formed a line. Rice or coffee sacks were then placed over their feet, pulled up, and tied at the waist. Another sack with a hole in it was then placed over each head, allowing it to protrude, but at the same time, being tied at the waist, preventing the soldier from moving his arms. The largest man in the group quickly took the lead, but tripped and fell "flat on his face, from which the blood flowed freely." The winner's prize was five dollars. A foot race followed, but as the only prize was the "fancied honor of possessing the biggest chest and the strongest legs," there was little interest.[21]

One of the last physical contests was called "bucking." Two men were placed in the center of the ring and bucked—a process that was sometimes used as a punishment. It entailed having one's hands bound together with the arms stretched out alongside both bended legs. A stick was placed over the arms and under the bent knees, locking all snugly in place. The two men were then "set up by their respective 'seconds,'" whence they proceeded to maneuver in this fettered condition in an attempt to push their opponent over. "Their movements are of the most ludicrous order," said

20. *Ibid.*
21. *Ibid.*

Kenderdine. "This performance was conducted and closed amid the greatest and uncontrollable merriment." The winner received ten dollars.[22]

The final contest of the day involved a "wheel of fortune." This consisted of a revolving wooden cylinder about twelve feet long and six feet in diameter, held about ten feet off the ground by a wood frame on both ends. The object was for the soldier to climb up one side of the frame, walk across the cylinder, and retrieve the ten-dollar bill at the other side. Normally, the cylinder was made to turn so freely that passage over it was nearly impossible. In this case, however, the wheel turned so sluggishly that the first contestant was able to scamper over and snatch the bill. Neither the wheel nor the piles of hay placed expectantly beneath it saw further use.

By early afternoon the affair had slowed, and the Zouaves headed back to camp at a quickstep. It was a day they would not soon forget. Sergeant Fox wrote to his parents, "Yesterday was a great day with our Division. I suppose there will be an account of it in the papers so I need not tell you the particulars but if it ain't in the papers you tell me when you write again and I will give you the details. There was an accident happened. A Col. in our Division was thrown from his horse."[23]

As winter gave way to the increasing warmth of an early Virginia spring, Collis returned to command his regiment. Brigadier General Charles Kinnaird Graham had arrived to take command of Birney's First Brigade in early April. "He is from the Excelsior Brigade," wrote Private Murray, referring to Graham's colonelcy of the 74th New York, which had been part of Major General Sickles' famed Third Corps unit. Graham had fought through the Peninsular Campaign with his regiment, but ill health then forced him to be placed on recruiting duty for almost a year. The men of his new command quickly found that things would be different.[24]

When the Zouaves awoke to prepare for picket duty on Easter Sunday morning, April 5, they peered from the "white-fringed openings of [their] tents" to find that an early-spring snowstorm had blanketed the ground with a covering that was growing deeper seemingly by the minute. The men formed up with their knapsacks and equipment but were delayed in

22. *Ibid.*

23. Fox to "My Dear Father & Mother," March 28, 1863, in Fox Collection, HSP.

24. Murray to "Dear Father & Mother," April 9, 1863, in Murray Collection, FSNMP.

moving out. While standing in the freezing sludge, "manifesting that patience that is the mark of the veteran soldier," they learned the reason: General Graham had insisted that the number of men in line for picket duty be equal to that shown on the regiment's morning report as fit for duty. "It took nearly an hour to correct the balance sheet," recalled Kenderdine; but the bugle finally sounded and the men moved off at right-shoulder-shift. Graham sent the Philadelphians an additional two days' rations, and kept them on picket for a total of five days. Fortunately, the weather rapidly improved during that time.[25]

Upon returning from their stint on picket duty, the Zouaves were informed that a review by the president would be held the following day. President and Mary Todd Lincoln, along with their son Thomas ("Tad"), had arrived at Aquia Creek Landing aboard the dispatch boat *Carrie Martin* on Easter morning while the Zouaves were standing in the snow preparing to go out on picket duty. The presidential party had already reviewed the army in a massive display on April 8; but now the group was departing, and its route would be lined with cheering troops. The 114th was marched out along the corduroy road and deployed in line on both sides. After they had waited for about an hour, the airborne sounds of distant cheering gave notice of the guests' approach. "The ranks are no place for one to witness to fullness a sight like this," complained Kenderdine. "The 'head erect' and 'eyes to the front' interfered much with our chance of observation, so I had no more than one glance. . . . In almost an instant, and almost before we had got our three cheers and 'Zouave' on the air, they passed away."[26]

In the letters home from Private Murray, the affair merited only passing mention. "We were reviewed by the President and his family the other day," was the extent of his observation. Many had doubtless not even seen the president as he rumbled past in his enclosed carriage. The men returned then to their campsite. The company streets, along which the Zouaves' huts were neatly aligned, had been festively decorated with pine trees, while the entrance to each hut bore an elaborate pine bough arch. Watching from the hill that descended into the camp as the companies filed into their respective streets, Corporal Kenderdine thought that the

25. "From the 'Zouaves D'Afrique,'" Bucks County *Intelligencer*, April 28, 1863, p. 1.
26. *Ibid.*

contrast of the red trousers and white turbans against the greenery rendered the scene "romantically picturesque."[27]

When he returned from picket duty on April 9, Murray had penned a letter to his parents in which he passed on a rumor that he had heard. "The talk is that we will lay around here all summer but I cannot tell whether it is so or not," he wrote. Of course it was not so. Lincoln's visit had meant more than just a social call designed to raise the spirits of the troops. A confident General Hooker was preparing to put his men to hard use, and the president had come down from Washington to see about his plans for a spring campaign. Hooker intended to move his cavalry over the upper Rappahannock and far into the Confederate rear to get on Lee's line of supply. A part of his infantry was to create a diversion at Fredericksburg, while his main force crossed at Kelly's Ford and swept down on the rear of the befuddled Rebels.[28]

In mid-April, the Zouaves turned in their blankets and extra clothing, except for one change. They put five days' rations in their knapsacks and three in their haversacks, and prepared to march once again. The Dixie weather proved unreliable as usual, however, and the entire movement was canceled when rain began to fall steadily. "Fighting Joe" Hooker had learned a valuable lesson from his predecessor's error. There would be no repeat of January's mud march, at least not for the infantry. In retrospect, Hooker made the right decision: the rain continued for several days. The Zouaves returned to camp, where they were reissued their blankets. Over the next few days they received their long-awaited pay; however, as a movement was imminent, most of the men paid off the sutler and sent nearly all of the rest of their money home. On Sunday, April 21, the Keystone Staters were reviewed by General Sickles and "several Swiss officers from the Peninsula." They would be the last to see the Zouaves so numerous.[29]

On April 28, the Philadelphians again departed Camp Sickles with eight days' rations. The inactivity of the past several months had apparently been too much for at least one disgruntled Zouave. An officer in the 105th Pennsylvania recalled that forty-year-old Captain Severin A. Bar-

27. Murray to "Dear Father & Mother," April 12, 1863, in Murray Collection, FSNMP; "From the 'Zouaves D'Afrique,'" Bucks County *Intelligencer*, April 28, 1863, p. 1.

28. Murray to "Dear Father & Mother," April 9, 1863, in Murray Collection, FSNMP.

29. Murray to "Dear Father & Mother," April 26, 1863, *ibid*.

thoulot of the 114th barged into his tent early that morning, exclaiming in a heavy French accent: "What you think, cap-tan? I can no c-a-r-e-e 8 days ra-she-one, I go to General: I say Gen-e-rul: I kin no carrie 8 day ra-she-one: you gib me hoss, Gen-e-rul." The "short, plump, ruddy-faced" captain was likely disappointed, though, as company-grade officers were not authorized mounts. Sergeant Fox estimated that the men marched with their weighty provisions about four miles below Fredericksburg, again in a continual rain. There they took up position in dense woods near the river as support for the troops of the First and Sixth Corps that were to cross there. Far upstream, the Eleventh Corps was also crossing, followed by the Twelfth and Fifth Corps.[30]

The following morning, the men steeled themselves for the coming battle. They awoke to the sound of musketry and cannonade as their companions fought to gain the opposite bank of the fog-shrouded Rappahannock. But the Zouaves were not called upon to fight that day. Instead, they moved about a mile upriver and again lay all day in a pine woods, where they heard an encouraging message from their commander. Hooker's dispatch to his troops rang with confidence, although many of the men in the army thought it just so much "chin music," or braggadocio. Private Coburn, however, must have been impressed by General Orders Number 47 on hearing it, for he accurately recalled its message that "the efforts of the past 3 days had been a series of successes, & that the enemy must either ignominiously fly, or come out from his stronghold & give us battle on our own ground where nothing but destruction awaited him."[31]

Colonel Collis had been in Washington on leave when his regiment began to move, and he caught up to them on April 30. The day was yet another rainy one. The men were mustered for pay that morning, and by early afternoon were started once again upriver toward the fords where the main body of the army was crossing. Along the way they passed the detritus of an army in motion. The Union force was slowly getting into light marching order and had filled the roadside with discarded clothing and equipment. The Zouaves halted that night within a few miles of United States Ford. With Collis now returned, they had a full complement of field-grade officers for this campaign. Lieutenant Colonel Cavada had

---

30. Memoirs of Samuel A. Craig, April 28, 1863, in *CWTI* Collection, USAMHI; Fox Diary, April 28, 1863, in Fox Collection, HSP.

31. Coburn to "Dear folks at home," May 1, 1863, in Coburn Papers, USAMHI.

recovered from his injury and also returned to the regiment by that time, although, by order of General Birney, he was placed under arrest and confined to the limits of the brigade until word was received reporting the disposition of his case.

Early next morning, the Zouaves were roused quickly and pushed forward to the river, where they "found two splendid pontoon bridges lying ready for [their] passage." The men crossed the turbulent stream under a cloudy sky and wound carefully up the steep bluffs on the opposite bank. Along the way, they passed long lines of abandoned rifle pits and redoubts and wondered why their adversaries had fallen back with little resistance. "It was a good omen, we poor, short-sighted mortals thought," Corporal Kenderdine later wrote.[32]

After a short rest at the top of the bluffs, the Red Legs headed off south from the ford, picked up the Mineral Spring Road, then turned west on the Orange Plank Road to support the Eleventh Corps. They were placed in line of battle along the road, where they remained until late afternoon, when they were ordered to retrace their steps and take up a position near the stately brick Chancellor House. The large, two-story building was surrounded by a generous clearing, but dense woods and thickets lay beyond that. The house had only recently been cleared of civilians. When some of the first Union troops had arrived the previous morning, they were greeted by ladies dressed in what appeared to be light summer clothes. These women had stood on the upper porch and "with characteristic Southern female bravado reviled us audibly, and wanted to know why we did not go on as General Lee was anxious to extend the hospitalities of the country."[33]

By the time the Zouaves arrived there, they had already sampled some of this so-called hospitality. Rebel artillery shells had screamed over their heads as they passed along the Orange Turnpike, and Kenderdine thought the sound "a horrific screech . . . very similar to a diabolical trill of the letter R." Though several men of the brigade were killed in the shelling, there were no casualties among the Zouaves. When they arrived at the Chancellor House, they took up position on the brow of a nearby hill in

32. "From Collis' Zouaves—114th P.V.," *Bucks County Intelligencer*, May 19, 1863, p. 2.

33. Frank A. Donaldson to "Dear Brother," May 9, 1863, in Frank A. Donaldson Papers, CWLM.

Chancellorsville, May 2–4, 1862

support of a battery of New York artillery, which was posted in the front yard.[34]

The Zouaves had no sooner positioned themselves when they came under a severe fire from Rebel artillery. Shells suddenly churned the earth about them, sending great showers of dirt over the men. The Zouaves had stacked arms, not expecting an attack, but they were quickly ordered to fall into line and march about three hundred paces to the rear. This maneuver placed the men on the reverse slope of the hill, away from the exposed brow and out of immediate danger. But it was too late for Private George W. Young of Company F, a twenty-four-year-old baker and friend of Sergeant Given, who was struck in the leg by the first rounds that landed among them. Given ran to his aid, cutting off the wounded man's accouterments with a sharp knife. Two stretcher-bearers, one of whom was the injured soldier's nineteen-year-old brother, George D. Young, a musician in company A, placed the wounded Zouave on a stretcher and carried him to the hospital that was then set up at the Chancellor House. "I bade George be of good courage and bear up manfully," said Given, but the leg was "fearfully mangled" and had to be amputated below the knee. When the Chancellor House later caught fire, the wounded Zouave was carried out and placed under some nearby trees, where he remained for two days without further medical attention. After the battle, he was brought back to the Union lines and the leg was again amputated, this time above the knee. He was too weak by that time to recuperate from another operation and he soon succumbed. "I had known [him] from boyhood," recalled Given; he "enlisted with me. A brave good soldier." Given was consoled by the thought that "his dear mother was with him in his last hours." She took her son's body home to Roxborough for burial.[35]

The artillery duel continued until sundown, after which the Zouaves rested fitfully on their arms through the night. Hooker's main force was now concentrated around the intersection where the Chancellor House stood. Mostly, they faced south, and east toward Fredericksburg. Despite his initial success in outmaneuvering the great southern general, Hooker had backed off that first day and handed the initiative to Lee. Hooker's

34. "From Collis' Zouaves—114th P.V.," Bucks County *Intelligencer*, May 19, 1863, p. 2.

35. Given Diary, n.d., in Given Collection, CWLM. Musicians typically filled the role of stretcher-bearer during this war.

troops moving east along the turnpike and Orange Plank Road that morning had been confident of success. Thus his lieutenants were utterly flabbergasted when he ordered them to withdraw and take up a defensive position near the Chancellor House crossroads. Sickles' Third Corps was being held in reserve. In the woods some distance to the east, Fifth Corps pickets could hear the southerners talking loudly. Accompanied by a banjo, one confident Rebel was overheard singing a song to the tune of "Other Side of Jordan":

> Ho, ho, ho, ha, ha, ha,
> The Louisiana boys *air* a coming,
> Never mind the Yanks,
> > but get upon their flanks,
> And you'll send them to
> > the other side of Jor-dan.[36]

Little could the listeners know, but the homespun lyrics accurately revealed the planned movements of the Confederate army. Lee and Lieutenant General Jackson had met that evening and boldly determined to divide their forces in the face of Hooker's overwhelming numbers. Jackson proposed to take nearly his entire available corps on a circuitous westward march around Hooker's army and strike his exposed right flank. Lee's cavalry had discovered that the Eleventh Corps was strung out along the Turnpike to the west of Chancellorsville, their flank unanchored on any defensive terrain. It was hung out in midair, just waiting to be rolled up like an old carpet. The entire corps faced generally south behind strong entrenchments. Only two regiments were refused, facing west, the direction from which Jackson's attack would come.

In the morning, the weather had cleared. The Zouaves left the battery posted near the house and moved once again along the plank road to their right between the Eleventh and Twelfth Corps. Federal observers were reporting the movement of a large body of Confederate troops westward along the Catharine Furnace Road directly to the front of Sickles' Third Corps. Evaluating this intelligence, Hooker apparently believed that Lee's army was only doing the sensible thing under the circumstances: retreating west to Gordonsville. Strangely, though, even from his perspective, Hooker sent only the Third Corps forward to attack the Rebel column at

---

36. Donaldson to "Dear Brother," May 9, 1863, in Donaldson Papers, CWLM.

Catharine Furnace. At about 10 A.M., the Zouaves were ordered forward about three-quarters of a mile to support a battery trained on the passing Confederates. "We had a full view of a retreating rebel wagon train," wrote Corporal Kenderdine. "The teams went plunging along at headlong speed, the latter sensibly increasing as shell upon shell poured upon them from our talking Parrots."[37]

Throughout the afternoon, the Zouaves continued to move forward toward the furnace in support of skirmishers and sharpshooters, who were by then engaged with the Georgia and Mississippi regiments sent to relieve the pressure on Jackson's rushing columns. By late afternoon, however, Jackson's lead regiments were starting to form a line of battle across the Turnpike in the woods west of the Eleventh Corps line. Still, Hooker was unaware of the disaster about to befall him, and the men of the Third Corps were ebullient at their success. "We were ordered forward at a double quick march," recalled Sergeant Given of the late afternoon's events. "We were driving the enemy and felt quite elated and cheered mightily."[38]

The Zouaves, along with three other regiments of their brigade, had advanced along the road past Catharine Furnace, moving into an open field south of an unfinished railroad cut near the Welford house. There, General Graham received orders to fall back immediately. Jackson's flank attack had shattered the Eleventh Corps exactly as planned and sent them scurrying eastward toward Chancellorsville in a panic. Some of the Zouaves apparently thought that all was yet well, and that the Rebels were still attempting to get away. "Toward night we were thrown far to the right," reported Kenderdine, "where [Captain George E.] Randolph was pouring grape and canister right and left into the retreating enemy." However, they soon came to the realization that the battle was not proceeding so smoothly as thought. "Here there appeared to be a turn in the tide," recalled the incredulous corporal, while Sergeant Fox remembered that "on account of another Corps meeting with surprise we were ordered to fall back on a quick time."[39]

37. "From Collis' Zouaves—114th P.V.," *Bucks County Intelligencer*, May 19, 1863, p. 2. Kenderdine's "talking Parrots" refer to the Parrott gun: a rifled, muzzle-loading cannon developed by Captain Robert Parker Parrott. The rifling provided greater accuracy than smoothbore artillery pieces, and the range was nearly doubled.

38. Given Diary, n.d., in Given Collection, CWLM.

39. "From Collis' Zouaves—114th P.V.," *Bucks County Intelligencer*, May 19, 1863, p. 2; Fox Diary, May 2, 1863, in Fox Collection, HSP.

The men retreated in silence, their rifles turned down at trail arms to prevent the moon from gleaming on the shiny barrels. They were "disagreeably surprised" to find the division seemingly surrounded by enemy troops. Graham threw out the 141st Pennsylvania as pickets, and then ordered the 114th to go forward to fill a gap in the picket line, connecting his flanks to those of the existing line. Collis moved rapidly to comply with this order, but when the Zouaves arrived, they found that the gap had already been filled. They withdrew to a position on the right of the brigade at Hazel Grove and tried to sleep. "We laid down to sleep with the enemy on three sides of us," recalled a soldier in the 57th Pennsylvania. "It seemed as if nobody knew where the enemy was or from which side he would be likely to attack."[40]

They had not long to rest before the sounds of battle began anew, however. General Sickles issued orders for Birney to drive the enemy from the woods between him and the turnpike to the north. Birney dispatched his second and third brigades, along with the 63rd Pennsylvania of Graham's brigade, to participate in a confused fight in the eerie moonlight. "Oh how awful did that sound," recalled Sergeant Fox. A soldier of the Corn Exchange Regiment remembered listening in the darkness as the steady tramp of his comrades' footsteps grew louder. Soon he could hear the sounds of commands being given as the men prepared to move forward to the attack. "Forward, guide centre march," was heard. The order "was quickly followed by a tremendous musketry firing followed by a crash of artillery that fairly shook the earth beneath us, then deafening cheers this time from our men and the battle was on again in all its wild fury, and raged in fierce tumult all night long." The midnight charge failed to dislodge the Confederates, but it succeeded in reestablishing solid contact between the Third Corps lines at Hazel Grove and those of the main body at Fairview and Chancellorsville. Despite the setback, Hooker's contracted lines were in a strong position to renew the battle on Sunday morning.[41]

Soon after daylight on May 3, Confederate forces hidden in the nearby woods poured a "murderous fire" into the front and flanks of Graham's brigade "Hissing of round shot and flutter of shell was our reveille," re-

40. Fox Diary, May 2, 1863, in Fox Collection, HSP; C. Collis to Read, May 6, 1863, in Read Papers, HSP; Strauss to "Dear Mother," May 10, 1863, in *CWTI* Collection, USAMHI.

41. Fox Diary, May 2, 1863, in Fox Collection, HSP; Donaldson to "Dear Brother," May 9, 1863, in Donaldson Papers, CWLM.

called Kenderdine. "The buzzing of Minie balls betokened the near approach of the revengeful foe." By that time, Hooker had made the terrible
mistake of ordering Sickles to withdraw from his commanding position at
Hazel Grove. His corps was in the process of doing just that when Brigadier
General James Jay Archer's gray-clad troops burst forth from the woods
bordering the clearing on the west. Graham's brigade was the only force
left to face this onslaught. Collis later recalled that his men made a gallant
fighting retreat: they withdrew under a "terrible fire, . . . never once moving at a double quick." Brigadier General Joseph F. Knipe, commanding
the First Brigade, First Division, Twelfth Corps, had a different view of
things that morning. "A regiment of red-legged Zouaves came pell-mell
from our left, with less than half their number of the enemy close at their
heels," he complained; "I endeavored to arrest the fugitives and induce
them to defend themselves from behind the rifle-pits, over which they had
just retreated," but he was unable to do so. A soldier in the 5th New Jersey
also recalled the hasty retreat of the Zouaves, no doubt made more noticeable by their conspicuous dress and supposed prowess in battle. "Their
officers called upon us to fire into them," he claimed. "We did not obey
the order. The Red Leggs started the rest . . . leaving us in a bad position."
Despite the speed with which they fled the field, and Collis' claims to the
contrary, it should be noted that the 114th was falling back under orders
from General Birney to do so.[42]

In the confusion of the retreat, however, at least one Zouave became
separated from the regiment. Corporal Kenderdine turned to see the Rebels filing around the brow of the hill. "The shot was too tempting to a
soldier deaf with the whistle of Minies," he later recalled. After firing a
few quick rounds at the oncoming foe, Kenderdine turned and found to
his amazement that his gaudily dressed comrades were nowhere to be seen.
"Not a red-leg offered a tempting shot to the rebel rifles save a pair in my
immediate vicinity," said the astonished Zouave. He made a hasty retreat,
finding that he was the "distinguished object of their generous donations
of lead." Kenderdine sprang into a rifle pit held by the 27th Indiana,
Twelfth Corps. A Hoosier in that unit recalled the passage of Graham's

---

42. "From Collis' Zouaves—114th P.V.," Bucks County *Intelligencer*, May 19, 1863, p.
2; C. Collis to Read, May 6, 1863, in Read Papers, HSP; OR, Vol. XXV, Pt. 1, p. 687;
Alfred Bellard, *Gone for A Soldier: The Civil War Memoirs of Private Alfred Bellard*, ed. David
Herbert Donald (Boston, 1975), 213–14.

men as they were streaming past minutes earlier: "A regiment or two, however, came pellmell through the bushes, and passed through our ranks. They were not panic stricken or demoralized, as those of the day previous, yet in little if any better order. Part of them were zouaves, having baggy red pants, and phez caps, with long tassels."[43]

The Indianians, along with the rest of Brigadier General Thomas Howard Ruger's Third Brigade, brought Archer's advance to a halt. Kenderdine attempted to join in the repulse but found that the barrel of his rifle had become packed with dirt. He had stumbled in his haste to reach the safety of the breastworks and thrust the muzzle into the ground. But seconds after this discovery, "a poor Indiana boy" was struck down in the storm of flying metal, and the Zouave was armed once more. Ruger's brigade advanced and drove Archer's Confederates back. By that time, however, the strategic importance of Hazel Grove had become clear to all. Southern artillery now commanded the field from that vital eminence and played havoc on Ruger's flank. Still the men in blue surged forward against the soldiers from Alabama, Tennessee, and North Carolina, until, finally, Ruger began to receive word of ammunition running low in his regiments; he reluctantly issued the command to begin an orderly withdrawal. Kenderdine advanced with the Hoosiers and was "thunderstruck" when he turned and saw the 114th "coming up in gallant line" to their relief.[44]

As the Hoosiers remembered, the retreat of Graham's brigade had been somewhat disorderly. Collis contended that large numbers of men from other regiments were pushing through his lines in their haste to get to the rear and save themselves. As a result of the confusion, the 114th and 105th Pennsylvania became separated from the rest of the brigade. Because of the distinctive dress of the 114th, Collis claimed he was able to keep his regiment together and "well in hand." He observed nearby Major General Hiram Gregory Berry, commander of the Third Corps, Second Division, and sent Major Bowen to him for instructions until he could be reunited with his own brigade. Before Berry could place the men in position, however, Graham had spotted the distinctively dressed Zouaves and sent word for them to join his other regiments and pull back farther, to the rear of

43. "From Collis' Zouaves—114th P.V.," Bucks County *Intelligencer*, May 19, 1863, p. 2; Edmund Brown, *History of the 27th Indiana* (Richmond, 1899), 330.

44. "From Collis' Zouaves—114th P.V.," Bucks County *Intelligencer*, May 19, 1863, p. 2.

the batteries at Fairview. Berry rode off north across the turnpike and was killed by a Rebel sharpshooter. The Zouaves quickly followed the 105th to the rear of the batteries.[45]

Once Graham re-formed his brigade in division columns, he advanced them to support the hard-pressed Ruger. Graham sent the 105th ahead at a double-quick march and dispatched his aides to hurry the other regiments behind them. The general went forward with the 105th for about 100 yards, then turned and saw that the 114th was not yet coming up behind them. Graham sent a lieutenant with the words: "For Gods sake . . . go back, & tell Col Collis to execute his movement with celerity. . . . He is entirely too deliberate!" The Zouaves thereupon rushed up in rear of the 105th, with the other regiments following closely. Together they pushed forward across the clearing at Fairview and into the woods where Ruger was holding back repeated Confederate attacks. When they reached the crest of a small hill in their front, Graham formed the brigade in line of battle. The 105th held the left, followed by the 114th, 68th, 57th, 63rd, and 141st Pennsylvania to the right. It was then that Kenderdine observed his regiment marching up to relieve his new comrades. The brigade came to a halt while Graham rode forward to consult with Colonel Silas Colgrove of the 27th Indiana. Colgrove told the general that his ammunition had not yet been entirely exhausted and that he would prefer his regiment to remain in position for a short time longer until it was. Graham assented and brought his brigade forward to join them.[46]

The artillery fire on part of the line was so intense that some of the regiments were ordered to lie down. A captain in the 105th Pennsylvania recalled the horror of the barrage:

> I could actually see the black disc of the ten pound cannon balls as they came towards us. The top of the head of a soldier in my company, on my right, was scooped out by one of them. I turned him over and his face was not disfigured a bit. I then saw a black disc coming right at *me*, but it hit the ground a few feet in front of me, throwing mud in my face and went over me. A young fellow next to me said, "Cap, I thought that chap was for you."[47]

45. *OR*, Vol. XXV, Pt. 1, p. 423.

46. Testimony of Brigadier General Charles K. Graham, May 26, 1863, Colonel Charles H. T. Collis Court-Martial Proceedings, in Court-Martial Records, Record Group 153, NARA.

47. Craig Memoirs, n.d., in *CWTI* Collection, USAMHI.

After holding that position for about forty-five minutes, according to Graham's estimate, the brigade went forward at a charge to drive the enemy from the breastworks they were holding. Collis ordered his men to fix bayonets, and the Zouaves joined the frenzied dash for the works. Colonel Colgrove recalled that in some places, a hand-to-hand fight took place, but the Rebels soon gave way and were "thrown into the utmost confusion. . . . I can safely say that I have never witnessed on any other occasion so perfect a slaughter." A large number were taken prisoner, and Collis himself received the swords of one or two officers.[48]

The 114th was crowding onto the flank of the 27th Indiana at that time. Collis ordered his regiment to move by the right flank so that they would clear the Hoosiers and occupy a larger portion of the breastworks. Collis sent Sergeant Thomas J. Rice of Company I to relay that order to Major Chandler, but Rice found that officer lying on his back with a bullet hole just above his eyebrow. Captain Elliot of Company F and Lieutenant George M. Cullen of Company G were also down, mortally wounded, Elliot with a shot to the hip. All of the other officers in Cullen's company were wounded, Captain George J. Schwartz seriously. The field was strewn with Zouaves, their red trousers dotting the somber terrain with splashes of color. "The brave boys [fell] like leaves to the blast of autumn," wrote the unscathed Kenderdine, while Collis moved up and down his line encouraging the men to shoot low and not waste ammunition.[49]

The position was becoming exceedingly hot for the Union men by this time. Confederate reinforcements were arriving, about to turn the tide once more. Brigadier General George Doles's Georgians were pushing past the left flank of Graham's line, while the 141st Pennsylvania on the right was taking the brunt of an attack by Brigadier General Stephen Dodson Ramseur's Tar Heels. Graham pleaded for reinforcements but was finally compelled to send the Zouaves on another movement by their right flank to buck up the sagging 141st. "With as much coolness as could have been done on parade this movement was executed," recalled the general. Nevertheless, it was not enough. North Carolina troops poured out of the

48. OR, Vol. XXV, Pt. 1, p. 712; Testimony of Brigadier General Graham, May 26, 1863, Collis Court-Martial Proceedings, in Court-Martial Records, Record Group 153, NARA.

49. C. Collis, *1st Brigade*, 27; "From Collis' Zouaves—114th P.V.," Bucks County *Intelligencer*, May 19, 1863, p. 2; Testimony of Captain E. Forrest Koehler, June 1, 1863, Collis Court-Martial Proceedings, in Court-Martial Records, Record Group 153, NARA.

woods onto the Pennsylvanians' front and exposed right flank. That portion of the line began to break and fall back. The Zouaves retreated with
the entire brigade behind the crest of the hill from which they had earlier
advanced.[50]

Reaching the relative safety of the reverse slope, the men were ordered
to lie down. The regiments formed as ordered, but "a great deal of confusion still existed in the 114th," recalled a staff officer. Soon the enemy
advanced again on the exposed right flank of the brigade, and again the
line started to give way. The Zouaves began to fall back, but Collis took
the colors from Sergeant Benjamin I. Baylitts' hands and planted them on
the ground. Grabbing another man by the shoulder, Collis placed him as
a marker and called for his men to rally. "Do not let a man of my regiment
pass by this flag," he shouted loudly as the enemy's deadly projectiles sang
by. "Rally here, men!" Collis called for Captains Koehler, of the color
company, and Bowen, of Company B, to assist him. Bowen said that he
had been wounded. "Never mind that," replied the colonel. "I am likely
to be too."[51]

At that time, Koehler stated, one of General Graham's aides, Captain
Fitzhugh Birney, rode up to Collis and called out: "It is no use now. We
are outflanked." Private Thomas Wallworth observed Birney approaching
and ran up to hear what the order was, but "a bullet struck him, sending
him spinning like a top and yelling 'Oh, Captain Eddy! Come to me!'"
Eddy hotly replied that if he had been "paying attention to his own business he would not have been struck." "Tommy was carried off," said Sergeant Given. "I never knew what became of him." By then, the advancing
North Carolinians were within fifty yards of the now ragged line of Zouaves
and approaching on the flank. Collis ordered his men to retire from the
field. The entire brigade streamed back toward the Chancellor House,
"having been flanked on both sides and a Battery playing almost in our
rear," recalled Graham. "We retired rapidly & in comparative confusion,"
he admitted. The Pennsylvanians formed in the rear of the brick house,
once again in support of the batteries in front.[52]

50. Testimony of Brigadier General Graham, May 26, 1863, Collis Court-Martial Proceedings, in Court-Martial Records, Record Group 153, NARA.

51. Testimony of Captains Fitzhugh Birney, E. Forrest Koehler, and Edward R. Bowen,
May 27, June 1, 1863, Collis Court-Martial Proceedings, *ibid.*

52. Given Diary, n.d., in Given Collection, CWLM; Testimony of Captain Koehler and
Brigadier General Graham, June 1, May 26, 1863, Collis Court-Martial Proceedings, in
Court-Martial Records, Record Group 153, NARA.

As they approached the Chancellor House, all was chaos and disorder. Confederate shells had set the building on fire. One soldier likened it to a "'War is Hell' picture": "the timber and brush were burning, the house flaming from every door and window; in front crowds of retreating soldiers, shells bursting and roaring, wounded and struggling horses, dead and dying horses lying about; smoke everywhere thickly in the air; on our left a shell bursts right among a crowd of soldiers, horrible the sight."[53]

In place of Birney's collapsing division came Major General William Henry French's Third Division of the Second Corps. The 8th Ohio participated in this movement and drove the attackers back across the Turnpike and out of the rifle pits they had occupied to the south of the road. A large number of happy Zouave captives were there to greet them. Colonel Samuel S. Carroll of the 8th Ohio stated that his men "released a regiment of Zouaves belonging to the Third Corps that was held as prisoner behind those pits." The actual number of Red Legs taken captive was probably less than a full company; but in the seesaw battle, the Buckeyes had spared the Philadelphians from the danger and monotony of life in a Rebel prison camp or cell.[54]

Confederate artillery at Hazel Grove continued to hammer the Federals, driving them back. While supporting the battery at the Chancellor House, the 114th came under a terrific fire from the enemy guns. Fortunately, the barrage had little effect, other than on morale. The eighty or so remaining Zouaves hugged the earth as a "storm of shot, shell, grape and canister . . . flew around us. Limbs of trees and dirt flew in all directions but most of the shells burst too late," recalled Kenderine. Finally, the men were ordered back from this position, joining a new defensive line about one-half mile back, near the intersection of Mineral Spring and Ely's Ford Roads.[55]

They were shelled once more in their new position, but the heavy fighting was over. Though the army was yet full of fight, the commanding general was not. Hooker had been defeated. "We were worsted here, from whatever cause, not from any want of courage or willingness to fight . . .

53. Craig Memoirs, n.d., in *CWTI* Collection, USAMHI.

54. *OR*, Vol. XXV, Pt. 1, p. 365.

55. "From Collis' Zouaves—114th P.V.," Bucks County *Intelligencer*, May 19, 1863, p. 2.

but rather the lack of leadership," observed a soldier in the 105th Pennsylvania.[56]

Over 400 Zouaves had marched out of winter quarters just several days prior to the battle. Now, 181 of them were casualties. In the fields and woods around Chancellor House, 13 Zouave officers had been struck down. Of these, 3 were dead, and several others severely wounded. Among enlisted men, 18 had been killed, and 115 others wounded; 35 were missing. Among the wounded were Sergeant Fox, who was struck on the top of the head by a shell fragment, and Private Murray, who took a rifle ball in the shoulder that fractured his right clavicle. During one phase of the fighting, Private William Colbridge of Sergeant Given's company had been shot in the head, the bullet passing through the jaw and cheekbone. Given sent two of his men to carry Colbridge's body to the rear and bury him. "His head was swollen as large as two heads," recalled the sergeant. But when Colbridge reached the rear, he revived and was taken to a field hospital. He survived.

Colonel Collis, though unwounded, was carried from the field on a stretcher early that evening due to "insensible suffering from exhaustion."[57] As he passed to the rear, a man in the Corn Exchange Regiment thought the scene curious. On seeing the officer being carried on a stretcher, he recalled, his captain had called out

> and wanted to know whom they had. They replied, "Colonel Collis of the 114th Pennsylvania." "Is he shot," said the Captain. "Shot in the neck," remarked one of the men, whereupon they put down the stretcher and Colonel Collis rose, and upon Colonel Prevost asking where his regiment was, replied "just ahead, Sir, heavily engaged, and I being sick was obliged to turn over the command to Major Chandler and go to the rear." He exhibited his sword scabbard, much bent, as having been struck by a bullet. . . . his whole appearance and demeanor at this time denoted fear of the most abject kind. The men smiled contemptously as they passed him by, and I felt exceedingly sorry they had witnessed the humiliating loss of honor and self-respect of a man so widely known as Colonel Collis.[58]

56. Craig Memoirs, n.d., in *CWTI* Collection, USAMHI.

57. Given Diary, n.d., in Given Collection, CWLM.

58. C. Collis to Read, May 6, 1863, in Read Papers, HSP; Donaldson to "Dear Brother," May 9, 1863, in Donaldson Papers, CWLM. The phrase "shot in the neck" was a contemporary euphemism for intoxication. It should be noted that Donaldson was apparently a

In truth, Collis was then suffering from typhoid fever, and the illness had caused his performance that day to appear to many less than satisfactory. For the 114th, the battle was over; for Collis, however, a battle more bitter than the one just fought was about to open. He was about to be accused of cowardice. The issue would be settled by a court of his peers.

---

teetotaler, and throughout his letter he derided all officers for their propensity to drink. The conversation supposedly overheard by Donaldson must have been at least partly fabricated by him. Collis had already turned over command of the regiment to Lieutenant Colonel Cavada and of course knew that Chandler was dead.

8

In the Scale of Justice

Hooker's entire force at hand was withdrawn to a rough, U-shaped defensive position, the ends of which were anchored securely on the banks of the flowing Rapidan and Rappahannock Rivers to the north of Chancellorsville. Collis' Zouaves lay behind hastily prepared breastworks throughout the fourth and fifth of May. They were heavily shelled for a short time—losing one additional man—but there was to be no more hard fighting for the infantry.

Rain began to fall once again on the afternoon of May 5. It doused the last of the brushfires that had horribly consumed a number of unfortunate men who were wounded too badly to escape the licking flames. For the survivors, it was a night of misery. The torrent quickly soaked them through to the skin. A few were fortunate enough to find some shelter from the weather, but not from the projectiles that still whizzed and whistled past with great regularity. A captain in the 118th Pennsylvania recalled that one of his fellow officers had set up a tent in the open field behind the regiment's rifle pits, and after dark had been so bold as to light a candle to enable him to read a newspaper. When water dripped into his shelter through a newly made bullet hole, "his shadow pictured him as reaching up and stopping it with paper." To repeated commands to snuff out his candle, the Irish-born officer, who had served in "Injee" with "Her

Majesty's Foot," simply replied that he "didn't care a devil for the firing as he would rather be shot than drowned entirely."[1]

Sergeant Given had retained his half of a shelter tent, though he found that his usual tentmates were among the missing, wounded, and dead. He finally located someone from his company with another half of a tent. Given and Lieutenant George P. Anderson buttoned their halves together, drove two bayoneted muskets into the ground, and fashioned a shelter for themselves. They invited Captain Henry M. Eddy of Company D to join them, and the three "tired, wet, hungry and disheartened" men huddled together in the makeshift tent. Given soon withdrew from his jacket pocket the small Bible that his wife had given him, and began to read to himself. The words of John 14:1 brought him "great joy and comfort": "Let not your heart be troubled: ye believe in God, believe also in me." Anderson soon observed that Given "was having good from [his] little book," and asked if he too could read from it. The lieutenant began to read aloud, and soon both he and Captain Eddy "acknowledged that they had not lived as they should have lived, but that hereafter they would live good lives if spared to get out of this fearful battle." Though one of them would not survive the war, they were all to escape the carnage at Chancellorsville. Hooker had decided to pull back to the safety of the northern bank of the Rappahannock. The battle was over.[2]

By nightfall on the fifth, the men in the rifle pits knew that a movement was imminent, but they knew neither the purpose nor the direction. Many hoped for a renewal of the conflict, for they thought that "we will whip them yet." Still, they feared that they were about to be betrayed. "Things look strange to me," wrote Colonel Henry J. Madill of the 141st Pennsylvania. "There is something that is not right. Have orders to push up and be ready to march at a moment's notice. I hope it is not to evacuate."[3]

Early the following morning, however, their questions were answered and their fears confirmed. The Zouaves, along with the rest of the brigade, were ordered to fall back quickly and hold onto their tin cups and accouterments to avoid the telltale clatter that invariably accompanied a large body of soldiers on the move. The rain and the passage of hundreds of

1. Donaldson to "Dear Brother," May 9, 1863, in Donaldson Papers, CWLM.
2. Given Diary, n.d., in Given Collection, CWLM.
3. Diary of Henry J. Madill, May 5, 1863, in Greg Coco Collection, USAMHI.

wagons, guns, and horses had churned the roads into a morass. Consequently, the march was a difficult one. In places, the mud was up to the knees of the struggling soldiers. Hundreds of trees had been felled to make way for the wagons and artillery pieces, inadvertently creating an abatis for the retreating army. The Zouaves plodded toward the river, stumbling and climbing over the obstacles in an effort to avoid the quagmire. At last, they reached the mist-shrouded river and the pontoon bridges that would lead them to safety. Thousands of saddened and dejected men were poised to cross, yet they waited patiently and without complaint; perhaps many hoped that some officer would ride up to tell them that there had been some mistake and that they were to turn about and pitch into Lee's army once more. The men in the ranks had been roughly handled, but, man for man, most thought they gave as good as they got. Not the Army of the Potomac, only its commander, had been defeated at Chancellorsville—though one man admitted that there were some hard feelings for those charged with anchoring the army's right flank. "Whenever a crescent badge [of the Eleventh Corps] was seen, it was hooted."[4]

Once across the river, the 114th headed in the direction of its old camp near Falmouth. On the way, the Zouaves passed their fellow Philadelphians of the 99th Pennsylvania, then assigned to the Second Brigade of Birney's division. Sergeant Given was hailed by an old friend, George Roberts of the 99th. At home, the two had been members of a local section of the Cadets of Temperance. Now, reunited, they shared Roberts' cup of hot coffee and hardtack on sodden ground far from that home. It was an act of kindness not soon to be forgotten. Many years later, Given recalled with fondness his friend's offer of food and drink: "George has gone to his reward, but as long as I live will I remember this big-hearted boy."[5]

On the way back to Falmouth the rain ceased, but the men's spirits remained dampened. The bright spring blossoms on the dogwood and cherry trees seemed to mock them as they passed dejectedly. "We called it going home," recalled Given. "But, my how different!" Though dispirited, many Zouaves felt some relief at reaching their old camp. It was "as though we had found the roof-tree of our home," wrote Corporal Kender-

4. Given Diary, n.d., in Given Collection, CWLM; "From Collis' Zouaves—114th P.V.," Bucks County *Intelligencer*, May 19, 1863, p. 2; Craig Memoirs, n.d., in *CWTI* Collection, USAMHI.

5. Given Diary, n.d., in Given Collection, CWLM.

dine. For many of the men, however, the arrival at camp might be likened to returning to an abandoned home. Indeed, many of this soldierly "family" were gone. Men who had lived, laughed, marched, and fought together with those now returning would never do so again. The saddened survivors of the battle gazed forlornly at the piled logs that marked their old homes and looked about for new messmates. Neither of Sergeant Given's former tentmates had returned. Thirty-five-year-old Private Thomas Collins had been wounded and taken prisoner by the Rebels, and twenty-nine-year-old Matthias Chadwick had also been captured; both eventually would return to duty. But for the time being, Given called twenty-two-year-old Corporal John T. Shuster to him, and—as he, too, had no mates—invited him to share his quarters. "He was a good soldier and Christian man and we lived together for many months," recalled Given. "I had him made a sergeant."[6]

The Zouaves spent many of the ensuing evenings gathered around their campfires recounting the dangers and escapes of the recent fight. Their storytelling brought them to marvel at their common escape from the torrent of metal. They showed their bullet-torn clothing, their mangled accouterments, and their shell-bruised bodies; they tallied their losses and told how each fell. There was thirty-four-year-old Private William Weber, of Company B, who received a serious wound to the left arm. He would undergo three operations before being discharged on January 27, 1865. Private Albert Colcher, of Company D, sustained a gunshot wound to the head that lacerated his scalp and fractured his cranium. At the hospital, fragments of bone were removed from the wound, from which his brain was protruding, but the twenty-year-old succumbed on May 8. Private William W. Davis, of Company E, also twenty, received a head wound as well. The ball entered his mouth, fracturing his jaw, destroying his upper teeth, and tearing out a two-inch portion of his cheek. Though he survived, he suffered severe deformity and neuralgia in damp weather for the rest of his life. Private George Messenger, a thirty-four-year-old cooper of Company K, also was shot in the face. His wound was less serious, however, as the ball entered the lower right jaw and passed around to exit on the left side. The edges of the wound were sewn together by hare-lip suture, and though deformed, Messenger was eventually transferred to the 24th

6. *Ibid.*; "From Collis' Zouaves—114th P.V.," Bucks County *Intelligencer*, May 19, 1863, p. 2.

Regiment, Veteran Reserve Corps. Corporal Samuel Hensel, a thirty-one-year-old carpenter, was struck by a musket ball in the center of the left buttock. It was no less serious than the facial wounds, however, as the bullet fractured the femur and resulted in the shortening of his left leg by about three and one-half inches. Hensel was transported to Armory Square Hospital in Washington, where his wound was probed daily. After two weeks, the bullet moved close enough to the wound entrance to be extracted. For several weeks thereafter, pieces of bone and haversack were also emitted from the wound. Hensel was eventually able to walk with the assistance of a shoe support, an iron brace, and a cane. Five years after the injury, he could walk only one-half to three quarters of a mile, and had to stop to rest for several minutes once or twice while covering that distance. The long-term impact of the wounds incurred by some of the Zouaves was undoubtedly discussed in gatherings around the campfires those first few weeks of May. The men could only conjecture about a wounded soldier's prospects for recovery. Nevertheless, they could at least take some consolation in knowing that a friend had been accounted for ; many still were not.[7]

Eventually, the regiment began to receive word from those who had been captured, but still there were several men of the 114th who seemed to have disappeared. No one ever learned what became of them, and "they were swept off with the thousands of other brave men whose bodies were never recovered." Among those unaccounted for were two men from Given's company: twenty-five-year-old Private George Rutter and twenty-one-year-old Private George Howell, the latter an English-born weaver. Both men were listed as killed, though no one was certain of their fate.[8]

In addition to giving accounts to one another around the campfires, many survivors of Chancellorsville wrote quickly to friends and family to reassure them of their own safety and to tell of the fate of others known to them. A private in the 57th Pennsylvania wrote to his wife of the confused fighting near Hazel Grove and of one unlucky man in his company: "I guess [he] run into the rebels' lines and was taken prisoner for I have not heard from him. . . . The last I saw him he was making tracks to

7. Joseph K. Barnes, ed., *The Medical and Surgical History of the War of the Rebellion* (1861–65), (2 vols.; Washington, D.C., 1870), Vol. II, Pt. 1, pp. 296, 348, 367, Pt. 3, pp. 75–76, 959.

8. Given Diary, n.d., in Given Collection, CWLM.

the rear he thought but it was towards the Rebel lines for we were surrounded . . . on every side. We got out by the skin of our teeth." Sergeant Fox, of the 114th, wrote his parents from Carver Hospital in Washington on May 9 concerning his own lot:

> On Sunday morning May 3rd while in an engagement I received a slight wound near the top of my head from a piece of shell and I managed to get conveyed to Washington. I am little the worse for it but still I am not as I should be.
>
> . . . I would like to be home for about thirty days. I think at the end of that time I will be very near able to join my poor broken Regiment. I suppose you have heard the horrid news about our Regiment. We stood our ground like men while the shot and shell flew thick among us. Many of my poor companions on that never to be forgotten Sunday fell to rise no more among the number. God knows it makes my heart ache to record that of Capt Elliot, as brave and fearless a man as was ever born.[9]

Private Murray, having suffered a serious wound to the shoulder, was also in Washington but at Harewood Hospital. He was fortunate to have been visited by his father not long after his arrival in the capital. On May 18, though, he wrote his uncle saying that his mother had better not make the trip to see him. "She would be apt to miss me, as they talk of sending us all away soon as a new load comes in from the front." Fortunately for Murray, his parents disregarded his advice. They arrived in Washington on May 30 to find their son in worsening condition. "He was not receiving proper attention he having got very bad and having had a hemmorrage of the Lungs in consequence of mistreatment," wrote his father, William. Murray had by that time been moved to another barracks at the hospital, where he apparently was receiving better treatment. "The surgeon of the Barracks where he now is informed me that when he came under his treatment at first he thought he could not live." William returned to Philadelphia the following day, leaving his wife, Margaret, to look after their son. He thought that George's condition had improved somewhat, but he wrote his brother that "It is impossible to tell for a few days what may be the issue, we must hope for the best but not raise our hopes too high." Ultimately, Murray did recover, but he was unable to perform military

9. Granger to "Dear Wife," May 16, 1863, in CWMC, USAMHI; Fox to "My Dear Father and Mother," May 9, 1863, in Fox Collection, HSP.

duty for nearly a year after his wounding. He joined the Veteran Reserve Corps in April, 1864, and also served aboard the hospital steamer *Connecticut* before rejoining his regiment that October.[10]

Much of the news that was relayed home after the battle was only hearsay that later proved inaccurate. Corporal William F. (Willie) Williams wrote to his brother Edward soon after the fight mentioning that he heard that Captain Elliot was then in the division hospital with a severe wound to the groin. In fact, the captain had been killed, and his body left on the field. It was later learned that a sympathetic Confederate soldier had come across the wounded officer and subsequently gave the captain's watch and memorandum book to a woman who forwarded them to Elliot's wife. Willie Williams also wrote that one of the oldest enlisted men in the regiment, forty-four-year-old Private George Carel, a Philadelphia innkeeper, had been captured and paroled: "Old Carls" had received a bad wound in the "ancle and got the Eraciples in it." This information was true. Carel recovered and was discharged with his regiment two years later. He was, however, the source of an incorrect story. He claimed to have seen Owen Daily, of their company, lying face down in a puddle of water. If he had been thus prone, Daily was only faking, for the thirty-six-year-old Irish-born laborer returned to the regiment and was later promoted to corporal. Carel did speak accurately about twenty-one-year-old Private David G. Hutchinson, a farmer from Philadelphia, who was said to have been buried by the Rebels. Hutchinson had been wounded during the fighting and lost the forefinger of his right hand. "He got his turban and tied it up and tried to fight but could not pull the trigger so he went to the rear," wrote Willie Williams. That wound, or another received afterward, proved fatal.[11]

Another prominent topic of discussion among the men was the conduct of the officers of the regiment. Some of them, like Major Chandler and Captain Elliot, had died swift, heroic deaths; many had received less serious wounds that placed them out of commission for some time. Still others were accused of less than honorable behavior.

10. Murray to "Dear Uncle," May 18, 1863, and William A. Murray to "Dear Brother," June 1, 1863, both in Murray Collection, FSNMP.

11. William Williams to Edward Williams, n.d., in Sidebotham Collection. Erysipelas, also called "St. Anthony's fire," is a skin disease caused by a streptococcus infection and marked by spreading inflammation of the skin and subcutaneous tissue.

Lieutenant Edward Williams had been wounded seriously on the morning of May 3, when he sustained a bullet wound to the right knee. He was sent to Philadelphia, and Company K was left without an officer. There was little of the company left to command: Willie Williams claimed that they were able to muster only a six-man front when they fell into line. Nevertheless, Second Lieutenant Augustus W. Fix of Company E was placed temporarily in command. Other companies were in similar straits. Captain Bowen, of Company B, had received a slight wound and was then absent. "[He] ain't thought much of. His courage is doubted by a good many," wrote Corporal Williams. "He left the field with a wound in the shoulder *strap*." Captain George J. Schwartz had been wounded too, but, to add insult to injury, he soon afterward received notice that he had been dismissed from the service. The order that dismissed him had been in effect for several weeks before it reached him. "Poor Jake," wrote Williams about Schwartz. "It is a real shame. He has been dismissed a month nearly and got wounded and all and was out of the service and did not know it."[12]

Corporal Williams also felt sympathy for Company A's Captain Barthoulot, though for a much different reason. "Poor old Capt Bartholo. He is under arrest for cowardice. He run away . . . and never came to the regt until we crossed the river." The portly Frenchman finally succumbed to reality: he simply was not cut out to be a soldier. He was discharged on a surgeon's certificate the month following his arrest. First Lieutenant John S. Crawford, of Company I, also received poor reviews, though he had been serving on detached duty as part of General Graham's staff. "Lieut. Crawford the Gallant has been sent back to his company and he don't like it a bit. When the General wanted him he could not be found. He fell back to the River."[13]

The patriotic Given expressed similar contempt for the behavior of some officers of his own company, including his former tentmate on the scarred battleground: "We had a first Lieutenant by the name of George P. Anderson, but he left us after the battle saying he was struck in the foot with a shell. He never came back. We had a 2nd Lieut by the name of Alfred Steele who was reported wounded but never came back. This left our company without officers." The absence of Sergeant Major William M. Blanford, however, proved beneficial for Given. Blanford had been

12. *Ibid.*
13. *Ibid.*

sent to a hospital at Alexandria and was later discharged on a surgeon's certificate. Lieutenant Colonel Cavada was then in command of the regiment, and he ordered Given to act as sergeant major until Blanford's return. When Blanford was discharged, Given was promoted to that rank.[14]

On May 16, General Birney promulgated an order in which he thanked his division for their "achievements" during the battle. The division, he stated, had added to the reputation gained at battles from Williamsburg to Fredericksburg. He went on to list the names of 463 recipients of a new divisional decoration called the Kearny Cross, created in honor of former commander Major General Philip Kearny, who had been killed at Chantilly on September 1, 1862.[15]

The previous March, Birney had ordered his regimental commanders to submit to him the names of men to be considered for the award. The lists included only enlisted men from the regiments who had distinguished themselves in the battles in which the division had participated. Birney cautioned that the lists of candidates should be carefully prepared and scrutinized by the orderly sergeants, and company and regimental commanders were to ensure that "only brave and worthy soldiers" were considered. To be eligible, a soldier need not have performed a particular noticeable act—though many did—but needed only to have been present at all of the division's battles and performed his duties honorably.[16]

The medals were provided at General Birney's own expense. They were bronze Maltese crosses suspended from red ribbons that were sewn to two bronze bars at top and bottom. The words KEARNY CROSS appeared on the obverse, and BIRNEY'S DIVISION on the back. Twenty-five men were selected from the 114th, along with the regimental vivandiere, Mary Tepe, who had received a slight wound in the ankle at Fredericksburg.[17]

On May 27, the entire division was paraded at 3 P.M. for the presentation of the awards. As each recipient stepped forward to receive the medal, it was pinned to the left breast above the red patch of the Third Corps. In addition, each was given a copy of Birney's order, which closed with this admonition: "This cross is in honor of our old leader and the

14. Given Diary, n.d., in Given Collection, CWLM.

15. *OR*, Vol. LI, Pt. 1, pp. 1275–83.

16. Stanley S. Phillips, *Civil War Corps Badges and Other Related Awards, Badges, Medals of the Period* (Lanham, Md., 1982), 121–22.

17. *Ibid*. See Appendix herein for a listing of the Kearny Cross recipients.

wearers of it will always remember his high standard of a true and brave soldier and will never disgrace it."[18]

This statement revealed the hope of the divisional commander that the medal ceremony and awards would build the morale and confidence of the men; however, not everyone reacted in quite the same spirit. Though the men who had not been awarded the medal were generally pleased to see others from their regiment receive the recognition, those who wore the new cross felt a little embarrassed by the whole presentation. Many believed that the award cast "a reflection upon the men who stood shoulder to shoulder with them, and [were] worthy of the same mark of heroism." Many recipients never wore their medals again. Even "French Mary" declined to don her award, remarking that "General Birney could keep it, as she did not want the present."[19]

Another member of the 114th besides its recipients of the Kearny Cross was both happy and proud on that day. A week earlier, on May 20, President Lincoln had remitted the sentence imposed on Lieutenant Colonel Cavada, and he had undoubtedly received the good news by then. The results of his court-martial had been forwarded to Washington sometime around February 18, after General Hooker had reviewed and endorsed them. Hooker made the recommendation "that from the circumstances of the case . . . and the good character proven by Lt Col. Cavada, the sentence be remitted."

The president might also have taken into account a letter from Cavada, in which he wrote of his predicament. The anxious officer explained, "On the day of the battle of Fredericksburg, I, being Brigade Officer of the Day, made an urgent request to be allowed to go into the fight with my Regiment. This request was finally granted, but I was at the same time to be held responsible that my Guard did its duty: through my overzeal to discharge both these duties at once, I exposed myself to fail in either." Cavada also pointed out that, as a Cuban, he had forsaken his slaveholding family and enlisted "in this cause" because he believed "it to be the cause of all

18. *Ibid.*

19. Rauscher, *Music on the March,* 68. Mary Tepe was known to have worn the Kearny Cross on at least one occasion. An undated photograph shows the famous vivandiere in full uniform, replete with wooden brandy keg, pistol, and Kearny Cross; see Lawrence G. Bixley, "Gettysburg Mystery Photo: A 2nd Look," *Military Images,* IV (July–August, 1982), 25.

humanity." His countrymen in the southern army, he continued, had sacrificed "the broad principle of humanity to a narrow and pitiful geographic necessity," and he had "been pointed at by them for sustaining Northern principles. I was proud of their scorn, but I never dreamed of a disgrace to which their jeers must give an added keenness." He begged to be "tried by the only Court-Martial which is infallible: the field of battle. Let me be assigned . . . to the post of danger, where I have always tried to be, and I will prove by my conduct that I speak the truth."[20]

Though he thought that he had rebutted all of the points raised against him at his trial, Cavada still feared that the result would be adverse to him. "I defended myself," he wrote to the president, also admitting that "I am no lawyer, and may have made a lame defense." Whether Cavada's heartfelt entreaty had any influence on the president's decision is not known. The commander in chief simply endorsed the proceedings with the words "Sentence Remitted," and affixed his signature to them. In all likelihood, Lincoln would have done the same merely on the strength of Hooker's recommendation. In any event, the ordeal was ended: Cavada was restored to full duty.[21]

His colonel, however, now found himself in similar straits. Collis' difficulty ostensibly stemmed from his behavior on the battlefield on May 3, but there were other complications. On May 6, still feeling the effects of the onset of typhoid fever, Collis filed his official report of the engagement of May 2–3. The detailed account ran seven handwritten pages. He bluntly criticized the conduct of the campaign, and particularly condemned the seemingly senseless deployment and handling of his regiment. He wrote: "During this march I constantly received orders from staff officers of the most conflicting character ; one minute ordered to move forward, the next by a flank to the right, and the next to fall back; once ordered to form a line diagonally to the Regiment in front, when the order intended was parallel to the line. I was also pained to see a lack of unity of action amongst the different members of the staff of the Brigadier." Collis went on to describe the participation of his regiment in the fighting of May 3, but—perhaps in an earnest effort to point out to General Graham the deficiencies he perceived on the part of the general's staff—he emphasized

20. Federico Cavada to "His Excellency, the President of the United States," n.d., Cavada Court-Martial Proceedings, in Court-Martial Records, Record Group 153, NARA.
21. *Ibid.*

that staff's "lack of unity of action." He even went so far as to name Captain Fitzhugh Birney, General Birney's younger brother, as the one who rode up to him and told him that "it was no use we were outflanked." In essence, he was blaming Birney for panicking his regiment and causing the disorderly retreat on the morning of May 3. Later in his report, Collis detailed another instance of confusing leadership. While obeying an order by General Sickles to come to the support of a battery near the Chancellor House, "[I] was ordered away by a Staff Officer whom I presumed was properly authorized, I having received orders from staff officers all day." Always the politician, however, Collis chose to end his report by "pledging the thanks of myself and Regiment to Gen. Graham for the coolness and bravery he displayed upon this trying occasion." He also complimented Captain Birney on his "cool courage."[22]

Collis' report was written in such a way as to deflect criticism from himself and his regiment. Like most reports written by officers during the war, it emphasized the regiment's good performance and provided justification for any behavior that might be construed as inadequate. Yet Collis went a step further. In pointing out the deficiencies of General Graham's staff, Collis was indirectly implying that Graham himself was somehow accountable for the confused direction of the brigade, since it was Graham who was ultimately responsible for the actions of his staff officers. Though he was youthful, it is difficult to fully attribute Collis' actions to naiveté or inexperience. After all, he had been in the army for nearly two years. During that time he had intimate contact with General Banks and others, from whom he must have learned something of the proper protocol used in military reports. It thus seems more likely that Collis was conscious of the impact his report would have. He may have thought that he was merely doing his duty in calling these problems to the attention of his superiors. On the other hand, he might have been preempting the backlash that he anticipated from his handling of his regiment on May 3. By blaming Captain Birney and by portraying the conduct of the battle as a muddled series of movements, Collis could make it seem as though his own less than superlative performance had resulted from confusion not entirely of his own creation.

In fact, Collis had an idea as early as May 4 or 5 that he was to be questioned about his actions. It was at that time that he received an in-

22. C. Collis to "Captain [Fitzhugh Birney]," May 6, 1863, in Read Papers, HSP.

quiry from General Sickles, through General Birney, "asking an explanation from Commanding Officers of the 1st Brigade, as to their conduct in
leaving their commands upon the field of battle." When the document
reached Collis, it had been endorsed at brigade headquarters "by a call for
an explanation of this 'disgraceful and *cowardly* conduct.'" Under the circumstances, Collis wasted no time in forwarding his contentious report of
the battle. He then set about answering the inquiry from General Sickles.[23]

Collis moved quickly to answer the accusation that his conduct in
leaving the field had been "disgraceful and *cowardly*." He began by col-
lecting documents and testimonials from those with knowledge of his behavior. The most influential pieces of evidence gathered by the colonel
were probably the statement from Assistant Surgeon David W. Bartine
and the affidavits from Privates Henry C. Kelly and John Hocker, the
stretcher-bearers who had carried him from the field.

Bartine wrote that he had examined Collis "about daylight" on Monday, May 4, and found him to be "really unfit for duty. He was vomiting
and unable to retain anything in his stomach. There was every symptom
of an overtaxed nervous system, resulting in complete prostration of all
vitality." Despite the colonel's enfeebled condition, Bartine further wrote
that Collis "was anxious to leave early and rejoin his Regiment." The
surgeon advised him to rest longer, and Collis stayed at the hospital until
about 8 A.M. Bartine then accompanied him back to their regiment, "the
Col. being compelled to rest upon me."[24]

Privates Kelly and Hocker, of Company D, signed a sworn statement
on May 7, telling of Collis' condition on the third. Kelly told of being
detailed by Lieutenant Colonel Cavada to carry Collis to the rear at about
5 P.M.

> He was insensible & flighty. Several persons spoke to the Col, but he did
> not recognize them. Once a couple of guns were fired and the Col. rose up
> to a sitting position and said "up and at them boys; they are on to us." The
> regiment was then a mile and a half distant. I told the Col. the regiment
> was not there, and he insisted upon being carried back to it but we would
> not take him. We left him at the Hospital near the river at half past one
> on Monday Morning.[25]

23. C. Collis to "Major [Henry W. Brevoort]," May 13, 1863, Collis Court-Martial
Proceedings, in Court-Martial Records, Record Group 153, NARA.
24. Exhibit 7, letter from David W. Bartine, May 7, 1863, *ibid.*
25. Exhibit 7, statement of Henry C. Kelly and John Hocker, May 7, 1863, *ibid.*

In addition to gathering the evidence of his medical condition in support of his reason for leaving the field, Collis also obtained a letter from
Lieutenant Colonel Calvin A. Craig, of the 105th Pennsylvania, that testified to his behavior on the battlefield. Craig wrote that he saw and spoke
with Collis on several occasions on May 3. Most notably, Craig recalled
an exchange after their regiments had driven the Rebels from the breastworks that they had charged; and later, he depicted Collis "*with the colors
in your hand rallying your men,*" after they themselves had been driven back
from those breastworks. Craig concluded with the statement that he had
no knowledge that Collis went to the rear. "If you did," he reassured Collis,
"it certainly was not during the engagement."[26]

From his fellow officers in the 114th, Collis secured a copy of a set of
resolutions purported to have been adopted on the battlefield on May 4.
Signed by Lieutenant Colonel Cavada and thirteen of the remaining Zouave officers, the document praised the "gallantry and enthusiasm of the
men," which was "attributable to the spirit of confidence and invincibility
infused into them by our brave young Colonel." The resolutions went on
to acknowledge that the officers and men owed to Collis "a debt of sincere
gratitude . . . for his undaunted courage, intrepid bravery, untiring zeal,
and unflinching determination to win for our Regiment an imperishable
name." They also praised him for remaining with them on the field while
being "entitled to be carried to the rear." The flowery statement ended
with a renewal of "our pledges of fidelity to our gallant Colonel," and a
declaration of their willingness to "follow him at any moment against the
enemies of our Country, and we pray to God his life may long be spared
to add fresh laurels to his own name and to the name of the Regiment he
so ably commands."[27]

Apparently, neither General Graham nor General Birney found Collis'
excuses to be satisfactory. In contrast, they deemed that Colonel Andrew
H. Tippen, of the 68th Pennsylvania, who also had been asked to explain
why he left the field, had sufficient reason to do so. Tippen claimed that
he had lost his horse and had been on foot for nearly two days. He turned
over command of his regiment to the major of the 68th, then went to the
rear to seek medical treatment. He claimed to have been "completely
prostrated." No action was taken against Tippen, but Collis was promptly

26. Exhibit 7, Craig to "Dear Col.," May 7, 1863, *ibid.*
27. Exhibit 7, testimonial to Collis, May 4, 1863, *ibid.*

placed under arrest. When General Birney filed his official report three
days later, on May 9, he made sure to mention that Tippen's excuse was
"well supported" but that Collis' was not. He further added that Collis was
then under arrest, and intimated that General Graham had found the
colonel's performance lacking.[28]

General Graham filed his report of the campaign on May 10. In it, he
made no mention of Collis' leaving the field. He simply stated that the
114th had been ordered to move to the right to aid the hard-pressed 141st
Pennsylvania, but that they had fired only one volley before they broke
and fell back. "This and the increasing numbers of the enemy necessitated
the retiring of the whole line," he wrote. Graham seems to have made a
particular point of minimizing the role of the 114th in the battle. He
specifically mentioned that during the initial advance on the morning of
the third, he ordered the 114th to lie down, as the 27th Indiana had filled
their place in the brigade line. In addition, all of his regimental commanders merited some mention and praise in his report, with the exception of Collis and Tippen. While he naturally praised the efforts of his
staff, he conspicuously mentioned Captain Birney, noting the "rapidity of
his movements and the coolness and self-possession of his conduct."[29]

In addition to indulging in injudicious finger pointing in his report,
Collis forwarded an impertinent letter through the chain of command in
response to Birney's inquiry. There he objected to the accusations leveled
against him: "In answer to Special Order No 100 . . . calling upon me to
explain my conduct in leaving my command on the field of battle and
reporting to the hospital as unfit for duty, I have the honor to report that
I did neither the one nor the other and I feel indignant at being called
upon to explain a course of conduct which thank God is endorsed by every
officer and man of my Regiment and every officer of my Brigade." Thinking, perhaps, that his best defense against his accusers would be a strong
offense, Collis continued with an aggrieved attack: "Trifling and insignificant as the imputation in Special Order No 100 is to do harm to the
reputation of an officer who has devoted his untiring exertions and his life
for the Common Cause, its spirit is nevertheless calculated to weaken the
confidence in which an inferior should hold his superiors." As if the foregoing insubordination was not bad enough, Collis closed his letter by

28. OR, Vol. XXV, Pt. 1, pp. 410, 420.
29. *Ibid.*, 414–16.

stating that he would "permit *no man living* to accuse [him] of a want of courage or devotion to the Cause, whenever and wherever called upon." Although the irate tone of his statement obviously was designed as an emphatic rebuttal to the implication of the inquiry, it served to inflame again the anger of those to whom it was addressed. The letter constituted another reason for his superiors' finding his excuses unsatisfactory.[30]

Within days, however, the colonel began to have second thoughts about his method of responding to the question of his leaving the field. On May 13, he wrote Major Henry W. Brevoort, acting adjutant general of his division, stating that he had seen the endorsement returned with Colonel Tippen's excuse and was thereby "convinced . . . that Special Order No 100 . . . was not intended to impeach [his] character for courage." He, therefore, "respectfully" asked "permission to withdraw [his] communication of the 7th inst, with the exception of the two affidavits and medical certificate." He went on to disclaim any intention to seem disrespectful to General Birney. "If my language was harsh, it was intended to rebuke the unknown slanderer whom I believed had poisoned the ear of my Commanding Officer." Collis closed this letter with the hope that his explanation of his recent conduct, which had been based upon the belief that his honor and courage had been indicted, would satisfy the general's inquiry, and "that no further steps may be taken in the matter."[31]

By May 15, Collis had received an answer to his request that his previous communication be withdrawn. Birney intended by then to see Collis court-martialed; thus, the papers that the colonel sent to him would constitute part of the evidence in the proceedings. Birney therefore declined to return the document and endorsed Collis' request with the statement that the colonel would learn by further experience "that such communications cannot be sent with impunity thro official channels, or withdrawn at pleasure."[32]

Meanwhile, Collis had received a letter from Captain Birney, who voiced his displeasure at being named in Collis' report as the one who exclaimed that the men had been flanked. "The idea it conveys," he wrote, "is that owing to my telling you 'it was no use, we were outflanked' your

30. Charges and Specifications, May 26, 1863, Collis Court-Martial Proceedings, in Court-Martial Records, Record Group 153, NARA.
31. Collis to "Major," May 13, 1863, *ibid.*
32. *Ibid.*

Regiment ceased rallying and began falling back." Birney then wrote that, according to his recollection of the affair, Collis, at one point, came up to him as he was riding along the line "urging the men to stand fast," and "said as nearly as I can remember, 'There is no use do you not see that they are flanking us.' to which I replied 'You are right now; they have flanked us.'" He further recalled that the Zouaves, along with the rest of the brigade, were not rallying at that time, but were falling back. Birney asked Collis to strike out that portion of his report, or alter it, so that it "cast no imputation on me. Why the matter should be mentioned at all, I cannot see," he wrote, "inasmuch as the whole line was falling back."[33]

Collis received Birney's letter on the afternoon of May 16. He sat down immediately to pen his response. "I do not recognize anything which casts an imputation upon you," he asserted, "nor did I insert it with any such intention. (If what you said was true & it was your duty to communicate it to me.)" He went on to praise Birney's attributes as a soldier, but still contended that his own recollection was correct. He could not, he stated, "especially under existing circumstances" remove the comment from his report, but he gladly agreed to "shape it in such a manner that no possible injustice can be done to yourself." Specifically, Collis affirmed that it was necessary for his statement to remain as part of his defense. He reminded Birney that he had submitted his report on the day before charges were filed against him. In essence, he believed, his report had preempted the charges that it was he who had "alarmed" his command by telling his officers that it was no use holding their ground, because the brigade had been flanked. He called it a "fortunate coincidence" that he had "*officially reported what* was said and who said it, before I dreamed of having it laid at *my* doors."[34]

Collis again praised the captain by stating that he would gladly aid him if he thought that his character needed support. He then returned to the attack: "My feelings towards you are well known throughout the Brigade. I did believe those feelings were reciprocated but was surprised to find that a whispered, confidential, communication that 'my little handful of men were so dispirited from their heavy loss that I was glad we had not to

33. Birney to "Colonel C. H. T. Collis," May 14, 1863, Collis Court-Martial Proceedings, in Court-Martial Records, Record Group 153, NARA.

34. Collis to "Captain," May 16, 1863, *ibid.*

march again to the woods' or words similar should have been made the subject of a charge. I thank you however for doing me the credit to embody in it that I said 'I would do all man *could* do.' This was kind indeed." Collis made it clear that he knew who his friends were, and that many of them were willing to come forth to testify in his behalf. He evinced little fear of the outcome of his prospective trial. "My present position cuts me to the heart," he told Captain Birney. "But the time will come when I shall sit in the scale of Justice and my accusers will kick the beam."[35]

Though Collis already knew of Generals Birney and Graham's intention to follow through with court-martial proceedings, he received official confirmation of that fact on May 17 in a notice forwarded through Captain Birney. "I am directed by Genl. Graham to say that since you have refused to withdraw or modify your report, he will forward it, calling Genl. Birney's attention to the misstatements you have made. At the same time he desires me to acquaint you with his determination to prefer charges against you for the romance, with which it abounds, and more serious shortcomings."[36]

In the meantime, Collis had been writing to his friend Judge Read, seeking advice and assistance on the matter. The politically powerful Read advised his young colleague to write immediately to the influential Republican senator Charles Sumner, perhaps in hopes that Sumner could exert some pressure on Birney or his superiors to have the matter dropped. Read also counseled Collis to "remain perfectly cool and say nothing to [his] superiors." Judge Read may have thought the incident was not so serious as was portrayed by Collis, but the colonel responded that "There is little doubt that B—— is terribly in earnest. His influence over all who look to him for aid, is immense. Gen. Graham who spoke kindly of me to every one seems to have chopped around."[37]

Collis informed the judge that Graham had asked him to alter his official report, and he again referred to his belief that he was fortunate that his report had been forwarded prior to any charges being lodged against him. How could he now withdraw it, he asked, when the very staff officers accused in his report of exhibiting a "lack of unity of action" were now

35. *Ibid.*
36. Birney to "Colonel C. H. T. Collis," May 17, 1863, in Read Papers, HSP.
37. C. Collis to "My dear Judge," May 18, 1863, *ibid.*

witnesses against him? In addition, he was accused of using the words that he would "prove by a host of witnesses came from Capt. Birney himself."[38]

Collis also complained to Read that Birney was unduly restricting his movements. He had denied Collis permission to leave camp to visit those of his Zouaves still at the division hospital, only one-half mile from his own tent. And when Collis had asked for ten hours' leave to consult with his counsel, Lieutenant Joseph G. Rosengarten—a Philadelphia attorney then serving on the staff of Major General John Fulton Reynolds of the First Corps—Birney allowed him only five hours to make the twelve-mile round trip. The colonel was successful, however, in obtaining forty-eight hours' leave for his father, who would return to Philadelphia with correspondence for Read and consult with the judge about the proper course of action. William Collis also appeared to place great stock in the judge's abilities and influence. Charles wrote of his father, "Throughout this whole affair his advice to me has been 'Act precisely as though Judge Read was at your elbow.'"[39]

Collis had not long to wait, however, before the issue was to be decided. On May 22, he again wrote Judge Read, informing him that he had received notice from the judge advocate that evening—"(who came to me to night blind drunk)"—to appear for his trial at 10 A.M. the following morning. His first action, though, would be to ask for an adjournment for one week so that he could consult with his counsel, prepare his evidence, and ensure that witnesses for his defense would be able to appear on his behalf. He further informed Read that, although he had not received a copy of the detail for the court-martial, he had ascertained its members to consist of the following officers, all of whom were Birney's supporters:

> Genl. J. H. Hobart Ward, great friend of B. is a New York sporting character—very brave—but influenced entirely by B.
> Col. [Samuel B.] Hayman—[37th NY]—strongly backed by B. for promotion but I think a most truthful honorable man.
> Col. [Byron R.] Pierce—3rd Michigan—a perfect tool of B. such is his well known reputation.
> Col. [Thomas W.] Egan—40 NY Vols.—the prosecutor—a professional gambler & a drunkard—expects to get promoted on B's recommendation.

38. *Ibid.*
39. *Ibid.*

Lt. Col. [Edwin] Burt[—]3 Me Vol—I think an honorable man *is chief of B's staff.*

Col. Asher L. Leidy 99PV was a druggist at 9 & Filbert—has figured extensively in Police Gazette.

Major Taylor—[20th Indiana]—Judge Advocate—rather fond of whiskey—is in Ward's Brigade & Ward will no doubt brow beat him.

In addition to planning to request an adjournment to consult with his attorney, Collis also had a few other delaying tactics in mind. As an attorney, Collis planned to take a weighty role in conducting his defense. "Telegraph me if you think I am right," he wrote to Judge Read. "You can rely on my being able—I don't think I shall have a fool for a client."[40]

The general court-martial convened the following day at the headquarters of the Second Brigade, First Division, Third Corps. All of those appointed were present with the exception of Colonel Leidy, who had sent a statement to the court that he was sick and unable to attend. This absence ultimately worked to Collis' advantage. First, when he was asked whether he objected to any member of the court, he replied that he objected to Colonel Egan "on the ground that he had signed the charges against him." The court cleared for deliberation, after which it sustained Collis' objection. Next, Collis objected to Colonel Peter Sides "on the ground that he is on the list of witnesses for the prosecution." Again he was sustained. As a result of the three-member absence, there was no longer a quorum present, and the court was unable to proceed. It was adjourned until May 26.[41]

Collis wrote to Read soon afterward, informing him of the first day's proceedings. "I have got rid of two ugly customers," he told the judge. "Fortune seems to favor me." He also told Read that volunteer witnesses in his behalf were streaming forth to offer their services. He claimed that Generals Meade, Stoneman, Robinson, Geary, and Alpheus S. Williams were among those willing to testify. "I do not like to boast," he wrote. "But I think the result of this trial will be to give me an excellent reputation."[42]

40. C. Collis to Read, May 22, 1863, in Read Papers, HSP.

41. Collis Court-Martial Proceedings, May 23, 1863, in Court-Martial Records, Record Group 153, NARA.

42. C. Collis to Read, May 25, 1863, in Read Papers, HSP.

The members of the court reassembled on the twenty-sixth with three replacements: Colonel Philip Regis Denis de Keredern de Trobriand of the 38th New York, Colonel Elijah Walker of the 4th Maine, and Colonel Moses B. Lakeman of the 3rd Maine. When asked again whether he had any objection to the members of the court, he answered that he did not. In support of this decision, Collis later wrote to Read that he had confidence in all three of the new men.[43]

Once the court was duly sworn, Collis introduced his counsel and requested a copy of the order convening the court-martial, along with a list of the detail for the court. He then asked for an adjournment so that he could consult with Lieutenant Rosengarten. The court opined that Collis' want of the specified documents was insufficient cause for an adjournment. He then asked the court to decide on the question of whether he was entitled to have the court appointed by his corps commander, General Sickles. He contended that as Birney had ordered the court-martial, he could not appoint the members of the court. In addition, Collis stated that if he wished to call General Birney as a witness for the defense, he would be unable to do so, "as he is already a party to [the] proceedings" of the court. The officers of the court again deliberated for some time before overruling Collis on these points.[44]

Collis was then arraigned. The first charge against him was "misbehavior before the enemy." It was alleged that he left his command and went to the rear while his regiment was under fire, and that he screened himself from danger by hiding behind a tree. The second charge was "conduct prejudicial to good order and military discipline." Here Collis was accused of alarming his men by calling out that they were outflanked, failing to exert himself in rallying his men, and stating to Captain Birney that he "could not promise to lead his men under fire, that he would do all man could do, but doubted his ability to make them follow." In addition, he was accused of returning to his superiors an "insulting communication" when called upon to explain his behavior. The final charge against him was "disobedience of orders." Under this heading, the colonel was accused of mishandling his men when ordered to make an oblique change of front.

43. C. Collis to "My Dear Judge," May 26, 1863, *ibid.*

44. Collis Court-Martial Proceedings, May 26, 1863, in Court-Martial Records, Record Group 153, NARA.

His error, it was alleged, had thrown the brigade into temporary confusion. Finally, it was said that Collis again failed "to use the proper exertions" in rallying his men and forming his line between the 57th and 63rd Pennsylvania.[45]

Although he was overruled on his objection concerning General Birney's ability to convene the court-martial, Collis refused to enter a plea at this time. By not doing so, he thought that he would avoid admitting "that the court was of competent jurisdiction." The court then entered the plea of not guilty on Collis' behalf and called General Graham as the first witness for the prosecution.[46]

After some preliminary questioning, Graham was asked directly what he knew about Collis' leaving the field while under fire on May 3. His response was that he knew "nothing of [his] own knowledge" about it. Concerning Collis' behavior on May 3, Graham stated that he "thought his conduct unequal. He appeared to be thoroughly himself, at another time confused, at another time almost prostrate." Graham also testified that at one point, when issued an order for an oblique change of front, Collis appeared confused. "I think a portion of his Regiment changed front forward on left company and a portion changed front to rear on right company." Soon afterward, Graham testified, he left orders with his staff officers for them to inform his regiments in the rear to form in double column and advance. Graham rode forward with the 105th Pennsylvania, and stated that he turned and saw the 114th forming double column but not advancing. He had to send another staff officer with a message to speed up the movement.[47]

Later, Graham testified, after the brigade had driven the enemy from their breastworks, he observed Collis "covering himself by a tree." Graham rode up and spoke to the colonel. "He told me that he had been very unwell that morning suffering from an attack of virtago [*sic*] and scarcely felt able to perform his duty." Not long after, Graham observed Collis again at the head of his regiment. He had captured one or two Confederate officers and had their swords in his possession. Finally, when the brigade had fallen back to the Chancellor House, Collis asked Graham whether

45. Charges and Specifications, May 26, 1863, *ibid.*

46. C. Collis to "My Dear Judge," May 26, 1863, in Read Papers, HSP.

47. Testimony of Brigadier General Charles K. Graham, May 26, 1863, Collis Court-Martial Proceedings, in Court-Martial Records, Record Group 153, NARA.

he had any objection to his sitting down in the rear of the house. Graham assented, stating that Collis "appeared to be very much exhausted and greatly affected by the loss of Major Chandler and the other galant [*sic*] officers and men that he had lost." Graham admitted that the colonel was "evidently not himself," for upon asking for the time of day, Collis expressed surprise that it was about 11 A.M. He thought it was about 5 P.M. Again Collis complained about suffering severely from vertigo, and hoped that Graham had no ill feelings because of his lack of energy. Graham stated that later that afternoon, Collis asked if the general had any objection to his going to the rear and leaving his regiment under the command of Lieutenant Colonel Cavada. Graham testified that he had not had an objection to that. "I took it that we had retired from the engagement," he said. Under cross-examination, Graham clarified that Collis had been behind the tree on the battlefield for fifteen or twenty minutes, and that the tree was within twenty-five or thirty feet of the center of the regiment, which was then protected by an abatis of felled logs. The trial was then adjourned until the following day.[48]

On May 27, the prosecution began by calling Captain Birney as its next witness. Birney's testimony corresponded fairly closely to that of Graham. However, Birney interjected his belief that Collis had not made sufficient effort to rally his men after they fell back from the breastwork. While the other regiments quickly took up their assigned positions, he stated, "considerable confusion" persisted in the 114th. He claimed that he rode up to the color guard and ordered the Zouaves to "halt and face about, which they did." After that, he said, Collis "manifested more desire to rally his men." When the brigade was attacked a second time, recalled Birney, Collis came up to him and said: "What is the use of staying here, do you not see that they have outflanked us?" At that time, the brigade began to fall back. Birney testified that he found Collis' actions on May 3 to be "very strange, such as to lead me to suppose that he was either worn out by fatigue or frightened." While they were retreating, said Birney, Collis told him that he could not promise to lead his men into the fight again.[49] The court then adjourned until the following day.

But on May 28, Collis produced a note from his regimental surgeon

48. *Ibid.*

49. Testimony of Captain Birney, May 27, 1863, Collis Court-Martial Proceedings, in Court-Martial Records, Record Group 153, NARA.

requesting an additional day's adjournment due to ill health. During the preceding days of the trial, the colonel had been plagued by "violent headaches." On May 26, he had written to Read that he was "much fatigued & not in good health by any means." The exertion required of him for his defense would soon overcome him completely, though his protestation of illness on May 28 may have been a ploy that provided him with a valid excuse for delaying the trial until May 29. On that date, Collis introduced Samuel C. Perkins, Esquire, of Philadelphia. While Judge Read may have had confidence in his young friend's abilities as a lawyer, he took no chances. Read had dispatched Perkins to assist Lieutenant Rosengarten in conducting Collis' defense.[50]

The trial continued for several more days. Lieutenant Colonel Cavada appeared in order to testify that Collis left him in command of the regiment on the afternoon of May 3. Later, reported Cavada, Collis was brought to him supported by a man on either side. "He appeared very much exhausted," recalled Cavada. "He was very pale and spoke incoherently, as though he was not in his right mind." Cavada ordered the colonel carried to the rear on a stretcher. Then Colonel Peter Sides of the 57th Pennsylvania appeared and testified that he also thought he heard Collis remark that the brigade was flanked. He admitted that he did not see Collis but thought that he recognized the latter's voice. Sides ended the testimony for the prosecution.[51]

In his defense, Collis first called Colonel Tippen of the 68th Pennsylvania. Tippen stated that on May 3, he "saw nothing that could detract from [Collis'] character as a brave officer." Tippen also addressed the confusion caused in the brigade when the 114th failed to carry out the oblique change of front promptly. He testified that he supposed that "the Captain of Companies had mistaken the order," but that the movement "did not confuse [him] in the least."[52]

Collis then called two officers of the 105th Pennsylvania, Lieutenant Colonel Calvin A. Craig and Major Jacob W. Greenawalt. Each attested to Collis' good behavior in rallying his regiment. Craig stated that he

50. Collis to "My Dear Judge," May 25, 26, 1863, in Read Papers, HSP.

51. Testimony of Lieutenant Colonel Federico F. Cavada, May 30, 1863, Collis Court-Martial Proceedings, in Court-Martial Records, Record Group 153, NARA; Testimony of Colonel Peter Sides, May 30, 1863, *ibid.*

52. Testimony of Colonel Andrew H. Tippen, May 30, 1863, *ibid.*

observed Collis take his colors and call out to his men to gather around it. "His regiment was kept in good order until we commenced to retire," he told the court. "At that time there was a good deal of confusion in all the Regts of the Brigade." Craig also stated that he thought Collis' bearing to be "soldierly. I heard him encourage his men frequently, he used every effort I think to encourage them." Major Greenawalt also testified to being similarly impressed. "He appeared to be cool, steady, and brave all the time that I saw him under fire," he said.[53]

On the following day, Collis called as a witness Captain E. Forrest Koehler of Company C. The captain testified to Collis' exertions in leading the Zouaves on May 3, and told of the colonel's taking the colors and ordering the men to rally. He further stated that he heard Captain Birney ride up and call out that they were outflanked. "I was right along side of Col. Collis at the time," he said. "[The] Colonel then ordered us to fall back." After the regiment fell back to the rear of the Chancellor House on the morning of the third, continued Captain Koehler, Collis asked how many men were left. When the captain found out and reported the number to Collis, he replied: "Well, we have got enough to give them another turn anyhow." Koehler closed his testimony by saying that Collis had been on foot since April 30 as a result of his horse's being lame, and "was very much exhausted." When asked under questioning whether Collis could have been behind a tree for fifteen or twenty minutes without his knowing it, Koehler replied that he could not have. The regiment was at the breastworks for only about twenty-five minutes, recalled the captain, and for most of that time, he was with Collis, "walking and talking to him." Finally, he stated, he saw Collis having a conversation with General Graham, "who was also in the rear"; immediately after that exchange, Collis ordered the movement by the right flank to support the 141st.[54]

Collis then called Captains Edward R. Bowen and Henry M. Eddy of the 114th. Both gave testimony similarly relating the untiring efforts of Colonel Collis to rally his men on May 3. Captain Eddy, however, testified that he did see his colonel "lying at the foot of a tree, completely worn out by fatigue." This rest occurred not at the time that the regiment was advanced to the breastworks, though; it was at about 1 P.M., when the

---

53. Testimony of Lieutenant Colonel Calvin A. Craig and Major Jacob W. Greenawalt, May 30, 1863, *ibid.*

54. Testimony of Captain E. Forrest Koehler, June 1, 1863, *ibid.*

Zouaves were ordered to move from their location behind the Chancellor House to a position farther to the rear. Thus far, the witnesses for the defense had refuted every serious allegation concerning Collis' behavior.[55]

The next several witnesses called by the defense on June 1 testified to Collis' character as an officer and to his past performance. The witnesses included his former brigade commander, John C. Robinson, and Brigadier General John W. Geary, then commanding the Second Division of the Twelfth Corps, who remembered Collis' service in the valley. A letter from General Meade telling of Collis' gallantry at Fredericksburg was also introduced.

During that last day of testimony, Collis had become so weak from his debilitating fever that he was unable to sit. Instead, he was forced to lie all day on a stretcher placed in the courtroom. Still, he was confident of the trial's result and hoped soon to be able to obtain a leave of absence for fifteen days to recruit for his regiment in Philadelphia. He would, in fact, be returning to the city: not to recruit, but to recover from the serious illness that was quickly overwhelming his body's defenses.

The trial concluded on June 1, and Perkins wrote to Judge Read the following day, informing him that the court-martial had ended. "The Judge Advocate," he related, "was kind enough to say to me this morning of his own accord that the Col. had made a very strong defense indeed." Later that day, the court returned a verdict of not guilty on all of the charges and specifications save three. One offense dealt with Collis' behavior in taking shelter behind a tree. Since it was admitted that he had done so, but not while the regiment was in its advanced position, the court had no choice but to find him guilty. Because of "the peculiar circumstances of the case," however, the court attached no criminality to the charge, and he was acquitted of the offense of "misbehavior before the enemy."[56]

Collis was also found guilty of the specification that related to his telling a member of Graham's staff that he could not promise to lead his men into action again. The colonel's debilitated condition, however, and the testimony concerning his physical condition on May 3, led the court again to attach no criminality to the offense.

55. Testimony of Captain Henry M. Eddy, June 1, 1863, *ibid.*

56. Samuel C. Perkins to Read, June 2, 1863, in Read Papers, HSP; Verdict, June 2, 1863, Collis Court-Martial Proceedings, in Court-Martial Records, Record Group 153, NARA.

The only offense for which he was penalized concerned the "insulting" May 7 letter that was sent to Generals Graham and Birney, in which Collis explained his actions on the third. The court refused to allow into evidence his subsequent letter of May 13, which had sought to withdraw the communication. For the letter of May 7, the court sentenced the colonel to be reprimanded in general orders by the division commander. The court was then adjourned.

The proceedings of the trial were forwarded to General Birney for approval and administration of the sentence. Birney, however, declined to implement the censure. "In consideration of the previous good conduct of this officer" (to which several of his fellow generals had testified during the trial), "and of his youth, the sentence is remitted and Colonel C. H. T. Collis will resume his sword."[57]

Collis and his supporters considered the results to be a complete victory. The colonel's impertinent letter, they felt, indicated only a "lack of discretion." Some later believed the lapse to have been justified on the ground that "any soldier of spirit would have been prompted to do the same thing."[58] Soon, the event was apparently forgotten, but it would not remain so. Years later, Collis would be forced on several occasions to address the charges lodged against him that spring. The court-martial was an ordeal that would follow him for the rest of his life.

57. Endorsement of Major General David B. Birney, n.d., Collis Court-Martial Proceedings, in Court-Martial Records, Record Group 153, NARA.
58. Taylor to "My Dear Collis," March 4, 1891, in C. Collis, *1st Brigade,* 23.

9

Mr. Sherfy's Farmyard

When Colonel Collis' trial concluded, General Birney not only declined to carry out the recommended sentence, but he also permitted the colonel to return to Philadelphia on leave. Whether his stature in the army had been advanced as a result of his nearly complete vindication—as he thought might happen—is not known. Perhaps General Birney's seemingly cordial treatment of him resulted from a fear of political repercussions at the hands of the young colonel's powerful friends. Birney sent his personal ambulance for Collis' own use in traveling to the railroad depot. His men, however, insisted on carrying the colonel the distance on a stretcher. Coincidentally, when they arrived at Aquia Creek, where Collis was to board a ship bound for the capital, they were met by the regimental band. The musicians had just disembarked, and were en route to rejoin their comrades. On seeing the Zouave stretcher bearers, the band members called out to them. When they found that it was Collis who was being borne to the rear, they expressed their sadness at finding him in such condition, and no doubt pondered the other changes they would find after the campaigns of the preceding weeks.[1]

After seeing Collis safely situated on the northbound steamer, the band members marched off toward the Zouave camp near Potomac Creek. They found the place nearly deserted, as the regiment was then out on picket

1. C. Collis, *1st Brigade*, 7; Rauscher, *Music on the March*, 66.

duty; but they were greeted by Lieutenant Colonel Cavada, who had been left in command. Cavada informed the musicians that the men were expected back at camp at any time. The band members, however, decided to surprise their friends by marching out and lying in wait along their route. As the returning infantrymen approached the place on the road along which the band members were hiding, the musicians filed out in front of them and took the lead, "striking up a spirited piece, which was received with welcoming cheers by the battleworn men." It was a new tune, which an enthused drummer had named "Hell on the Rappahannock."[2]

The following morning, the Zouave musicians were rudely reminded of their return to the army when they were suddenly awakened by the buglers blowing reveille. Soldiers dozing in the chill morning air sometimes heard the call played in the distance by the corps bugler. The sound would reach its crescendo as it passed on to the division, brigade, and regimental buglers, until only the most weary of men could ignore its nearby strains. It would take some time for the recently returned bandsmen to adjust to the routine of camp life. Their army experiences of the last several months had been very different from those of the infantrymen.

After being captured at Fredericksburg on the morning of December 16, the Zouave bandsmen had been marched into the Rebel lines, where they encountered Brigadier General James J. Archer. The general instructed the Zouaves to lay down their instruments and fall in with the other prisoners. One of the bandsmen took the liberty of calling the general's attention to the fact that the instruments were not government property, but belonged to the musicians themselves. Archer refused to hear their plea, however, and the Zouaves marched off empty-handed. The men were then taken to General Jackson's headquarters, where they signed the parole papers by which they gave their promise not to bear arms against the Confederacy until properly exchanged. They would be bound by this oath until they were exchanged, man-for-man, for an equal number of Rebel enlisted men captured by the Union army. After signing their paroles, the men were sent to Libby Prison to await their exchange.[3]

The Zouaves waited for transportation to Richmond aboard the overtaxed southern rail system, and after several days they finally arrived in

2. Ibid., 67.
3. Ibid., 36–39.

the Confederate capital. One of the men recalled that they received a discourteous greeting. While marching to the prison, they were forced to endure the insults of the "rabble" and were "upbraided by others who profanely prefixed the word 'Yankees' as we approached them." Once there, the men were herded to the second floor of the brick tobacco warehouse that served as a prison. They found not a stick of furniture in the overcrowded facility, and at night were forced to lie down on the filthy floor like "boxed herring."[4]

As the Zouaves began to wonder at the delay in their exchange, their suffering increased. Smallpox and measles soon broke out in the prison, and each morning several lifeless bodies were carried out. The prisoners rapidly became infested with lice; and the rations of black bean soup twice each day, with a small piece of meat and bread every third meal, were barely enough to sustain men with hardy appetites. Fortunately, the Zouaves had not been relieved of their money. Several enterprising men had even sold some of their belongings to their captors, receiving payment in Confederate money. One sold a three-dollar rubberized blanket for twenty-five dollars, while a pair of half-worn shoes fetched six dollars. Most of the men thus had enough cash to supplement their meager fare with food sold by hucksters who came each morning to the prison windows.[5]

The Zouaves soon learned that the delay in the prisoner exchanges had resulted from a dispute over the exchange of African American soldiers fighting for the Union. With the enlistment of black men, who had been promised by their government the same protection and courtesies of warfare as those extended to white soldiers, the cartel reached an impasse. To many southerners, the black man in uniform embodied their greatest fear: slave revolt. It was precisely this fear that shaped the Confederate president's policy in dealing with captured soldiers of the United States Colored Troops. Captured blacks were to be turned over to state governments to be tried for insurrection.[6]

At first, the controversy put an end to all exchanges. Eventually, enlisted men were again freed, though officers were not. The issue would not be decided until later in the war; but for the Zouaves, the temporary res-

4. *Ibid.*, 41–42.

5. *Ibid.*, 42–43.

6. *Ibid.*, 45–46; Joseph T. Glatthaar, *Forged in Battle: The Civil War Alliance of Black Soldiers and White Officers* (New York, 1990), 201–204.

olution meant an opportunity for freedom. In January, 1863, after several days of rumors and dashed hopes, the musicians were finally released. "We really wept with joy on being removed from that horrible place," recalled one of them. Still, their return to their comrades would take nearly five more months.[7]

Rather than returning the band members home, the army sent them to Camp Parole, near Annapolis, Maryland. The army had adopted this practice of sending released prisoners to Camp Parole because experience had shown that many men were unwilling to report promptly back to duty when called. Therefore, no paroled prisoners were permitted to leave the camp on furlough. The bandsmen found the new accommodations to their liking; in addition, they seemed to appreciate the fact that there was "practically nothing to do," especially after their recent ordeal farther south. Soon, however, the band members petitioned the camp commander, Colonel George Sangster, for permission to return to Philadelphia to obtain new instruments. The colonel told them that there was nothing he could do for them, as there were to be no exceptions to the order against furloughs. He was apparently not a rear-echelon martinet, however, for he hinted to them that if they did not know how to get home, it was not his business to tell them.

Buoyed by the knowledge that the camp commander would not miss them should they suddenly disappear, the musicians embarked on a daring adventure designed to carry them to Philadelphia. They made it nearly as far as Baltimore before being captured by the provost guard and sent to Fort McHenry, "in comparison with which Libby Prison was a parlor," recalled a bitter Zouave. After twenty-four hours confined in the "despicable hole," the men were returned to Camp Parole. The Zouaves profited from their experience and quickly devised another means to get past the suspicious provost guards. They sent home for civilian clothing, and upon its arrival took the train to Philadelphia unmolested.[8]

After procuring new instruments and uniforms in Philadelphia, the band returned to Annapolis. They brazenly marched into the camp and past Colonel Sangster's quarters while playing a stimulating rendition of "John Brown." The band soon made itself immensely popular, not only

7. Rauscher, _Music on the March_, 46.
8. _Ibid._, 52–54.

with the officers and men at the camp, but with the citizens of Annapolis as well. Their popularity was enhanced by the fact that there were then no other bands in the town. In addition, the Zouaves flattered Sangster and other dignitaries with successive evening serenades that exposed their musical abilities to the local citizens. Eventually, Sangster found that the band had value as a military tool as well. He put them to work greeting the shiploads of paroled prisoners arriving at the city docks. The normally dispirited and straggling masses of men were charmed into formation, marching off smartly behind the rousing band. Colonel Sangster attempted to have the band permanently detailed to Camp Parole, but the request was denied. The musicians later claimed to be glad of this denial.[9]

By early May, after receiving news of the battle of Chancellorsville, the bandsmen also claimed to be anxious to return to their comrades. Their motivation was undoubtedly increased by the arrival at the camp of numerous paroled men of their own regiment. While the musicians were happy to renew old acquaintances, it must have been difficult for them to face the battle-scarred Zouaves who had gone into the thick of the fight once again while they themselves were contentedly tootling in Annapolis. Thus it was that the bandsmen found themselves again near the banks of the Rappahannock, which separated the two opposing armies.

The work of putting the Zouaves back in fighting trim commenced shortly after their return to camp from the brief but brutal foray south of the meandering river. Directing this work were the few remaining regimental officers; and in his new position as commanding officer of the 114th, Lieutenant Colonel Cavada proved to be both able and likable. Cavada took the men out to drill, and Corporal Willie Williams recalled that "everything went as well as you could wish. He explained everything and went smiling along the line and everyone took an interest in the Drill." Periods of regimental drill supervised by Cavada were less strenuous than those to which the Zouaves were accustomed. Williams wrote to his wounded brother Edward that Cavada permitted the men to rest after the practice of each movement, and even allowed them a half-hour respite during which they were able to stack arms and lie down. Even to seasoned marchers, the repetitious practice of drill, which often required moving at the

9. *Ibid.*, 55–56, 65.

double-quick, proved a tiring experience. The men were apparently pleased by the relaxed pace set by Cavada.[10]

Williams found several other reasons to admire his new commander. Cavada was probably making an effort to be personable, but the men apparently were not in the habit of being engaged in conversation by their field and staff officers. They must have found the attention unusual, or at least noteworthy. While Corporal Williams was on guard duty, for instance, Cavada came to him and told him to allow several of the men on the detail to go over to the hospital to burn the rubbish that had accumulated there. "Then he stood talking to us and telling us the reason sickness got into the camps." He then went down to the hospital himself and distributed lemons to those who were sick. "He is a nice man," wrote Williams. "They say a new broom sweeps clean. If he only keeps on he will be the best man ever lived."[11]

The recovery of the Zouaves from their ordeal at Chancellorsville was assisted by the relocation of their camp to a more healthful and scenic area. The regiment packed its belongings and moved off in heavy marching order for about two miles, halting on a small hill overlooking the army's busy supply depot at Belle Plain. From the camp, the men could look out on Potomac Creek where it begins to widen and flow into the river of the same name. They were surrounded by Virginia's verdant late-spring greenery, in contrast to the trampled ground and woodless landscape of their previous site. In these sylvan surroundings, the thoughts of battles past could more easily fade into memory. The expectation of battles yet to come, however, must have weighed heavily on their minds.

On June 5, the men could hear heavy cannonading in the distance, toward Fredericksburg. Rumors abounded that thousands of Union soldiers had been sent across the river and had participated in another "sharp" engagement at that place. "The probability is that Sickles' fighting Corps must go up and have a hand in the work," wrote Corporal Kenderine. Others expected the same. Corporal Williams wrote that "there ain't no use telling you I am well for you know that old Joe is feeding us up again with bread and potatos. Bully for him. I expect he will fatten us up for killing day again." Still, they maintained their Zouave bravado. Those who had been captured and paroled returned with stories from the Rebels. Their enemies had told them that they didn't like to fight the Red Legs.

10. William Williams to Edward Williams, n.d., in Sidebotham Collection.
11. *Ibid.*

Willie Williams reported, "They say we look like Devils and fight too hard. They say we try our best to kill and I think they are about right." [12]

The men were right about the impending movement and battle. But they were not expecting to head in the opposite direction, northward. General Lee had refused to sit and wait for another attack by the numerically superior Federals. Instead, in the wake of his most spectacular victory, he would carry the war northward once again, this time to the heart of Pennsylvania. The general had been able to convince Confederate President Jefferson Davis and Secretary of War James A. Seddon that, at this crucial juncture of the war, a drive into northern territory would help to accomplish their grand strategic purpose. That goal was to relieve pressure on the Rebel capital at Richmond as well as on the beleaguered force holding the important Mississippi River stronghold of Vicksburg. Lee contended that rather than reinforce the western army that was holding out against Major General Ulysses S. Grant's forces, it would be better to preserve the integrity of his own Army of Northern Virginia, push rapidly into Pennsylvania, and draw off Union troops from the siege of Vicksburg. At the very least, he thought, such a move would compel Hooker to follow him north, and thus provide farmers in the war-torn area of central Virginia a breathing spell during which their agriculture could recover. His defeat on the battlefield in Pennsylvania, however, was destined to thwart his scheme to relieve Vicksburg and to render short-lived the recovery of Virginia's farms. It was a defeat that Collis' Zouaves would do their part to ensure.

Hooker's cavalry soon discovered that Lee was mobilizing his troops from their lines south of the Rappahannock. In response, the Federals moved to shadow their adversary, seeking to discover his intentions. Hooker believed that the Rebels were merely attempting to turn his right flank, but it was necessary to keep his army in a good position to block the main avenues of advance on Washington.

The bugle sounded "Pack up!" for the Zouaves on June 11, when they marched westward with the army to Kelly's Ford. Private Donnaker took the opportunity to write his father on June 12. After nearly a year with the Zouaves, he still felt it necessary to reassure his family that certain elements in the army had not corrupted his morals. "You know what the

---

12. "From Collis' Zouaves—114th P.V.," Bucks County *Intelligencer*, June 23, 1863; Willie Williams to Edward Williams, n.d., in Sidebotham Collection.

army is made up of—plenty of rascals in it, for they are generally the
rowdies of the city, but I am the same as ever. I suppose you know that is
backward as ever but I can swear a little more than I used to but when I
get home again that will wear off." The twenty-year-old private would find
himself at home sooner than he expected. The next day, in the intense
heat of a late Virginia spring, Donnaker and his fellow Zouaves resumed
their "extremely annoying" trek. It was to take them to a battle on the
soil of their native state, a battle from which Donnaker would emerge
walking wounded on crutches for several months. Along the route they
followed to Bealton Station on the Orange and Alexandria Railroad, water
was scarce. At Bealton, however, the soldiers were able to unburden themselves. All unnecessary equipment was put on the trains destined for Washington. In lighter marching order, the Zouaves pushed on, following the
railroad line for several miles until they arrived at Catlett's Station at about
7 o'clock that night.[13]

The Philadelphians were able to catch their breath and recover at Catlett's, where they remained all day on June 14. The march continued early
the next morning, and still the torrid weather was nearly unbearable. The
sun beat down on the wool-capped men as they plodded onward over the
dusty roads, the still air giving them little comfort. Heat exhaustion and
sunstroke left several men gasping by the roadside long before the regiment
reached the day's destination of Bristoe Station. There the Zouaves settled
in wearily for a stuporous rest. By 7 o'clock the next morning, they were
on the road again; but the end of that day's march brought them some
relief when they reached the gently winding stream known as Bull Run.
Many of the men took the opportunity to bathe and cool off. It was a
much-needed respite from the stifling heat and dust, and grizzled veterans
splashed and swam happily in the current.

The Zouaves moved only a few miles past Bull Run on the following
day. A rumor was sweeping through camp that day that Hooker was sick
and General McClellan had resumed command of the army. It was only
hearsay, of course; but once again, with the prescience typical of the army's
soldiers, their murmurs predicted the fate of their current commander. He
was soon to be removed—though not because of illness—and replaced
by another: not McClellan, as many of the men hoped, but Major General
George G. Meade.

13. Rauscher, *Music on the March*, 75–76; Donnaker to "Dear Father," June 12, 1863,
in Donnaker Papers, CWMC, USAMHI.

The men remained encamped all day on June 18 amidst the evidence of defeat on the old battlefield of Bull Run. They again enjoyed some relief from the oppressive heat when it began to rain that afternoon. The following day they remained inactive, until the order was received to be on the road by 3 P.M. Instead of sweltering in the heat, this time the men were soaked through by a drenching rain. The temperature dropped sharply, and the now shivering Zouaves trudged on until midnight. Their destination was Gum Springs. It was a difficult march in the mud and darkness: they had left the roads and forced their way through woods, over stumps and fallen trees, and across turgid creeks and freshets. From their hurried pace, the men realized that the movement must be of some great importance. Like pieces in a large and deadly chess game between the commanding generals of both armies, they were being maneuvered into some strategic position. In fact, they were being set up to protect the Union capital by blocking all routes of access. Hooker kept the men forming this protective perimeter until he learned that Lee was still moving northward.

On June 25, the Zouaves headed north again, marching from Gum Springs, probably on the road leading to Leesburg. Along the way, the soldiers passed many large plantations. On hearing the regimental band, one musician recalled, crowds of former slaves "became wild with excitement. . . . For miles they would keep along with us, dancing, jumping and yelling with delight."[14]

The regimental band, though often called upon in the evenings to serenade various commanders, was providing more than just amusement on the march into Pennsylvania. After crossing into Maryland at Point of Rocks, General Birney put the band to more functional use. As the division entered towns along their route of march, he placed the Zouave musicians at one of the main intersections and directed them to play until the entire division had passed. "By this means the men kept precise step, and besides making an imposing appearance before the inhabitants, it prevented the men from straggling, as they became imbued with the pride of making a soldierly display."[15]

Birney may also have hoped to prevent repetitions of what he must have observed at Point of Rocks. When his forces entered the Union town,

14. Rauscher, *Music on the March*, 79–80.
15. *Ibid.*, 80.

they were greeted by residents armed with "horrid pies, and cakes that were even worse." The change from the dreary army diet was too tempting for the soldiers, and they paid exorbitant prices for the delicacies. Many of the Zouaves bought onions, "which were also sold on the gold premium principle." In short, the sight of friendly Unionist faces offering refresh-ment or conversation likely proved disruptive to the integrity of the marching columns.[16]

The march continued for the next few days, passing through Jefferson, Middletown, and Frederick. It was a novel experience for the Zouaves, for along the route they were constantly greeted by Marylanders loyal to the Union. Women waved red, white, and blue flags and banners; threw bou-quets of flowers; and by their encouragement steeled the men to march bravely onward and defend their home soil. The patriotic residents of the state also derived some immediate benefit from their friendly and enthu-siastic treatment of the passing soldiers. The men were generally better behaved than when amongst southern sympathizers. After passing through Frederick on June 28, for example, the Zouaves encamped near Walker-ville. There, a wise local farmer provided them with firewood, thus saving his fences. In a more southerly location, the men might have spurned secessionist firewood and set the fence rails blazing in a spiteful pyre.[17]

By June 28, the Confederate Third and First Corps under Lieutenant Gen-erals Ambrose Powell Hill and James Longstreet were already in the area of Chambersburg, Pennsylvania. The Second Corps, commanded by Lieu-tenant General Richard Stoddert Ewell, was even farther north at Carlisle. General Lee, with the army near Chambersburg, was operating at a serious disadvantage at this time. His trusted cavalry commander, Major General James Ewell Brown ("Jeb") Stuart, had seemingly disappeared. A misun-derstanding of orders had sent Stuart on a circuitous raid around the rear of the Federal armies. Lee had not heard from the horseman since June 24. As a result, the Confederate commander had no current information concerning the disposition of the Union forces. He thought that Hooker was still south of the Potomac.

Lee learned late on the night of the twenty-eighth that his adversary was not in Virginia, as he himself had supposed, but within a day's march,

16. *Ibid.*
17. Rauscher, *Music on the March,* 82.

at Frederick, Maryland. This adversary, moreover, was no longer Hooker, but Meade. The order appointing the latter had arrived that very day. "I have no promises or pledges to make," wrote the new commanding general in his first address to the army. Rather, he recognized the gravity of the events about to unfold, and he cautioned his troops to bear that urgency in mind. "Let us have in view constantly the magnitude of the interests involved and let each man determine to do his duty," he wrote. There were no grandiose musings about great victories in his order: simply a grim recognition of the awful test to which the soldiers must again put themselves. The country looked to these men "to relieve it from the devastation and disgrace of hostile invasion."[18]

At 6 o'clock the next morning, the Zouaves again headed northward, through Woodsborough and Ladiesburg. The latter town was aptly named, thought one of the Philadelphians, as the men were cheered by "three pretty young ladies [who] stood on a porch and sang 'John Brown'" while the soldiers passed. The day's march ended about a mile past Taneytown, Maryland, close to the Pennsylvania border. The Zouaves had been welcomed heartily by the residents of Taneytown, who "received us as though we were their deliverers"; and on the following morning the camp was crowded with well-wishers from the town and countryside. At 2 P.M., the Zouaves left their congenial surroundings and headed northwest toward Emmitsburg, Maryland, where they halted for the night. As they passed Mount Saint Mary's College near Emmitsburg, several of the men left the ranks and climbed over the wall. They soon returned "with their gun slung over their shoulder and a large loaf of fresh-baked bread under each arm." Their comrades quickly surrounded them, each begging for a piece of the rare treat.[19]

In the early afternoon of July 1, General Birney was ordered to take his First and Second Brigades and push on to Gettysburg to support Major General Oliver Otis Howard's Eleventh Corps. Howard's men had joined those of the First Corps in forming a defensive line north and west of that strategic crossroads town. The low, rolling thunder of distant artillery fire drifting over the undulating countryside soon told the Zouaves that the battle had been joined. Some must have wondered at first whether they

18. OR, Vol. XXVII, Pt. 3, p. 374.
19. Rauscher, *Music on the March*, 85; Given Diary, n.d., in Given Collection, CWLM.

were the rumbles of a far-off summer storm, for the rain had begun once again the previous night. Rain and the passage of the two corps that preceded them had turned the roads into treacherous, mud-slick paths. The march was another trying one. Though the weather had been warm during the day, the nights had been cool, and many of the men still wished to keep their overcoats. Nevertheless, the constant marching convinced them to lighten their loads by discarding anything other than necessities. A number of men had been cutting away the tails of their overcoats inch by inch in an effort to reduce the weight of them. Some were so short by then that they resembled jackets rather than overcoats. Sergeant Given recalled trying to give his coat to a passing farmer. "Look here neighbor," he called to the man. "How would you like to have an overcoat?" The farmer declined the offer, but said he would save it for him. "I threw it to him. [I] suppose he is saving it for me as I never saw him afterwards that I knew."[20]

Despite the difficulty of the march, the soldiers made every effort to accomplish it quickly. Often, they were ordered to move forward at a double-quick pace—about the speed of a slow jog. Soaked by rain, sweat, and mud; their woolen uniforms plastered to their bodies; chafing, cursing, stumbling; onward they pressed toward the sound of the guns. As they approached the site of the battle, they encountered long lines of fleeing citizens. "The faces of our men grew pale with shame and indignation at the idea of our own people being driven from their firesides," recalled one of the marching Zouaves. "They saw that the tables were being turned upon them, and many were heard to swear that 'A man not willing to fight his best now, will never fight!'"[21]

It was nearly dark when the Zouaves arrived near the scene of the day's battle. It was quiet by then, and the men filed up the Emmitsburg Road toward Gettysburg while the campfires of the enemy burned brightly only a short distance to their left. Many of the Philadelphians stopped at a local farmhouse owned by a Germantown man, George W. Rose. They gathered around Rose's well and helped themselves to the refreshing cold water. Continuing up the Emmitsburg Road, the men filed right, through a peach orchard, to Seminary Ridge. There, they fell into line with the rest of the army and waited to see what daybreak would bring.

20. Given Diary, n.d., in Given Collection, CWLM.
21. Rauscher, *Music on the March*, 86.

Meanwhile, at a resort hotel near Pottsville, about a hundred miles north-east of Gettysburg, Colonel Collis was fretting over the fate of the country and lamenting his inability to take the field. After arriving in Philadelphia, Collis spent several days regaining his health and recovering from his trip north. Seeing firsthand his young friend's fragile condition, Judge Read made arrangements for Collis to move temporarily to the country and stay at the Mansion House in Mount Carbon. There, he would be looked after by one of Read's friends and fellow judges. Collis, his wife, and their infant daughter, Amelia, departed for the restorative climate of Schuylkill County as soon as the colonel felt well enough to endure another trip.

Collis was not a very large man, his normal weight being only about 138 pounds; but his weight on June 24—the day after his arrival at Mount Carbon—was only 115 pounds. Read's friend insisted that Collis drink quantities of eggnog, and the colonel soon admitted that he thought the prescription benefited him. He quickly regained his appetite as well and eagerly anticipated his daily dinner of spring chicken; on at least one occasion he thought it remarkable that he had consumed an entire bird. The hardy food and drink seems to have launched the ailing patient down the road to recovery.

Collis corresponded daily with Read and speculated in his letters on the meaning and object of Lee's latest campaign in the North. On one hand, he seemed convinced that the Rebels were streaming north only to replenish their supplies. The countermeasure to this drive, he asserted, was to sever the supply line west of the Blue Ridge Mountains. "On every little stream is a mill," he wrote of the rich Pennsylvania countryside. "These will all be set in motion & the flour sent in wagons to Staunton, from whence it will go by rail to Gordonsville & perhaps Richmond. *This line of communication should be cut.*"[22]

On the other hand, the colonel placed little stock in the proposition that the Pennsylvania capital was the object of Lee's march. " 'The Rebels are advancing on Harrisburg' say the newspapers. How absurd! Who would be fool enough to cross a river *a mile wide,* which rises with every shower." He also dismissed the notion that Lee would turn toward Pittsburgh. There would be no danger of that, "if they ever expect to get back alive," he claimed. "For every mountaineer would be a bushwhacker."[23]

---

22. C. Collis to "My dear Judge," June 24, 1863, in Read Papers, HSP.
23. C. Collis to "My dear Judge," June 25, 1863, *ibid.*

On June 27, Collis commented to Read on Governor Curtin's call for 50,000 men to enlist for three months to protect the state. He thought it important to accomplish such a move quickly but criticized the proposed method of doing so. "If he wants to have them in the field in ten days he must receive them by *squads* and *companies*. If he wants to occupy *three months* in raising them, let him give every Tom, Dick, & Harry authority to raise a *Regiment*." Collis, however, did not say who should officer these troops, but he might have wished that the men be used to fill out the ranks of depleted regiments or be enlisted in under-strength militia units. His final comment may reveal a jealousy for those who would soon cover themselves in glory in the defense of their state. Probably he feared that some newly minted officers would fare so well that they would be promoted over him. "It is of the last importance that *no man* should be permitted to recruit more than a *company*," he stated. Companies, of course, would be commanded by captains.[24]

In addition to his definite ideas about how the governor should conduct the defense of state, Collis had some military advice for the commander of the recently created Department of the Susquehanna, Major General Darius Nash Couch. Collis had read an account that asserted that the Rebel forces were at Duncannon and York. "If they have divided their forces thus, Couch ought to whip them in detail," he wrote. Couch himself, however, had not sufficient force to deal with the invasion. The men called for by Governor Curtin to compose a corps for the Department of the Susquehanna would, for the most part, be ill trained, ill equipped, and poorly armed. Nevertheless, the men were enlisting. "I think Pottsville will put Phila to shame," wrote Collis of the response of that town's citizenry. "The whole population seemed disposed to volunteer *en masse*." The ailing colonel likely would have joined them if circumstances had been slightly different. He hinted wistfully to Read of his desires for promotion, as well as the possibility of a miraculous recovery. "How I wish Mr. Lincoln would put a star on my shoulder & order me to report to Gen. Couch," he wrote. "I would start early tomorrow."[25]

The following day, June 29, Collis learned that General Meade had been appointed to command the Army of the Potomac. He was pleased with the choice, and optimistic about the results. "I think now I see the

24. C. Collis to "My dear Judge," June 27, 1863, *ibid.*
25. C. Collis to "My dear Judge," June 28, 1863, *ibid.*

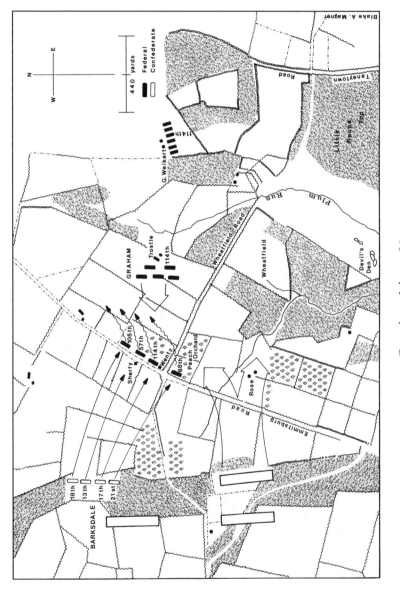

Gettysburg, July 2, 1863

beginning of the end," he wrote to Read. "He is an accomplished, scientific soldier, cool under the most trying circumstances, brave as a lion." He went on to describe his own experiences with Meade, touting the latter's handling of his troops in battle. Finally, he was hopeful regarding not only the country's fortunes, but his own as well. He felt sure that Meade, who was well aware of Collis' recent trouble with General Birney, would now transfer his regiment to Brigadier General John C. Robinson's Second Division of the First Corps. He anticipated sympathy from the new commanding general because he knew that Meade was "no friend of B's, [while] Robinson being an old Army Officer is well known to him." [26]

Collis continued to hint to Read of his ambitions for promotion, but at first only subtly. "The desire to be in a sphere of usefulness *somewhere* keeps me in a state of nervous anxiety," he wrote. "I should prefer being with Gen. Couch & among the *Penn* troops, but I suppose that is impossible." The day after penning those lines, however, he could contain himself no longer and bluntly appealed to Read to use his influence in seeking his promotion from colonel to general officer. Collis had been informed that the War Department intended to appoint general officers to command the state troops then being raised. As there were a number of brigades in the army then commanded by colonels, from where were the generals to come? he inquired. "Mr. Lincoln," he asserted, "will be compelled to make promotions." In these speculations, Collis was not merely guessing. He had received a letter from General Robinson, who reported that a friend in Washington had heard the president say that he was willing to make promotions if the army needed generals. Accordingly, the Philadelphia colonel considered the time propitious to ask a favor of the politically powerful judge.

> Now I hate to ask you to do more for me than you have already done out of the kindness of your heart & almost without solicitation, and I dislike even to suggest your writing Mr. [Charles] Sumner or Mr. Jos. J. Lewis or anyone else in whom you have confidence, "to go & see the President." In these times of course you would not go to Washington yourself, everyman's place is *here*.
>
> But *now* is the time; & *Pennsylvanians* will have the preference. During the coming week many promotions & assignments will be made, in fact

---

26. C. Collis to "My dear Judge," June 29, 1863, *ibid.*

must be made, & if some one in Washington would just at this moment bring my case again before the Prest. I should receive the appointment.

You know best how to act, & whatever *you* do will please *me*.[27]

Thus unburdened, Collis returned to the subject of the current dispositions of the army. Being unable to join in the action, he amused himself by predicting the movements in the campaign to defend his state from Lee's army. It was a part of a young officer's military training, he thought, after studying events carefully, to make such predictions. On the night of July 1, while his men were resting fitfully on Cemetery Ridge in the shadow of Little Round Top, Collis wrote Read that he had thus far made five judgments, three of which had been verified by recent events, and two of which promised soon to be.

First, he claimed, he had predicted that Lee would move north and again invade Maryland. Second, he had said that Lee did not intend to fight, only to gather crops, cattle, and horses. Third, he posited that Lee would never cross the Susquehanna River. Next, he contended, Meade would catch Lee and force him to fight near Gettysburg. Finally, having argued with many people in the area about the size of the Army of the Potomac, he claimed that its effective fighting strength was 95,000 men. Others insisted that the number was far less. He stuck to his figures, which he had calculated by subtracting from the number of rations drawn before the fight at Chancellorsville the number of teamsters and noncombatants, the losses at Chancellorsville, and the loss of several nine-month and two-year regiments. Despite the skepticism of those with whom he disagreed, Collis persisted. His opinion was eventually upheld by a colonel in the adjutant general's office. That officer settled the argument by stating that on June 30 the army's Commissary General had told him that "Meade had exactly 94,500 exclusive of Heintzelman, & had since been reinforced by 10,000; but . . . the Army of P. *proper* was 94,500 *fighting men*." To Collis, the subject was more than just a topic of conversation; it was a matter of

27. C. Collis to "My dear Judge," June 30, 1863, *ibid.* Joseph Jackson Lewis was a prominent attorney who had run a successful prewar law practice in West Chester, Pennsylvania. Of strong antislavery sentiment, Lewis strengthened his reputation by defending the rights of escaped slaves in the case of *United States* v. *Castner Hanway*. He was a delegate to the 1860 Republican national convention and presented Abraham Lincoln's name for the nomination at that convention. In 1863, Lewis was the U.S. commissioner of internal revenue.

pride and a vindication of his stature as a military expert. "My opinion has enhanced in value up here a hundred per cent," he told the judge.[28]

In answer to his daily letters to Read, Collis had not received any correspondence from his friend since his arrival at Mount Carbon on June 23. In his letter to the judge on July 2, Collis claimed that his health had been completely restored with the exception that his knees remained a little weak. The medical expert who examined him that day disagreed. He told Collis that he could certify without reservation that he was yet unfit for duty. Seeing that the colonel was anxious to resume his command, however, the doctor opined that four more days of horseback riding would probably strengthen his legs sufficiently to allow him to return to the army.

Collis also learned that day of the death of Major General John Fulton Reynolds, which he likened to the "loss of 10,000 men at this critical hour." The event seemed to sober him momentarily, causing him to adopt a slightly more pessimistic, though still hopeful, attitude. "Our poor Army of the Potomac has been so often beaten, that a grand success such as I pray for seems improbable. But we are fighting on our own ground under an excellent chief. Our time may have arrived at last."[29]

By July 7, the battle of Gettysburg had been fought and Lee's army forced back to the safety of the Shenandoah Valley. With the immediate crisis past, Collis must have felt no pressing need to return to the army. He was examined by a doctor again that day. This time, however, he received a certificate of health stating that in consequence of the "general debility" resulting from typhoid fever, he was unfit for duty and would remain so for at least another twenty days.[30]

Despite the passage of the emergency that required the calling out of the state militia, Collis still hoped to pursue his chances for promotion. Perhaps he felt that he could better wage his campaign for advancement from his present location. Not long after Gettysburg, he received instruc-

---

28. C. Collis to "My dear Judge," July 1, 1863, in Read Papers, HSP. While compiling the *Official Records of the Union and Confederate Armies* in 1886, the war records office of the war department calculated the effective strength of Meade's army as 93,500 men. In *The Gettysburg Campaign: A Study in Command* (New York, 1968), however, Edwin B. Coddington arrived at the somewhat lower estimate of 85,500. See Coddington, 242–50, for a discussion of the difficulties in accurately tallying the number of men available in both armies.

29. C. Collis to "My dear Judge," July 2, 1863, in Read Papers, HSP.

30. Certificate of Health signed by F. J. Kern, M. D., July 7, 1863, *ibid.*

tions from Read telling him to forward a detailed account of his military
career to the Washington offices of Joseph J. Lewis, U.S. Commissioner
of Internal Revenue; the account would support the circulation of his
name before the proper parties in the capital. Whatever may have been
done for him, the promotion was not forthcoming. He would return to his
depleted regiment in mid-August, distressed, no doubt, by the losses having resulted from the fighting on July 2.

While Collis was amusing himself by speculating on the outcome of Lee's
invasion, his Zouaves were playing a major—and costly—role in turning
back the southern advance. On the morning of July 2, the men of the
114th had been roused from their bivouac on Cemetery Ridge. They had
spent the night as comfortably as possible in a wooded area near the Wei-
kert Farm, but at dawn a blazing red sun rose causing the temperature to
climb. There was not much for breakfast. Sergeant Given sent one of his
men to the Trostle house to see if he could buy some flour. The man soon
returned to say that nothing was left to eat there. Given eventually found
a small bit of flour, which he quickly mixed with water and heated in his
tin cup. He was able to bolt the pasty mixture before the order came to
form up; but his tentmate, Sergeant Joseph DeHaven, was not quick
enough and had to throw his portion away. Though there had been little
time to eat, there had been time to conduct the daily prayer. Given and
his comrades were in the habit of reading scripture and praying each morning while in camp, but during the course of the march the group simply
knelt and prayed together. When they arose from prayer that morning,
DeHaven voiced an ominous prediction. "Boys," he said, "this is the last
time we will pray together."[31]

Not long after rising, the Zouaves were formed into line. They moved
out across the fields to the west, toward the Trostle Farm. Trostle's buildings
were situated between the Emmitsburg and Taneytown Roads, about six
hundred yards from the former. There, the regiment formed a line of battle
with the rest of the brigade. The line faced the Emmitsburg Road and was
arranged in columns doubled on the center. The front line was composed
of the 68th, 141st, and 57th Pennsylvania, while the 114th was positioned
to the left and slightly to the rear of the 57th. The 105th Pennsylvania
was behind the 57th and to the right of the Zouaves, and the 63rd had

31. Given Diary, n.d., in Given Collection, CWLM.

been deployed earlier as skirmishers. Immediately in front of the 114th was Captain A. Judson Clark's Battery B, 1st New Jersey Light Artillery. The brigade remained in that position throughout the early afternoon with little movement.[32]

The Third Corps position that afternoon stretched from Devil's Den on the left through a wheatfield to a peach orchard, where it made an abrupt right turn and continued north along the Emmitsburg Road. General Sickles' Third Corps front covered nearly 3,200 yards of ground, almost twice that proposed by General Meade's plan of placing the corps on the crest of Cemetery Ridge. There, its left would have rested on Little Round Top, while the right would connect to the Second Corps line on the ridge. Sickles' decision to move his men into what he thought was a more defensible location left a 500-yard gap between the right of his corps and the left of the Second.

Sometime around 2 P.M., Clark threw six or seven rounds into a Confederate column that was moving across the Emmitsburg Road to the south. Clark's guns were then moved across the brigade front, nearer the peach orchard, and aimed southward toward Emmitsburg. The 141st Pennsylvania was taken out of line and ordered to support the battery. Not long afterward, the rest of the brigade was ordered to advance. The 114th reached an oat field near the Emmitsburg Road and deployed into line with the brigade. The 68th now occupied the extreme left, the 114th and 57th the middle, and the 105th the right. First Lieutenant John K. Bucklyn's Battery E, 1st Rhode Island Light Artillery (Randolph's Battery), deployed along the road in front of the brigade and immediately opened fire in response to the Confederate batteries that were supporting their attacking infantry near the wheatfield. The fire of the artillerists naturally brought a response from the Rebels, and for nearly two hours the Zouaves were forced to lie in the open field and endure the terrible shelling. The infantrymen were powerless to respond to the barrage. No enemy yet appeared on their portion of the field, and one of the men recalled that there was "nothing to do but to remain in our position, having no protection of any sort or kind."[33]

32. OR, Vol. XXVII, Pt. 1, pp. 497–506, 585; "Collis' Zouaves," Philadelphia *Weekly Press*, June 22, 1887, p. 1.

33. OR, Vol. XXVII, Pt. 1. pp. 589–90; "Collis' Zouaves," Philadelphia *Weekly Press*, June 22, 1887, p. 1.

Across the field to the west, Brigadier General William Barksdale's Mississippi Brigade, consisting of the 13th, 17th, 18th, and 21st regiments, was enduring a similar ordeal as Union shells crashed into the woods around them. While the Zouaves were preparing themselves to receive an attack on their position, the Mississippians were waiting to cross the open fields and assault the bristling Federal lines. They were anxious to make the attack, and no one exuded more impatience than their commander. Seeing Lieutenant General James Longstreet ride up, the impulsive Barksdale pressed him for the order to move. "I wish you would let me go in, General," blurted out the former Mississippi congressman. "I would take that battery in five minutes." Longstreet must have smiled inwardly with pride, knowing that Barksdale would surely do exactly as he promised. "Wait a little," he replied. "We are all going in presently."[34]

Finally, at about 6 P.M., the artillery fire began to slacken. Barksdale ordered his men forward, and 1,400 Mississippians burst forth from the woods with a furious Rebel yell, heading directly for General Graham's brigade and the 114th Pennsylvania. It was obvious that the battery positioned in front of the 114th would be captured if the line did not advance. Captain George E. Randolph, the Chief of Artillery, rode up to the Zouaves and requested them to advance and protect the guns. "You boys saved this battery once before at Fredericksburg," he said to Captain Bowen. "If you will do it again move forward."[35]

Randolph had been unable to locate either General Graham or Lieutenant Colonel Cavada, but the critical situation forced him to order the men forward on his own responsibility. The entire brigade sprang up to meet the advancing enemy. The Zouaves quickly passed through the guns, reached the Emmitsburg Road, and clambered over a rail fence. A portion of the fence had been torn down earlier, but the obstacle had delayed the right wing of the regiment. Once on the road, the men stopped and reformed their line, then advanced into John and Mary Sherfy's farmyard.

Sergeant Given ran up to the Sherfy buildings in advance of the regiment and knelt looking out between the house and barn. Cavada, kneeling next to him, asked if the Rebels were coming. "You bet your life they are

---

34. J. S. McNeily, "Barksdale's Mississippi Brigade at Gettysburg," *Publications of the Mississippi Historical Society,* XIV (Oxford, 1914), 239.

35. "Collis' Zouaves," Philadelphia *Weekly Press,* July 22, 1887, p. 1; *OR,* Vol. II, Pt. 1, p. 502.

coming," said Given. With that, the sergeant got up waving his sword and ran down the pathway "calling to the men to fire out between the house and barn." The Zouaves were loading and firing furiously as they advanced, and the Mississippians were apparently doing the same thing. The musketry was tremendous. "Give it to them boys," yelled Private Joseph S. Beaumont of Company F. "We have them on our own ground!" Men were quickly falling in clusters. Captain Francis Fix of Company E fell with a serious wound to the knee that would prove fatal. Scores of others dropped around him. Sergeant DeHaven, who had not even been afforded the opportunity to eat a final meal that morning, was among them; and there were to be no more rambling, poetic letters to the Bucks County *Intelligencer* from the perceptive young teacher, Corporal Robert Kenderdine. He too lay dying in Sherfy's yard. Sergeant Henry H. Snyder of Company C was near Kenderdine when the latter was struck down. Snyder later recalled that the ranks of the 114th were so thin and scattered by then that he was able to observe one of Barksdale's Mississippians take deliberate aim at Kenderdine, who fell mortally wounded. Snyder quickly fired back but missed. A comrade "drew on him with better luck, for the rebel fell apparently dead."[36]

Barksdale's tightly packed lines surged onward against the vastly outnumbered men of Graham's brigade. The 68th and 114th Pennsylvania bore the brunt of the attack, especially at the place where their overextended lines tenuously joined near the Wentz farmyard and the intersection of the Emmitsburg and Wheatfield Roads. The 21st Mississippi advanced on the 68th, but the well-aimed fire of the Pennsylvanians brought the attackers to a standstill. Soon, the 17th Mississippi moved into position, threatening the right flank of the 68th. The Zouaves, meanwhile, along with the 57th Pennsylvania, were fighting furiously around the Sherfy house and barn against the 18th Mississippi. The breach between the thin lines of the Pennsylvanians, however, allowed the 17th and 13th Mississippi to pour through and deliver murderous volleys into their flanks. Neither the 68th nor the 114th could do much to combat this calamity, and both were forced to withdraw.

As the left flank of the 114th began to crowd over onto the right, the combination of casualties and confusion impelled the remnants of the

36. Given Diary, n.d., in Given Collection, CWLM; Kenderdine Papers, HCWRT Collection, USAMHI.

regiment to break up and seek safety. The only avenue of escape for the few remaining men was northward, parallel to the Emmitsburg Road. Captain Bowen finally ordered Sergeant Benjamin Baylitts with the national flag, and Private Harry Hall with the state flag, to start off in that direction. Bowen, then acting as major, enlisted the aid of Captain Eddy and attempted to rally the Philadelphians around the flags. He succeeded in gathering only a few men, amounting to little more than a color guard.

The confusion caused by the smoke, noise, and devastation did not entirely render futile these attempts to rally the men. Small groups were able to maintain their coherence. Sergeant Given told the men who remained with him to retreat slowly while loading and firing. Bowen ordered the men around the colors to do the same. Thus, these small fragments of the once proud Zouave regiment stood firmly, blazing away, while the color-bearers retreated a short distance to the rear. As the Rebel masses closed in on the men again, they followed the colors and re-formed. This maneuver was repeated several times, and the flags were saved. The Confederate forces driving back the Union lines suffered no less grievously. Private Robert A. Moore of the 17th Mississippi recalled the carnage in his diary entry for July 2. "Our loss was heavy, in the Regt. 233 killed and wounded, in our Co., [G] 29. Several of them were my dear friends. Every man acted the hero. Miss. has lost many of her best and and bravest sons. How thankful should all be to God who have escaped. OH! the horrors of war."[37]

After retreating up the Emmitsburg Road, the men turned off into a field and made for Cemetery Ridge. Captain Henry M. Eddy, of Company D, took a ball in the chest as they entered the field. Fortunately, it was nearly spent when it struck the officer, and his men were able to get him up and assist him in continuing. They passed a small frame dwelling used as a shoemaker's shop, and there Given and Bowen both observed Lieutenant Colonel Cavada sitting on the back doorstep. They asked if he was wounded, and when he replied that he was not, they urged him to get up and go on with them to the rear. Cavada declined. He was too weak to continue, he stated, and he refused the assistance of the men, urging them to save themselves. "There was no time to parley," recalled Given, and the officer was left behind with the enemy quickly closing in.[38]

37. James W. Silver, ed., *A Life for the Confederacy* (Jackson, Tenn., 1959), 153.

38. *OR*, Vol. XXVII, Pt. 1, p. 503; Given Diary, n.d., in Given Collection, CWLM.

Crossing the open field to the rear at that particular moment was an extremely hazardous undertaking. The retreating men were pursued hotly by the exuberant Rebels, and the lead flew thickly through the air while shells burst overhead. Two Zouaves and a wounded comrade whom they had been assisting across the field were all killed when a shell landed in their midst. Thirty-eight-year-old Private Henry S. Strouse of F Company was shot through the leg in the yard of the shoemaker's shop. Fortunately for him, Sergeant Given was nearby. Given "caught him by the back of the neck and ran him out of the side gate." Strouse was able to get aboard an empty ammunition wagon headed for the rear, and thus made his way to safety.[39]

The retreat must have grown even more confused from this point as the command fragmented in its rush to safety. Given and twenty-five-year-old Matthew Bradley of F Company wound up near the Twelfth Corps portion of the line. The two had no idea where to find their regiment by then. They asked several men whether the Red Legs had passed that way, but no one could help them. One Twelfth Corps soldier who was sitting beneath a tree offered them some of his dried apples, which the grateful men quickly accepted before pushing on. Eventually, they reached the Baltimore Pike. By then it was dark, and the road was crowded with men. They soon found themselves among their comrades of the Third Corps, the remnants of which had been positioned in the fields lying between the Taneytown Road and Baltimore Pike. When they found the Zouaves, Given counted only about sixty-two men remaining, though several more dragged themselves in during the night. Bowen was especially pleased to see that Given had rejoined the men. His proficiency in his administrative duties as Sergeant Major had made him an indispensable member of the regimental staff.

Of course, a great many men of the regiment would never reunite with their comrades. Though many of the missing had been captured in the smoky turmoil of the battle, nearly one hundred had been killed or wounded. Many of the wounded had found themselves in a difficult position. Some of those too badly hurt to move were lying helplessly in the road when a Confederate artillery battery came thundering toward them. The officer commanding the guns kindly stopped and had his men remove the wounded soldiers from the road. Others crawled, walked, or were car-

39. Given Diary, n.d., in Given Collection, CWLM.

ried to the shelter of the buildings on the Sherfy farm. Most would find
no safety there, however. Later during the battle, most of Sherfy's buildings, including the barn, were burned to the ground by fires that resulted
from the incessant artillery shelling. Three days later, the 20th Maine
moved across the scarred fields and past the burned-out farm. In the ruins
of the barn were scattered the charred bodies of the wounded who had
sought safety under its rafters. Some were burned to skeletons. On the
grounds surrounding the farm were scores of bodies. Some were clad in
blue, some in gray, and scattered among them were the bright red hats
and trousers of the fallen Zouaves. It was a scene of such carnage as to
horrify even the veterans of the terrible conflict on the slopes of Little
Round Top.[40]

Though Given had found the regiment, it was apparent that the dis-
ordered withdrawal had separated more than just individual men from
their commands. The Zouaves had only a vague idea where the rest of
their brigade might be. Given took Company C's first sergeant, Samuel
Smith, and set off in search of them. By daybreak on July 3, they had
found the Third Corps field hospital, set up in a large barn. In the center
of the barn was an operating table, around which "arms, hands, legs and
feet lay in piles." The ghastly scene reminded Given of a slaughterhouse.
The horror was completed by the "fearful" groaning of the wounded and
dying men lying around the grounds so thickly that it was difficult to
maneuver through the place without stepping on one of them. Two
women, who Given supposed from their ages were mother and daughter,
assisted the hospital stewards and doctors in attending the wounded.[41]

The men continued their search for the brigade while the sun rose
higher in the sky. "As the daylight broke through the branches of the
trees," recalled Given, "so did the bullets and shells of the enemy come
crashing through filling the air with the most unearthly sounds I ever
listened to." They finally located the brigade near Little Round Top, "in
the shelter of the great rocks." The regiment was directed to the site, and
acting quartermaster Lieutenant John S. Crawford brought up rations for
359 men. There were perhaps 65 Zouaves present at that time. Though
tired and ragged, the men were hungry enough to begin cooking coffee
and frying fat pork, which they quickly ate with hardtack. By some strange

40. John H. Pullen, *The Twentieth Maine* (Dayton, 1984), 133–34.
41. Given Diary, n.d., in Given Collection, CWLM.

circumstance, a barrel of whiskey had also been delivered to the regiment. The men soon had the barrel head staved in and were freely imbibing when Captain Bowen brought the fiasco to a halt. He began to issue the potent liquid in small portions, "as he thought best." Given, though not a drinker, filled a half-empty bottle of Jamaica Ginger so that he could dispense the mixture to the wounded.[42]

Captain Bowen was apparently too late to prevent at least one man from becoming very drunk. Nineteen-year-old Private Michael Duddy of Company K "got crazy drunk and made a dash at Captain Henry M. Eddy to kill him." Given intervened and threw the private to the ground. Bowen ordered him to be bucked, which was accomplished with a bayonet and gunstrap. He soon became so abusive, however, that he was ordered to be gagged as well. Another bayonet was placed lengthwise in his mouth and tied behind his head. He was left in this position under guard until he sobered up. "It was too bad," recalled Given. Duddy had been a "good brave soldier, and [when] sober ever proud to obey orders. But it was the old devil 'Whiskey.' "[43]

The brigade was soon called on to come to the support of their fellow Philadelphians of the 69th, 71st, 72nd, and 106th Pennsylvania. These regiments of Second Brigade, Second Division, Second Corps were known as the Philadelphia Brigade, commanded by Brigadier General Alexander S. Webb; their position on July 3 placed them at the focal point of the attack of Major General George Edward Pickett's division. The Zouaves moved off to their assistance at a double-quick pace, carrying haversacks bulging with excess rations. Their brigade was then commanded by Colonel Andrew H. Tippen of the 68th Pennsylvania; General Graham had been wounded and captured in the previous afternoon's engagement. Tippen moved the brigade to the right during a tremendous cannonade that preceded the Confederate attack. Captain Bowen, years later, recalled Tippen's command of the brigade as something of a whimsical interlude.

> Whether it was that the brave Colonel didn't know his right from the left, or just which way it was he was ordered to go, or whether it was that his soldierly instinct led him to lead the brigade towards the enemy, doubtless glad of an opportunity to repay them in the same coin for the way they had served us on the previous afternoon the writer does not know, but this much

42. *Ibid.*
43. *Ibid.*

he does know, that in less time than it has taken to tell this we were in the midst of a most severe shower of flying missiles of all sorts and kinds, one of which struck colonel Tippen's horse, and placed the doughty Colonel hors-de-combat.[44]

Colonel Henry J. Madill then assumed command and withdrew the brigade "from the exposed position Colonel Tippen's indiscretion had placed it." It seems likely that Tippen had simply moved too close to the rear of the regiments he was to support. The Confederate gunners had been overshooting the infantrymen of the Second Corps, making the rear areas more dangerous than the front line. Soon after, the barrage began to taper off, and long lines of men in gray and butternut appeared from the woods on Seminary Ridge. Madill was ordered to send two regiments to the right and front to assist in repelling the attack by Pickett's division. The 114th and 141st trotted off and took up position in the second line of defense. The 114th was formed in the rear of the 69th Pennsylvania. The Philadelphia Brigade was successful in repelling the attack, however, and the Third Corps regiments were not required to assist them. The Zouaves, moreover, were partially under cover during the attack, and no casualties occurred among them.

Sergeant Given again became separated from the regiment as they moved into position that afternoon. The previous day, he had lost the scabbard for his sword when jumping the fence at the Emmitsburg Road; so when he observed a Union lieutenant of the 72nd Pennsylvania lying dead with a bullet in his chest, he buckled on the officer's sword and belt and left his own stuck in the ground next to the fallen soldier. While he was making this exchange, he recalled, another man nearby called out to him for help. Both of the soldier's legs had been shattered, and he wished to have his feet propped up. Given piled discarded articles under the man's mangled limbs and offered him water and a taste of the whiskey and Jamaica Ginger. Another wounded man nearby asked for water, and Given administered a dose of the whiskey to him as well. The second soldier had been shot through the bowels and was dying. In his hands was a photograph of his wife, which he asked Given to return to her in Maine. "Good bye dear Wife. Good bye," he said as he kissed the picture and handed it over. "Are you prepared to die?" inquired the pious sergeant. The soldier looked up at him. "Yes," he replied. "I never left that until now," he

44. "Collis' Zouaves," Philadelphia *Weekly Press,* June 22, 1887, p. 1.

commented about the photograph Given now held in his hands. Given bade him farewell, put the photograph in his pocket, and hurried off to find his regiment.[45]

After the repulse of Pickett's division, Given led a detail of Zouaves onto the field at the spot where some of the heaviest fighting had taken place. They were to pick up the weapons lying in the field and to return them behind the Union lines. Sorting through the carnage of the attack was no easy task, even for veterans. Men who had bravely charged into the mouths of waiting cannons were heaped in piles, bodies horribly mangled. Wounded men begged for deliverance from their awful suffering. Sergeant John Guiness of Company E took pity on one of the wounded men and leaned over to offer him a drink from his canteen. The canteen was held over Guiness' shoulder by its cotton strap, in which a knot had been tied to shorten it to waist level. This arrangement was adopted in order to keep the precious fluid safe under the arm, and to prevent chance spillage or annoying banging against the leg during a march. The wounded man reached out to grasp the proffered canteen and pulled it to his lips. As he did so, Guiness was drawn so close to him that their faces almost met. At that moment, the man was gripped by the "paroxyam [sic] of death," and his arms and hands tightened into an iron hold. Guiness quickly reached out and sliced the canvas strap with a sharp knife, then stumbled off leaving his canteen in the dead man's lifeless clutches. "Sergeant Guiness was a brave man," Given recalled. "But this was more than he could bear for he almost collapsed as he told me."[46]

45. Given Diary, n.d., in Given Collection, CWLM.
46. *Ibid.*

10

They Are Small in Number but Are All Veterans

In the aftermath of the devastation that marked the high tide of the Confederacy, the stunned Zouaves had little time in which to evaluate their straits. Theirs was not an unusual predicament among the armies that summer of 1863: how to rebuild a nearly decimated regiment after such severe losses of men? Many regiments by that time had been nearly destroyed by the ravages of warfare. Without reinforcements, another battle such as the one just passed would virtually ensure the dissolution of the proud Zouave unit. Over the course of the previous year, the numbers of the regiment had been steadily decreased by sickness, desertion, details, wounding, and death. The 114th had arrived on the field of Gettysburg on July 2 with approximately 341 men and officers present for duty. Two days later, only about 184 of them remained to answer to their names at roll call. According to these estimates, their casualties—including those who were killed, wounded, missing, or captured—amounted to 46 percent of the men engaged.[1]

The number of casualties that the 114th suffered at Gettysburg was only slightly less than those it had borne at Chancellorsville. The loss on May 2 and 3 had been 168 of the 536 men present for duty on those days. This casualty rate amounts to 31.3 percent. The real impact of the loss at

---

1. Regimental Casualties, Records of the 114th PV, Record Group 94, NARA; Bates, *Pennsylvania Volunteers*, III, 1184–97.

Chancellorsville, however, can be realized only when one considers that a much lower proportion of casualties there registered in the missing or captured categories than were accounted for in that manner at Gettysburg. Chancellorsville had been mostly a bloodbath, with only about thirty men reported as missing or captured. Mass slaughter occurred at Gettysburg as well, but the rapid descent of the Mississippians on the left flank of the regiment resulted in a comparatively high number of men being taken prisoner. The number of men missing or captured at that battle was estimated at 59. On both occasions, several of those who were captured were also wounded, though at Gettysburg many were not.[2]

It is more difficult to estimate the number of casualties suffered by the 114th in their first battle. No compiled statistics concerning the regimental losses at Fredericksburg survive. There are only scattered notations in the books and records of the regiment that probably do not reflect the true rate of casualty. Many who were only slightly wounded and not admitted to hospitals were probably not counted as a matter of record. The best assessment of the Zouave losses on December 13, 1862, using only those verifiable sources that are available, would be approximately fifteen men. With the exception of the regimental band, which had been captured when the army withdrew north of the Rappahannock, none of the Zouaves were taken prisoner. Since the strength of the 114th at Fredericksburg was probably near 700 men present for duty, this estimate of loss would support a casualty rate of only 2.1 percent. Several men other than those officially reported wounded undoubtedly would have been injured slightly and not have required extended medical attention. Although it is impossible to make a numerical estimate of these men, the figure could not be large and would raise the casualty rate by an insignificant amount. The numbers would in no way compare to the losses from the two subsequent battles.[3]

The regiment had passed through its worst ordeals by the summer of 1863. It would continue to suffer casualties, of course, but nothing like those inflicted at Chancellorsville and Gettysburg. Not until April 3, 1865, when the Zouaves participated in the final attack on the Rebel defenses of Petersburg, did they again suffer losses in any significant num-

2. Regimental Casualties, Records of the 114th PV, Record Group 94, NARA; Bates, *Pennsylvania Volunteers*, III, 1184–97.

3. Regimental Casualties, Records of the 114th PV, Record Group 94, NARA; Bates, *Pennsylvania Volunteers*, III, 1184–97.

ber. There were about 288 men present for duty on that spring day; 33 of them were killed or wounded; none were captured. Thus, the casualty rate reached about 11.5 percent. Though this percentage was less than half the rate for men killed and wounded at Chancellorsville or at Gettysburg, the loss was very likely felt more keenly by the survivors—both in the regiment and at home—because the end of the war was so near. Their suffering must have been intensified by the thought that so many men who had passed safely through some of the heaviest fighting of the war had fallen on victory's doorstep, the final goal within reach.[4]

Word of the death of a loved one in the army was never easily received, no matter how much those at home thought they had prepared themselves for the possibility that it might arrive. Though death was no stranger to families of the mid-nineteenth century, those it touched were not inured to grief. By August, 1863, most families had been affected by the war-related death of a close friend or relative. The death rate for military-aged men in Philadelphia during the war years has been estimated as approximately three times the normal peacetime death rate. Religion and family support played important roles in allaying the survivors' grief, but for many it was a difficult time. The recollections of one Pennsylvania soldier whose brother fell at Chancellorsville may illustrate the prevailing mood.

> Although not entirely unlooked for, yet when it came it well nigh crushed the spirit of my mother. I believe those were more trying times for the friends at home, who had fathers, husbands and sweethearts in the army, than for the soldiers themselves. They were anxious and worried all the time, and after each battle they were eager for letters from the front, but every seal was broken with great fear and trembling. The brave, selfreliant soldier seldom worried about himself, and when the fatal bullet snuffed him out, he became unconscious of years of grief and sorrow but just beginning at home.

Some men were fortunate to have family members present during their last hours. Corporal Kenderdine, severely wounded at Gettysburg, first had the company of a fellow Zouave, Private James S. Priest, who "did all he could to make him comfortable" until Kenderdine's father located his dying son on July 10. The young corporal had lain without medical attention

4. Regimental Casualties, Records of the 114th PV, Record Group 94, NARA; Bates, *Pennsylvania Volunteers*, III, 1184–97.

until the wounded were recovered from the field on July 4. Then Robert Kenderdine was taken to a field hospital on Rock Creek, where his father found him. According to Private Priest's recollection, "Robert recognized [his father] for a moment, but soon wandered off in the delirium which had clouded his mind since his arrival from the battle-field." Perhaps he had lingered in hopes of seeing his loved ones one final time. Robert died on July 10, soon after his father's arrival.[5]

Many of the casualties suffered by the Zouaves were due not to death or wounding but to capture. Numerous men were taken prisoner in the confused battles, where suffocating smoke, deafening noise, and imminent danger often caused soldiers to be separated from their comrades. Sometimes, those who stood fast were simply overwhelmed. Most of the men of the 114th who were taken prisoner during the war were later paroled and exchanged. Many of them returned to the regiment to fight again, and were mustered out with the other veterans in May, 1865. By discounting the number of men in this category, and tabulating only the number of killed and wounded, it may be more precisely estimated that the Zouaves suffered about 295 casualties in battle. This figure amounts to about 29 percent of the total number in the regiment. When one subtracts from the total number of men in the regiment those who died of disease, deserted the ranks of the 114th, or were otherwise not available on the battlefield, the percentage of killed and wounded appears somewhat higher—possibly as great as 40 or 45 percent.[6]

An examination of the ages of those who became casualties reveals that the average age at enlistment of those killed was 20.8 years old. The median age was 21. For those who were wounded, the average age at enlistment was 23.9, while the median was only 22. Taken together, then, the average age at enlistment of those either killed or wounded was 22.3 years. The median age was 22. (See Table 8.)[7]

5. Rice Papers, 1863, p. 77, USAMHI; Kenderdine Papers, HCWRT Collection, USAMHI. See Gallman, *Mastering Wartime*, 54–60, for a discussion of mourning in wartime Philadelphia.

6. The war department's adjutant general's office estimated in December, 1889, that 330 men of the 114th Pennsylvania were either killed or wounded during the war. Its estimate of the strength of the regiment was about 1,100 men, making the casualty rate 30 percent. See John P. Nicholson, ed., *Pennsylvania at Gettysburg* (4 vols.; Harrisburg, 1914), II, 974–75.

7. Records of the 114th PV and CMSR, Record Group 94, NARA; Bates, *Pennsylvania Volunteers*, III, 1187–96.

Table 8
Average and Median Ages of Killed and Wounded

	Number	Number with Known Age	Median Age	Average Age
Killed	75	67	21	20.8
Wounded	220	210	22	23.9
Total killed and wounded	295	277	22	22.3
Entire regiment	1016	863	22	25.0

The median age of those who were killed or wounded corresponds exactly with the median age of the members of the regiment as a whole. The average age, however, is 2.73 years younger than that of the regiment as a whole. This difference likely reflects the fact that officers, NCOs, and older privates did not constitute a high number of the total casualties. It seems significant that the average age of those killed or wounded is fully 2 years less than that of even the youngest group of men, privates. Of the 295 casualties, 77 were above the average age for the entire regiment, but even those men could not raise the average age of casualties enough to correspond to that found for the privates in the regiment as a whole.

As younger men composed the largest portion of the regiment, it hardly surprises that they suffered the most casualties. It is surprising, however, that in an age of battle when the role of officers was largely to inspire their men by their conspicuous presence on the battlefield, a higher number of officers were not among the killed and wounded. This curious phenomenon is undoubtedly accounted for by the fact that when deployed for battle in the usual fashion, a regiment formed a nearly solid double-line of riflemen; officers, by necessity, were positioned behind this line of men, where they could more freely, observe and encourage the men, and relay orders directing their fire and movement. Given that officers were generally older, it would seem that the death or wounding of more officers would have caused the average age of the total casualties to have corresponded more closely to that of the average age of the regiment as a whole. It is possible, however, that older men constituted a smaller number of the total casualties because their presence in the regiment was reduced by several intervening factors. Older men may have been more prone to experience sickness and to succumb to the adverse effects of life in the field. Thus, they may have been more often listed as sick, laid up in the hospital, or discharged for medical reasons. In addition, since older men composed a higher number of skilled and more semiskilled workers, it seems likely that they would have been called upon regularly for the types of details requiring persons with some degree of education and ability. Such assignments would have removed some of them from the ranks and reduced the likelihood of their becoming casualties.

Inspection of the occupations of those who were killed or wounded reveals that 10.3 percent of those killed and 12.4 percent of those wounded were skilled workers. Combining these groups, skilled workers constituted 11.9 percent of all casualties whose occupation could be determined, compared with a total percentage of skilled workers in the regiment of 16.7 percent. It must be remembered that the total percentage of workers in any category was derived only from the number of men whose occupation was specified in the regimental records. The number of men whose occupation could be determined was less than the total number of men known to be in the regiment, and also less than the total number of casualties.[8] When actual numbers are compared, it emerges that 30 of the total of 67 workers known to be skilled became casualties. By this calculation, 44.8 percent of all confirmed skilled workers were either killed or wounded. (See Table 9.)

Assigned to the category of semiskilled workers were 81.0 percent of those killed and 79.4 percent of those wounded. Semiskilled workers thus composed 79.8 percent of all casualties, compared with their overall representation in the regiment of 74.1 percent. Again, a comparison of actual numbers of semiskilled workers who were killed or wounded reveals that 201 of 298 became casualties. Thus, 67.4 percent of all semiskilled workers were killed or wounded.

When a distinction is made between more and less semiskilled workers, a breakdown of the casualties by occupation reveals that 39.6 percent of those killed and 41.2 percent of those wounded came from the category of more semiskilled workers. In all, 40.9 percent of all casualties whose skill level could be determined were more semiskilled workers, compared with a total of 51.7 percent of the semiskilled men in the regiment fitting

8. Records of the 114th PV and CMSR, Record Group 94, NARA; Bates, *Pennsylvania Volunteers*, III, 1187–96.

Table 9

Killed and Wounded at Known Occupational Skill Levels

Skill Level	Number in Regiment (%)	Number Killed (%)	Number Wounded (%)	Total Casualties (%)	% of Regiment
Skilled	67 (16.7)	6 (10.3)	24 (12.4)	30 (11.9)	(44.8)
Semiskilled	298 (74.1)	47 (81.0)	154 (79.4)	201 (79.8)	(67.4)
More	154 (51.7)	23 (39.6)	80 (41.2)	103 (40.9)	(66.9)
Less	144 (48.3)	24 (41.4)	74 (38.1)	98 (38.9)	(68.1)
Unskilled	37 (9.2)	4 (6.9)	13 (6.7)	17 (6.7)	(45.9)

that classification. The number of more semiskilled men who became casualties was 103 out of a total of 154. This outcome means that 66.9 percent of the regiment's more semiskilled workers were killed or wounded.

Among less semiskilled workers, 41.4 percent were killed and 38.1 percent were wounded, for a total casualty rate of 38.3 percent. Men in this category made up 48.3 percent of the regiment's semiskilled workforce. Of the total of 144 men of the regiment identified in this category, 98, or 68.1 percent, became casualties.

Finally, unskilled workers constituted 6.9 percent of those killed and 6.7 percent of those wounded. Unskilled workers thus totaled 6.7 percent of all casualties in comparison with a total of 9.2 percent of them present in the regiment as a whole. A comparison of actual numbers reveals that 17 of 37 unskilled workers were killed or wounded. This figure represents a casualty rate 45.9 percent among all unskilled workers.

A final method of viewing the casualty rate in comparison with various occupational skill levels entails examining the percentage difference between casualty rates and the proportion of men in each skill category. For skilled workers, the percentage of men who became casualties was 4.6 percent fewer than the total percentage of men in that skill category. For semiskilled workers, the rate was 6.9 percent greater than the total percentage in that category. Unskilled workers tallied 2.3 percent fewer casualties than the total percentage of men in that category. (See Table 10.)

The information presented indicates that those who bore the brunt of the casualties came from the most numerous class of workers, semiskilled;

Table 10

Comparison of Casualties at Known Occupational Skill Levels

Skill Level	Number of Men (%)	Number of Casualties (%)	% Difference
Skilled	67 (16.7)	30 (12.1)	(−4.6)
Semiskilled	298 (74.1)	201 (81.0)	(+6.9)
Unskilled	37 (9.2)	17 (6.9)	(−2.3)

and that men in that skill level suffered death and wounding at a number in excess of their proportional representation in the regiment. Decidedly, this working class of men fought with the greatest risk, for skilled and unskilled workers were, in contrast, killed and wounded at a number somewhat less than their proportional representation in the regiment. The most plausible explanation for this statistical deviation is that semiskilled workers, who composed the bulk of the regiment, had fewer opportunities to remove themselves from the front lines than did skilled workers, who may have been tapped for duties that permitted them to escape danger. Unskilled workers, on the other hand, may have individually created their own opportunities to remove themselves from danger.

Finally, a look at the place of birth of those who became casualties indicates that 51, or 20.0 percent, were foreign-born; while 203, or 80.0 percent, were born in the United States. Those born in this country suffered casualties at a rate 8.7 percent greater than their proportional representation in the regiment, while foreign-born Zouaves suffered 8.4 percent fewer casualties than their proportional representation in the regiment. (See Table 11.)

It may be concluded from the previous information that most casualties were suffered by men who were younger than average, semiskilled, and native-born. Older, skilled, unskilled, and foreign-born Zouaves suffered at disproportionately lower casualty rates than their presence in the regiment would suggest.

Another factor that served to reduce the number of men available in the regiment was desertion. The largest number of desertions from the 114th occurred in the first four months of the regiment's existence. After that,

Table 11
Comparison of Casualties by Birth

	Number in Regiment (%)	Number Killed (%)	Number Wounded (%)	Number Killed and Wounded (%)	% Difference
Native-born	241 (71.3)	49 (83.0)	154 (79.0)	203 (80.0)	(+8.7)
Foreign-born	97 (28.7)	10 (17.0)	41 (21.0)	51 (20.0)	(−8.7)

the number was considerably reduced and was spread over the remaining twenty-nine months of the war.

Desertions are difficult to calculate with accuracy. While some men deserted and never returned—which was the case with nearly all that occurred in the first four months—many others simply took advantage of the army's inability to prevent men from coming and going at will. Many weighed the consequences then resolved to take unauthorized leaves to visit home, with the intention of returning to the regiment after a short stay. Men were therefore reported as absent without leave, with the expectation that they would eventually return. If they did not come back within a reasonable period of time, they would be reported as deserters. This practice became increasingly risky for the soldiers as the war progressed and efforts to curb desertion became more severe.

Several factors other than opportunity probably influenced decisions to desert. One of these was boredom. Life in winter quarters gave ample opportunity for men to think long and often of home, or of holidays spent among loved ones. Such reveries frequently created an overwhelming desire to steal away for a visit, as did the two younger brothers of Company K's Lieutenant Edward E. Williams after the battle of Fredericksburg. Like the Williams boys, many of these men returned to the army afterwards and completed their term of service.

As might be expected, both the prospect of impending battle and the aftermath of battles fought also provided an apparent impetus for desertion. Men often dropped out on the march—especially when the route took them near convenient roads home, as during the Gettysburg campaign. Other men, disheartened by the carnage of the battlefield, made their way home in the confusion following the battles.

Battle also affected men in at least two additional ways. On one hand, wounded soldiers who were confined to hospitals, sometimes near their homes, invariably grew tired of the boredom and of the sporadic, ill-administered medical treatment. Several chose to leave the hospital and return home as soon as they recovered sufficiently. On the other hand, the death or wounding of a close comrade or relative also influenced soldiers' conduct. Nevertheless, close personal relationships probably factored into decision making even in the absence of death or injury, just as they had conditioned the decision of many to enlist. Family members often chose to desert together ; but instances of such behavior seem to prevail mostly when one of them had been killed, wounded, or otherwise rendered unable to continue in the service. This last phenomenon is illustrated by the interdependent actions of two Zouave brothers, Lewis and Charles B. Sloan. Charles, the thirty-year-old captain of Company H, was discharged on March 7, 1863, for medical disability stemming from the effects of bronchitis and diarrhea. His brother, Lewis, a twenty-four-year-old sergeant in the same company, deserted that same day. While he might have left with the intention of escorting his brother safely home, he evidently determined at some point not to return.[9]

Steps to curb desertions in the army during the first two years of the war were largely ineffective. It was not until March, 1863, that the groundwork for a policy change was laid. The Enrollment Act of March 3 required the provost marshal general in Washington to relay to the provost marshal of each congressional district all information regarding residents of that district who had been reported as deserters. All commanders—most importantly, those of the army's many regiments—were required to forward to the provost marshal general each month a descriptive list of deserters from their units. Eventually, the provost marshal was able to apprehend these men with the aid of soldiers of the Veteran Reserve Corps, a group of disabled men who were unfit for full duty in the field.

Ultimately, the one factor that seems to have decreased the incidence of desertion was the prospect of swift and sure capital punishment. The winter of 1863–1864 saw no repetition of the previous year's propensity

9. Records of the 114th PV and CMSR, Record Group 94, NARA; Bates, *Pennsylvania Volunteers*, III, 1187–96.

to desert. Men who chose to leave the army during the winter encampment of 1863–1864 ran a much greater risk of suffering the ultimate punishment. Hanging and death by firing squad were the preferred methods of administering this penalty, and the passage of a week without the spectacle of some lamentable fellow dangling from a scaffold or toppling bloodily backward into his own casket was rare. It had the desired deterring effect.[10]

Of the 274 known deserters gleaned from the regimental records of the 114th, 116 of them, or 42.3 percent, reneged on their commitment in the first four months of their enlistment, between July and November, 1862. While a number of these desertions may be attributable to the early September quarrel over the payment of the bounties, which led to a minor revolt, most of the men involved returned to duty and therefore were not reported or counted as deserters. Still, over 40 Zouaves left the ranks soon after taking the field in early September, never to return. By the time the Philadelphians departed their hometown on September 1, at least 47 of them had already chosen to remain at home. Perhaps some of these men had consciously made the decision to enlist with the intention of deserting after they had received the money offered by the city and state governments. There is no way to estimate the number of men of whom this might have been true, but it would have placed them among the earliest members of a despised group of men known as bounty jumpers. Later in the war, bounty jumping would become a lucrative, though hazardous, occupation.[11]

Of the remaining number of deserters, 89, or 32.5 percent, are definitely known to have deserted later than November, 1862. Unfortunately, the dates on which 69 others left the ranks could not be determined. This amounts to 25.2 percent of the total number of deserters. Since the majority of those whose date of desertion is unknown are also lacking any descriptive data, it seems likely that they also might have deserted early in their enlistment. This lack of descriptive data even suggests the probability that they deserted prior to the regiment's being mustered into Federal service in September.

10. Ella Lonn, *Desertion During the Civil War* (1928; rpr. Gloucester, Mass., 1966), 173–82.

11. Records of the 114th PV and CMSR, NARA; Bates, *Pennsylvania Volunteers*, III, 1187–96.

There are several possible reasons for the rash of desertions in the initial months of enlistment. I have already mentioned the possibility that some were bounty jumpers. In addition, as chapter 4 explains, the dispute over the payment of bounties, and the opinion of the men that the contract into which they had entered was not being honored, might have persuaded some that the government was not playing fair. Also to be considered, however, is the possibility that some men joined the regiment in the hope of being appointed or elected to a position of authority. As an example, a cooper may have been able to influence several of his coworkers to join him in forming the nucleus of a company in which he hoped to be made a sergeant. If, however, a seaman joined the company with the same intention, and was able to bring more of his friends and coworkers with him than those which the cooper was able to bring, the cooper may have found himself relegated to the lowest enlisted ranks despite his best efforts. The disgruntled soldier may then have decided to leave the regiment, and he could have influenced some of his friends to follow.

Similarly, a man may have discussed with his friends their desire to enlist in the 114th; but, upon enlisting himself, he may have found that their exuberance was not so strong as his, and that the sunshine patriots now declined to follow. The abandoned soldier would have been compelled to make new friends among his fellow enlistees, or desert. Finally, contributing to the attrition in ranks is the obvious fact that many men, once enlisted, found that the appeal of army life quickly wore thin. A brief taste of drill and camp life—including the offensive imperative to show respect to and to take orders from someone who, only days ago, would have been the butt of boyish pranks or jokes—may have been enough to drive several men away.

An examination of the known ages of 258 of the deserters reveals that the average and median ages at enlistment was 24.0 and 22 years old, respectively. The average age of deserters is very close to that of privates and NCOs in the regiment as a whole. The difference is only .5 years. This correspondence is likely due to the fact that no officers, who were generally somewhat older than enlisted men, were among the deserters; it also reflects the fact that most of the deserters belonged to the largest, and youngest, group of men within the regiment, privates. Again, the median age corresponds exactly to the median age of all members of the regiment. From this information, we may conclude that no particular age group was disproportionately prone to desertion, and that the propensity was evenly distributed among the men of the 114th. (See Table 12.)

Although the median ages for deserters and for those who became casualties correspond exactly, the average age of deserters was nearly two years older than the average age of those who were killed or wounded. This would seem to indicate that a larger number of older men deserted than became casualties. In this connection, recall that the foregoing discussion of the ages of casualties illuminated the fact that older men suffered death and wounding at a percentage somewhat less than their proportional representation in the regiment. To the reasons previously listed may be added the observation that older men were slightly more likely to desert than to appear on the casualty lists.

A review of the occupational skill levels of deserters found that 12 of those whose occupations could be considered skilled had deserted. This group amounts to 10.4 percent of the 115 deserters whose occupation is known, and is far less than the percentage of skilled laborers in the regiment, 16.7. In addition, under 18 percent of all skilled workers in the regiment deserted. This figure is the lowest of any of the occupational skill groups. (See Table 13.)

Semiskilled workers also deserted less frequently than their proportional representation in the regiment would suggest. Eighty-one, or 70.4 percent, of the deserters were semiskilled workers, as compared with 74.1 percent of the regiment who were classed in that category. Again, this was the largest group of workers represented, and the percentages for deserters in this category correspond most closely with the total number of semiskilled men in the regiment. The same is true both of more and of less semiskilled men. In general, only about 27 percent of semiskilled workers deserted.

Unskilled laborers, on the other hand, deserted in far greater numbers than their proportional representation in the regiment would lead us to expect. Though unskilled workers accounted for only 9.2 percent of the regiment, 22, or 19.1 percent, of them became deserters. Nearly 60 percent of all unskilled workers deserted. Perhaps for this reason, they are also under-represented in the total number of casualties.

Examination of the known place of birth of 114 of those who deserted indicates that 23, or 20.2 percent, were foreign-born, while 91, or 79.8 percent, were natives of this country. Non-native soldiers deserted in numbers fewer than their proportional representation, while native-born de-

Table 12
Ages of Regimental Deserters and Casualties

Regimental Group	Number	Median Age	Average Age
NCOs, privates	825	22	24.5
Deserters	258	22	24.0
Casualties	277	22	22.3

Table 13
Skill Levels of Deserters

Skill Level	Number in Regiment (%)	Number of Deserters (%)	% of Deserters
Skilled	67 (16.7)	12 (10.4)	(17.9)
Semiskilled	298 (74.1)	81 (70.4)	(27.2)
More	154 (38.3)	42 (36.5)	(27.3)
Less	144 (35.8)	39 (33.9)	(27.1)
Unskilled	37 (9.2)	22 (19.1)	(59.5)

serters exceeded their proportion in the regiment by 8.5 percent. (See Table 14.)

The number of desertions in the 114th Pennsylvania seems to far exceed the estimate made by the provost marshal general for the average among volunteer regiments. His report gave a figure of 62.51 per 1,000 for volunteers, and 244.5 per 1,000 for regular army troops. The Zouaves more closely matched the estimate given for the regiments of the regular army. The question of whether the number of deserters in the 114th was excessive remains open to further examination by comparison with the desertion rate in other individual regiments. The 114th may not have been dissimilar to other urban eastern regiments, whose desertion rate was purportedly swelled by bounty jumpers and foreigners. In the 114th, at least, the claim that foreign-born soldiers may have unduly added to the total number of desertions seems invalid.[12]

12. Lonn, *Desertion*, 219.

Table 14
Birth Origins of Deserters

	Number in Regiment (%)	Number of Deserters (%)	% Difference
Native-born	241 (71.3)	91 (79.8)	(+8.5)
Foreign-born	97 (28.7)	23 (20.2)	(−8.5)

No matter the cause of the absences from the regiment, the men of the 114th needed only to look around them to know that their numbers had been severely reduced. The Zouaves spent July 3, 1863, on the battlefield gathering the weapons that lay in great heaps on the blood-soaked Pennsylvania soil. Sergeant Given estimated that his men picked up over two thousand muskets. Captain Bowen thought the number was only about five hundred, but the pile in which the guns were placed was four or five feet high and fifty to seventy-five feet long.[13]

The 114th rejoined its brigade at about 7:00 P.M., but within an hour the exhausted men were sent out to the front on picket duty. They remained all night without being disturbed by firing and were relieved at 8 o'clock on the morning of July 4. With no opportunity to rest, the soldiers were again instructed to begin gathering up stray weapons. They were probably cheered somewhat by the appearance of the regimental band, which had been assisting at the division hospital. The musicians played a few patriotic airs in honor of the day, including "The Star-Spangled Banner." The sound must have traveled over the field and wafted into the Rebel positions. A solitary shell soon came whistling overhead, a reminder that those who currently pledged allegiance to the Stars and Bars were yet nearby. By noon, a violent summer thunderstorm had begun. This downpour called a halt to the work, and those fortunate enough to have a shelter half or poncho quickly arranged it and tried to rest underneath. Sergeant Given and Thomas P. Wilkinson picked up two bayoneted muskets, jabbed them into the ground, and stretched their oilcloth poncho between the guns. Each man held on to an end of the poncho to prevent it from blowing down, and in that position they promptly fell asleep.[14]

13. Given Diary, n.d., in Given Collection, CWLM; "Collis' Zouaves," Philadelphia *Weekly Press*, June 22, 1887, p. 1.

14. Rauscher, *Music on the March*, 99; Given Diary, n.d., in Given Collection, CWLM.

Across the scarred fields, the equally spent men in gray waited for a counterattack. It was not forthcoming. Lee had shortened his lines and concentrated his artillery in expectation of such an offensive, but his opponent refused to budge from the security of his present position. By the evening of July 4, with no indication of a counterattack in sight, Lee began moving his battered army toward the safety of the Shenandoah Valley. With his retreating force were some four thousand prisoners. Among them were a number of Zouaves, including Lieutenant Colonel Cavada. Brigadier General Graham had also fallen into the hands of the enemy.

It was not until July 7 that the 114th joined the desultory pursuit of Lee's forces. Their route carried them first through the renowned Peach Orchard, the scene of such terrible slaughter on the second day's battle. The once fragrant orchard was now a wasteland. Nothing remained but the jagged stumps of the fruit trees that had been blown apart in the hail of lead and iron. All around were the carcasses of dead artillery horses and the bodies of the slain who had struggled bravely for control of that small piece of Pennsylvania farmland. The repulsive stench of decay pervaded all. The men were glad to push on and escape the scene of carnage. Precipitation and the passage of the heavily laden wagons and artillery had again turned the roads to mud, and the men were forced into the surrounding fields. They slogged on in miserable weather, through Emmitsburg and on to Mechanicstown (now Thurmont), Maryland.

The following day saw the men reach Frederick, where they headed west on the National Road toward Middletown. By July 12, after passing over a portion of the battlefield of Antietam, the men again assumed a position facing the Rebel army. The Third Corps was to be held in reserve during the impending attack. If a Union assault was successful, the men could be called upon at any time to exploit a breakthrough; if unsuccessful, they could be tasked to stem the likely counterattack.

Unable to cross the rain-swollen Potomac, Lee had drawn his forces up in a defensive perimeter surrounding the river passages at Williamsport and Falling Waters. Meanwhile, his engineers labored to construct a pontoon bridge and waited for the turbulent river to subside. Meade, for his part, had intended to attack on July 13, but, being opposed by a majority of his corps commanders, he delayed. Thus unopposed, the Rebel general began crossing his army after dark on the thirteenth, and by next morning nearly all were safely across the river.

When he found the enemy gone from his front once again, Meade

started his army south, shadowing his opponent's march up the Shenandoah Valley. The Zouaves began moving south on July 15, with their
regimental band leading the march in each of the small towns through
which the column passed. At first, it was not a difficult march for the men.
In an attempt to evade the summer heat but still keep pace with the
retreating Confederates, each day's march began early. Reveille on July 16
was at 3:30 A.M. By the time the day's heat became unbearable, the men
had advanced for many hours and were resting in camp under whatever
shade could be found or improvised. There was no shortage of good water
along the route, and their meager diet was supplemented by tin cups filled
with the blackberries that seemed to grow everywhere in the area. The
Zouaves reached Harpers Ferry the following day, and the band was moved
to play "John Brown's Body" with "more spirit than ever before" as they
filed past the engine house that marked the bloody end of that aboli-
tionist's exploits. For several more days, the column plodded due south,
reaching Manassas Gap on July 23.[15]

The Third Corps was then commanded by Major General William
Henry French. General Sickles had been seriously wounded on July 2, but
the feisty New Yorker would soon return to duty with a wooden leg as a
reminder of his service at Gettysburg. The corps had been commanded
temporarily by General Birney; but Meade soon called on French, who at
that time was in charge of the District of Harpers Ferry. He had assumed
his position as head of the Third Corps several days before July 22, on the
evening of which he received orders to detach a division. The division
French chose would support the cavalry that had been detailed to wrest
control of the mountain pass from the defending Georgian brigade of
Brigadier General Ambrose Ransom Wright.

French immediately dispatched the First Division, temporarily commanded by Brigadier General J. H. Hobart Ward, to Manassas Gap. The
Zouaves were awakened at 3 A.M., and shortly after they began their march
to the foot of the Blue Ridge Mountains. General Ward deployed the
division in line of battle and posted a picket line in its front. The 114th
Pennsylvania was detailed to the picket force, on the right of the division. When French arrived later that morning with the balance of the
Third Corps, Ward advanced his line toward the waiting Georgians. The
lone brigade was no match for an entire Union corps, however, who

15. Rauscher, *Music on the March*, 109.

steadily drove them back from their defenses. This encounter would be no Confederate Thermopylae, and the Zouaves readily joined in the victory, pushing the enemy pickets off Wapping Heights on the right side of the gap.[16]

There was no need for a Spartanlike defense of the pass that day. By the time the Georgians fell back from the gap, they were able to fall in with the final southward passing corps of Lee's army. With Manassas Gap cleared, the valley lay open to Meade's men. Yet their triumph was a hollow one. The long line of Confederates had already passed up the Valley Turnpike to safety. It was not until the following day that the Zouaves moved through the pass and on to the vicinity of Front Royal. They found none of the rapidly moving Rebel forces there, however.

The corps filed back through Manassas Gap and headed for Warrenton, where they camped for several days. On July 31, the men marched a few miles to the south and went into summer quarters at Sulphur Springs. For nearly six weeks the Zouaves would enjoy the comforts of the fading resort, with its park area shaded by stately trees, its cottages, and, of course, the spring itself. The men were told by their doctors that it was safe to drink freely of the spring water. Within two weeks, however, boils began to appear on their bodies, and many of them nervously rushed to the regimental surgeons. The doctors reassured the men and jokingly remarked that it was merely the salt pork being flushed from their systems.[17]

As the Philadelphians swam in the cooling waters of the north branch of the Rappahannock River, whose banks were overflowing with blackberries, their rejuvenated bodies and minds felt the hardships and horrors of the past several weeks begin to recede. General Birney had returned to take command of his division, and he detailed the Zouave band to his headquarters. He subsequently detailed the entire regiment to headquarters duty. Though fresh bread, vegetables, and other long-desired foods finally were served with regularity, and the soldiers' physical well-being had much improved, little had been done thus far about the men's outward appearance. This last concern was especially important to the Zouaves, who could not easily obtain replacements for the tattered clothing that hung on them like rags. Many of them had found it necessary to discard parts of their badly worn uniforms and to clad themselves instead in var-

16. OR, Vol. XXVII, Pt. 1, pp. 489–96; Rauscher, *Music on the March*, 110.

17. Rauscher, *Music on the March*, 114–15.

ious pieces of regulation army attire. When the Third Corps was reviewed during the first week of September, the Zouaves were so unpresentable that they were sent on picket duty instead of to the review.[18]

Colonel Collis returned to his command on August 16 and received a warm welcome. The regiment was formed up, and the colonel "was presented with a beautiful sword as an appropriate symbol of his soldierly bearing, and in evidence of the esteem in which he was held by the rank and file." The sword bore an inscription: "In commemoration of his distinguished bravery at Chancellorsville, May 3, 1863." This, if nothing else, should have laid to rest any doubt abroad that Collis' behavior on that day had been less than commendable. Surely, no hard-fighting veteran who had seen many of his comrades fall at his side would have assented to bestowing such an honor upon one whose behavior did not come up to the expectations of those he led.[19]

When the ceremony ended, Collis visited with the members of the regimental band. The colonel commented on the comfortable arrangements that the men were enjoying at Sulphur Springs. Then, with his usual trenchant logic, he remarked that it was "rather too nice to last long." His inference was soon proved correct.[20]

18. *Ibid.*
19. Rauscher, *Music on the March*, 116; C. Collis, *1st Brigade*, 25.
20. Rauscher, *Music on the March*, 116.

I I

Campaigning with Uncle George

The sound of bugles pierced the warm, late-summer air, shattering the stillness of the day and ending the tranquil repose of the veteran Zouaves. Those standing on the banks of the nearby stream, their soiled clothing boiling in kettles, stared wide-eyed at one another, scarcely believing that the unexpected call to "pack up" was summoning them. Nevertheless, their period of inactivity was at an end. The regiment was on the move again. It was September 14, 1863, and General George Meade's army was probing southward to see whether reports of a Confederate withdrawal were accurate. A brief cavalry engagement on the previous day had indicated that a portion of Lee's army had indeed been withdrawn, but the Rebel line at the Rapidan River was still a formidable one. Meade moved his troops across the Rappahannock to Culpeper Court House.[1]

The march of the Zouaves on September 14 was an easy one. They advanced only a few miles from Sulphur Springs. The next day they covered over twenty miles, passing southward through Culpeper and encamping on the right of the main road leading from the town. The regiment would remain there for some time, and though the accommodations did not measure up to the standards of their previous camp, the men were surely happy to continue their respite from hard marching and fighting.

A few days after their arrival, the band members were notified that

---

1. Rauscher, *Music on the March*, 117; OR, Vol. XXIX, Pt. 1, p. 9.

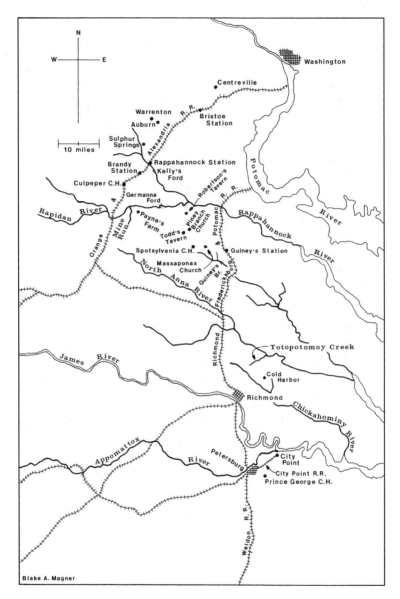

Area covered by the Zouaves while assigned as headquarters guard for Major General Birney (August, 1863, until March, 1864) and as headquarters guard for the Army of the Potomac commanded by Major General Meade (March, 1864, until April, 1865)

their sorely needed new instruments had arrived at Culpeper. The musicians left excitedly to collect them; when they arrived back in camp, they found that they had been honored with an invitation to play for General Meade at army headquarters. Colonel Collis, who had been elevated to command the First Brigade, started off immediately with the band. The bandsmen must have been slightly apprehensive about playing for the "critical audience" comprised of the "large and distinguished military family" at Meade's headquarters. They found the encampment to be set in a carefully selected location and meticulously maintained. The tents formed a semicircle, with the commander in the center, the chief of staff on his right, and the adjutant on the left. "The remainder of the retinue [had] positions according to their rank," recalled one Zouave.[2]

Notwithstanding the musicians' fears for the success of the concert, their playing was warmly received. With candle bearers at their sides to light the difficult sheet music, they began with a rendition of "Hell on the Rappahannock," followed by several selections from various operas, and wound up their introductory set with a rousing galop. Such eclectic music was rarely performed by army bands. While most of the army bands were able to play popular tunes with varying degrees of skill, none, apparently, could offer the selection of operatic numbers that the talented Zouave musicians presented. The distinctiveness of their program and the skill of the musicians tended to make them popular among the officers of the various headquarters. Collis and the bandsmen were complimented lavishly that evening by the pleased audience. This performance was long to be remembered.[3]

Throughout the remainder of September and the first week of October, 1863, Meade's forces lay in position near Culpeper, with two corps advanced south to the banks of the Rapidan River. Earlier in September, Meade had dispatched the Eleventh and Twelfth Corps to the west, shoring up the Federal defenses at Chattanooga, Tennessee. Sometime before that move, Lee likewise had weakened his own army by sending an entire corps to bolster the southern forces to the west. With the help of General James Longstreet's First Corps, the Confederates had seemingly scored a much-needed victory at Chickamauga Creek in Georgia on September 20. To follow up that incentive in his own theater of operations, Lee proposed

2. Rauscher, *Music on the March*, 119–20.
3. *Ibid.*, 121–22.

to move on Meade's right flank, with a view to forcing him to retreat and to give battle while on the move or in the open.[4]

What became known as the Bristoe Campaign, named for the resulting contest at the Orange and Alexandria railroad depot of that name, began on October 9. Meade immediately began the withdrawal of his army once Lee's intentions became known to him. His objective was to reach the strong defensive positions at Centreville, less than twenty miles from Washington. Over the next several days, a series of skirmishes and engagements ensued along the line of the retreating army, but Lee was never able to catch the rapidly retreating Meade or to marshal enough force to bring the northerners to decisive battle.

On October 13, as the Third Corps neared the village of Auburn, dismounted Rebel cavalry poured a volley into the head of the column in an apparent attempt to slow its crossing of the bridge over Cedar Run. General Birney, whose First Division led the column, quickly had Collis form his brigade across the road along with a portion of de Trobriand's Second Brigade. Collis led the men forward in a charge that "speedily dislodged" the enemy from their position. The Zouaves lost five enlisted men who were wounded in the resulting skirmish, while Company C lost their second lieutenant, William J. Miller. Miller had been a twenty-three-year-old plasterer when he enlisted. He probably had a difficult time resuming his occupation after his discharge in 1864; he was severely wounded in the shoulder.[5]

The following day, the Second Corps, at the rear of Meade's retreating army, took position behind the railroad embankment near Bristoe Station and easily repulsed an ill-conceived attack by Lieutenant General Ambrose Powell Hill's Third Corps. Hill lost about 1,400 men and five guns, while the Federals suffered fewer than 600 casualties. Though he blamed himself for attacking too hastily, Hill knew that the quickly moving column would have been gone from his front had he waited longer. "In that event," he wrote, "I should equally have blamed myself for not attacking at once." It was a gamble that did not pay off. Meade won the race to the fortifications at Centreville, where, Lee realized, any further attempts to

4. Freeman, *Lee's Lieutenants*, III, 239; Emory M. Thomas, *Bold Dragoon: The Life of J. E. B. Stuart* (New York, 1986), 264; *OR*, Vol. XXIX, Pt. 1, p. 410.

5. *OR*, Vol. XXIX, Pt. 1, pp. 311–12; Casualty Lists, Records of the 114th PV, Record Group 94, NARA.

flank him out of that position would be compromised. The Union army would beat another hasty retreat to the defenses of Washington and Alexandria, which the Confederates were in no condition to surround. Consequently, Lee began heading his destitute army back to the Rappahannock, tearing up the Orange and Alexandria Railroad along the way.[6]

From his headquarters near Centreville on October 17, General Birney published an order thanking the officers and men of his division for their "admirable conduct" during the retreat from Culpeper. "Especial credit is due to the First Brigade, Colonel Collis, for its gallantry in repulsing the enemy's attack . . . at Auburn," he wrote. He went on to compliment the colonel for "his skill and promptitude in making the dispositions ordered." Given this praise, relations between the two officers may have seemed to be on the mend, but they were not so.[7]

Collis had, in fact, been conspiring with Judge Read to have his regiment transferred to Brigadier General John C. Robinson's Second Division of the First Corps. Read wrote to General Meade on at least two occasions in reference to the subject. His first letter, probably written sometime in September, 1863, apparently had been referred to General French, who approved the change. Meade failed to act, however, and Read again wrote to him on October 4. "I regret troubling you again," he told the general. "But I am so convinced of the propriety and necessity of the transfer that I would respectfully request you to have it made notwithstanding any opposition that may be made to it."[8]

Read had also been in contact with Birney. On the same day that he first wrote to Meade, he also wrote again to Birney, telling him of his request to have Collis and the 114th transferred to Robinson's command. It was, he said, "a measure which I think under the circumstances you will agree is expedient and proper and to which I trust you will give your approval." In order to speed the process he was recommending, Read also included a carefully veiled threat in this letter: "I expect to pay a visit to Washington before our election and I hope to hear the transfer has been made before I reach there." From these words, it was clear, at least to Birney, that Read would oppose his confirmation to the rank of major general if he did not expedite the transfer. Birney's apparent good will

6. OR, Vol. XXIX, Pt. 1, pp. 407–11, 426–27.

7. *Ibid.*, 313.

8. Read to "General [Meade]," October 4, 1863, in Read Papers, HSP.

toward Collis was thus probably only a screen designed to ward off the wrath of the powerful Philadelphia judge.[9]

The events of the Bristoe campaign put such matters on hold, however. Before they could be acted upon again, incessant pressure from Washington had compelled Meade to pursue Lee and to take some offensive action. By early November, he had ordered his army to be divided into two wings, one commanded by Major General John Sedgwick, the other by French. Each wing was to move southward from Warrenton: Sedgwick's to Rappahannock Station, and French's to Kelly's Ford. From these points, they were to cross the Rappahannock River and converge on Lee at Brandy Station. The plan enacted would be known as the Mine Run Campaign, and its results would greatly damage French's reputation, thus depriving Collis of the support of a powerful ally.

The advance began on the morning of November 7, and the divided army accomplished the crossing of the Rappahannock with little delay. The surprised Rebel defenders were easily swept aside, and by noon, French's wing was on the road to Brandy Station. The 114th incurred no losses that afternoon, and the Zouaves appeared in better fighting trim than they had done for some time. Many of the men captured at Chancellorsville and Gettysburg had recently returned from Camp Parole. There were also a number of new recruits engaging in their first campaign. Among the latter was a small group of Frenchmen who had been brought from their homeland through the efforts of an enlisting agent. Disgruntled, these foreign-born men soon found that they had been misled. When they had enlisted, they thought that their Zouave regiment was composed of their countrymen. They were disappointed to find only a few men with whom they were able to converse in their native tongue.[10]

Meade encamped near Brandy Station and began rebuilding the vital railroad and the bridge across the Rappahannock. The army's southward movement would not get underway again until November 26, when an advance designed to turn the right of the Confederate line along the Rapidan River was begun. It was during this advance that General French encountered difficulties in complying with Meade's orders. The inability of the engineers to complete the pontoon bridge had quickly delayed the crossing of the Rapidan. The river, it seems, was somewhat wider than

9. Read to "General [Birney]," October 4, 1863, *ibid.*
10. Rauscher, *Music on the March*, 132–33.

supposed, and the engineers had underestimated the number of pontoon boats needed to span it. The bridge was one boat short of the opposite bank. By the time the engineers had constructed a makeshift trestle, French's advance was far behind schedule. In addition, the trestle could not support the weight of the artillery or ammunition wagons, which had to be sent across at Germanna Ford, a few miles downriver. It was an inauspicious beginning.

When the Third Corps encountered enemy resistance near Payne's Farm on the afternoon of the November 27, Birney's division was at the rear of the column. French ordered Birney to form his line in rear of Brigadier General Joseph Bradford Carr's Third Division. Birney placed Egan's brigade behind the center of Carr's line. He then positioned Ward's brigade to the right rear of Egan's, and Collis' brigade to the left rear. Carr's line was soon hotly engaged, and Birney eventually was forced to send Ward to support his right flank. Next it was the center of the line that became hard pressed. Birney moved Egan's brigade up to the relief of that portion of the line. With the enemy then attempting to turn the left flank, Birney moved Egan's men in that direction and ordered Collis' brigade into position in the center of the division line.

Collis, meanwhile, had detached the 114th earlier in the afternoon with orders to support Clark's Battery B, 1st New Jersey Light Artillery. But when the fighting along the line became heavy, Collis realized that his brigade might need the help of the Zouaves. He sent Major Bowen an order to bring up the 114th and rejoin the brigade. The Zouaves had "considerable difficulty" locating their brigade, however, and by the time they took position, the battle was nearly over. The Red Legs relieved the 141st Pennsylvania near dark, and remained there in line of battle throughout the night.[11]

Though his regiment largely had been spared during this engagement and had suffered no loss, Collis himself had remained at the front of his brigade during the heaviest fire. He recalled it as "one of the sharpest and best fought affairs of the war."

> The musketry was the most terrific any of us had ever heard, and the chances of getting off without a decent wound was about as poor as it could possibly have been. No sooner had I ridden to the front on my handsome grey than a hundred rifles erupted themselves at me—half a dozen men

11. OR, Vol. XXIX, Pt. 1, pp. 756–57.

standing near me went through a series of gyrations . . . Only one ball hit me and that, passing through all my wardrobe to the damage of about $50 worth of Irish frieze and broadcloth, came to a stop in my horse's neck on the off side.

I thought at first that I was badly hurt and clasped my hip with my right hand, when [First Lieutenant Frank C.] Grugan (my A. A. G.) with criminal coolness touched his hat and mildly asked "Shall I go for Col. [Henry J.] Madill Sir." [12]

The prospect of being hit by one of the many projectiles that flew about the battlefield seemed to Collis to be great. He perceived the whistling iron and lead to be coming closer with each passing fight, and he thought it likely that in the next battle one shot would find its mark and see him "get a thirty day fellow." Many men hoped that when finally struck down, they would be wounded only slightly. If they could escape with a minor wound, they imagined, the odds of being struck again were greatly reduced. Others less inclined to play the odds probably hoped to be injured just enough to be sent to the Veteran Reserve Corps. It would be some time before Collis or the 114th would be asked to play the odds again. [13]

On the morning of November 28, Meade discovered that the Confederates had pulled back to a defensive position behind Mine Run. The Zouaves withdrew from the scene of the previous day's battle and marched with the brigade southward to the vicinity of Mine Run. The 114th moved along the Orange Turnpike some distance past Robertson's Tavern, where they filed off to the left of the road and formed in support of Randolph's battery that evening. At daylight on the twenty-ninth, Randolph's guns moved forward and went into battery preparatory to an assault on the Mine Run defenses. The Zouaves deployed on the battery's left flank and quickly began constructing breastworks as protection against the fire that the artillery would draw. It proved to be an uneventful day for the infantrymen, however, and they rejoined their brigade after being relieved on the morning of December 1. By daylight on the second, they were back on the north side of the Rapidan, the unsuccessful Mine Run Campaign at an end. The Zouaves had suffered no loss at all, while the rest of Collis' brigade lost a total of thirty-seven men and three officers. [14]

12. C. Collis to "My dear father," December 15, 1863, in Collis Papers, HSP.
13. *Ibid.*
14. *OR*, Vol. XXIX, Pt. 1, pp. 756–57, 681.

Meade withdrew his army to the vicinity of Culpeper once again and went into winter quarters. The vast array of blue-coated soldiers spread over the fields and woods around the vital railroad link at Brandy Station, while General French established his headquarters at Henry Miller's house at the base of Fleetwood Hill. From here, French would answer the inquiries into his blundering behavior during the Mine Run Campaign, often commiserating with his friend Colonel Collis, who still had troubles of his own.

Judge Read was yet attempting to use his influence both to secure the transfer of Collis' regiment to Robinson's division and to have the colonel elevated to the rank of brigadier general. "Do your duty steadily and it will enable me to act for you," wrote the judge. Collis had been further encouraged earlier in November when he was informed by French that he intended to seat the colonel "firmly in the saddle" by giving him permanent command of his brigade.[15]

Collis was fortunate that French, a relative of Judge Read, had been assigned to the corps. The colonel was in great need of an ally in his camp, for he was at odds with a number of his fellow officers. Much of the difficulty undoubtedly derived from the debated circumstances at Chancellorsville; but those events had only deepened the incipient and mutual dislike between Collis and Birney. By virtue of his rank and position, of course, Birney had attracted a following of ardent supporters. Collis believed that this clique was intent on destroying his reputation and career; hence his importunity in seeking a transfer and promotion. He set forth many of the perceptions regarding his vexatious predicament in a heartfelt letter to the judge. Birney's outward cordiality, he thought, resulted from his professed motto of "you pat me and I'll pat you."[16]

Collis also harbored some political beliefs that differed from those of his chief. "I am a Republican of 1856," he wrote to Read. "And I am fighting to day, first to abolish slavery—and second to restore the Union." He did not align himself with those in his party who questioned the passage of the Emancipation Proclamation and sustained it only because it had become law. Rather, he considered slavery "as much an instrument of war, as the Merrimac, and as much a target for our bullets." Collis also believed that he had been the first officer to request permission to raise a

---

15. C. Collis to "My dear Judge," November 18, 1863, in Read Papers, HSP.
16. *Ibid.*

"Regiment of Africans" when he petitioned the secretary of war in a letter dated May 10, 1862. Captain Robert Gould Shaw, with whom Collis had consulted, followed his example and, with the influence of Massachusetts governor John A. Andrew, was successful in fielding a black regiment.[17]

As an ardent Republican with strong antislavery feelings, Collis certainly belonged to a minority in the corps. Both Birney and Graham had been personal friends of General Sickles, a prominent Democrat. Though Sickles had been silent in the dispute prior to his wounding at Gettysburg, Collis thought that he had used his power to push for the promotion of colonels in his Excelsior Brigade. It was Collis' opinion that Sickles hoped to become governor of New York by securing the allegiance of officers from that state. Sickles also might have hoped to secure a nomination for the presidency with the help of the War Democrats. These political aspirations gave rise to an organization known as the Third Corps Union. The organization had been inaugurated at Birney's headquarters on September 2, 1863, and Sickles was elected in absentia. Other officers elected to positions at that time were New Yorkers: Captain James C. Briscoe, Birney's aide-de-camp; Major Henry Edwin Tremain, Sickles' aide-de-camp; and Brigadier General Gershom Mott of New Jersey, commander of the Third Brigade, Second Division, Third Corps. Though described by its founders as a benevolent organization, the union came to be perceived by Collis as useful only in advancing Sickles' and Birney's careers.

Collis had probably generated some resentment among his fellow officers when he refused to participate in the Third Corps Union, of which Sickles and Birney were president and vice-president, respectively. While at Sulphur Springs, shortly after returning from his illness, Collis, too, had been offered a position as one of the six directors of the organization. He was told that, among its other goals, the union's purpose was to send home the bodies of deceased officers and to support widows and orphans. The flattered colonel innocently accepted the position. But after conferring with General French, who had not been tendered an office in the union, Collis discovered the true purpose of the organization. Collis had not known French prior to his arrival as commander of the Third Corps, but he soon found that he was not only a relative of Read's, but "a gentleman of the first order—a giant compared to the Lilliputians who were plotting against him." Trusting French's view, Collis tactfully declined his recently

17. *Ibid.*

acquired directorship by noting that General Graham was expected to return to his command in a short time and that the position rightfully should be his.[18]

After terminating his connection with the union, Collis learned that General Meade had issued an order prohibiting such meetings among his officers. But his order was ignored—at least in Birney's command. It was obvious to officers of the Third Corps that General Birney harbored a dislike for the commanding general. "Mead[e] is not liked in this Corps," wrote one of the officers. "And is especially disliked by General Birney." Meade undoubtedly knew of the dissension among and disobedience of those officers. The men continued to meet once a week, where "the subaltern and Maj. Genl. are hail fellow well met, discussing the merits of their superiors." As for the professed benevolent intentions of the union, Collis scoffed at them, recalling that he had spent an entire night without rest in an effort to have returned to Philadelphia the body of one of his staff officers who had been killed at Kelly's Ford. Two days later he learned that the man had been a member of the union.[19]

The notion that he was surrounded by enemies and fellow officers whom he distrusted must have greatly depressed Collis. Eventually, such feelings overcame him, and he wrote to Read of his disgust with the entire situation: "I have had a good childish cry. I couldn't help it. Oh to think that my fair name should be tarnished by these miserable politicians. Ask the men who carry the muskets and stand in the front rank—they will tell you that I am always with them through thick and thin." He further claimed that his entire brigade, "*to a man*" wanted him to command them.[20]

Judge Read did his best to relieve the unease of his young friend and to satisfy the wishes of Collis' men. On December 4, he again wrote to Secretary of War Stanton concerning the colonel's promotion. He had appealed several months prior to that time, and had submitted a number of "testimonials of the strongest character" in support of his request. This time, he enclosed a letter of recommendation from French, endorsed by

18. *Ibid.*

19. Levi Bird Duff to "Dearest Harriet," June 29, 1863, in Levi Bird Duff Papers, Robert L. Brake Collection, USAMHI; C. Collis to "My dear Judge," November 18, 1863, in Read Papers, HSP.

20. C. Collis to "My dear Judge," November 18, 1863, in Read Papers, HSP.

Meade. He also noted that Collis had been commanding a brigade for several months past and should be advanced to the rank of brigadier general. "I ask this as a personal favor to myself," wrote Read, "knowing that he will never disgrace our National Flag."[21]

General French, in the meantime, was being questioned about his conduct during the recent campaign below the Rapidan. He had received notice on December 3 that Meade considered the delay in the Third Corps's movements and its failure to reach its objective on November 27 to have exerted "powerful influence" on the subsequent unsuccessful maneuvers. He called for an investigation into the causes for French's delay and requested a full explanation.[22]

French sent an immediate response to Meade's chief of staff, Major General Andrew Atkinson Humphreys. In it, he listed the reasons for the delay in his movements. Among them was the fact that the artillery had been sent to cross the river at Germanna Ford and was thus late in reaching him. He further stated that the head of his column lacked a guide and had lost its way. They were forced to backtrack to what they thought was the correct route, but soon found their way blocked by a large Confederate force near Jones's Cross Road and the Payne Farm. When the Rebel force withdrew on the night of November 27, French continued his march, arriving at his objective, Robertson's Tavern, a full day behind schedule.[23]

Collis, of course, had a great interest in supporting General French. He dined with the general several times each week and assisted him in preparing his reports. The two became "great friends," but Collis feared for the results of the investigation ordered by General Meade. So long as French remained in command, the colonel wrote, "I shall be very comfortable." "But if he goes away, woe be unto me." Collis took it upon himself to defend French from negative comments appearing in the press. He wrote the editor of Philadelphia's *Inquirer* that the report that General French was held under arrest was erroneous "and unjust to this gallant soldier."[24]

As for French, that general felt no particular anguish about the result

21. Read to "Dear Sir," December 4, 1863, *ibid.*

22. Andrew Atkinson Humphreys to "General [French]," December 3, 1863, *ibid.*

23. French to "General [Humphreys]," December 3, 1863, *ibid.*

24. C. Collis to "My dear father," December 15, 1863, in Collis Papers, HSP; C. Collis to "My dear Harding," December 17, 1863, in Read Papers, HSP.

of the investigation—provided that it remained public. He dreaded, however, the possibility that "his enemy [would] endeavor to accomplish his
purpose at Washington *secretly.*" In order to prevent that outcome, Collis
kept Read informed of events as they transpired and sent copies of all the
pertinent documents that were received and sent. French wanted the president and secretary of war to know that he, too, had friends and that Read
was one of his supporters. Read also set out the facts for Senator Charles
Sumner, and further assisted by ensuring that Meade had promptly forwarded French's report of the campaign to the War Department. Collis
had sent the general's report in duplicate, so that no delay would affect
the receipt of his rendition of events. The recriminations must have grown
embittered over time; for in one of his letters to the War Department,
French placed the blame for his stalled march on "one of his division
commanders," whom he did not name.[25]

General French never was disciplined formally for his tardiness during
the Mine Run Campaign. However, when the army was reorganized a few
months later, on March 23, 1864, he was left without a position. The
Third Corps was disbanded, and Birney's division was designated the Third
Division, Second Corps. Collis' brigade was also dispersed. The 141st
Pennsylvania went into Ward's First Brigade, while the 57th, 63rd, and
105th Pennsylvania were placed in Brigadier General Alexander Hays's
Second Brigade. The 114th and 68th Pennsylvania were attached to
Meade's headquarters.

To the men in the ranks, the winter encampment at Brandy Station was
another welcome respite from the rigors of marching and the unpredictable
weather. Collis' brigade reached its former campsite on the evening of
December 3. "We found our tents all standing and so we moved right in
and now we are once more as comfortable as soldiers could wish to be,"
wrote one man in the 57th Pennsylvania.[26]

The men soon began to erect huts for more permanent quarters, but
they had little time to enjoy the fruits of their labor. During the first week
of January, 1864, the entire brigade was ordered to move a few miles deeper
into the woods. Having spent several backbreaking days clearing the

25. C. Collis to "My dear Judge," December 12, 16, 1863, in Collis Papers, HSP.
26. Strauss to "Dear Mother," December 4, 1863, in *CWTI* Collection, USAMHI.

ground and building their shelters, the men received the news with dismay. "They were considerably enraged about it, officers and men alike," recalled one Zouave. Their camp had been on the property of John Minor Botts, a staunch Union sympathizer who supposedly was hated by Rebel cavalryman J. E. B. Stuart; now he was maligned by the men of the Third Corps as well. Botts surely appreciated having the blue-clad soldiers nearby—but not too close. The men had been "too neighborly, or as the darkey expresses it 'too familious like,'" and Botts feared that his fences and livestock would soon disappear altogether. The soldiers railed against Botts's lack of patriotism as they trudged through six inches of snow to their new camp.[27]

While an icy wind blew down off the Alleghenies that night, the men of the 141st Pennsylvania stood around a campfire and, with typical good humor, vented their frustration. We "howled ourselves hoarse (singing we called it) with the tune 'Dixie' and the following doggerel which we call 'Botts's Land'":

> Way down South in the Old Dominion,
> Land of darkeys and persimmons
> Look Away! Away! Away! Away!
> There lived a man whose name was Minor
> Thought he was a "whale" but was only a "shiner"
> Look Away! Away! Away! Away!
> Away down South on Botts's land
> Hurra! Hurra!
> On Botts's land we took our stand
> And thought we'd stay on Botts's land
> Away! Away! Away down South on Botts's.
> But Birney's boys were very cruel,
> They took old Botts's rails for fuel,
> Look Away! etc.

The song went on for several more verses, culminating in an appraisal of their current situation.

> The winds blow cold and the snow lies deep,
> No tents put up! No place to sleep!
> Look Away! etc.

27. Rauscher, *Music on the March*, 144.

> And the boys are mad and spend the night,
> Cursing old Botts by campfire light,
>   Look Away! etc.

The men may eventually have felt some satisfaction on learning that one of Botts's daughters had become pregnant by a sergeant in a Massachusetts regiment: Botts must have suffered an intense degree of emotional anguish. Years later—probably unknown to any of the Pennsylvanians—the Virginia supreme court of appeals ruled that Botts had fraudulently obtained the deed to his property. It was returned to the original owner.[28]

Many of the men in Collis' brigade were able to obtain furloughs that winter. Some of them received a leave of thirty-five days after reenlisting for three more years. The 57th Pennsylvania was one such regiment in the brigade whose initial period of enlistment was slated to end in spring, 1864. "You will perhaps feel grieved to hear that I have enlisted again without even asking you," wrote a soldier to his mother. He tried to console her: "I have studied the matter carefully and you can rest assured that I did not rush into it blindly." He cited his motives—"Patriotism and Self-Interest," noting that the reenlistment of a large number of veterans "will have a terrible effect on the South, and also upon the Cowardly Copperheads of the North." In addition, he was confident that the rebellion would be brought to an end within the next year. "There fore I think it will not make our term of Service any longer than it would be if we did not reenlist."[29]

Colonel Collis, still fretting over his chances for promotion, was afraid to absent himself from the army that winter lest someone else grab the opportunity to "ask promotion on the ground that he was commanding a Brigade." Instead, he invited his father, who had left the army by then and returned to Philadelphia, to come down and visit. His wife Septima arrived with the new year, and the happily reunited couple spent several days in surroundings that Mrs. Collis later termed "the most picturesque home I have ever lived in." Two army tents—one serving as the parlor, the other as a bedroom—were all that constituted the humble quarters. Their bucolic lifestyle was soon cut short by the arrival of their young

28. "Extract from a Soldier's Letter," undated newspaper clipping (*ca.* January, 1864), in Coburn Papers, USAMHI; Clark B. Hall, "Season of Change: The Winter Encampment of the Army of the Potomac, December 1, 1863–May 4, 1864," *Blue and Gray*, VIII (April, 1991), 50.

29. Strauss to "Dear Mother," January 1, 1864, in *CWTI* Collection, USAMHI.

daughter, and the family moved into the Culpeper home of a Mr. Yancey, whom Mrs. Collis recalled as being "an awful rebel."[30]

Those not able to obtain a furlough or to receive a visit from loved ones settled into the dreariness of winter quarters and sought occasional distractions from their increasing boredom. There was a large chapel in the brigade in which services were held each evening by "eminent Clergymen from Philadelphia assisted by the Chaplains of the different Regts in the Brigade." The services were attended by a large number of men, both enlisted and officered, and it was thought that they would "tend greatly to improve the Morality of the Brigade."[31]

Despite such feelings among some of the Pennsylvanians in Collis' brigade, gambling was reported to be rife throughout the army at that time "to a demoralizing extent." Groups of soldiers could be seen gathered at various places throughout the camps playing a game called "sweat-box." Even "French Mary" had been tempted to try her luck, but she was soon fifty dollars poorer for the experience. General Birney was finally compelled to issue orders directing the camp guards to drive the players from the field whenever they were observed.[32]

Unlike their comrades, the regimental band members were not at all bored. They were engaged in a busy performance season that winter, playing each night at various headquarters at the request of their respective commanders. The bandsmen had received a number of offers to attach themselves to those headquarters, including Meade's. When the men of the 114th learned of the attempts to separate the band from their regiments, they immediately voted that the band should be permitted to belong to no other than the regiment that brought it to the field. The issue was temporarily settled when both the band and the regiment were detailed to Meade's headquarters. Shortly after the army's reorganization, the delicate question was resolved conclusively. At the daily dress parade on March 31, 1864, an order was read attaching the regiment and the band permanently to the headquarters guard, Army of the Potomac.[33]

The elimination of the Third Corps and the subsequent rearrangement of Birney's division left Collis without a brigade to command. Just as

30. C. Collis to "My dear father," December 15, 1863, in Collis Papers, HSP; S. Collis, *War Record*, 29–33.

31. Strauss to "Dear Mother," December 21, 1863, in CWTI Collection, HSP.

32. Rauscher, *Music on the March*, 139–40.

33. Fox Diary, March 31, 1864, in Fox Collection, HSP.

French was displaced from command of a corps, so Collis was from command of one of Birney's brigades. In a letter that spring, Birney revealed his true feelings about Collis and his glee at being able to squeeze the colonel out of his position as brigade commander.

> As to Collis, my opinion is unchanged. He was sustained by Judge Read on all occasions, and gave me much annoyance. In the reorganization I had the power to divide my division into two brigades, and I killed him off in the reconstruction, by placing in the brigade colonels to rank him. He immediately applied for the cowardly, ignoble position of guarding the headquarters train, cattle and matters around provost marshal's. General Meade offered me another regiment in their place, and I accepted instanter. . . . I am glad to be rid of him; he was thoroughly despised in my command.[34]

The ousted colonel was not "killed off" so easily, however. Though he would no longer serve under Birney, Collis quickly found a position—as implied in the general's letter—commanding the Headquarters Brigade. Whether it was a "cowardly" and "ignoble position" is open to debate; but with French gone and his chances for promotion vanished with his former brigade, Collis certainly chose the most practical assignment available to him. In fact, as his regiment was already temporarily detailed to Meade's headquarters, the only place for the colonel to go at that time was back to the 114th.

Even before these structural changes took place, on a dreary and wet March 10, General Meade had been paid a visit by the newly appointed commanding general of the army, Ulysses S. Grant. Grant held the recently revived rank of lieutenant general and would command all the armies of the Union. Meade was to be retained in tactical command of the Army of the Potomac. Grant, however, would make his headquarters with that army as well. The 114th formed in full-dress uniform on the sodden field to welcome the lieutenant general, and the band struck up "Hail to the Chief" as he approached. There was no fear that Grant would detach the band for duty at his headquarters, no matter how high the quality of their performance; he was tone deaf and had little appreciation

---

34. Charles H. T. Collis, *The Case of F. F. Cavada* (Philadelphia, 1866), 5. Collis had access to this letter written by Birney through Cavada's stepfather, Samuel Dutton, who had quoted from it in a published letter to buttress his own attack on Collis' character and to deflect attention from Collis' condemnation of Cavada after the war. Birney was by then deceased. See the account of this dispute in Chapter 13.

for fine music. According to one of the musicians, the news of Grant's appointment to commanding general was received with little enthusiasm. The men had confidence in Meade, contended the musician; they were pleased when they learned that he was to remain with them. At the same time, they were doubtless pleased by the thought that some desk-bound general in Washington would no longer interfere with the armies on campaign. Grant would command from the field.[35]

By mid-April, as the sun warmed the Virginia countryside and began to dry the roads saturated by rains and melting snow, the Union army began to show signs of activity. The brigade chapel was dismantled; field tents replaced the winter tents at headquarters; baggage was sent to the rear along with the sick from the field hospitals; and row upon row of boxes, barrels, and other containers were piled near the busy railroad depots. The straining engines brought not only supplies, but men as well. The army was growing steadily as each arriving train raucously disgorged members of newly formed regiments along with reenlisted veterans returning from their furloughs.

On April 22, the Zouaves turned in their extra clothing, overcoats, and blankets. The regiment then formed in the field adjacent to their camp on Fleetwood Hill for a photograph. It was not the first time the colorful Zouaves had attracted the attention of a photographer. In March, several photos had been taken of the band and of companies formed for the daily ritual of guard mount. With their log and canvas shanties providing the backdrop for one of the March photos, the turbaned Zouaves stood in two ranks at parade rest. In full-dress uniform, their rifles resting against their bodies, white-gloved hands clasped together holding them securely in place, the men stared stiffly ahead. To their right, separated by a short interval, stood twelve members of the band with instruments poised; while in front of the regiment, with their backs to the camera, were the Zouave Officer of the Day and Officer of the Guard, resplendent with swords and sashes in place.[36]

The Zouaves were issued rations on May 3, 1864, and on the following day the spring campaign began. The men crossed the Rapidan River at Germanna Ford and soon found themselves in the area known as the

35. Rauscher, Music on the March, 152–53.
36. Fox Diary, April 22, 1864, in Fox Collection, HSP.

Wilderness. They resumed their march at noon on May 5, and shortly afterward they heard the sounds of battle. The fighting kept up until after dark and at intervals throughout the night. From their position on the Germanna Plank Road near Meade's headquarters, the Zouaves listened to the roar of the conflict. Heavy fighting began early on May 6 and persisted throughout the day except for "an intermission of about 4 hours from 12 till 4." The sounds of rifle, shot, and shell would be heard nearly continuously for almost a month.[37]

General Grant's grand strategic scheme called for all the armies of the North to move against their adversaries in a concurrent campaign designed to prevent one southern force from reinforcing another. As for the Army of the Potomac, Grant hoped to push those soldiers through the tangled Wilderness before Lee could bring forces to bear against him. But Grant was unable to preempt Lee here, and for two days the opposing armies battled in seesaw fashion through the smoky, fire-scarred woods and knotted underbrush.

The Army of the Potomac sustained over seventeen thousand casualties during the brutal fighting in the Wilderness. Nevertheless, on May 7, rather than retreating—as had all of the army's previous commanders after such stalemates—Grant decided to push on and try to get around Lee's right flank. Some heavy skirmishing occurred on that spring Saturday, but by night the Union army was on the march to a crossroads village called Spotsylvania Court House. The Zouaves advanced in the darkness with the headquarters brigade to the vicinity of Todd's Tavern and encamped near the road leading to Piney Branch Church. None of the Philadelphians recorded their thoughts on this occasion, but many other northern men did. Despite the suffering occasioned by the past few days, the veterans' morale soared when the men realized that Grant intended to resume the offensive. The general had promised Lincoln that there would be no turning back. Soldiers who were eager to end the war, and astute enough to realize that only the defeat of the Confederate army would bring about that result, were gratified by the continued movement southward.

Lee, however, was not an obliging opponent. Moving quickly on interior lines, his men were able to assume strong defensive positions around Spotsylvania before Grant could seize the crossroads. For several more days the Union general would probe and assault his adversary's defenses to no

37. *Ibid.*, May 5, 1864.

avail. Of this fighting, the Zouaves at headquarters saw little. One of the men noted that "the Rebs made a feint of an attack on HQ," on May 9, but nothing came of it. The results of the fighting around them, however, sometimes appeared vividly, as when the body of the much-loved Sixth Corps commander, Major General John Sedgwick, was carried into camp on May 9. "There was an indescribable silence and sadness that took possession of every one," recalled a member of the band. In addition, field hospitals sprang up everywhere; and the passage of mangled, wounded, and dying men en route to them was endless. Many of the Zouaves undoubtedly marveled at their good fortune in the face of such slaughter, but they probably did so privately, lest their fortunes suddenly change.[38]

The Army of the Potomac lost over eighteen thousand men in the carnage at Spotsylvania, but Grant constantly replenished his supply of manpower by drawing on the regiments garrisoning the defenses of Washington. The Zouaves were in a position to witness the arrival of these men, who reported first to army headquarters, whereupon they were dispatched to the various brigades. One Philadelphian thought that the replacements numbered at least thirty thousand men, among whom were a few oversized regiments of heavy artillery now converted to infantry. With such forces at his disposal, Grant was able to embark on another movement designed to turn Lee's right flank and force the Rebels to abandon their formidable breastworks and fight in the open. On the night of May 20, Grant started the Second Corps southward toward the North Anna River on a route that would eventually take them to a sleepy crossroads town: Cold Harbor.

Collis' Zouaves broke camp at 5:30 A.M. on May 21, marching off with the headquarters wagons toward Guiney's Station. Sometime around 11:00 A.M., Grant and Meade halted the headquarters column at Massaponax Church. There, staff members hauled pews into the front yard, and Grant sat in the shade of the trees writing a dispatch to General Burnside and discussing plans with Meade. Photographer Timothy O'Sullivan captured the scene in a series of five photographs. One of them, taken from the Telegraph Road, pictures the church itself and the surrounding area, including a number of Collis' Zouaves. Sergeant James Madely and Private William D. Gilmour of Company D, along with Sergeant Alvah J. Anderson of Company A, went into the church and left their names inscribed in the wall. While O'Sullivan preserved the historic scene outside, the

38. Rauscher, *Music on the March*, 165.

three little-known Philadelphia Zouaves left tangible evidence of their presence inside that is still visible today.[39]

Later that afternoon, the column had moved forward again some distance when Collis received a report advising that a force of Rebel cavalry was in their front. He sent the 114th and the 68th Pennsylvania to the head of the column and pushed forward. He soon discovered that the cavalry had retired to the vicinity of Guiney's Bridge, which spanned the Pony River near the Richmond, Fredericksburg, and Potomac railroad station. The headquarters component of the army had become somewhat isolated between the Second Corps, positioned to its front, and the Fifth Corps, which trailed some distance behind. Members of Grant's staff suggested that the commanding general withdraw to a safer position and await the arrival of the Fifth Corps. He declined, however, characteristically stating that rather than his going back, it would be better to hurry the Fifth Corps forward. Meade, in all likelihood also fearing for Grant's safety, rode up to Collis and instructed him to "drive the enemy from the bridge and hold it." The two generals then calmly lit cigars and watched the action while seated on the top rails of the whitewashed fence that surrounded Guiney's Station.[40]

The colonel formed his own regiment and the 68th Pennsylvania in a line of battle and sent the 68th forward to assault the Confederate position. The Rebel cavalrymen, however, had taken the precaution of barricading the bridge, and the Philadelphians were unable to drive off the enemy. Collis then ordered Major Bowen to take the 114th downstream, ford the river, and come up rapidly on the enemy flank. "This movement had the desired effect," the colonel later wrote, and he soon had his entire force across the river and in pursuit of the Rebels. A squadron of the 1st Massachusetts Cavalry, which had been attached to the headquarters guard, arrived at that time, and Collis ordered the troopers to head off into the woods and attack the right flank of the remaining Confederates. The Bay Staters became mired in the swampy ground, however, and the attack never materialized.[41]

The headquarters guard was finally relieved by arriving elements of the Fifth Corps, and Collis disengaged his men and returned them to their

39. William Frassanito, *Grant and Lee: The Virginia Campaigns, 1864–1865* (New York, 1983), 116–19.

40. OR, Vol. LI, Pt. 1, p. 243.

41. *Ibid.*

normal duties. The Confederates lost a few men killed or wounded, and two officers and nine men were taken prisoner. Again there were no casualties among the Zouaves, though the 68th lost one man killed and two wounded in the skirmish. Grant's aide-de-camp, Lieutenant Colonel Horace Porter, later recalled that Collis was afterward "complimented and thanked by both General Grant and General Meade for the handsome manner in which he had behaved." Collis, he wrote, "always acted with the greatest gallantry, and commended himself highly to his superior officers."[42]

That evening, the headquarters tents were pitched in the rear yard of the stately home of George Motley, just down the road from the Chandler farm, where Stonewall Jackson had died the previous year. The Zouaves encamped nearby; and some of them might have taken the time, as did Grant, to visit the small outbuilding where their nemesis had crossed over the river to "rest under the shade of the trees."[43]

Despite Grant's continual efforts to outflank Lee, the southern general was able to utilize his interior lines to parry every move. At the North Anna River, Totopotomy Creek, and Cold Harbor, Grant found Lee's men entrenched and waiting. On June 3, Grant ordered yet another full-scale assault on the Confederate defenses at Cold Harbor. It was the worst Union disaster of the war. Lee's veterans had learned well the science of defensive warfare. The attacks cost the Union 7,000 casualties, while the Rebels suffered fewer than 1,500.

Finally, on the night of Sunday, June 12, Grant began another attempt to move around Lee's right flank. This time, however, his destination was the city of Petersburg, south of Richmond. With Union cavalry screening his movements and other Federal forces creating distractions to the west, Grant slipped away across the Chickahominy River. It was a difficult march through the swamps of the Virginia Peninsula. Drinking water was scarce and roads were poor. Sergeant Fox, of Company F, recalled passing "over a swamp road so narrow that about 12 of our wagons went down an embankment."[44]

---

42. Horace Porter to "Dear General [Christian Thomsen Christensen]," March 21, 1891, quoted in C. Collis, *1st Brigade,* 32.

43. Horace Porter, *Campaigning with Grant* (New York, 1897), 133; Freeman, *Lee's Lieutenants,* II, 682.

44. Fox Diary, June 12, 1864, in Fox Collection, HSP.

The Zouaves crossed the Chickahominy the following day and reached the banks of the James River on June 15. Engineers had already completed a 2,100-foot-long pontoon bridge over the treacherous river below Wilcox's Wharf, and Union forces had begun crossing on June 14. The tenacious Grant had finally outmaneuvered Lee. If the first Union troops who arrived on the outskirts of Petersburg on June 15 had only known that they faced little more than a skeleton of a Rebel army, Petersburg would have fallen. Instead, Grant's lieutenants stalled and procrastinated while Lee desperately urged his men southward. By June 18, the exhausted Rebels filed wearily into the trenches surrounding the city, and the opportunity was lost. The siege of Petersburg would consume ten months' time and countless lives.

12

Soon with Angels I'll Be Marching

Collis' Zouaves crossed the James River on June 16 and marched within two and one-half miles of Petersburg. Over the next few days, their comrades in the front lines made several costly attacks against the Confederate defenses, which proved only that frontal assaults would be ineffective. The army began to settle into the drudgery and danger of siege warfare.

Even the men of the headquarters guard would be called upon to fill the trenches on occasion. Sometimes these calls were false alarms. As early as June 23, Collis was ordered to take all the available infantry from the headquarters and picket the Jerusalem Plank Road south of the city. Reports had arrived indicating that Rebel cavalry was advancing on the road. Ten minutes afterwards the order was rescinded. "Never mind sending out the infantry guards at headquarters," General Humphreys wrote. A few days later, however, the entire "Provisional Brigade was ordered out into a line of Breast works which the 6th Corps had left to go down on the left." The 114th supported Captain Edwin B. Dow's 6th Maine Battery near the Williams house, west of the Jerusalem Plank Road. They returned to the headquarters the following night, but as the army moved in an ever-expanding line to the south and west of the city, the headquarters moved accordingly. The Zouaves were sent into the trenches intermittently during these movements, and the regiment took part in the operations against the Rebel lines near the Weldon Railroad. Their stay in the trenches usually proved to be short, however, lasting only a day or two at a time.[1]

Typically, the duties of the Zouaves entailed the mundane tasks of providing security for the army's headquarters and supply trains. Often, they guarded prisoners or escorted them to the rear. Even when they occupied the trenches, the Zouaves were seldom in a position of great danger. Private George Murray of Company B had returned to the regiment in October after serving aboard a hospital steamer during his recovery from the wound he received at Chancellorsville. A few months after his return, he wrote lightheartedly to his parents that his regiment had been out in the breastworks: "but we were not engaged as they never put us in a dangerous position. We have what we call a Headquarters fight, that is we always manage to leave when they get engaged."[2]

Though Murray undoubtedly was often in somewhat more danger than he might have liked his parents to believe, he was comparatively safe. The regiment participated in no assaults and repelled no desperate enemy charges. Rather, they performed duties like the one that a detail of Zouaves completed on July 14. Several of them were sent to build a gallows on which two soldiers were executed the following day for raping a woman in Prince George County. This was not the first execution witnessed by the men since their arrival at Petersburg. On June 20, in the midst of a brief artillery duel, they were called out "to see a darkey hung who had committed rape on a girl in Kent County." The man was Private William Henry Johnson of the 23rd United States Colored Troops. Again, the scene was preserved by the photographers traveling with the army, but this time the Zouaves were not pictured.[3]

Although the 114th was seldom exposed to the hazardous circumstances faced daily by their comrades in arms, they endured much the same suffering from the intense heat and resultant thirst as the men in the trenches. Those who had cursed the rain and mud on previous occasions now hoped for an end to the forty-seven-day dry spell that lasted from June 3 until July 19. Springs, creeks, and ponds had been dried completely

1. *OR*, Vol. XL, Pt. 2, p. 335; Fox Diary, June 16, 1864, in Fox Collection, HSP.

2. George Murray to "Dear Father & Mother," February 19, 1865, in Murray Collection, FSNMP.

3. Fox Diary, June 20, July 14, 1864, in Fox Collection, HSP; Frassanito, *Grant and Lee*, 216–23.

by the brutal summer sun. The dust rose so thickly that, as one Zouave remembered, it was sometimes difficult to tell the "white from the colored troops."[4]

Though they were well supplied with army food, the men were undoubtedly overjoyed to receive the fare that was occasionally dispensed by the United States Sanitary Commission. On July 6, perhaps in a delayed celebration of Independence Day, Sergeant Fox wrote that the men "lived high on Sour Kraut, pickles, canned meats, crackers, tomatoes, and milk" that the sanitary commission had provided. The feast made a welcome change from the usual meal of hardtack and salted pork, or worse yet, fly-blown beef. Eventually, however, brick ovens were constructed at the rapidly expanding supply base of City Point, and trains carried fresh-baked bread the short distance to the front. As the siege wore on and supply lines into the Rebel stronghold were cut, the smell of hot loaves of bread arriving in the Union camps must sometimes have overpowered the stench of the battlefields and sent sharp pains of hunger into the bellies of Lee's nearly starved soldiers.[5]

The Zouaves continued to be thrown into the trenches on occasion throughout the remainder of the summer, but the passing weeks proved generally uneventful. An exceptional day in this pattern was Saturday, July 30, when the men could hear the terrible cannonading and explosion of one of the Confederate forts that had been blown up by miners of the 48th Pennsylvania. The Battle of the Crater was yet another Union disaster, however, and the siege dragged on.

The men at headquarters heard another terrible explosion on August 9, this time at City Point, the vast Federal supply port east of Petersburg where Grant had established his headquarters. The explosion of an ordnance boat, later discovered to be a work of sabotage, destroyed much of the dock, killed 43 men, and wounded 126. Grant was fortunate to have escaped injury, but some of his staff were wounded. The dock was reconstructed, this time farther away from the commanding general's quarters.

As the summer wore on and gave way to autumn, the Zouaves maintained this pattern of existence. During periods of heavy fighting, they were often called upon to man the trenches where the lines had been weakened by the removal of those participating in the attacks on the Rebel

4. Rauscher, *Music on the March*, 194.
5. Fox Diary, July 6, 1864, in Fox Collection, HSP.

defenses. Otherwise, the regiment was posted as a guard around the head-quarters, or they escorted prisoners to City Point, sometimes picking up new recruits and convalescents there and taking them to the front. In the intense summer heat, the marching was difficult and wearing. Though disappointed that the war had not yet ended, the men were glad to see the torrid summer heat yield to the more temperate conditions of fall. Their blankets and overcoats were distributed to them on September 22 in anticipation of yet another season of cold weather.

The war's death and destruction were relentless that fall. The Confederates hung on desperately, in hopes that the terrible toll of dead and wounded would propel war-weary northerners to oust Lincoln from office and replace him with a conciliatory peace Democrat. The election was a much-discussed topic that fall. "Every time one of the big guns goes off the men have a saying among them, there goes another vote for Abe," wrote Private Murray on October 24. For its part, the army did not support a Republican defeat. The men at the front intended to see the war through to victory. "You can see by the papers that the soldiers are not so fast for peace as many that stay at home, reaping the benefits of what we are fighting for," wrote one man. In the state elections that fall, Private Murray thought that there had been only about twenty-five Democratic votes cast in the regiment. "The army I think went republican," he noted. Voting results in the presidential election in November were probably similar. Sergeant Fox's company tallied thirty-nine votes for Lincoln, and two for McClellan, his Democratic opponent. Private Murray's company "went 19 Union and 8 Democratic. The regiment went republican but I forget how much majority."[6]

The army that voted overwhelmingly for Lincoln's reelection in 1864 was, in many ways, very different from the army that had fought some of its hardest battles. Thousands of its veterans had been killed or wounded, many in the unprecedented horrors of the spring and summer campaigning of 1864. Many of those men had been replaced by entire regiments that had spent the war garrisoning defensive works, while others were replaced by soldiers who had been drafted or been paid exorbitant bounties to enlist.

6. George Murray to "Dear Father & Mother," November 17, 1864, FSNMP; William T. Lobb to Mr. C. Thomas, October 17, 1864, in Lewis Leigh Collection, USAMHI; Fox Diary, November 8, 1864, Fox Collection, HSP. Seventy-eight percent of the army voted "Union," as some Republicans styled their party, while the civilian vote was only 53 percent in favor of returning Lincoln to office. See McPherson, *Battle Cry of Freedom*, 804.

Morally, many replacements belonged to a different breed from that which originally filled the army's ranks. Bounty jumping became an endemic evil.

A large number of men whose enlistments expired in 1864 chose not to reenlist, including many from Company A of the 114th, who had joined the Zouaves d'Afrique in 1861. Bereft of its backbone of hard-bitten veterans, the army took on a new character. Those who remained and had passed through the ordeals at the Wilderness, Spotsylvania, or Cold Harbor could no longer easily be coaxed into making futile frontal assaults against heavily defended works. They attacked, to be sure, but soldiers with little confidence in the success of their endeavor seldom achieve their objective. So it was with the army in 1864.

To combat the problems associated with the inordinate number of bounty jumpers in the army during this period, a military court was established at City Point. Collis was placed in charge of it, and the first trials it conducted were those of seven men accused of the aforementioned crime. All were convicted and sentenced to death by firing squad. Playing the "Dead March," the Zouave band accompanied the open-topped army wagons in which the condemned men were seated, each atop his own coffin. At the execution site, the coffins were removed from the wagons and the men seated again on their tops. At the tap of a drum, a detail of soldiers fired their muskets, and seven men fell on or into their coffins. One band member described it as "a repulsive scene."[7]

In addition to assuming new duties at City Point, Collis soon won his long-sought promotion, although it was something less than what he had hoped for. He received word on October 28, 1864, of his brevet to the rank of brigadier general, United States Volunteers, for "gallant and meritorious service." Collis undoubtedly would have been happier with more than just a brevet promotion, which in many respects was only an honorary title. In his case, however, the title assumed more significance and legitimacy. An 1806 article of war stipulated that a brevet rank would receive the recognition accorded to actual rank when the officer was serving on courts-martial duties. In addition, the act further provided for recognition of actual rank when the officer was serving with provisional formations composed of different regiments. Because Collis was serving on the court at City Point and also commanding the headquarters brigade, he was entitled to such recognition on both counts.

7. Rauscher, *Music on the March*, 204–205.

There were rumors in early November that he would soon replace Major General Marsena Patrick as provost marshal general. The rumor proved false, but Collis eventually was placed in charge of the bustling port of City Point. There, as winter approached, his wife and little daughter Amelia joined the general in the field once again. The family occupied the home of Doctor Peter Epps in the town of City Point, where Mrs. Collis had the luxury of a few female servants. It was a crisp, dry season, and the general's wife spent a good deal of time riding while her husband was occupied with his duties.

City Point could not have been a healthy or attractive environment for the little family; the place had become, in Septima Collis' words, "one vast hospital for suffering humanity. As far as the eye could reach from the doorstep of my humble home, the plain was dotted with tents which were rapidly filled with wounded men, Northern and southern, white and black without distinction."[8] There were seven hospitals operating at City Point at that time. The largest, Depot Field Hospital, was spread over a two-hundred-acre tract and held as many as ten thousand men. Also in close proximity to the Collis home was a prison camp called the Bull Ring. It was a horrible, vermin-infested stockade that offered little shelter and few sanitary facilities for the prisoners. Some of them were Union soldiers awaiting trial at General Collis' court; at times, many of those confined there were captured Confederates awaiting transportation to permanent prison camps in the North.

While Collis was at City Point, his regiment remained with General Meade's headquarters. The 114th again fell under the command of Major Edward R. Bowen. Although Lieutenant Colonel Cavada had returned from his confinement in Libby Prison, he had resigned from the army that summer after learning that Collis intended to file charges against him again, this time for his behavior at both Chancellorsville and Gettysburg.

Collis later alleged that Cavada had "disappeared" when the first shot was fired at Chancellorsville on the morning of May 3, 1863. A few hours later, Collis charged, he was located "sitting in the woods more than two miles distant from the line of battle." When asked by Collis for an explanation of his conduct, Cavada supposedly replied that he had lost the regiment early in the fight and, being unable to find it again, took command of the 109th Pennsylvania. Collis determined this excuse to be false.

8. S. Collis, *War Record*, 29–33.

He also contended that, although Cavada had been placed in command of the 109th by a general officer in the rear, that regiment was marching away from the front at that time and did not fire another shot that day. Collis claimed that an officer of the 109th later told him that when the regiment was ordered to return to the field, Cavada was suddenly attacked "with a severe headache and, being unable to accompany the regiment, remained at the rear."[9]

Other observers of Cavada contributed to Collis' case against the officer. Some who had seen Cavada prior to his capture at Gettysburg alleged that he had allowed himself to be captured by the onrushing Mississippians on July 2 rather than risk retreating across the shell-swept field. In a letter to Collis written shortly after the battle, Major Bowen described Cavada's actions: "I saw nothing in Cavada's conduct to induce me to change the opinion I formed of him at Fredericksburg and which was afterwards confirmed at Chancellorsville. I can see no excuse for his having been taken prisoner except to avoid danger."[10]

Cavada spent several months in Libby Prison prior to his exchange. When he returned to Philadelphia, he promptly challenged Major Bowen to a duel, though the major was then over two hundred miles to the south. Cavada was arrested immediately and confined to the Continental Hotel. While there, he began gathering his notes and drawings from his prison confinement and putting them together for publication. His memoirs of his days in Rebel hands were published in 1864 under the title *Libby Life: Experiences of a Prisoner of War in Richmond, Va., 1863–64.*[11]

On May 17, 1864, Cavada was ordered to report for duty on the staff of Major General Birney. Within a month, however, he had tendered his resignation from the army, citing poor health. Cavada's brother, Adolpho, then serving on the staff of Major General Humphreys, hand-carried the letter to Second Corps headquarters on June 20, where it was promptly approved. It cannot be known for certain whether Cavada's health was really too poor for him to continue in the army; or whether, on learning that Collis had filed charges against him on June 8, he decided to leave the service to avoid facing another court-martial. Before the war's out-

9. C. Collis, *Case of F. F. Cavada*, 11–12.

10. *Ibid.*, 12.

11. See F. F. Cavada, *Libby Life: Experiences of a Prisoner of War in Richmond, Va., 1863–64* (Philadelphia, 1864).

break, Cavada had accompanied an expedition to Panama intended to survey a route for the Panama Railroad. It is certainly possible that he contracted malaria while on that expedition, or even while campaigning with the present army. Malaria, known among the soldiers as the ague or, more familiarly, as "the shakes," was one of the more common illnesses in the Union Army throughout the war. In fact, General Birney himself would be dead within a few months of Cavada's departure, struck down by a particularly virulent strain of the disease. A recurrence of the disease in Cavada would have made it difficult for him to continue on active campaigning. Cavada's later adventures as a leader in the Cuban Revolution would seem to indicate that he had at least some appetite for battle, and it is possible that some forces were working against him within the 114th.

When Collis learned of Cavada's resignation, he immediately sent a letter to the adjutant general of the Army of the Potomac, Major General Seth Williams. Though Collis had already filed charges against Cavada, no action had been taken because of the continual movement of the army. He asked General Williams for a copy of the order accepting Cavada's resignation, "so that it may appear on record in this office that the vacancy exists, and also for information as to what disposition was made of the charges."[12]

Upon receiving Collis' inquiry, General Williams wrote to Birney to find out whether the resignation had been accepted. Williams made it plain that if it had been, Meade would not be pleased. "As he belonged to a regiment on duty at these Head Quarters, and was but temporarily assigned to your staff," wrote Williams, "the Commanding General considers the resignation should have been referred to him for consideration."[13]

Birney, who had been temporarily in command of the Second Corps, responded that he had been absent from headquarters when the resignation of Lieutenant Colonel Cavada was accepted; in addition, he averred that his adjutant general had no knowledge that Cavada's regiment was on duty at headquarters or that the charges were pending against him. Upon learning this information, Meade could do nothing but return the

12. C. Collis to "General [Williams]," July 19, 1864, Records of the 114th PV, Record Group 94, NARA.

13. Maj. Gen. Seth Williams to "Maj. Genl. D. B. Birney," June 25, 1864, *ibid*.

charges against Cavada without action, noting that Birney had accepted
the resignation without his knowledge. When he forwarded a copy of
Cavada's resignation to the War Department on June 27, he noted the
circumstances and recommended that Cavada "should not be permitted
to re-enter the Military Service of the United States." By that time, the
troubled Cuban native was long gone.[14]

The onset of cooler weather did not slow the pace of campaigning. The
Zouaves' duties still included being sent into the trenches periodically. On
October 18, they provided an escort for Secretary of War Stanton "and
several other large men," and a few days later they moved about three
miles across the Weldon Railroad with the headquarters. On October 27,
the men again were ordered into the front line of breastworks, while heavy
fighting raged on their left. When the regiment moved, they were fortunate to be able to throw their knapsacks into the headquarters wagons.
Private Murray estimated the number of wagons at the headquarters to be
"about two hundred," adding that there was "a corrall of about two hundred extra horses."[15]

By early November, when the army camps were filled with civilians
acting as commissioners for the election, the Zouaves began building their
huts for winter quarters. There were plenty of trees in the area. "You
cannot find a field large enough to fight a battle on," wrote one of the
Zouaves. "It is almost like a wilderness." The officers even appropriated
some of the horses and wagons from the headquarters and sent the teams
to Prince George Court House to gather bricks. They then constructed
brick chimneys for their huts, which was a vast improvement over the
usual wooden chimneys. The latter invariably caught fire at the most in-
convenient times.[16]

Most of the huts were finished by mid-November. Private Murray described his as rising to the height of about nine logs, which came about
to his shoulders. Two pieces of shelter tent provided the roof, and the
interior contained a large fireplace and a bunk large enough for three men.

14. Endorsement to Resignation of Lieutenant Colonel F. F. Cavada, June 27, 1864,
ibid.

15. Murray to "Dear Father & Mother," October 19, 30, 1864, in Murray Collection,
FSNMP; Fox Diary, October 27, 1864, in Fox Collection, HSP.

16. Murray to "Dear Father & Mother," November 4, 1864, in Murray Collection,
FSNMP.

The other shanties in the regiment were probably similar to Murray's, and in these surroundings the men consumed a sparse Thanksgiving dinner. Each company received a few pies and turkeys that night, "but they were so small that it was hardly a bite." The men in Private Murray's mess had already made other arrangements, however, and they enjoyed a good stew with potatoes and onions. For most men, whose companies had received only two turkeys and pies, the meal was a disappointment. The sanitary commission fell into disfavor as a result, and Private Murray urged his parents not to give money to them "or any other kind of Commission as they are humbug." As Christmas neared, he feared a repetition of the Thanksgiving fiasco.

> I hope the people of the North will not dirty themselves by sending another dinner down here as that thanksgiving dinner was a disgrace and a humbug. The people of the North had better save their money and stuff and give it to the orphans and widows of the soldiers. . . . If the people only knew what fun the soldiers made over their dinner they would not send any more, one fellow said he was going to put his piece of turkey in a letter and send it home. Another fellow said that he had a hollow tooth and he put his piece of pie into his mouth expecting to have a feast but he lost it in the hollow of his tooth. . . . If you have anything to give to the soldiers give it to them yourself.[17]

Apart from having "good warm dry and comfortable quarters," that winter, the Zouaves found this season to be in other ways unlike the previous cold-weather encampments. They were kept busy with a variety of activities. Private Murray reported: "We was on guard Monday, come off Tuesday morning, dress parade at night, go on guard again Wednesday, come off Thursday, dress parade again, fatigue duty Friday, and dress parade, guard Saturday again and off Sunday morning, and so on week in week out. We have no drills as we have no time for it."[18] Although they were occupied a good deal more than they expected to be, the weather was generally not bad during the first part of the winter. December even was warm enough to be compared to Indian summer, and flies swarmed so

17. Fox Diary, November 24, 1864, in Fox Collection, HSP; Murray to "Dear Father & Mother," November 24, December 3, 1864, in Murray Collection, FSNMP.

18. Murray to "Dear Father & Mother," December 3, 1864, in Murray Collection, FSNMP.

thickly in the daytime that the men could not sleep without covering their faces. It soon turned colder, however, and men wrote home asking relatives to send mittens, socks, and scarves as quickly as possible.

The Zouaves were on guard duty once more on Christmas Eve. At about 9 P.M. they could hear church bells ringing from the direction of Petersburg, where starving Rebels were celebrating the holiday for the last time under the Confederate flag. While the Philadelphians feasted on treats sent in boxes from home, the revelry among their foe must have been strained. Many of the gray-clad soldiers were starting to despair. With Petersburg nearly surrounded, the Shenandoah Valley laid waste, Atlanta captured, and an entire army of westerners ready to march north and join Grant, the Confederate cause seemed doomed. "The rebs are coming in very fast," wrote Private Murray in January. "They give a doleful account of things. They say they do not get enough to eat." By late February, Murray wrote that Rebels were deserting at a rate of about fifty per day, and that they brought horses and guns with them, for which they received payment.[19]

Still the Confederates tested the strength of the Union lines and were tested in return. Early in February, the Union army made another movement to the left, further lengthening the enveloping lines, forcing the Rebels to stretch theirs even farther and spread their remaining troops dangerously thin in spots. Even the Federal line was sometimes hazardously weak. "We were hurried out to the breastworks in front of Headquarters," recalled Murray after one such occasion. "When we got out there were no troops in them. It is so every move that the army makes we have to fill up a gap." The Zouaves lay in the trenches that night and awoke with ice and snow covering their blankets the following morning.[20]

Although the Zouaves continued to fill up gaps in the entrenchments, they were not engaged in any of the fighting that raged along the lines to the west. Many of the men, like Private Murray, repeatedly reassured loved ones at home that their assignments were not dangerous. For the family of one man in the regiment, however, disaster struck that winter not on the battlefield, but at home. Drummer Joseph H. Ware of Company K learned in February that fire had destroyed his house in Philadelphia. He immediately was given a ten-day furlough, wrote Private Murray, "but his

19. Murray to "Dear Father & Mother," January 22, February 25, 1865, *ibid.*
20. Murray to "Dear Father & Mother," February 9, 1865, *ibid.*

mother, two or three of his sisters, and two brothers have died or are expected to die soon." Ware mustered out with his company later that year, but his homecoming must have been a somber affair.[21]

The constant dress parades, escort duties, and ceremonies required of the headquarters guard meant that the Zouaves had to keep their uniforms and equipment in presentable condition. This requirement proved especially difficult when they were called to man the trenches. To improve their appearance, they drew new uniforms that winter and also received new flags. The men claimed that they did not like the new colors so much as their original flags, nor were they so proud of their pristine condition. The old colors had been torn and shredded by shot and shell during the hard-fought battles in which many of the Zouaves had fallen. "You ought to see the old ones," wrote Private Murray. "The union has very nearly seceded from the stripes. A solid shot or something has very nearly carried it out."[22]

The veteran Zouaves also claimed not to be very fond of the new recruits that the regiment was receiving. Most of the new men had drawn large bounties. Many of the Zouaves had heard of the poor performance of some of the army's regiments during the latest fighting and placed the blame on the men who were enticed into the army by the large bounties being offered. "It is just ruining the army," wrote Murray. "No regiment with many of them is good for anything." Moreover, the new recruits were discredited by a prevailing notion in the regiment that they had enlisted in the 114th only because they knew that the regiment would not have to go to the front. Some veterans also feared that if enough men enlisted to return the regiment to its former strength, they *would* have to go to the front.[23]

In spite of the pessimistic outlook on the condition of their own forces, the Zouaves were coming to apprehend their enemies' weakness. They were in a position to observe the many Confederate prisoners who came daily into the Union lines. So many prisoners were gathering that details from the regiment had to be sent to assist the provost guards at City Point. One detail even escorted a large group of prisoners to Washington. From these prisoners, the Zouaves often received insight into the enemy's pre-

21. Murray to "Dear Father & Mother," February 19, 1865, *ibid.*
22. *Ibid.*
23. *Ibid.*

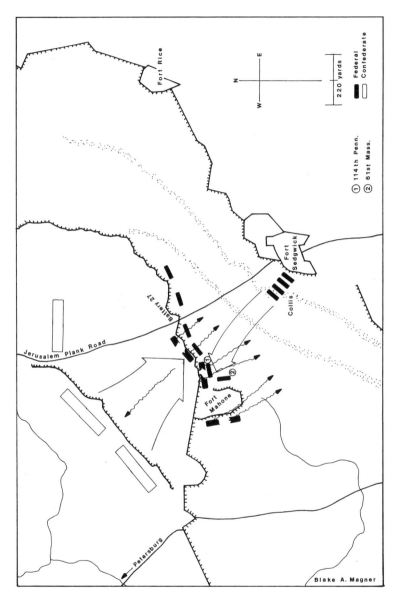

Petersburg, April 2, 1865, and the assault on Fort Mahone

Blake A. Magner

carious situation. One of the Rebels told them, for example, that for every man who came over to the Federal camp, one hundred more deserted to the rear. It was also said that Lee was constructing a corduroy road to haul off the army's guns. "So some fine morning we will find them gone," forecast Murray.[24]

Collis remained on duty at City Point in his capacity as commanding officer of the bustling port and as assistant provost marshal. His courtroom docket was often filled with the cases of men who were accused of bounty jumping or of more serious crimes, and executions were performed at a brisk rate. Though busy, the general had time to meet the president when the latter arrived near the end of March. His wife later recalled the "tall gaunt figure of Abraham Lincoln" as he passed among the wounded soldiers, "his moistened eyes even more eloquent than the lips, which had a kindly word of cheer for every sufferer."[25]

The other Zouaves were also able to glimpse the president on his visit to City Point. The Rebel prisoners had become so numerous by then that the entire regiment had been detailed to assist in guard and escort duties at the post. The Zouaves pitched their tents on a hill overlooking the Appomattox River and began their new task of guarding prisoners and periodically escorting groups of them by ship to the capital. This duty was destined to end soon, however, as the Confederacy was breathing its last desperate gasps that spring.

By late March, Major General John Grubb Parke's Ninth Corps had been selected to lead an assault on the Confederate line opposite Fort Sedgwick. Despite the general weakness of the enemy defenses in that sector, the point of the attack was to be directed against one of the most imposing positions still facing the Federal line. The approaches to the Rebel defenses were swept by numerous batteries, including a three-sided earthen fort

24. Murray to "Dear Father & Mother," February 28, 1865, in Murray Collection, FSNMP.

25. Record of C. H. T. Collis, No. 8636, MOLLUS, New York Commandery (N.Y., January 15, 1892), CWLM; S. Collis, *War Record*, 60. See also Robert I. Alotta's *Civil War Justice: Union Army Executions Under Lincoln* (Shippensburg, Pa. 1989) for a discussion of some of the cases over which Collis presided. In several of them, more than one defendant was found guilty on the same day and sentenced to execution. As a result of his position on the court at City Point, Collis had the unfortunate distinction of having presided over more courts-martial in which the sentence was death than did any other officer in the army.

variously dubbed Fort Mahone or Fort Damnation. At 4:30 A.M. on April 2, after a deafening barrage of artillery fire, Parke's men surged forth to the attack. His troops fought valiantly against the stubborn southern defenders, and they managed to capture several defensive works and to gain a foothold in Fort Mahone.

The assault began to lose its momentum in the confusion, however, and a number of fierce Confederate counterattacks threatened to turn the tide of battle. By 3 P.M., the Rebels had mustered the personnel necessary for a concerted and vigorous attack against Parke's men, whose toehold on the Confederate defenses was growing weaker. After the disorderly fighting in the many trenches and traverses around the Rebel position that day, the Ninth Corps was losing its cohesion; it was also running short of ammunition. When a Confederate brigade slammed against the left flank of the Union line, the disheartened and segmented Union force near Fort Mahone began to retreat. Captain David F. Ritchie of Battery C, 1st New York Light Artillery, whose cannoneers had come up to work the captured Rebel guns in Battery 27, to the right of Fort Mahone, blamed the retreat on the disgraceful behavior of the one-year regiments. He later wrote that among these officers and men, there seemed to him to "be a total lack of discipline. The arrival of General Collis' brigade and their good conduct in charging up to the fort at the time of the panic contributed to restore the courage of our troops."[26]

On Sunday morning, April 2, General Collis had risen and dressed early, before the gray light of this miserable day shone. After he bade good-bye to his wife and sleeping child, he slipped out of City Point to join the headquarters brigade in the field. Collis found that the brigade had been ordered to Meade's Station on the City Point Railroad. He relieved Colonel Tippen of the 68th Pennsylvania and assumed command of the four infantry regiments that composed the brigade. With him that day were the 20th New York State Militia (80th New York Infantry), the 61st Massachusetts Volunteers, the 68th Pennsylvania, and his own Zouaves, then commanded by Captain Henry M. Eddy of Company D. Collis directed his command to move southward to the vicinity of the Avery house, then set off on horseback in search of General Parke. He finally located Parke directing his troops from Fort Rice, about a mile southwest of Avery's. Parke ordered Collis to continue his route southward and report to Briga-

26. OR, Vol. XLVI, Pt. 1, p. 1082.

dier General Simon Goodell Griffin, then commanding Parke's Second Division from Fort Sedgwick.

Collis' brigade reached Fort Sedgwick at about 2 P.M., and Griffin requested that the general move his men forward into the front line near Fort Mahone, then held by Griffin's Ninth Corps troops. As he was forming his brigade in the picket lines in front of Fort Sedgwick preparatory to an advance, Collis noticed that Griffin's line near Fort Mahone was starting to give way in the face of the concerted Rebel counterattack. He sent his brigade forward quickly across the open field swept by defending fire, leading the 114th himself. One desperate Ninth Corps soldier recalled the advance of Collis' brigade: "It was a thrilling sight. We battled to hold on and prayed for supports; the thought was 'can they make it?'—'will they make it?'"[27]

The Zouaves swept forward through the withering fire, recapturing the disputed portion of the line and losing a number of veterans in the effort. As the men made their way through the defenses of the tangled field and across the trenches and traverses, Captain Eddy was mortally wounded. The officer sustained a horrible head wound and would linger in great agony until April 11, when death finally took him. Lieutenants Andrew J. Cunningham of Company A and Edward T. Marion of Company I were also killed. All three of the officers had been members of the original company of Zouaves d'Afrique. The total loss in the regiment from this charge was six killed and twenty-seven wounded.

Also among the slain was Company F's first sergeant, Isaac Fox. Most likely, his younger brother and sister at home had recently received the letter he had written to them on March 15. In it, he described the desolation of war and the effect it had on the barefoot and starving children of Petersburg whom he had seen come into the Union lines. As a religious man, Fox was affected powerfully by such scenes, and he asked his siblings to "pray with me that the Lord will watch over us and help us to whip the Rebels this Summer, so that all the Soldiers can come home and so that these poor Southern children wont have to suffer so much. . . . My Dear little Sister and Brother, God bless you both and keep you and me until I shall come home again." He had signed his letter, "From War, Isaac Fox, Co F 114th P.V." Though saddened by his death, the family of the

27. *Ibid.*, 1091–93; C. Collis, *1st Brigade*, 34–37; Noah Andre Trudeau, *The Last Citadel: Petersburg, Virginia, June 1864–April 1865* (1991; rpr. Baton Rouge, 1993), 365.

twenty-eight-year-old sergeant bore the hope that they would one day be reunited. An anonymous poem appeared shortly after his death. The work was fraught with the religious symbolism that was the constructive channel of so much of the grief felt by war's survivors. The final stanzas provide a glimpse of how those survivors commonly rationalized the death of loved ones as the work of God's hand:

> Mysterious are the ways
> That mark Thy sovereign will,
> And our poor finite reason fails
> To comprehend thy skill!
> Teach us the rod to bear,
> And, when our work is done,
> May we, through Christ's redeeming grace
> All meet around Thy throne.

Such consolation as their beliefs provided undoubtedly went a long way toward healing the grieving hearts of the sergeant's family members.[28]

Although the Zouaves and the rest of Collis' brigade had succeeded in shoring up the defenses and stemming the tide of the latest Confederate attack, they were still under heavy fire from Rebel troops inside Fort Mahone. The three-sided fort had thus far proved impossible for the Federals to hold. The fort was open to the rear, and behind it lay the Confederate second line of defense. From those secondary defensive lines, the Rebels were able to pour a murderous fire into Union troops attempting to occupy the interior of the fort. Nevertheless, Collis requested permission to take his brigade around to the rear of the fort and attack from that direction. He sent a note to Griffin, seeking a brigade for his support.

Collis received authorization to carry out his attack at about 4:30 P.M., and was told that a brigade of the Sixth Corps along with two additional Pennsylvania regiments were moving to his support. Griffin, however, soon had second thoughts about the plan's chances for success, as did Parke, and the assault was canceled. Instead, Collis directed the 61st Massachusetts to begin building a breastwork on the brigade's left flank. The work ran perpendicularly from the outer defenses of Fort Mahone toward Fort

28. Fox to "My Dear little Brother and Sister," March 15, 1865, in Fox Collection, HSP; "On the Death of 1st Serg't Isaac Fox, Co. 'F,' 114th Regiment, Pa. Vols. . . . ." undated clipping, in Fox Collection, HSP.

Sedgwick. If the Rebels mounted another attack, Collis reasoned, the left flank at least would be well anchored and defended.

The incessant shooting slowed to a desultory pace after dark, and the Rebels made no further efforts to drive the Federals from their advanced position. Fires soon began to illuminate the sky over Petersburg, indicating that an evacuation was underway and that supplies were being abandoned. By 2:30 A.M., with reports from deserters that the Rebel lines had been evacuated, Collis sent out skirmishers to feel the enemy positions. The 61st Massachusetts quickly returned with confirmation of the deserters' reports.

Thus encouraged, Collis rapidly formed his men for an advance into the city. The general prepared to deploy his Zouaves as skirmishers and ordered their commander, Captain John R. Waterhouse of Company F, to advance toward the flames but to retreat firing should they meet with heavy opposition. Not knowing what force the Zouaves might meet, and perhaps fearing that the Rebels had simply further constricted their defensive lines, Collis ordered the Zouaves to leave their colors with the other regiments. He then sent word to Parke that he was advancing into the apparently deserted Rebel works and requested that the regiments on his flanks be cautioned not to fire into his men. By this time, however, it was nearly 4:00 A.M., and Parke sent word for Collis "not to be too hasty, as a general advance was ordered for 5:00 A.M." [29]

Collis delayed his advance until nearly 5 o'clock, when he sent the Zouaves forward at a double-quick pace. The 114th had the honor of being the first Union regiment to enter the city from the east; but because their flags were not readily available, the other regiments of the brigade were first to raise the colors over Petersburg. Colonel Jacob B. Hardenbergh of the 20th New York Militia ordered his flags hoisted on the roof of William Cameron's house. "I think I can safely say that this was the first American flag that floated over the city after the foul rebel rag ceased to wave there," he claimed in his official report. The 61st Massachusetts planted their flag on the courthouse roof but made no claim to its primacy in the city. [30]

The rear guard of Lee's army was just vacating Petersburg as Collis' brigade streamed in. The general led the Massachusetts regiment in pursuit at a run, but they were too late. When they reached Campbell's Bridge

29. OR, Vol. XLVI, Pt. 1, p. 1092.
30. *Ibid.*, 1097.

over the Appomattox River, they found it already blazing and the south-erners safely on the other side. Collis and the Bay Staters made an effort to beat out the flames, but the fire spread so quickly that the bridge col-lapsed within minutes after their arrival. Several of the men were seriously burned. This action concluded the brigade's participation in the fall of Petersburg, for orders soon reached Collis directing him to return to City Point immediately. The number of Rebel prisoners there was increasing rapidly, but there were few infantrymen to guard them. The hard-pressed remnants of the provost guard at City Point were forced to call on the Marines aboard nearby ships for assistance in guarding the prisoners. The five hundred marines provided by the navy were sent to the front, from which they soon returned with three thousand captured Confederates.

Subsequently, Meade and Grant moved through Petersburg in pursuit of the retreating Confederates, and the ensuing days proved somewhat confusing for Collis. On April 6, the general informed his superiors from City Point that Major General Godfrey Weitzel had been sending him orders indicating that he was to be relieved by a brigade of United States Colored Troops and that he was then to report to General Meade by telegraph. When the relief brigade arrived, however, details from Collis' command were scattered between City Point, Point Lookout, and Wash-ington. Forty officers and over one thousand men were then absent from the brigade. This number constituted nearly one-half of his entire force. Collis therefore stated in a report to the assistant adjutant general at City Point that he would be unable to join General Meade until he could reassemble his men. Brigadier General Charles Sawyer Russell, command-ing the brigade sent to relieve Collis, apparently received a different story. He wrote Weitzel that Collis refused to be relieved on the grounds that he had been placed in command by Meade and did not see how an order issued from Weitzel's Army of the James could take effect in the Army of the Potomac. Collis further told Russell that he wanted to receive an order from Meade before relinquishing control of the post. Weitzel finally sent a message to Grant, asking him to issue the necessary order replacing Collis.[31]

But even the order that Collis received directly from Grant on April 8 did not resolve Collis' problem. Grant's order instructed him to send for-ward all the troops under his command to meet the Confederate prisoners

31. OR, Vol. XLVI, Pt. 3, pp. 615–16, 658–59.

who had been taken thus far. He was to take charge of them and escort them to City Point. Yet nothing was said about being relieved from command at that place. Collis next received another order from Meade's assistant adjutant general, Colonel George David Ruggles, ordering him to proceed with his command to Farmville to guard the wagons there. He quickly responded that Provost Marshall General Patrick had already requested him to escort prisoners to New York City and Coney Island. Meade then instructed Collis to disregard any orders from Patrick, to turn his prisoners over to the nearest troops from the Army of the James, and to report immediately to his headquarters. In the meantime, Major General George Lucas Hartsuff, commanding all forces in the Petersburg area, issued an order relieving Collis and appointing Russell. General Patrick, however, still sought to keep Collis at City Point, despite the wishes of Grant and Meade that all forces belonging to the Army of the Potomac be forwarded to their assistance and that troops from the Army of the James be detailed for duties in the Petersburg area.[32]

The unfortunate Collis, caught in the middle of the army's confusion, was barraged by a succession of contradictory orders. The issue was finally resolved when Meade's latest instructions were received, and the Zouaves set off for Farmville. Soon after, the 114th was ordered to report to the Fifth Corps; and on April 24, Special Orders Number 93 assigned them to the First Brigade, Second Division. By that time, the war in the eastern theater was ended. Lee had surrendered the battered remnant of his once formidable army to Grant on April 9.[33]

Collis undoubtedly had been disappointed to leave his assignment at City Point. It had become the scene not only of much confusion, but of much excitement as well. Distinguished visitors thronged to the port during the last weeks of the war, and the ever-ambitious Collis probably sought to make the best use of his exposure in such a situation. One of the visitors was Governor Curtin. When he left, he escorted Collis' wife and daughter home to Philadelphia, along with a few cats that Curtin took back to Harrisburg. Collis wrote the governor from Burkeville on April 21: "I trust . . . that Mrs. C. and the little one did not trouble you. How are the tabbies? I am sure they will prove good mousers if they adopt the

---

32. *Ibid.*, 660, 679, 697–698.
33. *Ibid.*, 923.

'unconditional surrender' principle of the school in which they were educated." [34]

Though Collis wrote these sentences to Curtin in a lighthearted fashion, the foregoing week had been one of great sadness among the men. In spite of their hard-won victory, the death of President Lincoln at the hands of an assassin had cast a pall over their spirits. "The sad National calamity . . . has filled the soldiers with a sadness of heart of which I little thought them capable," Collis also observed to the governor. "Old friends met and shook hands in solemn silence." News of the disaster had been greeted at first with skepticism, but when it proved true, "all the bands commenced playing dirges, minute guns were fired, and by order all unnecessary work was suspended." [35]

The Zouaves commenced their new assignment, and within days the army began retracing its steps, first to Petersburg, then slowly northward to Washington. Though they all had seen the last of fighting, they had not yet experienced the last of the wet and chilling conditions of life on the march. The Virginia mud that had often plagued them in the past did so again on the long trek homeward. The Zouaves broke camp on May 1, tramped through Petersburg, and arrived near Richmond on the fourth. The following day was spent preparing for a grand review through the former Rebel capital. The 114th, with its band leading the way, took position at the head of the brigade and marched proudly through the city. At the reviewing stand, recalled a member of the Zouave band, "one of the men stepped out of ranks and proposed three cheers for 'Uncle George,' which found a prompt response from the soldiers, who loved Meade." [36]

The march continued over the next several days, with the men becoming increasingly angry over the rapid pace at which they were prodded homeward. They suspected that the forced march resulted from nothing more than a wager between two generals to see whose corps would reach the capital first. When they finally reached Arlington Heights on the afternoon of May 12, the men were completely worn out. Years later, the

34. C. Collis to "My dear Governor," April 21, 1865, Records of the 114th PV, Record Group 19, PHMC.

35. *Ibid.*; Rauscher, *Music on the March*, 246.

36. Rauscher, *Music on the March*, 250.

memory of their mistreatment on that march still burned within them, causing the Zouaves' historian to write in 1892 that "No matter where or on whom the responsibility should have been saddled, it was enough to know ... that a victorious army of veterans ... was so inconsiderately treated."[37]

A few days of rest and full rations soothed the men considerably, but not for long. They were anxious to return home and had no desire to continue their unnecessary stay in camp. They felt disgust at having to perform camp chores. "They had seen enough of the glory of war on the field, and they no longer cared a fig for its glitter in camp," recalled one. Still, the men prepared for one final display of martial grandeur. The grand review of the Army of the Potomac was scheduled for May 23, and the Zouaves were slated to march at the head of the First Brigade, which would lead the Second Division of the Fifth Corps.[38]

The men fell into line shortly before 4 o'clock on the morning of May 23 and marched to the staging area near Pennsylvania Avenue. At 9 A.M., the Army of the Potomac began its final march down the cobblestone avenue, past the reviewing stands, as cheer after cheer arose on the air. "Ladies waved their handkerchiefs, and in the dense crowd men and boys held up their hats and shouted. There was no end to the enthusiasm of the spectators," recalled one of the Zouave musicians. The veterans of the 114th stepped proudly at the head of the Fifth Corps's Zouave Brigade, and a photograph captured that final official gathering of the men as the column halted opposite Market Square on Pennsylvania Avenue. The grand review was a fitting honor for a proud and victorious army. It was a fitting end to their service as well.[39]

37. *Ibid.*
38. Rauscher, *Music on the March*, 258.
39. *Ibid.*, 260.

Conclusion

How Shall We Rank Thee on Glory's Page?

On June 1, 1865, thirty-four months after receiving its rousing send-off to war, the 114th Pennsylvania Volunteers reached Philadelphia with their Zouave cornet band proudly leading the way. Nearly one-third of the men who marched off with the regiment to preserve the Union in 1862 either had been killed or now bore some physical scar as a reminder of their service. Those returning to Philadelphia left behind them on the battle-fields of Pennsylvania and Virginia more than just the hallowed memory of their dead. Many of them left behind their youth and innocence as well, for they had done more than embark on a new stage of their lifecourse; they had changed the meaning of their lives forever. As the 20th Massachusetts's captain Oliver W. Holmes, Jr., eloquently expressed it, in their youth, their "hearts were touched with fire." They truly had learned early that life was a "profound and passionate thing." War had been an experience that would bond them forever in fraternity with those who understood the ordeal through which they had passed: those who had stood shoulder to shoulder in the smoke and din of battle and seen their comrades fall in a hail of lead and iron; those who had passed wearily along dust-choked or mud-slicked roads en route to battles and been cheered by the sight of their generals galloping to the front; those who had shared cups of hot coffee, pieces of hardtack, and pipes of tobacco with friends who had none; those who shared stories, songs, and jokes around campfires on countless cold winter nights when boredom and loneliness leavened with thoughts of loved ones far away meant a pain more searing than that which any wound could inflict. Those who had not been among them could never understand the camaraderie, the love, these men bore for one another. They were different: different from the men they would have been had no war occurred; and different from their peers whose life experiences were not informed by the rigors of military service.[1]

Within days of reaching home, many of the men donned their Zouave regalia for the last time to march through the streets of Philadelphia in yet another grand review. In a driving rainstorm on June 10, locally recruited regiments were led by General Meade and the First Troop, Philadelphia City Cavalry, along a route that ran southward on Ridge Road from Camp Cadwalader through the city to the Volunteer Refreshment Saloon near the Delaware River. There, the citizens of Philadelphia had prepared a farewell meal for the soldiers. Over two hundred of the Zouaves participated in the parade that day, led by their former colonel, Charles H. T. Collis.

Just before the Zouaves returned to Philadelphia, General Grant had requested that Collis be brevetted to the rank of major general. The promotion was made retroactive to March 13, 1865, for "meritorious service during the war." Near the end of April, Collis also had recommended several men of his brigade for brevet promotion as a reward for their service in the final attack on Petersburg. To major, he recommended Captains Benjamin C. Shermer and Alfred S. Newlin. The regimental quartermaster, First Lieutenant James Hartley, was recommended for brevet to captain.[2]

In addition, Collis had recommended other officers for permanent promotion to fill vacancies in the regiment. Major Bowen, for instance, had struggled for months after Cavada's departure to obtain his rightful promotion to the rank of lieutenant colonel. Unfortunately for Bowen, the numbers of the 114th had been so reduced that for some time there were not enough men on the rolls to warrant mustering a lieutenant colonel. Replacements eventually boosted the number of men to the required amount, and the major's name was submitted for promotion. Still, by the time the 114th was returning to Philadelphia, many of the long-sought

1. Bartlett, comp., *Familiar Quotations*, 14th ed., s.v. "Oliver Wendell Holmes, Jr."

2. Record of C. H. T. Collis, No. 8636, MOLLUS, New York Commandery (N.Y., January 15, 1892), CWLM; *OR*, Vol. XLVI, Pt. 1, pp. 1093–94.

commissions had not been received. Knowing that the nominees were nearing the end of their term of service, Collis wrote Governor Curtin and asked that any forthcoming commissions be sent directly to him. "I intend to keep up the organization when I return home," he said. Not all of the requested commissions materialized, however, and several of the men had to content themselves with brevet promotions. The attempt to maintain the ties of the organization in the postwar period resulted in the formation of the Survivors' Association. Whether it was formed by Collis himself or whether it resulted from a communal desire among the former Zouaves for such an organization is not known.[3]

One of the veterans' last formal gatherings in Philadelphia took place on Independence Day, 1866, when an elaborate parade and ceremony were staged during which each regiment would return its colors to the state. A large amphitheater holding five thousand people had been erected across from Independence Hall for the occasion; it was filled with, among others, children from the Soldiers' Orphan Schools and families of soldiers who had been killed. At 10 A.M., the parade started off from Broad Street, north of Arch Street, and headed for Independence Hall. The men were led by Major General Winfield Scott Hancock, a native of nearby Montgomery County. The First Troop, Philadelphia City Cavalry, again served as escort, along with the Henry Guards, another local militia unit. The Zouave detachment marched with the parade's Second Division, led by Major General Robert Patterson. The Fourth Division was composed of cavalrymen led by Major General David McMurtrie Gregg, who escorted Major General Meade and his staff. In the Sixth Division of the parade were carriages filled with more orphaned children, escorted by city firemen. When the regiments assembled at Independence Hall, honor guards turned over their colors to General Meade, who presented them in turn to Governor Curtin. The conclusion of the ceremony was marked by salutes fired from artillery stationed in nearby Washington Square. Other guns were fired throughout the course of the day from Fairmount Park and Penn Square, and fireworks provided an end to the day's celebration.[4]

The men of the 114th Pennsylvania would gather again on many occasions over the years, both at meetings of the Survivors' Association and

---

3. C. Collis to "My dear Governor," April 21, 1865, Records of the 114th PV, Record Group 19, PHMC.

4. F. H. Taylor, *Philadelphia in the Civil War*, 315–17.

as members of other veterans' organizations such as the Boys in Blue and the Grand Army of the Republic (GAR). Philadelphia members of the Boys in Blue were organized into ward associations that were represented in a general council, which had "more direct charge of the work required to advance the political interests of soldiers and sailors belonging to the Republican Party." The GAR professed to have a philanthropic purpose, although it, too, became a powerful political agent on behalf of the veterans. The organization supported efforts to care for and educate orphans of deceased soldiers, to assist their widows, and to aid those disabled by "wounds, sickness, old age or misfortune." Most importantly, however, the GAR became a vociferous proponent of veterans' benefits and pensions in their bid to "inculcate a proper appreciation" for the services of the soldiers.[5]

The first GAR post in Philadelphia was chartered on October 16, 1866. Major Edward R. Bowen was among the post's first members. General Collis, also a GAR member, was elected to the position of chaplain of Post Two in 1867. Collis' post contained many of the city's business and professional elite. By 1871, the GAR boasted over 30,000 members. The numbers decreased somewhat in succeeding years; then in 1878, as interest in the war revived, a steady growth in membership took place. By 1881, there were 87,718 members, and only seven years later, membership rolls showed that 361,779 former soldiers had joined. Giving voice to such a considerable voting bloc, the GAR became a champion of veterans rights, urging Congress to support legislation that funded pensions for the former soldiers and their survivors.[6]

Many of the former Zouaves benefited from the lobbying efforts of the GAR. One of them was William T. Abrams, a member of Collis' original company of Zouaves d'Afrique, who had been wounded in the right thigh at the battle of Cedar Mountain in August, 1862. Abrams became a park guard after the war. He married in 1868 and had nine children. His wife

---

5. Robert B. Beath, *History of the Grand Army of the Republic* (New York, 1889), 464–67. See also Stuart C. McConnell, *Glorious Contentment: The Grand Army of the Republic, 1865–1900* (Chapel Hill, 1992).

6. Beath, *History of the Grand Army of the Republic*, 466. See also Stuart C. McConnell, "Who Joined the Grand Army? Three Case Studies in the Construction of Union Veteranhood, 1866–1900," in *Toward a Social History of the American Civil War*, ed. Vinovskis, 139–70.

died in 1908, but the old veteran survived to see his son Albert go off to fight in World War I as a sergeant in Company B, 109th Infantry, 28th Division. Abrams' pension at that time was a modest thirty dollars per month.[7]

Another member of the original company, John Alff, received twelve dollars per month from 1890 until his death in 1900 at the National Home for Disabled Soldiers, Central Branch, in Ohio. Alff's pension application described him as having rheumatism, heart disease, and a hernia. Another former Zouave who died in a veterans' home was Joshua G. Bates. He was admitted to the National Soldiers Home of Virginia in 1908, where he lived until his death in 1912. He received a pension of fifteen dollars per month.[8]

The Bureau of Pensions apparently was very thorough in its investigations into the applications of veterans, requiring concrete evidence that illnesses or injuries stemmed from military service. Even Captain Charles B. Sloan of Company H, who had procured a discharge on grounds of a medical disability in 1863, had a difficult time obtaining a pension. He first applied in 1877, alleging diarrhea, bronchitis, and a double hernia. He stated to the pension examiners that in December, 1862, he had contracted pneumonia after the battle of Fredericksburg. In his weakened and debilitated condition, he claimed that he stumbled while marching with his regiment to Falmouth on the night of December 15. He fell flat on his face and stomach, which caused the hernia on both sides of his groin. Upon checking his disability certificate, which had been issued by Surgeon Jacob M. Cummins, the pension examiners found no mention of a hernia. The Bureau of Pensions sent a letter to Dr. Cummins, then living in Industry, Pennsylvania, seeking his recollection of the circumstances. Cummins apparently was dismayed by Captain Sloan's attempts to procure a pension, and wrote that he had no recollection of a hernia. In addition, he felt unkindly towards Sloan because of the latter's betrayal of the doctor's trust in February, 1863. Sloan had been very ill at that time, contended Cummins, but "the certificate of disability I gave [him] dated Feb 26th 1863 was to obtain a Leave of Absence and not a resignation." Cummins also expressed his exasperation at being called upon to support the claims of former soldiers now applying for pensions, when he had been

7. Pension file of William T. Abrams, NARA.
8. Pension files of John Alff and Joshua G. Bates, *ibid.*

compelled to turn over his complete medical records to the War Department in 1865 and had nothing to rely upon but his memory.[9]

Sloan persisted in his efforts, however, supplying clarification by stating that then Colonel Collis had been marching at his side, along with Major Chandler, and that both men knew of the injury, though Chandler had been killed at Chancellorsville. Collis wrote a letter on Sloan's behalf that was carelessly worded and ambiguous. Collis stated that Sloan had fallen and sustained a rupture and that the fact had been "reported to him," thus seeming not to support Sloan's claim that Collis had been present. Further inquiry produced another letter from Collis in which he stated that he had indeed seen Sloan fall, and it was only the fact that he had sustained a rupture as a result of the fall that was later reported to him. Sloan further alleged that the certificate of disability that had been completed by Dr. Cummins had been filled out prior to his fall and injury. By his own insistence, Sloan maintained, he declined to accept the certificate until after the impending engagement at Fredericksburg. When he saw the surgeon again after the battle, Cummins simply gave him the certificate that had already been prepared, despite Sloan's telling him of the hernia. Sloan also prevailed upon Cummins and helped the doctor to clarify his recollection of the events. Cummins either had a change of heart or was convinced that Sloan's version was the accurate one. He eventually wrote to the Bureau of Pensions stating that Sloan might have had a hernia at the time, but that he was so dangerously ill from other causes that he probably did not think it necessary to mention the hernia on the disability certificate. Sloan was granted a pension, receiving fifteen dollars per month until his death in 1892.[10]

At other times the Bureau of Pensions was faced with conflicting claims from survivors of the veterans. Corporal Henry C. Kelly of Company D, who had borne Collis from the field on a stretcher at Chancellorsville and later testified at his court-martial, was wounded in the right thigh at Petersburg on April 2, 1865. When he died in August, 1910, Kelly left a widow, Sarah, who continued to receive a widow's pension. The following year, however, the bureau received a rambling letter from one Catherine Kelly, who maintained that it was she who was the rightful widow: "I wish to know if a Woman Maried a man in the year 61 and he whent to the

9. Pension file of Charles B. Sloan, *ibid.*
10. *Ibid.*

war the same year and came home and lived with her until [18]70 and a
nother woman won him away from her and lived with him of and on until
he died . . . I called on her the day after he was Buried and asked her for
his Discharge and she said she would give it to me. please let me know if
she is drawing a pension for herself as she is not entitled to any as she is
not his Wife." Catherine received a response from the bureau stating that
their records showed Sarah J. Kelly of 1019 Snyder Avenue as Corporal
Kelly's widow. "If you are the legal widow of this soldier and you were not
divorced from him at the time of his death, you are at liberty to make
claim for pension as his widow," stated the letter. A blank claim form was
enclosed for that purpose, but Catherine apparently never followed
through with the claim. Perhaps she was merely bluffing and still harbored
resentment against Sarah, but she probably could produce no evidence of
her alleged marriage to Kelly. The bureau's records, however, indicated
that Henry Kelly and Sarah J. Robertson had been married on October
29, 1871, at St. Paul's Methodist Episcopal Church, 623 Catherine Street
in Philadelphia. Sarah continued to receive the pension, and was collect-
ing twenty-two dollars per month at the time of her death in 1922.[11]

Other veterans and their survivors were not always successful in convincing pension board officials that their plight was related to wartime
service. Alvah J. Anderson, one of the soldiers who had left his name on
the wall of Massaponax Church in the summer of 1864, died at Wills Eye
Hospital in Philadelphia on April 3, 1874, at the age of twenty-seven.
Anderson had worked as a machinist at an iron foundry before the war;
when he enlisted in 1863, he gave his age as eighteen. After his death,
his widow applied for pension benefits but had difficulty establishing the
veracity of her claim. Her husband, she said, had been wounded in the
knee at the battle of Chancellorsville. Two fellow Zouaves, Jacob Baugh
and John Tricker, provided affidavits further explaining that when Anderson fell from the leg wound, he struck his head on the stump of a tree.
It was the head injury, his wife maintained, that caused his death. Anderson had experienced frequent dizzy spells and eventually went blind. Despite her efforts, Mrs. Anderson's claim was denied.[12]

Sadness also clouds the circumstances of the death of "French Mary,"
the regimental vivandiere. Mary's service had been much touted during

11. Pension file of Henry C. Kelly, NARA.
12. Pension file of Alvah J. Anderson, *ibid.*

her time with the Zouaves. In addition to the Kearny Cross awarded her after the battle of Fredericksburg, a silver cup was given to her by Lieutenant Colonel Cavada with the inscription: "To Marie, for noble conduct on the field of battle." An officer of an Ohio regiment recalled seeing her at the battle of Spotsylvania in search of her regiment: "She was wonderfully courageous or else she did not understand the danger . . . the shower of musket balls, shrapnel, and every sort of projectile falling in the midst of us was trying the nerves of the coolest." Mary married Richard Leonard, a former Maryland cavalryman, after the war. She appeared at an 1893 reunion of the Zouave veterans in Philadelphia, where she had her photograph taken with the wooden keg that she had carried over her shoulder throughout the war. Little is known of her life in the intervening years, but on May 14, 1901, the aged vivandiere took her own life by ingesting the caustic pesticide and paint pigment Paris green. Death for the sixty-seven-year-old woman was slow and painful. One can only hope that few other Zouave veterans were overcome by such despair.[13]

Though a number of pensions, like Captain Sloan's, were granted as a result of illness or injury suffered while in the army, many others were granted to those whose bodies had been brutally invaded by Rebel lead and iron. One can only imagine the physical pain the wounded veterans suffered as they aged. Many lived long lives, though pension applications often indicate that their wounds eventually made it difficult for them to work. Some, however, were thankful to have survived. Sergeant John Waterhouse, for example, was wounded twice in the right thigh on July 2, 1863, at the Sherfy Farm near Gettysburg. Strangely, two bullets entered his thigh inches apart, just below his groin, and exited just below his buttocks. A few inches higher and the wounds would surely have proved fatal. When Waterhouse marched off to war at age thirty-seven, he left behind an already large family consisting of his wife, Sarah, and five children ranging in age from four to eleven years old. He remained hospitalized after his wounding until the spring of 1864 and mustered out with the regiment the following year. He received a well-deserved pension until he died at age seventy-eight in 1903 of "old age" and a "fatty heart."[14]

Private Thomas Egbert of Company D also was wounded twice, first in

---

13. Gladstone, "Gettysburg Mystery Photo," 18; Marie Varrelman Melchiori, "The Death of 'French Mary,'" *Military Images*, V (July–August 1983), 14.
14. Pension file of John R. Waterhouse, NARA.

the right thigh at Auburn on October 13, 1863; then just above the right ankle joint on April 2, 1865, in the final assault on Petersburg. After his first wounding, Egbert was transported to Judiciary Square Hospital in Washington, D.C., where he was also treated for gangrene. At Petersburg, Egbert was struck by a bullet four inches above the outside of the right ankle. The shot passed through his leg fracturing the fibula. He was discharged from the army in July, 1865, from a Baltimore hospital. Egbert moved to New York City after the war and found employment with the city's extensive transportation company as a streetcar operator. Eventually, however, his wound caused such discomfort that he could work only a few days each week. Egbert received a pension to supplement his reduced income, suffering with his impairment until his death from heart disease in 1903 at age seventy-six.[15]

Surprisingly, George Murray of Company B experienced only minor complications in later years as a result of his serious shoulder wound. Murray lived in Hainesport, New Jersey, after the war and worked as a carpenter. He applied for a pension in 1877, when he was thirty-three years old. At that time, the examining physician concluded that the bullet had entered Murray's right shoulder just below the clavicle, passed through the upper lobe of the lung, exiting through the scapula. Despite the nature of the wound, the results were less severe than might be expected. The doctor noted that "the motion of the arm is somewhat affected enough to cause numbness down under the elbow and in the little and ring fingers." Murray, who never married, died in January, 1910. He was receiving twelve dollars per month from the Bureau of Pensions.[16]

A number of officers of the 114th became members of another veterans' group, the Military Order of the Loyal Legion of the United States (MOLLUS). Union officers had organized the group in Philadelphia on the day following Lincoln's death. Its purpose was to perpetuate the memory of the fallen president, though it eventually evolved into a more elite version of the GAR *sans* national political clout. Locally, however, it exerted considerable political force. General Collis' application for membership in 1890 caused a furor in the organization when the details of his court-martial in 1863 resurfaced. He recalled, "Insidious efforts were made by a few personal enemies to resuscitate a dead slander, and to use this

15. Pension file of Thomas Egbert, *ibid.*
16. Pension file of George Murray, *ibid.*

noble organization to strike me a blow." It was not the first time that Collis was haunted by his past.[17]

Collis had resumed his law career in 1865 and soon after was appointed to the post of assistant city solicitor in Philadelphia. In 1871 and again in 1874, he was elected city solicitor. For fifteen years after his return from the war, Collis held a seat on the board of trusts that administered the public charities in this city. Then in 1883, he moved to New York City to become partner with his wife's brother in the law firm of Collis and Levy, where he remained until 1890. He involved himself in politics once again in New York City and became an influential member of the Committee of Seventy. He eventually was appointed deputy commissioner of public works, then assumed the office of commissioner in 1895 at a salary of $8,000 per year.[18]

Collis' predecessor had made an effort to remove corrupt Tammany Hall officeholders from the department of public works, and Collis promised that he too would ensure that the department was "run as free as possible from political influences." One of his first official acts, however, was to appoint as deputy commissioner Adelbert H. Steele, who was chairman of the campaign committee of the Republican Club. Perhaps the general meant only to keep his department free of Democratic political influence. Nevertheless, Collis accomplished a number of beneficial projects as commissioner, including the modernization of Fifth Avenue, the installation of new water mains, and the regrading and repaving of Park Avenue. He proved to be as feisty as ever while serving in the position of commissioner. When a newly elected mayor suggested that Collis had been negligent in his official duties, the old soldier sent a letter to him "stating that if such insinuations were again cast upon his character he should hold the man who made them personally responsible." In case the mayor failed to comprehend his meaning, Collis sent another note in which he "made it plain that he meant to chastise [the mayor] if the offense was repeated."[19]

Collis was undoubtedly sensitive about his honor, though for his actions at Fredericksburg on December 13, 1862, he received the nation's most prestigious military decoration, the Medal of Honor. The medal was

17. C. Collis, *1st Brigade*, 1.

18. "General Collis Is Commissioner," unidentified newspaper clipping, December 2, 1895, Philadelphia *Bulletin* Files, in Temple University Urban Archives.

19. *Ibid.*; "General Collis, Soldier, Life-Saver, and Fire-Eater," unidentified newspaper clipping, June 12, 1899, Philadelphia *Bulletin* Files, in Temple University Urban Archives.

awarded to him on March 10, 1893, at a time when requirements less stringent than those that would later prevail guided the recipient selection process. Despite the medal, questions occasionally arose concerning his actions on the battlefield. He probably grew tired of defending himself against allegations that his behavior at Chancellorsville had been cowardly. The court-martial was brought up and used against him, he maintained, "upon all occasions when it was necessary to throw some obstacle across my path in life." It became an issue during his election campaign for the post of city solicitor in Philadelphia, and it was "anonymously communicated to the Stock Exchange" in New York when he became a member there in 1880.[20]

In 1891, after nearly losing in his bid for membership in MOLLUS, Collis published a short booklet detailing his military career and containing many testimonials from eyewitnesses stressing his courage and good behavior while under fire. The objection to his membership in MOLLUS stemmed not only from his court-martial, but also from the allegation that he had been "hissed" by the men of his regiment after the battle. That charge, Collis stated characteristically—and in language reminiscent of that which composed his letter to General Birney in May of 1863—"I now hear for the first time in my life, and it is so absurd that I will challenge any man living to repeat it to my face." The general was saddened by the attack on him, and he wrote of his hope for an end to the slander that had plagued him for so many years: "I prefer that my posterity who may be called upon to defend my name when I am not here to do it for myself should be able to point to the archives of the Military Order of the Loyal Legion, and say that their ancestor's record was passed upon not only by a jury of his fellow-soldiers in the field, but by a Committee of the Legion appointed expressly for that purpose, who had all the facts before them."[21]

In addition to showing sensitivity about slights to his own honor, Collis expressed implacable disdain for those whom he thought deserved censure. Such was the case with his view of Lieutenant Colonel Cavada. In December, 1865, when he found that Cavada had been appointed United States consul at Trinidad de Cuba, Collis fired off a letter to President Andrew Johnson, informing him of Cavada's misconduct while attached

20. C. Collis, *1st Brigade*, 9.
21. *Ibid.*, 3, 9–10.

to the 114th Pennsylvania. "I consider it my simple duty to the many *gallant* soldiers now out of employment to bring these facts before you, and hold myself prepared to prove them," he wrote. A response from Cavada's stepfather, Samuel Dutton, rebutted the charges by recalling that Collis himself had been subject to a court-martial at Chancellorsville. Dutton's letter was published and widely circulated, prompting Collis to have the entire correspondence printed, including a final rebuttal in his own defense. The document concluded with a brief note signed by twelve former Zouave officers, who stated that they concurred with Collis' letter to the president. "Such of the facts therein referred to as came under our immediate observation are true, and those which did not we believe to be true," they wrote.[22]

Despite the opposition to it, Cavada's appointment was confirmed. And notwithstanding the reasons for the negative perceptions of his conduct during the Civil War battles in which he fought, he soon proved that he was far from cowardly. Cavada resigned his post in 1869 to take part in a revolution designed to free his native country from Spanish domination. Eventually, he succeeded former Confederate brigadier general Thomas Jordan as commander of the revolutionaries. Jordan, with a $100,000 price on his head, returned to the United States and founded the *Financial and Mining Record* of New York, where he died in 1895. His successor in Cuba, however, fared badly. On July 4, 1871, word reached New York that Cavada, known as the "Fire King," had been captured by a Spanish gunboat while attempting to flee the island. Understanding the usual fate of captured revolutionaries, Cavada's friends made frantic efforts to preserve his life. They enlisted the aid of Generals William Birney, Graham, and Philip Henry Sheridan; and they besought President Grant to plead for a postponement of any execution, particularly since Cavada was an American citizen. Their efforts were in vain, however, for they were seeking clemency for a dead man. On July 11, Cavada's supporters read that his death at Puerto Principe, Cuba, had occurred on July 1. When he faced his executioners, Cavada purportedly "flung his hat to the ground and uttered a patriotic cry. . . . Just before the fatal volley was fired, he cried out his last words—'Adios, Cuba! para siempre!'"[23]

---

22. C. Collis, *Case of F. F. Cavada*, 1, 14.

23. Unidentified newspaper clipping found in flyleaf of a copy of Cavada's *Libby Life* in CWLM. See Philip S. Foner's *Antonio Maceo: The Bronze Titan of Cuba's Struggle for Inde-*

Collis, of course, let the matter of Cavada's behavior in the regiment drop forever, and he probably regretted their past disagreements. When asked in 1876 for a copy of the pamphlet that he had published years earlier concerning Cavada's appointment to the Cuban post, he judiciously responded, "Since Col. Cavada's very sad death, I have carefully avoided any mention of his troubles in my Regiment; and would prefer not letting any of the pamphlets pass out of my hands, unless under a promise that no use should be made of it which could possibly open afresh wounds which time has done much to heal." The incident was never mentioned again in public by Collis.[24]

By the time Collis retired from public life near the turn of the century, his attention had been drawn to other matters. The general became increasingly involved with perpetuating the memory of his comrades. Collis was present among a group of about twenty veterans of the 114th who arrived at Fredericksburg, Virginia, on May 2, 1899, to dedicate a monument to their comrades who had fallen at nearby Chancellorsville thirty-six years earlier. On May 3, the group proceeded to the battlefield accompanied by members of the Chancellorsville Battlefield Park Association along with Ves Chancellor, who acted as guide. The group toured Salem Church, the Chancellor House itself, the Jackson Monument, and the site of Lee and Jackson's last meeting. At the monument to their former nemesis, the veterans placed a wreath and listened to speeches by General Collis and Private William Grew. After "three rousing cheers to Stonewall Jackson," the old soldiers walked across the Orange Plank Road to the site of their own monument, which they complained was improperly located. Again, Collis mounted the speaker's platform and delivered a stirring speech. The monument was unveiled, a floral arrangement was presented, and a prayer was said to conclude the ceremony.[25]

Though Collis had not been present at the dedication of a monument to his Zouaves at Gettysburg on November 11, 1888, he later took great

---

pendence (New York, 1977) for a brief discussion of Cavada's role in Cuba's Ten Years' War, including his direction of the revolt in Las Villas district starting on February 9, 1869, and his urging of the Cuban revolutionary government to follow the examples set by northern generals during the American Civil War. Most notably, Cavada proposed to emulate the wartime policies of Benjamin F. Butler and to disrupt Cuba's Spanish colonial economy by liberating slaves in territories invaded by the revolutionaries.

24. C. Collis, *Case of F. F. Cavada,* i.

25. Donald Pfanz, "History Through Eyes of Stone" (Typescript, 1983), 116, at FSNMP.

interest in the battlefield and was instrumental in securing land that became part of the Gettysburg National Military Park. Speeches at the dedication of the Gettysburg monument were delivered by Captain Alexander W. Given and Lieutenant Colonel Edward R. Bowen. The Survivors' Association of the 114th Pennsylvania Volunteers had the monument's stone pedestal erected at their own expense, but the state funded the bronze figure of a Zouave that was placed atop the stone.[26]

Collis devoted much of the remainder of his life to the development of a national park at Gettysburg. He even built a summer home there on West Confederate Avenue, not far from the site where General Barksdale's Mississippians would have formed on the afternoon of July 2, 1863, before crashing violently into the 114th and driving them from the field. Collis named the residence Red Patch, after the corps insignia he and his men had faithfully followed during the war. The home was occupied only by the general, however. Family lore holds that Collis developed a roving eye at some point in his life, and his infidelities led to a temporary estrangement from his wife. The couple reunited and produced another child in 1881, whom they named Charles. Young Charles well might have been named Charles Henry Tuckey Collis, Jr., had not a newspaper article concerning a much debated political issue appeared shortly before his birth in which the general was labeled Charles "Hot Tamale" Collis. The children in the family then consisted of nineteen-year-old Amelia and her younger brother, Lloyd, born in 1870. The general did not amend his ways permanently after being reconciled with his wife, however, and Septima finally separated from him for good. Their relationship must often have been a stormy one, for they both were strong-willed. The general, at least, was known to be quick-tempered, though Septima might well have given as good as she got. Family tradition also has it that when differences arose between them, she sometimes threatened to invoke her rights as a South Carolinian and the sister of a Confederate officer by joining the United Daughters of the Confederacy, a threat that she ultimately carried out. After the final separation, Septima spent a number of years in Europe and was living in France when she died in 1916. For his part, General Collis often stayed at his Gettysburg home in his final years. According to local legend, Red Patch was sometimes the scene of wild parties hosted by the general. More certainly, it was the site of a number of meetings of the

26. Nicholson, ed., *Pennsylvania at Gettysburg*, II, 604–19.

commissioners of the newly formed Gettysburg Battlefield Park Commission.[27]

On May 11, 1902, only a few years after the completion of the house in Gettysburg, Collis died at the age of sixty-four. The general passed away in Bryn Mawr, Pennsylvania, near Philadelphia, while his wife was in Paris. One of the old soldier's final orders was that he should be buried in the National Cemetery at Gettysburg with the men of his regiment who had fallen on that field thirty-nine years before. Though he was not with them in battle, he would rest with them forever.

The funeral service was held at Saint Stephen's Episcopal Church near Tenth and Chestnut Streets in Philadelphia. Many Zouave veterans filed by the bier, which was draped with the flag for which they had so proudly fought. Collis' sword lay on the coffin amid a mass of flowers; a crescent of red and white roses and asparagus vines provided by his men surrounded the casket.[28]

The general's body was taken the following day by train to Gettysburg, where a long funeral cortege started from the Western Maryland Depot and accompanied his remains to the National Cemetery. The Grand Army Band played a dirge as the procession wound its way through the cemetery to the gravesite. After a brief prayer by local pastor W. N. R. Ashmead, veterans of the regiment fired three volleys and laid their former leader to rest while the strains of taps floated sadly on the air.[29]

General Collis was gone, but he was not soon forgotten. On Saturday evening, May 12, 1906, four years after his death, members of the Survivors' Association of the 114th Pennsylvania Volunteers again stepped off the train in Gettysburg to pay one final tribute to their deceased leader. At about 8 o'clock that night, the men assembled near the Adams County Court House, gathering again around an open campfire. Major Bowen recited a short history of the regiment as the old Zouaves stood staring into the flames and reliving the glory of their martial past. At precisely 2 o'clock the next afternoon, after touring the battlefield, the veterans gathered at the cemetery. The old soldiers stood with Collis' two sons, Lloyd

27. Charles Collis (grandson of Charles H. T. Collis) to the author, December 12, 1995, and January 8, 1996, in possession of the author.

28. "Many Veterans at Gen. Collis's Funeral," Philadelphia *Public Ledger and Daily Transcript*, May 15, 1902, p. 3.

29. "General Collis Buried," *DEB* (now the Philadelphia *Evening Bulletin*), May 16, 1902, p. 2.

and Charles, and witnessed the dedication of a monument to honor the general. The youthful face of their former commander would evermore keep watch over their fallen comrades as it gazed stoically toward the horizon in the direction of Collis' beloved Red Patch.[30]

The life of Brevet Major General Charles Henry Tuckey Collis and the career of his regiment, the 114th Pennsylvania Volunteers, were inextricably entwined. Collis' professional stature in antebellum Philadelphia as well as his relationship with Judge John M. Read served to enhance the regiment's notability in the Army of the Potomac. Through his mentor, Collis had been able to develop close personal relationships with men in the army who could help advance his own career, and who would influence the fate of his regiment. Collis owed his promotions only partly to his efforts to perform his duties well. The influence of Judge Read and other political figures also assisted his elevation and helped fend off accusations that he had performed poorly on the battlefield. The accusations might have destroyed an officer with fewer powerful connections, but Collis was able to rally others to his support. Such political ties ultimately served to make Collis' service, and that of his regiment, somewhat distinctive within the army.

Collis professed to abhor the government's tendency to promote officers on the basis of political influence. Writing to John W. Geary of his promotion to major general, Collis noted that Geary's rank was well deserved and that he should be proud of that fact, unlike others who could claim advancement only on the grounds of political influence. That Collis should express such sentiments when he knew that Judge Read was lobbying intensely for his own promotion seems incongruous, yet the colonel probably believed that Read was merely assisting in bringing his case before those whose endorsement mattered. Once there, his record would speak for itself. As was seen by his defense after Chancellorsville, and by his castigation of Lieutenant Colonel Cavada, Collis believed his record and motives to be unimpeachable. He was not one to be haunted by self-doubts, and his actions were typically intemperate.

When Collis risked his life in 1899 by entering a burning building to rescue two women, one newspaper correspondent described him as "an aggressive, self-confident, likable man, with a characteristically Celtic tem-

---

30. "Col. C. H. T. Collis Memorial," Gettysburg *Star and Sentinel*, May 14, 1906, p. 1.

perament." It was probably as apt a description as could have been rendered. His behavior often led to difficulties for him, but somehow, he always managed to overcome them.[31]

As early as 1861, Collis' "Celtic temperament" had flared while he was attending the theater in Philadelphia. Fort Sumter had recently fallen, and in the patriotic fervor of the moment, one of the performers had been moved to sing "The Star-Spangled Banner" between acts. Several southerners who were students at the University of Pennsylvania hissed the song. Collis and his companions promptly ran the offenders out of the theater; but the entire group was met at the door by the police, and all were taken into custody. Friends of Collis' group quickly furnished the required bail money, and the patriots returned to the theater. There, they received an ovation and were called to the stage to take a bow. Such an incident could only have reinforced Collis' belief that he would be sustained in taking what he thought was commendable action, no matter how immoderate that conduct seemed to others. It was undoubtedly this belief that compelled him to criticize General Graham's staff officers at Chancellorsville. It had been a near-fatal error, but again he prevailed. He profited by his actions in nearly every case, and he never was inclined to restrain his emotions: witness his threat to "chastise" the mayor of New York City for casting aspersions on his character.[32]

The fact remains, however, that despite Collis' self-confidence, his aggressiveness, and his abilities as an officer, his record would probably not have attracted the attention necessary for rapid promotion had his case not been championed by Judge Read and other supporters. Ultimately, there was little to differentiate him from hundreds of other colonels in the army; without Read's assistance, he might well have remained a colonel throughout the war. Had he raised a regiment in some more rural area of the country, where acquaintance with a powerful political figure would have been unlikely, he might have been relegated to obscurity. The advantages of coming from the ranks of the professional elite in a large eastern metropolis weighed heavily in his favor. A person of stature in Philadelphia, he seemed naturally to assume a similar stature in the army. However, a man of equivalent qualifications from an obscure town would probably have had much difficulty extending his civilian prestige into his army experience.

31. "General Collis, Soldier, Life-Saver, and Fire-Eater," newspaper clipping.
32. "Rush Lancers' Reunion," Gettysburg *Star and Sentinel*, September 26, 1900, p. 3.

Collis was not the only member of the 114th Pennsylvania Volunteers who was politically astute. Many of the men had probably been involved in politics in some form in the antebellum city. The career of William "Bull" McMullen illustrated that neighborhood political figures such as ward bosses, aldermen, and their many underlings wielded great power in Philadelphia. Political power touched nearly every aspect of nearly everyone's life in the city, for little could be accomplished outside of this realm. Jobs could be had or denied at the discretion of political leaders; in the same way, money was loaned and promotions secured. Political influence was an inescapable fact of life in Philadelphia, and the city's soldiers brought their experience of it with them to war.

One indication of the Zouaves' political consciousness was their contention, soon after arriving at the defenses of Washington, that the government had violated its contract with them by failing to pay the stipulated bounties at the proper moment. While other soldiers might have griped and grumbled, the Philadelphians acted—with their feet. The mass exodus from the ranks that September served to put the government on notice that its promises must be upheld. Though they were censured for it, the action had the desired result. Those who returned to the regiment were pardoned, and the bounty was received.

The political consciousness of the Zouaves—along with most other soldiers recruited from urban environments—probably set them apart from the typical men serving in the army. Most of the country's soldiery hailed from rural areas and towns, and had less experience with the day-to-day effects of political patronage. Many of them probably were unaware of what politicians could accomplish on their behalf. To Philadelphia's officeholders and office-seekers, however, regiments such as the 114th represented a considerable bloc of eligible voters who could be ignored only at their peril. Those officeholders could little hope to influence directly the army's treatment of the soldiers; the leverage held by politicians and influential citizens at home was not with the army as an institution. Their power rather resided in the widespread knowledge that their influence could affect regimental officers at home. As evidenced by the complaints to the newspapers from the Zouaves d'Afrique concerning then-captain Collis' treatment of his men and his handling of the company's funds in early 1862, the soldiers obviously believed that the public exposure of such perceived improprieties would elicit a corrective response. Likewise, when they thought that Collis had abandoned them in the field and broken his promise to make all of them officers and NCOs in the new regiment, they thought nothing of writing a letter to Governor Curtin seeking a redress of their grievances.

Their occupational skill-level distribution also set the Zouaves apart from much of the rest of the army. The most common occupation among members of the Union forces was that of farmer, again a reflection of the rural nature of the army's recruits. The 114th Pennsylvania had its share of farmers too, but as the examination of occupational groups revealed, a high percentage of men from the 114th Pennsylvania were classified as skilled or more semiskilled workers. This finding may possibly mean that those men were more highly educated and of a higher social class than the largely unskilled workers who composed the majorities within rural regiments. It might be argued, however, that the presence of so few skilled workers in rural areas might have reduced the social impact of being classified as only less semiskilled or unskilled. These distinctions simply may not have made that much difference to rural dwellers. Nevertheless, it is significant that the 114th was composed primarily of more highly skilled workers. In Philadelphia, if not in rural areas, this status made a difference.

In addition to variations in occupational skill level, recruits for the 114th Pennsylvania also were found to be older than average. Finally, we saw that the regiment contained a smaller percentage of soldiers whose place of birth was outside the United States than might be expected of a group of men recruited in a large eastern city.

Further studies of rural and urban Civil War regiments, along with studies of those enlisting earlier or later in the war, will facilitate comparisons with the 114th Pennsylvania. Through such comparisons, a more complete picture of the composition of the Union army may be drawn, and the finding that the 114th Pennsylvania differed from the average regiment may take on added significance.

APPENDIX

Recipients of the Kearny Cross from the 114th Pennsylvania Volunteers

Company A
Hopkins, Francis (Zd'A,[1] discharged 1864). Sergeant.
Brontz, John (deserted 1864). Private.
Rohrig, Christian (Zd'A, transferred to Veteran Reserve Corps[2]). Private.

Company B
Stotz, Andrew J. (mustered out with company, 1865). Sergeant
Weber, William (transferred to VRC). Private.
Cass, Samuel N. (transferred to VRC). Private.

Company C
Baylitts, Benjamin J. (mustered out with company, 1865). Color Sergeant.
Miller, William J. (Zd'A, discharged 1864 as 2nd lieutenant). Sergeant.
Cannon, Michael (wounded at Gettysburg, discharged 1864). Corporal.

Company D
Gower, George W. (Zd'A, wounded, discharged 1864). Sergeant.
Grasley, Herman (Zd'A, transferred to 190th P.V., May, 1865). Sergeant.
McLaughlin, Brian (discharged on surgeon's certificate, January, 1863). Corporal.

Company E
Cunningham, Andrew J. (Zd'A, promoted captain, Co. A, killed April, 1865).
  Sergeant.

1. Refers to membership in the original company of Zouaves d'Afrique.
2. First organized in April, 1863, as the Invalid Corps and renamed the Veteran Reserve Corps (VRC) in March, 1864, it consisted of men unfit for full duty in combat units. Depending upon the extent of the soldier's disability, he might have been utilized for guard duty, or served as a nurse or cook in an army hospital.

Munns, Henry C. (Zd'A, promoted 2nd lieutenant, Co. G, mustered out with company in 1865). Sergeant.

Guinness, John (Zd'A, discharged 1864 as 1st sergeant). Sergeant.

Company F

Waterhouse, John (mustered out with company in 1865 as captain). Sergeant.

Fox, Isaac (killed April, 1865, as 1st sergeant). Sergeant.

Maguire, James (mustered out with company in 1865). Private.

Fowler, William (mustered out with company in 1865). Private.

Company G

Bates, Joshua (mustered out with company in 1865 as 1st lieutenant Co. K). Sergeant.

Burk, John A. (mustered out with company in 1865 as 1st sergeant). Sergeant.

Patton, Matthew (wounded April, 1865, discharged). Private.

Company K

McCarty, Henry C. (Zd'A, killed at Gettysburg). Sergeant.

Lackey, William (deserted from hospital in Philadelphia, April, 1863). Corporal.

Borie, Charles (wounded April, 1865, discharged as sergeant). Color Corporal.

Source: Phillips, *Civil War Corps Badges.*

BIBLIOGRAPHY

Manuscripts

Civil War Library Museum, Philadelphia

    Donaldson, Frank A. Papers.

    Given, Alexander W. Collection.

    Grew, William. "Fredericksburg, December 13, 1862." Leaflet printed to accompany the exhibition of an oil painting by Carl Röchling, n.d.

    Papers of the Military Order of the Loyal Legion of the United States.

Fredericksburg and Spotsylvania National Military Park, Fredericksburg, Virginia

    Murray, George. Collection.

    Pfanz, Donald. "History Through Eyes of Stone." Typescript.

Historical Society of Pennsylvania, Philadelphia

    Beale, Joseph Boggs. Diary.

    Benners, Henry C. Diary.

    Cavada, Adolfo. Diary.

    Collis, Charles H. T. Papers.

    Dougherty, Daniel. Diary.

    Fox, Isaac. Collection.

    Gardiner, Edward Carey. Collection.

    Gratz, Simon. Collection.

    Meredith, William M. Papers.

    Read, John M. Papers.

    Wharton, Katherine Brinley. Diary.

Library of Congress, Washington, D.C.

    Morning Reports of Captain Collis' Company of the Zouaves d'Afrique, Army of the United States, August 25, 1861–May 21, 1862, Ac. 6267.

National Archives and Records Administration, Mid-Atlantic Region, Philadelphia

    Ship Passenger Lists, 1800–1882. Microfilm Publication No. M425.

    Ship Passenger Records. Name Index, 1800–1906. Microfilm Publication No. M360.

National Archives and Records Administration, Washington, D.C.

    Court Martial Records. Record Groups 153 and 154.

Compiled Military Service Records. Regimental Records. Modern Military Records Division, Records of the 114th Pennsylvania Volunteer Infantry. Record Group 94.

Pennsylvania Historical and Museum Commission, Harrisburg
Records of the Department of Military Affairs, Office of the Adjutant General, Civil War. Records of the 114th Pennsylvania Volunteer Infantry. Record Group 19.

Jack Sidebotham, Private Collection, Philadelphia
Williams, Edward E., and Edmund Williams. Papers.

Temple University Urban Archives, Philadelphia
Philadelphia *Bulletin* Files.

U.S. Army Military History Institute, Carlisle, Pa.
Robert L. Brake Collection.
Duff, Levi Bird. Papers.
Civil War Miscellaneous Collection.
Baker, Joseph D. Papers.
Bricker, John. Papers.
Canfield, Stephen B. Papers.
Crandall Family Papers.
Donnaker, Jacob B. Papers.
Granger, Luter A. Papers.
Rockwell, Phillip. Papers.
Zahniser, Thomas C. Papers.
Civil War Times Illustrated Collection.
Craig, Samuel A. Memoirs.
Strauss, Ellis C. Papers.
Coburn, James Parly. Papers.
Greg Coco Collection.
Madill, Henry J. Diary.
Harrisburg Civil War Roundtable Collection.
Ester, Henry. Papers.
Kenderdine, Robert. Papers.
Williams, Edgar. Papers.
George B. Jarrett Collection.
Burling, George C. Papers.
Lewis Leigh Collection.
Lobb, William T. Papers.
Reeder, William C. H. Papers.
Rice, Nicholas. Papers.
Thomas W. Stephens Collection.

Newspapers

Bucks County *Intelligencer*, 1862–1863.

Carlisle (Pa.) *Herald*, December 26, 1862.

Gettysburg *Star & Sentinel*, 1900–1906.

Grand Army Review, 1886.

Philadelphia *Daily Evening Bulletin*, 1861–1902. Title changed to *Evening Bulletin* by 1902.

Philadelphia *Inquirer*, 1861–1862.

Philadelphia *Public Ledger and Daily Transcript*, 1902.

Philadelphia *Sunday Dispatch*, 1862.

Philadelphia *Weekly Press*, 1887.

Philadelphia *Weekly Times*, 1886.

Sandersville *Central Georgian*, January 14, 1863.

Government Publications

Barnes, Joseph K., ed. *The Medical and Surgical History of the War of the Rebellion (1861–65)*. 2 vols. Washington, D.C., 1870.

Davis, George B., Leslie J. Perry, and Joseph W. Kirkley. *Atlas to Accompany the Official Records of the Union and Confederate Armies*. Washington, D.C., 1891–95.

Eighth Census of the United States, 1860.

Report of the Commission Appointed to the Governor of Pennsylvania to Investigate Alleged Army Frauds, August, 1861. Harrisburg, 1861.

Seventh Census of the United States, 1850.

Statistics of the United States in 1860. Washington, D.C., 1866.

U.S. Civil War Centennial Commission. *The United States on the Eve of the Civil War As Described in the 1860 Census*. Washington, D.C., 1963.

The War of the Rebellion: A Compilation of the Official Records of the Union and Confederate Armies. 130 vols. Washington, D.C., 1880–1901.

Articles and Essays

"The Battle of Fredericksburg, December 13, 1862." *Blue and Gray*, I (January, 1984), 21–42.

Bixley, Lawrence G. "Gettysburg Mystery Photo: A 2nd Look," *Military Images*, IV (July–August, 1982), 24–25.

"The Bombardment and Surrender of Fort Sumter, April 12–14, 1861." *Blue and Gray*, I (May, 1984), 25–34.

Gladstone, William. "Gettysburg Mystery Photo . . . More Answers and More Questions." *Military Images*, III (March–April, 1982), 16–19.

Hall, Clark B. "Season of Change: The Winter Encampment of the Army of the Potomac, December 1, 1863–May 4, 1864." *Blue and Gray*, VIII (April, 1991), 8–62.

Hennessy, John. "The Second Battle of Manassas: Lee Suppresses the 'Miscreant' Pope." *Blue and Gray*, IX (August, 1992), 10–58.

Katz, Michael B. "Social Class in North American Urban History." *Journal of Interdisciplinary History*, XI (Spring, 1981), 579–605.

Kett, Joseph F. "Adolescence and Youth in Nineteenth-Century America." In *The Family in History: Interdisciplinary Essays*, edited by Theodore K. Rabb and Robert I. Rotberg. New York, 1971.

McNeily, J. S. "Barksdale's Mississippi Brigade at Gettysburg." *Publications of the Mississippi Historical Society*, XIV (Oxford, 1914), 231–65.

Melchiori, Marie Varrelman. "The Death of 'French Mary.'" *Military Images*, V (July–August, 1983), 14–15.

Rayburn, Ella S. "Sabotage at City Point." *Civil War Times Illustrated*, XXII (April, 1983), 28–33.

Robertson, James I., Jr. "Stonewall in the Shenandoah: The Valley Campaign of 1862." Special issue of *Civil War Times Illustrated*. Harrisburg, 1979.

Shy, John. "A New Look at Colonial Militia." *William and Mary Quarterly*, 3rd ser., XX (April, 1963), 175–85.

Swart, Stanley L. "The Military Examination Board in the Civil War: A Case Study." *Civil War History: A Journal of the Middle Period*, XVI (September, 1970), 227–45.

Weigley, Russell F. "The Border City in the Civil War, 1854–1865." In *Philadelphia: A 300-Year History*, ed. Weigley. New York, 1982.

Books

Agassiz, George R., ed. *Meade's Headquarters, 1863–1865: Letters of Colonel Theodore Lyman from the Wilderness to Appomattox*. Boston, 1922.

Alotta, Robert I. *Civil War Justice: Union Army Executions Under Lincoln*. Shippensburg, Pa., 1989.

Anderson, Fred. *A People's Army: Massachusetts Soldiers and Sailors in the Seven Years' War*. Chapel Hill, 1984.

Barton, Michael. *Goodmen: The Character of Civil War Soldiers*. University Park, Pa., 1981.

Bates, Samuel P. *History of Pennsylvania Volunteers*. 5 vols. Harrisburg, 1869.

Beath, Robert B. *History of the Grand Army of the Republic*. New York, 1889.

Bellard, Alfred. *Gone for A Soldier: The Civil War Memoirs of Private Alfred Bellard*. Edited by David Herbert Donald. Boston, 1975.

Blodget, Lorin. *Manufacturers of Philadelphia, Census of 1860*. Philadelphia, 1861.

Boatner, Mark Mayo, III. *The Civil War Dictionary*. 1959; rpr. New York, 1988.

Bonsor, N. R. P. *North Atlantic Seaway: An Illustrated History of the Passenger Services Linking the Old World with the New*. 5 vols. Prescot, Lancashire, 1955.

Braverman, Harry. *Labor and Monopoly Capital: The Degradation of Work in the Twentieth Century*. New York, 1974.

Bremner, Robert H. *The Public Good: Philanthropy and Welfare in the Civil War Era*. New York, 1980.

Brown, Edmund. *History of the 27th Indiana*. Richmond, 1899.

Burton, William L. *Melting Pot Soldiers: The Union's Ethnic Regiments*. Ames, Iowa, 1988.

Caldwell, James Fitz James. *History of a Brigade of South Carolinians*. Philadelphia, 1866.

Catton, Bruce. *The Army of the Potomac: Mr. Lincoln's Army*. Garden City, N.Y., 1951.

————. *The Army of the Potomac: Glory Road*. Garden City, N.Y., 1952.

————. *The Army of the Potomac: A Stillness at Appomattox*. Garden City, N.Y., 1953.

————. *The Centennial History of the Civil War*. Vol. I: *The Coming Fury*. Garden City, N.Y., 1961. Vol. II: *Terrible Swift Sword*. Garden City, N.Y., 1963. Vol. III: *Never Call Retreat*. Garden City, N.Y., 1965.

————. *Grant Moves South*. Boston, 1960.

Cavada, F. F. *Libby Life: Experiences of a Prisoner of War in Richmond, Va., 1863–64*. Philadelphia, 1864.

Clark, Dennis J. *The Irish in Philadelphia: Ten Generations of Urban Experience*. Philadelphia, 1973.

Coddington, Edwin B. *The Gettysburg Campaign: A Study in Command*. New York, 1968.

Collis, Charles H. T. *The Case of F. F. Cavada*. Philadelphia, 1866.

————. *1st Brigade, 1st Division, 3rd Corps*. New York, 1891.

Collis, Septima M. *A Woman's War Record, 1861–1865*. New York, 1889.

Commager, Henry Steele, ed. *The Blue and the Gray*. 2 vols. in 1. 1950; rpr. New York, 1982.

Craft, David. *History of the 141st Regiment, Pennsylvania Volunteers, 1862–1865*. Towanda, Pa., 1885.

Cress, Lawrence Delbert. *Citizens in Arms: The Army and the Militia in American Society to the War of 1812*. Chapel Hill, 1984.

Cullen, Joseph P. *The Siege of Petersburg*. Harrisburg, Pa. 1970.

Davis, Alan F., and Mark Haller, eds. *The Peoples of Philadelphia: A History of Ethnic Groups and Lower-Class Life, 1790–1940*. Philadelphia, 1973.

Davis, William C., ed. *The Image of War*. 5 vols. New York, 1981–83.

Douglas, Henry Kyd. *I Rode with Stonewall*. Chapel Hill, 1940.

Dusinberre, William. *Civil War Issues in Philadelphia, 1856–1865*. Philadelphia, 1965.

Dyer, Frederick H. *A Compendium of the War of the Rebellion*. Des Moines, 1908.

Farwell, Byron. *Balls Bluff: A Small Battle and Its Long Shadow*. McLean, Va., 1990.

Foner, Philip S. *Antonio Maceo: The Bronze Titan of Cuba's Struggle for Independence*. New York, 1977.

Frassanito, William. *Grant and Lee: The Virginia Campaigns, 1864–1865*. New York, 1983.

Freedley, Edwin T. *Philadelphia and Its Manufactures: A Handbook Exhibiting the Development, Variety, and Statistics of the Manufacturing Industry of Philadelphia in 1857*. Philadelphia, 1867.

Freeman, Douglas Southall. *Lee's Lieutenants: A Study in Command*. 3 vols. New York, 1942–1944.

Furgurson, Ernest B. *Chancellorsville, 1863*. New York, 1992.

Gallagher, Thomas. *Paddy's Lament: Ireland 1846–1847, Prelude to Hatred*. New York, 1982.

Gallman, J. Matthew. *Mastering Wartime: A Social History of Philadelphia During the Civil War*. Cambridge, Mass., 1990.

Glatthaar, Joseph T. *Forged in Battle: The Civil War Alliance of Black Soldiers and White Officers*. New York, 1990.

Goolrick, William K. *Rebels Resurgent: Fredericksburg to Chancellorsville*. Alexandria, Va., 1985.

Graham, Martin F., and George F. Skoch. *Mine Run: A Campaign of Lost Opportunities, October 21, 1863–May 1, 1864*. 2nd ed. Lynchburg, Va., 1987.

Harrington, Fred Harvey. *Fighting Politician: Major General N. P. Banks*. Philadelphia, 1948.

Hassler, Warren W., Jr. *Commanders of the Army of the Potomac*. Baton Rouge, 1962.

Hays, Gilbert Adams. *Under the Red Patch: Story of the Sixty-Third Regiment Pennsylvania Volunteers, 1861–1864*. Pittsburgh, 1908.

Hennessy, Juliette A. *The United States Army Air Arm: April 1861 to April 1917*. Washington, D.C., 1985.

Herking, Charles. *Dictionary of Disasters at Sea*. 2 vols. London, 1962.

Higginbotham, Sanford W., William A. Hunter, and Donald H. Kent. *Pennsylvania and the Civil War: A Handbook*. Harrisburg, Pa., 1961.

History of the Fifty-Seventh Regiment, Pennsylvania Veteran Volunteer Infantry, First Brigade, First Division, Third Corps, and Second Brigade, Third Division, Second Corps, Army of the Potomac. Meadville, Pa., 1904.

Jackson, G. Gibbard. *The Story of the Liner*. London, n.d.

Jones, Archer. *Civil War Command and Strategy: The Process of Victory and Defeat*. New York, 1992.

Jones, Terry L. *Lee's Tigers: The Louisiana Infantry in the Army of Northern Virginia.* Baton Rouge, 1987.

Lonn, Ella. *Desertion During the Civil War.* 1928; rpr. Gloucester, Mass., 1966.

————. *Foreigners in the Union Army and Navy.* Baton Rouge, 1951.

Luvaas, Jay, and Harold W. Nelson. *The U.S. Army War College Guide to the Battle of Gettysburg.* Carlisle, Pa., 1986.

Martin, James M., et al. *History of the 57th Regiment Pennsylvania Volunteer Infantry.* Meadville, Pa., n.d.

Matter, William D. *If It Takes All Summer: The Battle of Spotsylvania.* Chapel Hill, 1988.

McAfee, Michael J. *Zouaves: The First and the Bravest.* Gettysburg, Pa., 1991.

McClellan, George B. *The Armies of Europe.* Philadelphia, 1861.

McConnell, Stuart C. *Glorious Contentment: The Grand Army of The Republic, 1865–1900.* Chapel Hill, 1992.

McPherson, James M. *Battle Cry of Freedom: The Civil War Era.* New York, 1988.

————. *Ordeal by Fire: The Civil War and Reconstruction.* New York, 1982.

Miers, Earl Schenck. *The Last Campaign: Grant Saves the Union.* Philadelphia, 1972.

Mills, H. Sinclair, Jr. *Vivandieres.* Collingswood, N.J., 1988.

Mitchell, Reid. *Civil War Soldiers: Their Expectations and Their Experiences.* New York, 1988.

Murdock, Eugene C. *One Million Men: The Civil War Draft in the North.* Westport, Conn., 1971.

Murfin, James V. *The Gleam of Bayonets: The Battle of Antietam and Robert E. Lee's Maryland Campaign, September, 1862.* 1965; rpr. Baton Rouge, 1982.

Nicholson, John P., ed. *Pennsylvania at Gettysburg.* 4 vols. Harrisburg, 1914.

Paludan, Phillip Shaw. *"A People's Contest": The Union and Civil War, 1861–1865.* New York, 1988.

Peckham, Howard H. *The Colonial Wars, 1689–1762.* Chicago, 1964.

Pfanz, Donald. *The Petersburg Campaign: Abraham Lincoln at City Point, March 20–April 9, 1865.* Lynchburg, Va., 1989.

Pfanz, Harry W. *Gettysburg: The Second Day.* Chapel Hill, 1987.

Phillips, Stanley S. *Civil War Corps Badges and Other Related Awards, Badges, Medals of the Period.* Lanham, Md., 1982.

Porter, Horace. *Campaigning with Grant.* New York, 1897.

Pullen, John H. *The Twentieth Maine.* Dayton, 1984.

Rauscher, Frank. *Music on the March, 1862–65, with the Army of the Potomac: 114th Regiment Pennsylvania Volunteers, Collis' Zouaves.* Philadelphia, 1892.

Robertson, James I., Jr. *Soldiers Blue and Gray.* Columbia, S.C., 1988.

————. *The Stonewall Brigade.* Baton Rouge, 1963.

————. *Tenting Tonight*. Alexandria, Va., 1984.

Schildt, John W. *September Echoes: A Study of the Maryland Campaign of 1862.* Shippensburg, Pa., 1980.

Scott, Kate M. *History of the One Hundred and Fifth Regiment of Pennsylvania Volunteers: A Complete History of the Organization, Marches, Battles, Toils, and Dangers Participated in by the Regiment from the Beginning to the Close of the War, 1861–1865.* Philadelphia, 1877.

Sears, Stephen W. *George B. McClellan: The Young Napoleon.* New York, 1988.

————. *Landscape Turned Red: The Battle of Antietam.* New Haven, 1983.

Shy, John. *A People Numerous and Armed: Reflections on the Military Struggle for American Independence.* London, 1976.

Silcox, Harry C. *Philadelphia Politics from the Bottom Up: The Life of Irishman William McMullen, 1824–1901.* Philadelphia, 1989.

Silver, James W., ed. *A Life for the Confederacy.* Jackson, Tenn., 1959.

Smith, Philip Chadwick Foster. *Philadelphia on the River.* Philadelphia, 1986.

Steiner, Paul E. *Disease in the Civil War: Natural Biological Warfare in 1861–1865.* Springfield, Ill., 1968.

Survivors' Association. *History of the 118th Pennsylvania Volunteers, Corn Exchange Regiment.* Philadelphia, 1905.

Sutherland, Daniel E. *The Expansion of Everyday Life, 1860–1876.* New York, 1989.

Tanner, Robert G. *Stonewall in the Valley: Thomas J. "Stonewall" Jackson's Shenandoah Valley Campaign, Spring, 1862.* Garden City, N.Y., 1976.

Taylor, Frank H. *Philadelphia in the Civil War, 1861–1865.* Philadelphia, 1913.

Taylor, Richard. *Destruction and Reconstruction: Personal Experiences of the Late War.* New York, 1879.

Thomas, Emory M. *Bold Dragoon: The Life of J. E. B. Stuart.* New York, 1986.

Trudeau, Noah Andre. *Bloody Roads South: The Wilderness to Cold Harbor, May–June 1864.* Boston, 1989.

————. *The Last Citadel: Petersburg, Virginia, June 1864–April 1865.* 1991; rpr. Baton Rouge, 1993.

Vandiver, Frank E. *Mighty Stonewall.* College Station, Tex., 1957.

Vinovskis, Maris A., ed. *Toward a Social History of the American Civil War: Exploratory Essays.* Cambridge, Mass., 1990.

Warner, Ezra J. *Generals in Blue: Lives of the Union Commanders.* Baton Rouge, 1964.

————. *Generals in Gray: Lives of the Confederate Commanders.* Baton Rouge, 1959.

Weigley, Russell F. *History of the United States Army.* New York, 1967.

Westerman, Gerhart von. *Opera Guide.* 1964; rpr. London, 1973.

Whan, Vorin E., Jr. *Fiasco at Fredericksburg.* University Park, Pa., 1961.

Wiley, Bell Irvin. *The Life of Billy Yank: The Common Soldier of the Union.* Baton Rouge, 1952.

————. *The Life of Johnny Reb: The Common Soldier of the Confederacy.* Baton Rouge, 1943.

Wilkinson, Warren. *Mother, May You Never See the Sights I Have Seen: The Fifty-Seventh Massachusetts Veteran Volunteers in the Last Year of the Civil War.* New York, 1990.

Woodham-Smith, Cecil. *The Great Hunger: Ireland, 1845–1849.* New York, 1962.

Index